REVIEWS OF PREVIOUS EDITIONS

NEPAL, WHERE JOHN CROSS BELONGS

How strange a link it is that binds Britain and Nepal.

For 180 years, our army has recruited Hindus from an Asian kingdom that we have never even governed—and been repaid with a loyalty that we have not, recently, repaid to them, the Gurkhas.

With their headquarters and museum in Aldershot and museum in Winchester, Hampshire is thick with past and present British officers of Gurkhas. But only one has the hard-won privilege of retirement in Nepal—J P Cross.

His life story is unusual, even by Gurkha standards. He served with the Gurkhas for nearly 40 years, the last six recruiting in Nepal. He has adopted a Nepalese son—and so, in time, a family—together with many Nepalese ways and beliefs.

A Christian, he is happy, and welcomed at Hindu ceremonies. Things we call "paranormal" seem to him, as to most non-European societies, normal enough.

Once, he records, the spirit of a dying communist guerrilla in Malaya passed into him and had to be exorcised. He recalls many instances of telepathy.

He finds nothing odd in asking a wise man whether he and his son were father and son in an earlier incarnation (answer: no—brothers).

He was also, it's plain, a good regimental officer—he's written a book on jungle warfare—who trusted and was trusted by his men.

Many ex-Gurkhas have recorded this unlikely closeness of officers and men. John Cross went deeper than most in understanding his men's customs and language.

As a soldier in Malaya, he was the live radio commentator, in Nepali, on inter-Gurkha football matches. As a civilian, he was thought fit to update a classic Nepali dictionary.

His feelings for his own countrymen were less strong but, one may guess, just as outspoken. No wonder the army did not know quite what to make of Lt-Col Cross. Certainly not a general...

That was his gain. For all Nepal's bureaucratic frustrations and academic infighting, this is the tale of a man who, in retirement, with a view of 16 peaks above 20,000 feet, knows where he belongs.

Hampshire Chronicle, November 1996

HANDLE HIM WITH CARE

Cross's detractors will have a party with The Call of Nepal. Those schooled in modern social science will pounce on such comments as: "Burma had never been ours in the same way as India had been," and will decontextualise statements such as "a Gurkha has a limited imagination" to render them offensive. What they will miss, however, is that in good reflexive tradition, Cross then turns these statements around and redirects them towards his own society, his family and even himself. An "Anglo-Saxon" and a hill man from Nepal, he suggests, have "basic qualities [that] seem to be the same: both peoples are fierce, obstinate and untameable and both peoples need special handling to get the best out of them." A further excerpt may serve to prove this point: "I found that the eastern Gurkha is like a cat: friendship cannot be forced and the chemistry takes some time to work. The westerners are more like dogs: it was productive to make positive advances."

In short, his tendency to objectify, rarefy and categorise ethnic groups and individuals is neither barbed nor colonial, it is simply the way that he sees all those who are part of his world, and most of all himself. Understandably, Nepali readers may react against such comments since they smack of a time which is all too fresh in the collective memory when Nepal and her citizens were characterised in the English-speaking world according to their racial virtues. However, one hopes Cross's critics will read him carefully and note that, although conservative in many ways and one among the ever-dwindling survivors of an era that has surely passed, Cross is a man whose experience of Nepal and fluency in spoken and written Nepali remain unrivalled by most other foreigners who have made this country their home.

The colonel's sheer love for the country shines through his sometimes verbose accounts and he reminds us time and time again that "to settle in [Nepal] became something that I wanted more than anything else in the world." This wish was granted by royal decree, and Cross became the first-ever foreign citizen to be allowed to own land in Nepal. He writes that he has "never accepted a Nepali as less than an equal and never regarded myself as intrinsically in any way superior." Some readers may wonder if this can be true given the colonial flavour in his slightly archaic English, but Cross's deep friendships with Nepalis must bear testament to the truth of his claim.

Likewise, the author's handling of the subtleties of the relationship with his adopted and surrogate Nepali son, to whom he dedicates the book, is so gentle that his motives are beyond suspect. His love for Buddhiman, and his belief that their relationship was predestined is deeply touching. This is how he places the relationship: "we [are] as one tree, I the roots and he, with his wife, the branches." It is a tribute to Cross that he handles this personal story in the candid and careful way that he does.

Cross's astonishing autobiography is as challenging to read as it is difficult to review. Reviewing the book is tantamount to reviewing the man himself. He swings with great ease from racial stereotypes of Gurkhas to such fashionable concepts as "morphic resonance" and even telepathy, and genuinely seems to believe in both. It is this peculiar mixture of humility, self-effacement and honesty on the one hand, and contentedness and pride on the other, that makes the book such an extraordinary achievement.

... Cross has written an intensely, at times even embarrassingly, personal account and it is firmly rooted in an altogether different dimension—historically, politically, culturally and linguistically. For Colonel Cross, despite the changing social and political climate, the "Call of Nepal is still as loud as it ever was when I first heard it so many years ago."

Mark Turin, Himal South Asian, Vol 12 No 6,
June 1999

BLOWING ONE'S OWN TRUMPET

It is pointless to pretend that this review is unprejudiced. Colonel Cross does not hold Madhesis, or Indians, as he chooses to call them in Nepal, in very high esteem. The antagonism is mutual. This reviewer is a Madhesi and harbors a rather ambivalent attitude towards Gurkhas in general and their English officers in particular.

The Call of Nepal has been placed by its editor and publishers in Series II of Bibliotheca Himalayica, the category that deals with linguistics, biography and literature. In its attempt to be all three, it ends up being just a crude effort at self-glorification. Confusion is evident in its every page.

Take the linguistics part first. A mercenary, according to Oxford Dictionary, is a soldier hired to fight in a foreign army. Colonel Cross does not accept such "a strained interpretation" of the term. Instead, he chooses the terms laid down by an "Ad Hoc Committee of the United Nations" that was "considering a possible draft convention!" Some straining, that. With this kind of language, it is no wonder that the author failed almost every examination he took in his life. The fault never lay with him, of course. As he makes one of his characters say, "You did not fail. They did not pass you."

The book is only slightly better as an autobiography. As it is, it's extremely challenging to examine oneself. Thoreau once said, "It is hard to see oneself as to look backwards without turning around." An additional difficulty arises in this case because officers aren't the best of people to either look back or turn around. In a flash of candor remarkable for an English and even more so for a colonial soldier, the author admits, "None of us are as good as we think we are or would like to be and I was no exception." Correct the tense and replace "was" with "am" and you realize what a difficult read this book is.

"The two names taught in the village school were the King of Nepal's and mine." says the exalted colonel, who mentions without a twinge of embarrassment: "Men would come to me with bowed head for my blessings." The author is enlisted into the Indian Army as a BOR—British Other Ranks—and remains its phonetic equivalent all his life.

The literature part of the book is a little less insulting to the intelligence. Despite, or maybe because of the author's extraordinary lack of formal education, the prose sparkles with occasional wit and passages of noteworthy narration. Whenever he puts his argumentative style to rest and lets his observations do the listening and his emotions do the talking, the result is a pleasure to read. He is in his element telling the story of Buddhiman Gurung.

Yet the book abounds with many instances of intended slight. The author claims, without even making an attempt to hide his nastiness, "The living legend that is the military mark of Gurkhas' greatness is, to an extent, the reflection of the high caliber of British officers who have served selflessly with them for so many years." Elsewhere he observes that poverty is paraded almost proudly and then pontificates, "Before Nepal could be saved from Indian or Chinese hegemony, it had to be saved from itself."

Then there is Colonel Cross's rank ignorance to reckon with. For him, tika is a caste mark, though even an occasional tourist to Nepal knows it to be a religion-mark used by all castes. Such a man was a historian to our army and a researcher at the supposedly prestigious Center of Nepal and Asian Studies at the Tribhuvan University. Remember the moving stanza from Bhupi Sherchan's famous poem: we are brave, because we are stupid? Colonel Cross knows this only too well, hence has the gall to quote with glee, "To be tasty, radishes have to be buried; to be good, a Nepali has to be pressed."

The book should be made required reading for all those who favor the continuation of Gurkha recruitment; they would realize what a shame it is. Just as our grinding poverty cannot justify the selling of our sisters in Sonagachhi, selling our brothers in the name of obscure treaties and lack of opportunity in our country is indefensible.

"In comfortless camps, is sweltering offices, in gloomy dark bungalows smelling of dust and earth-oil, they earn, perhaps, the right to be a little disagreeable," wrote George Orwell in Burmese Days, way back in 1935. Colonel Cross asserts this right only too forcefully with his ramblings in the form of a book. "Nepalis have a touching faith in the sanctity and infallibility of written words," he observes, and hints darkly that he may be reborn as a Christian in the royal palace of Kathmandu and the leader of the country.

In a nutshell, this book is a load of crap, all two hundred and forty-one pages of it bristling with racial overtones and colonial snootiness. Read it to test your patience in taking insults and soldiering the brown man's burden of putting up with the white ones' ignorance coupled with impertinence.

C K Lal
The Kathmandu Post Review of Books
8 November, 1998, Vol.3, No.14

COMMENTS FROM INDIVIDUALS

...I can say quite honestly that I think your books have made an immense contribution to our understanding of the post-war events in the Far East. Historians and diplomats generally draw with a broad brush, leaving the autobiographical account to provide more detail and a personal slant. You have managed both John!

Lt Col Duncan Forbes, ex RAEC, letter of
21.01.1996

Prepare to be suitably but most honourably embarrassed! I have now finished The Call of Nepal and thoroughly enjoyed every minute of it. It is a marvellous read and you have succeeded brilliantly in weaving together a large number of complex themes in a most enjoyable and instructive way.

All that any reasonable man would want to know about the history of Nepal is there and you deal most sensitively but clearly with the huge question of the Aryan-Mongoloid divide. The history of Gurkha recruitment into the British Army is also most comprehensively covered with the traumatic events of Partition and the formation of the Brigade of Gurkhas in Malaya standing out as moving and instructive pieces of narrative. I also admired the story of your own treks in the Hills and the candid and open way in which you dealt with the setbacks and disappointments which life dealt you.

All wonderful stuff but the jewel in the crown in undoubtedly Chapter 6 in which by extensive use of Buddhiman's own words you open up a view of the real Nepal which most visitors completely miss. Having read it a number of times I really do feel I know Buddhiman's family including particularly his tough father and most courageous mother. I have been fortunate enough to trek widely in the Hills and have a better view than most of the reality of life at village level but it took your use of Buddhiman's words to bring home to me what "subsistence farming" really means. The grinding impoverishment, the dignity and pride of those who have nothing, the influence of the Gods, the customs and culture of the Gurung people, along with much much more are brilliantly described and I just wanted you to know how much I enjoyed and learnt from it.

I have just started "A Face Like A Chicken's Backside" but having read the opening couple of pages in which you describe your meeting with the dying Cpl Balbahadur Raid I know that I am going to relish reading that book also.

Please give my warm regards to Buddhiman. Thanks to your marvellous writing I feel I really know him, his family and indeed the whole village of Thuloswara! It was a great joy to entertain you at our home during your recent visit and, as ever, I very much look forward to our next meeting. I am in my fifth week as Quartermaster General and thoroughly enjoying every minute of it but I know that I will benefit greatly from my annual pilgrimage to the Hills in October. Many congratulations again on producing a brilliant book.

Lt Gen S Cowan, ex QG SIGNALS, letter of
05.06.1996

[The Call of Nepal] is a delight and I read it slowly and carefully. It is a love story of your devotion to people and country. I think Dhampu must be very proud that you have dedicated it to him. The photograph of him is really very good. I know him as Buddhiman...

Miss B Hirst, aged 98, letter of 01.07.1996

...I read your book [The Call Of Nepal]. It really is a most fascinating story (and I don't say that to flatter, I'm past the age where I can be bothered to be insincere with people I know; people one doesn't is another matter...)

It strikes me you have no reason—as I have—to regret a life that could have been differently spent, as whose couldn't; and you can be proud of it...

You plainly weren't—forgive—born to marry, which can be a source of great happiness as of its reverse (I've had both). But you seem to have found a most adequate family by other means; and grandchildren that my graceless but likeable sons show no signs of producing for me.

I'm reading Call of Nepal at present, and I must congratulate you on producing such a fascinating account of the independence of India and Pakistan and the effect on the Gurkhas. You certainly don't pull your punches...

I found The Call Of Nepal absolutely fascinating. How you coped with blindness is incredible—quite awe-inspiring... It was so interesting how you first met Buddhiman, his background and how your friendship developed. It is an enormous credit to you, and wonderful that he has responded so appreciatively... It is wonderful what you have done for each other...

I've finished reading The Call of Nepal—absolutely fascinating and moving.

The Call of Nepal...is an excellent book. If I may say so, there is a certain innocence in the way you write about yourself which is unique. When the polished memoirs of your contemporaries have been forgotten The Call of Nepal will still be read. Gurkhas at War is excellent too, but for quite different reasons. When it soaks in among the bien pensants of the academic world, I don't know what they will make of it. It is the anthropology they cannot write and probably cannot understand. It's unique and all the better for it. And Buddhiman deserves a great pat on the back.

N F Howard [archaeologist and author], letter
10.05.2002

Many thanks for your book The Call of Nepal. I enjoyed it very much and I especially took pleasure from feeling so much more or a friend, with reading about the parts of your personal family life. I also took the opportunity to purchase Whatabouts and Whereabouts in Asia before it became available in the bookshops and many thanks for putting my name forward to your publishers...I am so sorry you have renounced your British citizenship. Let me say that I think no worse of you for doing that and no matter what, you will always be one of the great English men. I must tell you that it is still a great thrill for me to find myself sitting and writing a letter to you, one of my real life heroes: I still have to pinch myself.

e-mail from Fred Hudson, ex-Loyals National
Serviceman, 13 July 2003

THE CALL OF NEPAL

My Life In the Himalayan Homeland of Britain's Gurkha Soldiers

By J. P. Cross

NIMBLE BOOKS LLC

ISBN-13: 978-1-934840-78-8

ISBN-10: 1-934840-78-5

Copyright 2009 J. P. Cross

Version 1.0; last saved 2009-08-29.

Nimble Books LLC

1521 Martha Avenue

Ann Arbor, MI 48103-5333

http://www.nimblebooks.com

Photographs courtesy The Gurkha Museum (front cover) and Zenith Photo (back cover, title page).

Maps by by Joseph Peter (deskcube.elance.com).

The cover font, heading fonts and the body text inside the book are in Constantia, designed by John Hudson for Microsoft.

♾ The paper used in this publication meets the minimum requirements of the American National Standard for Information Sciences—Permanence of Paper for Printed Library Materials, ANSI Z39.48-1992. The paper is acid-free and lignin-free.

Contents

J P CROSS

DEDICATION

To the tens of thousands of Nepalis with whom I have shared my life over the last sixty-five years and most especially to my surrogate son Buddhiman Gurung.

Dhampu

Figure 1. Photograph of Buddhiman Gurung.

1	ANNAPURNA, MT
2	BAGSILA
3	BHAKTAPUR
4	DHAULAGIRI, MT
5	EVEREST, MT
6	FISHTAIL, MT
7	GHANDRUNG
8	LAMJUNG
9	LUWANG
10	MANANG
11	MUKTINATH
12	MUSTANG
13	NALMA
14	PAKLIHAWA
15	PASUPATI
16	PATAN
17	SALYAN
18	THULOSWARA

Figure 2. Points of interest from the author's life in Nepal.

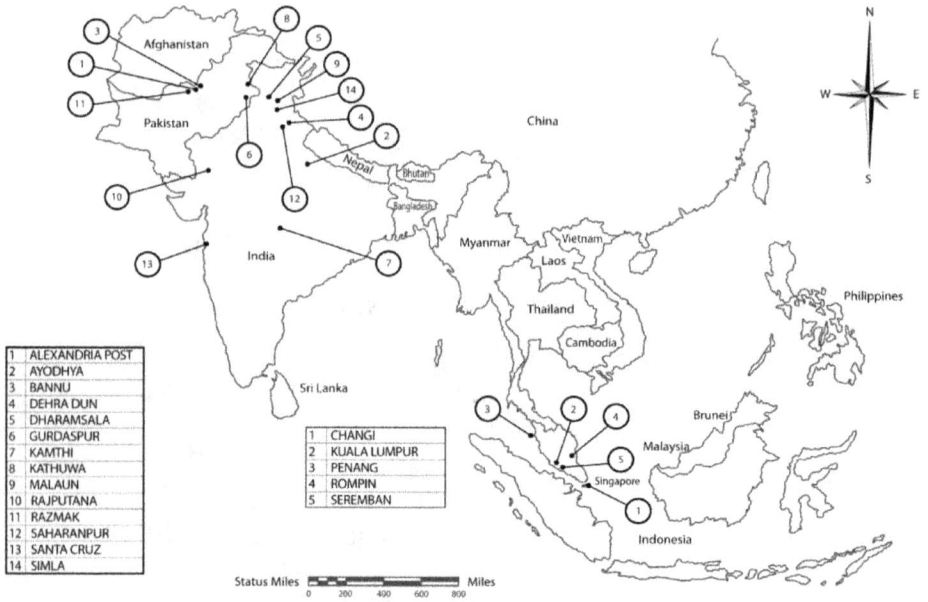

1	ALEXANDRIA POST
2	AYODHYA
3	BANNU
4	DEHRA DUN
5	DHARAMSALA
6	GURDASPUR
7	KAMTHI
8	KATHUWA
9	MALAUN
10	RAJPUTANA
11	RAZMAK
12	SAHARANPUR
13	SANTA CRUZ
14	SIMLA

1	CHANGI
2	KUALA LUMPUR
3	PENANG
4	ROMPIN
5	SEREMBAN

Figure 3. Points of interest from the author's tours of duty in India and Malaysia.

FOREWORD

No one is more qualified to talk about the history of Nepal than Colonel John Philip Cross.

After joining the British Army as a teenager at the end of WWII, Cross was assigned to the 1st Battalion of the 1st Gurkha Rifles, and thus commenced his life's work as a leader of the Gurkhas, "the traditional martial stock of Nepal," and as a student of the country's history and culture.

Now writing books on irregular warfare and Himalayan history that deserve to be read even though they aren't, he is a minor and very eccentric offshoot of a British imperial species that reached perfection in the person of the former soldier and literary travel writer Patrick Leigh Fermor. Both are inveterate walkers: Fermor across Europe, and Cross having covered 10,000 miles on foot through the Nepalese hills over the years.

In his book, *The Call of Nepal*, Cross portrays his profoundly personal journal, as he terms it, rooted not only in the physical – but deeply in the mental, emotional and spiritual.

During his lifetime Cross has long practiced linguistic and cultural immersion in Nepal both personally, and in the context of his time with the Gurkhas in what today's military analysts must clearly see as an integral component of military success. But with today's military pace, the time to achieve the depth of Cross's insight is not always affordable. A pioneer in many respects, Cross saw fluency and correct use of language

ix

not only as a tactical weapon but also as a vital, literally, element of command. It is this depth of knowledge, which also comes from understanding, living, and being part of Nepalese history that makes him and his writing such an invaluable resource.

Cross once told me: "You can't fight properly until you know that you are going to die anyway." That's extreme, but that's the gold standard....

Cross's experience includes counterinsurgency: In the late 1940s and early fifties, while teaching Gurkhas at the Army School of Education in Malaya, Cross discovered a Communist-inspired plot to penetrate Gurkhas and spread anti-British propaganda. He also operated against the Malayan Communists and against the Indonesians whose tactics were similarly based. Today, as India and its neighbors command so much more of the spotlight in global politics Cross's life work and his journey in *The Call of Nepal* become important and critical reading.

Robert D. Kaplan, May
2009

BACKGROUND TO THE CALL OF NEPAL

The first edition of this book appeared in England in 1996. Two years later it was published in Nepal. I had been asked by one close to the Highest in the Land to analyse where certain trends were leading the country and whence had they started. I felt such an approach by one such as myself was inapposite so I limited my response to what appears here; history, the present and the future, albeit with the caveat I am an observer and not a prophet. I have "played with time" to write history as "yesterday," my own time with the Nepalis as "today" and what I have to say for the future as "tomorrow." I have left "today" at 1996 as not only are events since then are too raw for rational, balanced and impartial judgement by one not born in Nepal but also "political correctness" veers like a weathercock.

By 2009 I had been with Nepalis, civilians and Gurkha soldiers, for nearly sixty-five years, from when I was nineteen years old, then bold and fearless, until, as I write this, an octogenarian, now old and hairless. This may not sound much but, since the Britain-Nepal military connection started in 1815, my uniformed service with Gurkhas counted as 23 per cent of that time and, as a civilian, it is just short of one-third. These years have seen my own long and very personal voyage of discovery in four-dimensions; physical, mental, moral and spiritual.

Since 1985 I have been allowed to settle in Nepal where I feel I belong. I am one of the most privileged foreigners ever to

1

be allowed to lead my life with such wonderful people and I pray, to whichever of the many gods that is nearest to me, that I may continue to live among them till the end of my days. *The Call of Nepal* is still as loud as it ever was when I first heard it so many years ago. I have tried to emulate what I believe the Fourth Wise Monkey might have had as its motto—write no evil, only the truth. I have tried factually to comment on the situation as I have seen it, not to harangue any imaginary reader or to offer unwanted advice—which a wise person does not need and a foolish one does not heed.

A Nepali song tells about "a lifetime is over in two days." I take mine as lasting only for one, so "morning," "afternoon" and "evening" neatly divide my story. I have also set the scene in "yesterday," explaining background reasons for the modern Nepalese mind-set, as I see them. Similarly, in an attempt to look into the future—always rash!—I have written a "tomorrow."

As I knew nothing either of Nepal or Gurkhas before I joined the army in 1943, I started off as a complete stranger and totally ignorant, seeing what I did from the outside. During the "morning" my first impressions were assailed by second thoughts as I experienced the many conflicting facets of a hill man's character. I try to relive this time (leaving aside the tail end of the Japanese war in Burma), in Malay and Borneo in peacetime conditions, in the jungle in a "limited war" setting and as a visitor in Nepal. This takes me up until 1956.

From then till 1976, the afternoon of my life, also gives glimpses of what it was like then as I strangely found myself more deeply involved in military work of a hard and sometimes hazardous kind, almost always with Gurkhas, to support me. In this section I have included a description of the first twenty years of the life of him who has become my surrogate son since 1976, Buddhiman Gurung.

The early evening of my life, starting in 1976, tells of what it was like working as a recruiter of Gurkha soldiers for the British Army, how I went blind, how I was so wonderfully led by Buddhiman and helped by all those Nepalis I came into contact with. That period over and finding myself a civilian after forty years, I was overwhelmed when asked to work on the staff of the Tribhuvan University by none other than the Vice-Chancellor, the late Ram Chandra Bahadur Singh, and approved by His Majesty himself. This was in 1982. I saw that as having been accepted as a true lover of Nepal and I learnt what life in Nepal was like from the inside, as it were.

I was assigned to the Centre for Nepal and Asian Studies where my first task was to write on The Role of the Brigade of Gurkhas in the British Army. I dedicated it to "The many thousands of Nepalese citizens whom I knew, loved, honoured, respected and worked with for the last 38 years of my Army Service, from 1944 to 1982 ... in the hope that, with the recording of your deeds, devotion and dedication, your fellow citizens will have a deeper understanding and greater knowledge of the part you have played to make the name Nepal stir other men's hearts and to increase and strengthen the ties between Britain and Nepal." I now wish to increase what I wrote there to include many, many others who have made my life the brighter, the happier and more worthwhile.

3

Apart from Dr. Vishnu Prasad Rajouria, MBE, Dr. Kumar Jang Bahadur Rana, and the late Pandit Bhimlal Sharma, close friends from the first part of my life, I want particularly to thank those of you who have become my friends since 1982. Whether you realised it or not, you made me aware of many aspects of life in Nepal in a way that immeasurably helped me become accepted as one of you and I am very grateful for this: Abhi Subedi, Ananda Shrestha, Bahadur Dwaj Rana, Chaitanya Misra, Dhruba Kumar, Dor Bahadur Bista, Gokul Prasad Sharma, Kumar Khadga Bikram Shah, Narayan Prasad Shrestha, Nirmal Man Tuladhar, Prayag Raj Sharma, Satya Narayan Manandhar, Shyam Kumar Bhurtel and Sridhar K Khatri, to say nothing of Generals Satchit Shamsher Jang Bahadur Rana, Garud Shamsher Jang Bahadur Rana and Narayan Chandra Malla. Special emphasis is due to the late Ram Chandra Bahadur Singh, without whom *The Call of Nepal* would still be unanswered. There are many more and, in not listing you personally, please do not think I have not appreciated your friendship. I have.

Included amongst you was one very old hill man with the power to see into the past and the future. He has twice said that this is not the only time I have been, or will be, with Nepalis in Nepal. He insists that my last incarnation was as a Nepali as will the next one be. When I learnt this all the events of my life to date fell into place like understanding a jig-saw puzzle. Over these many years not everything Nepalese has been positive, yet the attraction continued to attract and the repulsion did not repel me as much as it did others. Everything now makes sense, is satisfying and comforting. More than many other "foreigners" I can, and do, feel at home here in Nepal.

One very close Nepali friend told me that it was my duty to tell others of these years, so, hoping to be excused for what is much more than an exercise in the use of the First Person Singular, here it is. I have not only relied on my memory for many of the details but on letters I wrote home every week, less when I was on military operations, and those letters have been kept. Will those who read this book that see I love the Nepalis because I understand them or I understand them because I love them? Either will do..

Pokhara
January 2009

YESTERDAY

Nepal lives with very old and very deep roots. To discover when these were planted, what they are and how they still very much influence modern times, I have had to go back into the mists of history in my search for them. I found three what I have termed "time bombs," seminal events that have had, and still have, a lasting and profound influence here in Nepal. I made my journey forwards trying to establish "milestone dates" when other events occurred to try and see if the original effects had been modified and, if so, were they for the better or for the worse – but who is to be the judge of good or bad in any context? These, then, are my thoughts in simple terms, the bare skeleton without any flesh or blood.

Over the millennia everywhere has there been a slow, uneven but relentless focusing of human consciousness. Gradually people became aware that, as well as being members of a particular tribe, ethnic group may be the more politically correct description, each is indeed a separate individual who has an inclination to justify to himself aspects of tribal traditions, thoughts and temperament. This has lead to more and more individuals – in Asia essentially men rather than women – now making up their mind about the big choices in life and being responsible for these decisions. This modern phenomenon is altering many preconceived concepts of thought, if not of behaviour. Nepal, having been cocooned from the outside world for much of the time before, say, the mid-1950s, has had to face many new problems—or maybe old problems in new guises—and absorb most of them too fast for easy assimilation.

The point at which I started my forward journey was when the tribal family was supreme, the world was at one and the same time infinite, eternal, endless and constricted, parochial, fearsome. As the basic components of life, water, fire, air, could not be held in the hand without containers, other bodiless matters also needed to be contained and thus was god born as an animist concept to be revered in the image of natural things as any particular group felt apposite. The supernatural was present in many, if not all, aspects of daily life, to be wondered at, coaxed, blamed but never able to be ignored.

Spreading southwards from, inaccurately but simply, the general area of the Steppes, a slow, mass migratory movement of these tribal families composed of epicanthic peoples, those of "almond shaped" eye lids, crossed over the Himalayas and perched on the southern slopes, the earlier migrants being pushed even farther south by later arrivals. They ended up scattered from, in the west what is now modern Nepal, eastwards as far as the coast of northern Vietnam. The groups in the west contain those "traditional martial classes" known to the outside world as Gurkhas.

To their southwest, bound in physical isolation between the Himalayas and the seas, centuries of Aryan—"sacred-thread-wearers"—influence increased as invaders followed invaders from the west and these people were gradually absorbed therein, adopting what is now seen as basic Hinduism, a religion none of them worshipped before they arrived. These intruders all looked for a land kinder than that which they had left and, once absorbed, there was no going back, nor was there any going on farther east by land. By sea some reached as far away as Bali. Others moved as far as the lower reaches of the Himalayas but most of them had to stay where they were, in the "cow belt" of modern north India. It suited them to settle down to the humdrum rhythm of the seasons, raising their families and living as fulfilling a life as possible. Hinduism embedded them as firmly as though it were quicksand.

The "rip tide" between the two migratory groups is in central Nepal and the inter-fusion has exacerbated rather than placated social harmony. The adsorption of these two disparate groups, rather than absorption, was the first "time bomb" for modern Nepalese society: it is called ethnic tension. I suggest that the desire for permanence of superiority and social stability of the Aryan groups were the reasons behind the tract of religious Hindu thought called *Manusmrti*, the second "time-bomb."

Not including the founding of the world's great religions, my first "milestone date" is when a third "time bomb" with another very long fuse was lit in the far off city of Athens, when, in 508-507 BC—some 2500 years ago as I write this—democracy was founded.

Before I examine more "milestone dates" I need to assess, in brief, the ethnic mixture, democracy and the Laws of Manu, *Manusmrti*—Manu was the eldest of twelve sons of Brahma and the "laws" must have taken many years to evolve into their present codex –in that order, in the context of how both affect modern Nepal. I take ethnic tension first: the evil of ethnic intolerance is one of the crying sins of human nature, wheresoever it appears. One of the most common defects of biased and stubborn minds is to think too much of differences from others—fear or misplaced snobbery?—and too little of aspects in which they agree with others. Horrific examples of ethnic intolerance around us are so many and obvious that they need no added description.

As for "democracy", it is a weasel word in that it can mean so many different things to so many different people. Some of the world's toughest communist states call themselves "The Democratic Republic of ... " and all liberal governments see themselves as democratic. What is often not realised about the original Greek democracy—that occurred when society was rigid, with noblemen, middle classes and slaves—is that it is of two schools of thought. Demosthenes' version led to "Western" style while Aristotle's to Communist style. Modern democracy is seen by many as the only way to adjust "removable inequalities."

However, Aristotle put his finger on one of the prime virtues of democratic decision-making: "provided the mass of the people is not too slave-like, each individual will indeed be a worse judge than the experts, but collectively they will be better, or at any rate not worse." The pulse of a nation's wishes must be respected. In many countries this aspiration was only to be realised in very modern times.

My third point is the influence of *Manusmrti* here in the subcontinent. A Hindu was originally not so much a member of a particular religious faith but rather a member of the society living around the River Indus. Hinduism's upper echelon, Brahmanism, is an abstract expression that can be interpreted in different ways: as can democracy. Brahman values are a protection against the intrusion of foreign values, seeing the preservation of society as the first duty of society. Every detail of life in ancient Hindu times was invested with a religious sanction, a sacred ritual that regulated human action. This became law. Nothing could be changed, the system was one of "irremovable inequalities." The only way to withstand the assaults of more invaders was seen by the adoption of such a code of living. Core Hinduism is much more easily understandable by Christians as it did not have any caste system as practised today. Animists live under fear of evil spirits; Hindus likewise live under fear of unpropitiated forces. Fusion between the two was, therefore, not difficult as, in one respect, the latter is an extension of the former. In both cases, indifference of others plays a bigger part than either love or hatred does.

I believe it was the Muslim invasion of Nepal in and around 1349 AD, my next "milestone date", that was the cause of King Jayasthiti Malla of Kathmandu bringing Nepalese society into line based on the rigid caste system as laid down in *Manusmrti*, the better either to remain pure or to counter what was seen as the evils of another faith. It is impossible to say how much a part Hinduism played in the lives of those in what is now known as Nepal who then "wore their religion lightly." The effects of *Manusmrti* were slower rather than quicker in making themselves felt because in those times social intercourse was very much more restricted than it was later as, it is not unreasonable to suggest, the ethnic groups from the north were still living in hill top areas, not on the flatter ground nearer the larger rivers or in the uplands where strangers would not normally reach.

Some see *Manusmrti* as inviolate and divinely inspired. It is a system of irremovable inequalities, cramping originality by defining work levels in accordance with human levels by laying down complicated rules for social cohesion, dividing Hindus into four castes and thirty-six colours—as good a way to "divide and rule" as any the British were later to be accused of in India and a marvellous recipe for countless cases of superiority and inferiority complexes. Treat people like second, third or fourth class citizens and they will behave as second, third or fourth class citizens would be expected to, robbing the community of much potential the while.

(Buddhism—Sakyamuni preached his first sermon in 521 BC—does not come further into this equation than to say that the Vedic philosophy of unreality, *maya*, the illusion which considers the unreal universe as really existent and as distinct from the Supreme Spirit, has also spread to Buddhism. This basic philosophy has not always sat easily with extraneous religions, and tensions still arising from later arrivals on the religious scene, Islam and Sikhism, show up all too clearly from time to time. As for the earlier phenomenon of Christianity, the original Coptic Christians who arrived in India in the fourth century were accepted by Brahmans as equals. Since Abbé Dubois' proselytising foray in southern India for a quarter of a century from 1789, Brahmans have put Christians below the lowest of Hindus, calling them Mlechchha.

If Buddhism could the more easily cater for the needs of the traveller in the very early days by satisfying his religious instincts while not having to be tied to a particular location in order to carry out all that Hinduism ordained, Hinduism, with no formal religious hierarchy, has always been essentially static, inward-looking and self-centred, breeding a moral isolation that stands apart from others, not knowing their temptations, thoughts or aspirations. Therefore, even if such a person were wrong, he would be apt to believe that he was right. Such an outlook can never be adventurous, expansive or able to meet changing conditions. Where and when it has tried has been an aberration.

A Roman Catholic priest, wearing the saffron robe of a Buddhist monk and adhering to the code of conduct laid down by the Enlightened One, will not be unfrocked or excommunicated: he will be if he embraces Hinduism.)

India, as this area is now known and whose present boundaries were only fixed by the British in the last century, especially "cow-belt" territory, has always cast its long shadow over Nepal, particularly in the Tarai and the Valley, with much influence emanating from Rajisthan, Benares, Patna and Calcutta. Brahman intercourse through trade, travel, religion and learning, between India and Nepal has fostered Indian ideas in a Nepalese setting to a degree of penetration that has affected many strands of otherwise home-grown thought. No account of modern Nepal therefore can be taken in isolation from India. As Hindu thought spread it brought the tenets of *Manusmrti* with it into Nepal.

fManu, so long treated by Europeans as the key authority, is, to others, no more than a Brahman apologist, just as a great deal of Aristotle and Plato is an apology for Athens' leisured and educated class. Howsoever these laws are looked on, they lay down that those born within the Himalayan region, so, by definition, Gurkha soldiers of world fame, are of the lowest class. This can explain why military service with the British has been seen as the one honourable profession open to the Gurkhas. So it is that, no matter how good such a "low status" person is, he is proscribed from full fruits of any intrinsic worth. No wonder there is continuous stress, especially since education is now free for all and rigidities of the non-party Panchayat system were relaxed in 1990.

Rabindranath Tagore puts this from a Brahman's point of view: Hindu India had originally accepted the bonds of her social system in order to transcend society, as the rider puts reins on his horse and stirrups on his own feet in order to ensure greater speed towards his goal. Fine, except for when any member of a non-Brahman ethnic community is the horse with stirrups digging into him.

Manusmrti lays down the Brahman's four basic "rights" in life: religion, worldly goods, sex and salvation, in that order, on the inviolate and god-given authority that others lower down the system have no way of challenging if only because fatalism, induced and imbued by centuries of a rigid society riveted to unfathomable whims, is strong enough to discourage any such venture. All four rights need to be satisfied. In brief: religion is the strict retention of the caste system; what the western world looks at as bribery, sticky fingers or financial improbity come under the heading of worldly goods that are there for the taking if not for the asking—but never to the extent of, say, the American gold rush of the last century, Italian organised crime or Japanese politics in this; sex covers not loose morals but rather full enjoyment of a male-dominated relationship. One facet of its impact is seen in the epic poetry of such hedonistic amorous frolics as performed by Krishna and the cow-girls and "wanton sporting with other maidens", as Jayadeva wrote in Gita Govinda in the twelfth century. Fourthly, no matter how much human laws have been transgressed on earth, salvation for onward and upward progression is assured. Reading *Manusmrti* I understand that those who wear the sacred thread and whose ancestors penetrated the lower Himalayas are exempt from demeaning strictures.

It is only fair to say that, since 1854, the people normally thought of Gurkhas have been lifted from the bottom of the pile and are now slotted in between the twice born and the occupational groups.

India, the home of Hinduism and now much more of a united country than ever before the British arrived, has so many modern requirements for a successful industrial base "on home ground" that it is not wrong to ask why, in the late twentieth century, other countries less well endowed and also in Asia have left her behind in so many aspects of enhancement—land-locked Nepal also suffers and those of her citizens with an entrepreneurial bent of mind are penalised. I can see the inward-looking Hindu mind-set as being contrary to the needs of modern development. This is because the Hindu caste, or colour, system was designed with a political rigidity not unlike the bishop-clergy-laity syndrome that kept the early Christian church intact. Fear of unknown, unquantifiable and assertive elements of a fanciful cosmic world was so strong that basic survival needs could be given a religious, therefore a not-to-be-questioned, authority. It is a moot point where the religious and the superstitious separate and where they join.

Hindu values are all intimately and continuously influenced by the pantheon of countless gods and goddesses seeing all aspects of man's nature, good and bad, portrayed on a cosmic scale. Love and hate, sincerity and treachery, good deeds and sinful action are all aspects of the gods' behaviour, which can uplift man or bedevil him with destructive relentlessness. If the whim of the gods manifests itself adversely and cruelly by an individual not having paid due attention to making all the necessary oblations and sacrifices—however trite and trivial these be—it is the fault of the individual. Placating, warding off wrath and spite, and acting as a god's slave are constants: they whom the gods have made their heirs, the twice-born Brahmans, view those below them as the gods view mankind—an attitude that feeds on people's bigotry, superstition and callousness. Brahmanism also inculcates that sort of vanity that is apt to take disagreement as an affront—not a ready matrix for successful entrepreneurship.

There is also a continuous tension between all aspects of malevolence and benevolence. Never really knowing which side of the coin may be revealed and with an eye to the main chance, toadying, flattery, fawning and a subservient approach to one's seniors—far in excess of what normal politeness would require—along with bearing false witness, therefore ward off calamities more effectively than do accountability and a moral imperative. This produces tensions in a society in which the fortunes of men seem to bear practically no relation to their merits and efforts—not a ready matrix for adversarial politics.

Far be it from me to decry any belief nor to question doctrine, dogma or dictates of tradition. My belief is, in any mainstream religion—or political system, come to that—it has only been when rogue members of the elite have taken it into their heads that "ours is the only way" for matters to get so out of hand that misery for millions has resulted. This is in addition to the old conundrum of what happens when an unstoppable force meets an immovable body? Impelling power and restraining wisdom are as opposite as any two things and are rarely found together.

Getting back to Nepalese history, a "milestone event", exact date unknown but probably in the last two decades of the 15th century, occurred in the centre of the country, in Lamjung district, above the village of Thuloswara—the birthplace of the author's surrogate son. The background only needs touching lightly upon: the king to the north were too harsh on the local king, who went to the neighbouring district of Kaski to find one stronger. The family that was asked to provide the new king did so and the upshot of this was that one branch of the family stayed in Lamjung and the other, the forebears of the royal dynasty that was deposed in 2008, went east to Gorkha and set up its own kingdom. That was in 1559.

Two hundred years later King Prithvi Narayan Shah set out from Gorkha and conquered the Valley of Nepal, setting the seal on the unification of the country. To me, the most important aspect of this was that a Hindu king, not a Muslim, Buddhist, Christian, Jewish or animist king, established his religious beliefs as the state religion. Furthermore, King Prithvi Narayan Shah declared that Nepal was the true "Hindu-stan"—and also is reputed to have said, "Never trust the English but always be polite to them." The written constitution of Nepal declared the country as the only Hindu state in the world.

With Brahmanism being more powerful than any animism lurking in the hinterland of Nepal and more Brahmans being in higher positions than Buddhists, I believe Nepal's history can the better be seen not in isolation from Indian history. It is, therefore, germane to consider Indian political aspirations and reactions to the British because Nepalese and Indian Brahmans—always liable to be close to one another—are joined by general mental attitudes even if separated by governmental aptitudes.

The British presence in India, at a time when Mogul rule was disintegrating and conditions were in flux, sorely aggravated many Hindus who saw Europeans as veering towards Islam rather than towards Hinduism.

I do not think it is appreciated, certainly by the majority of Britons who still equate Nepal with Gurkhas, how residually unpopular the British are made out to be, chiefly among dissatisfied schoolteachers, who pass on their dissatisfaction, presumably embellished, to their students. There are two reasons for this, one historical and the other religious, both fostered by Indian-cum-Brahman antipathy. Both have been woven into a "Bible and Sword" interpretation of the Anglo-Nepal war of 1814-16, which has been the staple of all history students in Nepal. To discover why I needed to go back to the defeat of the French, at Arcot, in 1751—my next "milestone date"—before India was conceived as a modern nation.

When the British, the Grocers of Europe, turned into the Spice Traders of Asia, they started something that no one in their wildest dreams, to say nothing of any nightmares, could have imagined. Even at that time, Britain had taken five hundred years or so trying its hand at democracy. To think that Democracy according to the Gospel of St. Westminster should be suitable for countries of other continents and people of other mind-sets is, to my mind, taking too much for granted and unnecessarily arrogant.

Politics aside, the British did see that, without French competition, they would be much better placed for trade and that is why 1751 is such an important date. Not only that, if the French had been in India instead of the British, and I say this advisedly having seen the results of French colonialism in Indo-China, whatever the British did or did not do in India, the French would have done less. On leaving India, there were Indian generals, administrators, lawyers, judges, politicians and others in enough numbers to take over the reins of government in all aspects. When the French gave Laos its independence, there were few, if any, Lao military men who were higher than Warrant Officer and other professions were in a similarly derisory condition.

In 1757, the Battle of Plassey, was as momentous a victory for the English as that of six years previously. As for the inhabitants of Bengal, it has to be remembered that "the Mogul authorities regarded it as a suitable place for exile for the unscrupulous and rapacious"; it was referred to in court circles as "the hell well stocked with bread", that is to say, "the province whose fearful climate was mitigated by its easily garnered wealth and its opportunities for luxury and debauch." Historians tell us that many people helped personally with money degenerated, became spiteful and tenacious. This is still the case.

Nevertheless, Robert Clive's victory at Plassey gave the British enough treasure, loot, specie, call it what you will, to start the Industrial Revolution. England became the world's engine for industrial progress, stealing a march on everybody else but it was then also the centre of gravity in Europe—if not in the world—was a maritime nation and Britons had the spirit of marauding pirates. However much the Indians and other people may have railed against this, there was nothing that could be done. Some accepted this; in others resentment festered. Sadly, even when no reason exists, it still does.

Before Clive's victory the British had only been peripheral to the running of anything in the vast subcontinent. They traded from isolated coastal ports by precarious permission of native rulers, paying homage to the Mogul power in Delhi as subservient and temporary participants. It was only in the second half of the eighteenth century that the East India Company found itself administering possessions many times the size of England. Even then, it regarded this vast area as a windfall for its factors and shareholders. By mid-nineteenth century Britain was the world's wealthiest country.

Happenings thereafter, both in India and Nepal, set the scene for the Anglo-Nepal war from 1814 to 1816. All I would like to add to that is the effect English victory had on the mind-set of certain Nepalis. How is it, I ask, if the Aryan rulers from India, the "Gorkhalis", as government functionaries in Kathmandu styled themselves, thought so little of the English, their alleged cowardice, their perfidy, their administrative incompetence—to name but three negative attributes picked on by Nepali historians—so many hill men deserted the Gorkhali army by, initially between 1790 and 1814, moving down to Lahore to take service with the Lion of the Punjab, Ranjit Singh, and subsequently joining Ochterlony's force against their original Gorkhali army in 1815?

Inaccurate scholarship has it that "Better to die than be a coward" is the motto of all Gurkha soldiers to this day and the exceedingly high standards of Gurkha soldiers could in fact make that true. In fact, the originator of the quotation was not a "traditional martial class" hill man but an Aryan Nepali, Kaji Amarsing Thapa who at the age of 60 was made a General with hardly any, if any at all, active military background, at the beginning of the Anglo-Nepal War in 1814. He was a distant relation of Bhimsen Thapa, the Prime Minister, who started the war and also lost it. Amarsing was just not interested in fighting the East India company but, not wanting to appear against the most powerful man in Kathmandu, echoed, but did not originate, similar sentiments as expressed by a Sikh, Mokhan Chand, in 1809 when the local East India Company military commander, Ochterlony (later Major General Sir David, the victor in the war of 1814-16) moved from Delhi to compel the Sikh durbar to give up its recent conquests, "It is better to die in honour than to live in shame" and later by an Afghan, Muzaffar Khan, defender of Multan in 1818, "It is more honourable to die fighting than to capitulate without firing a shot."

Even so, it is ironic in the extreme for the British to castigate the "founder" of the Indian National Army, one Subhas Chandra Bose, for being a traitor when he allied himself and some Indian soldiers captured in 1942 in Malaya and Singapore to the Japanese in the Second World War yet to extol the type of person they enlisted after the Battle of Malaun in 1815 for the same tendency!

I believe the answer to the first point can be found in the sad fact that the Aryan "Gorkhalis" had no conception of "man management" for soldiers, only "officer management." Despite only once having found a hint of this in Nepalese writings, *Nepalko Sainik Itihas* (Nepal's Military History), when reference is made to the worry of officer casualties in the war in Tibet in 1791-92 but none to the "rank and file", as a military men myself I have noticed a tendency for all those in authority to take underlings for granted. Even the crisis in Nepal at the time of the Anglo-Nepal war could not prevent a significant degree of etiolation in regard to their feelings for the land of their birth. The English, for all their military warts, accepted courage and merit as more important in their rank and file soldiers than, for instance, social position of birth or religion; the Aryan Gorkhalis did not.

Another factor that could have caused those hill men to go over to the British was that, not coming from Gorkha, they were afraid of the excesses and atrocities of Bhimsen Thapa that, even for an age where human rights were never thought about, "knocked the nail out of sight."

As far as the Gorkhalis are concerned, the British wrongly linked the name with the traditional martial classes than with an extended ruling family from the place Gorkha. Gorakh Nath is the most holy Magar god there is and it is in Gorkha town. When the Shah family eventually arrived in Gorkha in 1559 (and founded a dynasty that would last until 2008), what would be more natural than to show appreciation of the senior god than by worshipping it and enhancing it? If my hypothesis is true, they therefore became Gorkhalis, a nickname that applied to all high caste Hindus of that area, whether of the conquering family or later by osmosis of all those living there. During the unification of Nepal, such was the dislike created by ruining the other petty kingdoms, known as the 22 Raj and the 24 Raj, that the Gorkhali dynasty became unpopular. Indeed, it could be argued that those hill men, despised as "non-sacred-thread-wearers", did not regard themselves as belonging to "Nepal"—which only referred to the Kathmandu valley until about the mid-1950s—but only to the states of their birth, Kaski, Lamjung or wherever. This lack of "country loyalty" is understandable to modern onlookers but was unforgivable to those Gorkhalis who had benefited from the situation, namely the officers of the Gorkhali army, almost all thread-wearers, then up on to the Head of State himself. One long-term consequence of unification was the absence of a squirearchy with the elimination of the many petty states that lay athwart Kathmandu, paving the way to a swing to the "left" after Absolute Rule was discontinued in 1990—as was this the direction of the swing after Czarist Russian rule collapsed in 1917.

It could well be that the genesis of the famous motto "better to die than be a coward", started in a letter dated 2 March 1815 to the King of Nepal, from Kaji Amar Singh Thapa, when he wrote; "If we are victorious we can easily adjust our differences, if we are defeated, death is preferable to a reconciliation of humiliating terms." Yet it only gained its current reputation as a result of a certain Bhakti Thapa's gallantry as, in the event, Amar Singh Thapa remained alive, despite having suffered a defeat that changed the history of the nation for all time. (Bhakti Thapa is the author's surrogate son's ancestor on his mother's side.) Can the motto's attraction have been as a result of a "sour grapes" riposte by the Gorkhalis who saw the hill men running to the beef-eating English as cowardice? It would be very interesting to find out when exactly it was that those who still thought of themselves as having roots in Gorkha as Gorkhalis now saw that name linked with traitorous and low caste behaviour, so pejorative and not to be used. How long after the 1815 blow to Gorkhali military pride did erosion set in?

On the brighter side of that coin, the ethnic minorities that did come over to the British side have made the name of Gurkha, however spelt, glorious in military annals and have won Nepal more friends and respect than any other aspect of other countrymen could have done. That is no mean feat.

As for events of the Indian Mutiny in 1857, only of peripheral interest to many Nepalis, after a thread-wearing Bengali soldier, Mangal Pandé, who was seen as firing the first shot of the Mutiny, became infamous in British eyes, "pandy" temporarily entered the English language as an "untrustworthy man", a "traitor", a "turncoat." After 1858 the East India Company army became the Indian Army and, although relations between the Queen's army and the Indian Army became strained and Indian soldiers were kept out of British soldiers' "wet" canteens, all Gurkha soldiers were always allowed in as equals. This "pandy syndrome" must have hurt many Brahmans' feelings considerably—and understandably.

During the century between 1850 and 1950 "Indianisation" of the Tarai, the "rice bowl" of Nepal, was intensified and encouraged. With the extension of this area in 1858, the area was almost wholly dominated by people ethnically close to their neighbours in northern India. Since the mid-1950s there has been some internal migration into the area, some government sponsored, some not. In any case, the results are tinder for ethnic tensions and by 2008 the fire was smouldering in some areas and raging in others.

Palace intrigues and the conflicting loyalties of the most powerful families in the Valley, ever bubbling, finally boiled over on 15 August 1846 when the Prime Minister, Jang Bahadur Rana, ruthlessly eliminated those who stood in his way to becoming the virtual ruler of Nepal. The Shah dynasty, while remaining senior for protocol purposes, became subservient and was eclipsed until 1951, its members being held as virtual prisoners and only allowed out only for special, mostly religious, occasions.

In the context of some Indians' increasingly vocal disenchantment with the British, maybe surprisingly I take 1905 as a "milestone date." This was when the Japanese defeated the Russians at Port Arthur. In this connection, it is opportune to note that Indians are said to be very impressionable and eager to act out what they are impressed by. The tremendous shock waves of realisation that an Asian power could inflict such a defeat on a European power spread through Asia, certainly India.

Also in 1905, the British tried to partition Bengal and modern resistance to British rule might be said to stem from then. Subhas Chandra Bose, inexplicably to the British a cult hero on Nepalese campuses in the 1980s and 1990s, who was born on 23 January 1886, was old enough to understand all this. He is almost bound to have read books about India's struggle for independence. It is not hard to see how some misguided patriots felt here was a man worth emulating, despite it being known how much embarrassment he caused to the Indian Congress Party during their campaign for Independence.

The Ranas ruled as despots and their power was ensured as long as the people of Nepal, especially those living in Kathmandu, acquiesced. Feudalism was the political idiom in many parts of Asia during the nineteenth century. In the first part of the twentieth century the desire on the part of the politically minded in neighbouring India to become independent from British rule had its mirror effect in Nepal where change from the autocracy of the Ranas was sought. A number of dissatisfied Nepalese found themselves in India, by choice or because they had been exiled. A few joined in the "Quit India" movement of 1942 and were jailed by the British. Some senior Indian socialist leaders tried to find asylum in the Tarai, but they were arrested and interned, only to be released by the mob. India seems to have been, and still be, the mainspring of matters not always in sympathy with Nepalitwa, the "Nepalese-ness" of conducting matters.

After 1950, with the emergence of Nepal from behind tightly closed borders, the need to define distinct national values, from political philosophy to dress and language, was felt because of Nepal's desire to keep aloof from what was seen as Indian political hegemony. The repeated declaration of a Hindu state in the constitution compelled the policy makers to define these values in relation to Hindu ideals and primarily high-caste Hindu values.

Only after the British left India did a "home-grown" Indian government have a different view on Indo-Nepal relations. If Nepal was not treated like one of India's twenty-two states, she was not so very far off being viewed as the sixth independent territory. Laws were enacted so that any Indian citizen who wanted to set up a business in Nepal was given enough land to do so. Factories and industries set up by these Indians attracted other Indians. Among other Indo-Nepal legislation, the following opened up opportunities for Indians in Nepal: the Peace and Friendship Treaty of 1950; the treaties of Trade and Commerce of 1950, 1960 and 1971: the Indo-Nepal Corporation Act of 1962, which allowed Indians to take back their original capital plus ten per cent; and the Irrigation and Water Development Projects Treaty of 1954. Indian migration, temporary or otherwise, into Nepal was further stimulated by the establishment of National Trading Ltd in 1962, which encouraged Indians to invest their money in Nepal. Foreign goods made enormous profits, black market flourished and a scandalous situation ensued. The Trade Promotion Centre (1971) and the Industrial Service Centre (1974) stabilised the position. The Citizen Act Law of 1952 gave foreigners citizenship after five years and in the general election of 1958, most Indian settlers, Nepalese citizens or not, were included in the voters' lists. This caused controversy.

Meanwhile great political changes were taking place. The years 1951 to 1955 saw many attempts at trying to institute one system or another that suited the Crown, the embryo political parties and those people (almost entirely of the Tarai and Kathmandu) who had an interest in how their country was run. India's role was either mediation or meddling, depending on individual perspective. In royal eyes the situation was not a revolution but a restoration from 1846 when King Surendra Bikram Shah was on the throne. The king now desired to administer the country according to a democratic constitution framed by elected representation and an interim council of ministers who would assist and advise. Framed around the settlement in Delhi the Interim Government of Nepal Act was promulgated on 30 March 1951 and the king became the real executive head of the country. Although parts III and IV of this act were almost bodily lifted from the Indian constitution, in effect the act restored the legal authority of the Crown as the source of all power in the land.

The Interim Government of Nepal Act, 1954, laid the foundation for royal absolutism and marked a new stage in Nepalese politics. On 18 February 1954 the king reconstituted the National Democracy Party cabinet. It was aimed at being a national cabinet but it soon started mutual bickering. Increased anti-Indian feeling was manifested and India was accused of interfering in Nepal's internal affairs.

King Mahendra dissolved the Advisory Assembly on 10 June 1955 and announced a general election for October 1957. However, there was civil disobedience and the election was postponed until 18 February 1959, Nepal National Day.

On 15 December 1960 the king ordered the arrest of the Prime Minister and, on the same day, issued a proclamation dismissing the government and dissolving Nepal's first elected parliament. The king accused it of, in effect, gross inefficiency. He formed a council of ministers under his chairmanship and banned all political parties. The constitution of 1959 was suspended, less a few provisions, and a new law, called Nepal Special Arrangement Act of 1961, along with renewals of periods of emergency, saw the country through until 16 December 1962 when a new constitution, based on the non-party system and known as the Panchayat Constitution, was promulgated.

It remained in force until 1990, after the third of three Indian-inspired trade embargoes.

Back in 1964 the government had realised that the policy of attracting Indians to settle in Nepal had been too successful and so a policy of discouragement was adopted. However, it had become very difficult to tell who was an "Indian" Indian and who a "Nepali" Indian as, apart from dilatoriness in producing any Proof of Citizenship documents at all, the ability to obtain false ones had resulted in no accurate records being available and no curb being effectively put on Indians who still wanted to enter Nepal, where, in any case, neither passport nor visa was required. Thus it was that some families of over hundred years in Nepal and who regarded themselves as Nepalis had to revert to being Indians and recent arrivals from India became "instant" Nepalis. By 1984 it was reckoned that one in every three inhabitants in Nepal was an Indian.

Anything done by Nepal to modify this situation had to be thought of in terms of what might happen to the very large Nepali colonies, not only near old regimental areas, but in many major Indian cities, as well as the seasonal migrations from the Hills of those in search of work in India and the relative size and strength of India compared with Nepal.

Events leading up to the installation of democracy in 1990 loosened much pent-up emotion which is still simmering. The modern ingredients of tourists, television and overseas travel to mention but three, are quickening the pace of change as never before, as bringing the fuses of all those three "time bombs" closer and closer to the detonator. "Explosion or damp squib?" was the question I was asking myself.

The answer was "explosion" with a 10-year Maoist armed revolution that almost completely changed the face of the country. In 2008 an election was held at which the Maoists won the most votes at just less than 30 per cent of the total cast.

J. P. CROSS

The future can only be turbulent but, as far as the personal story in this book is concerned, is should not impinge on the reader. After all, Nepal has always been turbulent—and maybe that is the key to producing such wonderful soldiers.

AT THE END OF THE DAY

1986

Colonel's Kingdom

> *GURKHA veteran Colonel John Cross*
> *has received a unique honour from the*
> *King of Nepal. He is being allowed to*
> *settle in the mountain kingdom, where*
> *Gurkhas are recruited for the British*
> *Army. Colonel Cross, who comes from*
> *Dorset, was chief recruiting officer for*
> *the Gurkhas until his retirement in 1982.*
>
> *He said: "I would like to spend the*
> *rest of my life there."*
>
> *DAILY EXPRESS [UK newspaper]*
> *Saturday, November 29, 1986*

That makes it sound so simple but, no, simple it was not. I had been serving with Gurkhas for thirty-four years when I started to go blind in 1979 and Nepal, as a sanctuary, with Gurkha hill men as my "eyes," was such a remote possibility that even to think of it was a waste of time. I was in Nepal then and had met up with a penniless and fatherless hill lad from the Gurkha heartland called Buddhiman Gurung, "Dhampu" to his friends. He had run away from home because there was not enough food for the whole family had he stayed there any longer. He had spent five years scraping a living to feed his younger brother and sister who, by 1976, were hungry enough to eat more food than there was. I ensured that he need never go hungry again and he looked on me as his father. Buddhiman guided and guarded me as I progressively lost my sight and I looked on him as my son, relying on him as I had never relied on anyone before except when I was a small baby. I thought I could never get cured and, brought up under the military code that officers don't go sick, kept on with my job for as long as I could, to within two hours of unescorted helplessness.

By the time my sight was restored we were as one tree, I the roots, and he, with his wife, the branches. To settle in his country became something that I wanted more than anything else in the world. It was a combination of survival, love and peace of mind; physical comfort was not a factor in the equation.

I am very proud to have been accepted by the Nepalis and ask: "Do I love them because I understand them or do I understand them because I love them? Whichever it be, it comes from the heart." Either way, I, a Christian Englishman, have been totally accepted by Hindu and Buddhist Nepalis. When asked how did it all come about, I say, "There is no simple answer but, in its way, it is a personal Nepalese odyssey in a different dimension ... "

When pressed for details I have to be more specific and this book is the story of how it all came about. It was not only in a physical context that I found myself away from England and in many countries in Asia other than Nepal. It was also a mental, emotional, spiritual and profoundly personal journey I found I was undertaking, often feeling incomplete, but looking for quite I knew not what, one which took me to peoples' minds and hearts in those countries. I managed both to get nine Asian languages "under my belt" and a name for eccentricity among my own countrymen; many Asians I came into close contact with over the years saw me as "different" from other Europeans and this resulted in a closer empathy with me that with other Europeans. To Asians, eccentricity is seen as an inner strength; to Englishmen, an egotistic but probably harmless desire "just to be different."

Initially it never occurred to me to write about my life, feeling others would not be interested in it even if I wanted to tell others about it. When my book on military Gurkhas was published, the blurb mentioned how I was in Nepal. That intrigued the British broadcasters five times, some British newspapers, local and national, and an author writing a book about the ten most eccentric Englishmen living in Asia—a chapter each—I being the tenth! The book was never published so I have yet to learn how he chose his ten.

I have been prevailed to tell my own story if only because none of those interested people could ever know all the facts, all the pieces of the jigsaw of my personal journey through life. During the more than fifty years I have been with them, I have come to know many more Nepalis better than I have people from the Land of my Birth, England. I can see a problem both as an Englishman can and as a Nepali can—a recipe for never have a duodenal ulcer from worry as well as for constant indecision! I have come to the conclusion that it is not so much what we and others are that causes difficulties in society but what we and others think we are that does. In other words, perception is all. I can also see Nepal in a way that, maybe, Nepalis cannot: phrases such as "wood for the trees," and "the spectator seeing most of the game" spring to mind. Why is this?

In late 1993 I was asked by the spokesman of a film crew on the point of making a film about Gurkha recruitment and training, what was the essential part of my relationship with the Nepalis? I answered straightaway that I never accepted a Nepali as less than an equal and never regarded myself as intrinsically in any way superior. And I have always been accepted.

The start of my army life was as a Private soldier. So much of what I saw and experienced then was frustratingly negative but it was an object lesson of what not to do to get the best out of people as individuals, how best to foster officer-man relationships, why to take the "rank and file," the backbone of any army, seriously. This period affected me so greatly I have included it in my story.

I left England for India in 1944 and the first of a number of visits to Nepal was in early 1947, the year of Indian independence. My last years as a soldier, from 1976 to 1982, were spent recruiting Gurkha soldiers for the British Army. After that I worked in the university in Kath-mandu, as an exotic appendage to higher Nepalese learning, from 1982 until 1986, when I came to Pokhara to live out the rest of my live; these periods I have described. So it is that the morning of my adult life, and its evening, are given in greater detail than the afternoon, despite its unusual challenges and problems.

Since 1985 I have been allowed to settle in Nepal where I feel I belong. I am one of the most privileged foreigners ever to be allowed to lead my life with such wonderful people and I pray, to whichever of the many gods that is nearest to me, that I may continue to live among them till the end of my days. The Call of Nepal is still as loud as it ever was when I first heard it many years ago.

The chemistry and empathy and love between me and the Gurkhas, the traditional martial stock of Nepal, started very early on. I got the best out of them and they of me, so I never had to "soldier on my men." As regards my brother officers and superiors, I was a puzzle. I did not fit the conventional mould so had to prove myself many times over before being taken seriously. So it was that, at the beginning of my journey through life, I quickly developed an urge to go a little farther, to learn a little more about the raw material of soldiering—men, to probe a little deeper, to try and understand a little more. As for the pull of wanting to get married—having fallen in love was it five or six times?—something always seemed to intervene to prevent anything concrete happening, almost as if I was being called away, being willed to do otherwise. Many times there seemed to be no sense in the way events were working out and it was only in the evening of my life that I was told why it all had to happen as it has done.

Looking back, I am fascinated by the series of coincidences, turning points, significant events, call them what you will, that brought me where I am now. I have always been fascinated in the way a chance encounter here, a few minutes late there or a few minutes early elsewhere can play such a tremendous part in a person's life, yet at the time be unnoticed. I am most intrigued in telepathy, a sixth sense and what the "head shrinkers" know as "morphic resonance," collecting thinking, which I heard about very late on, and how such imperfectly understood facets have also added their enigmas to bring me when I am.

Even now I am not sure if what I have learnt can be true although only it makes sense out of all that has happened to me, and to Buddhiman. Non-Asians laugh at me when I tell them. They do not believe it. Please bear with me as I tell this story and then see if you can believe it after all...

THE CALL OF NEPAL

MORNING

1: 1925-1947

My father's side of my family is descended from Cadwalon, King of the Britons in 656 AD—who himself was a direct descendant of Joseph of Arimathea, 24 generations later, down through Cynwyn, Prince of Powys; to the wife of Llewellyn, the last Welsh Prince of Wales killed by Edward I between 1282 and 1284. That gives the eldest son of each paternal generation the family name of Kynaston (son of a king) which has been "good," with a Lord Justice of Appeal, a Bishop of St. Helena, a venerable and honourable Archdeacon of Middlesex (with two Military Crosses), a world record holder for the half mile, a Governor of Tasmania and "bad," with a notorious highwayman and "neutral" for the name of a Berkshire fire engine. The highwayman lived a cave some way up the face of red rock. A secret path led up to it—I was never able to find the path but I did find the cave—and legend has it that he was never caught because he could jump his horse off the ledge of the cave and escape.

My mother's side has an obscure background but has French blood in it resulting from a by-blow of Louis XIV with one member, a suspect black-sheep great-uncle, becoming private secretary to the White Rajah Brooke of Sarawak. What it does show, however, is that the unusual, if not the unconventional, has been the hallmark, if not the curse, of both branches of the family for a long time so it is small wonder that I am a man who had no chance of being anything but unusual, if not unconventional, myself.

My paternal grandfather, Francis John Kynaston Cross, started life by making money in cotton in the north of England and spent the rest of it losing it farther south as a gentleman farmer in Berkshire. He set a world record for the half mile in 1 minute, 54.4 seconds, in 1880, only drinking a glass of milk a day as "extras" during training, was a cross country runner of no mean calibre and played football for Bolton Wanderers' second team. He was almost unbeatable out on the left wing because he somehow managed to run down the field keeping the ball in the air with his knees so could not be legally tackled. I can remember him saying that the grey-flannel trouser was the biggest social leveler of all time, and his definition of a gentleman remains with me yet; "one who is never unintentionally rude."

He married the Honourable Eleanor Mary, eldest daughter of Lord Phillimore, and their five children carried the gift of originality, or the curse of eccentricity, to a marked degree. My father, Philip Kynaston, was the eldest. He died from overwork still comparatively young at fifty-one. He had faked his age in the First World War, joined the Royal Field Artillery and won a Military Cross when adjutant of his battery. He too was a very good athlete. Before the Second World War broke out he rejoined the army: too old for active work, he became first cook then office runner before, eventually, rising high in the legal (Judge Advocate General's) department. The first time he had to defend a soldier at a court-martial was because the accused man had said he would rather work all day for a

German than an hour for an Englishman. Once in court, father asked him what his peacetime profession was? "Grave digger." Case dismissed!

He was a very kind man, with a strong sense of Victorian Christianity, the work ethic, patriotism and family life. He had a great sense of humour, could tell spine-chilling ghost stories, had a great love of the countryside, of animals, of hard exercise and of us children. He had a very good ear for music and would have made a good linguist. He was personal solicitor to Lord Portman, owner of Hyde Park Corner in London and what later became Bryanston School in Dorset, as well as to the Royal College of Surgeons. He was also a junior partner (the "Co") in the solicitors' firm, Wilde, Sapte and Co. It was he who pioneered the idea of making oneself or one's family into a limited company to try and limit the ravages to an estate caused by death duties. His work in London, initially on an income of £200 a year, kept him from the country life he so loved and ensured that mother's housekeeping had to be frugal and accurate.

My maternal grandfather, John Steed, was a Quaker by conviction and a doctor by choice. He met my grandmother, Constance Margaret, a nurse, in Hereford. Dr. Steed worked near or in Staunton-on-Wye, ten miles west from Hereford, for about forty years. He had the second car in Herefordshire, in 1906, which was unaccountably registered CJ 6.

My maternal grandmother was half French, one of thirteen children, ten of whom were girls. Longevity and poverty were common characteristics of them all. They kept close and enjoyable tags on each other until the very end. I only met a few of them and never managed to sort them out in my mind's eye.

My mother, Margaret Constance, was the eldest of four. Blessed with green fingers, a very strong constitution, indomitable fortitude and a fierce loyalty to her family, she and father sacrificed much, worked very hard and lived on a limited budget to give their four children the best they could. After father's death in 1949, mother looked after her youngest son until he married, then busied herself in her garden and social activities in the village of Child Okeford, Dorset, being awarded the British Empire Medal for the latter at the age of ninety-one.

I had two brothers and a sister: Timothy, the eldest, was born eighteen months before me, on 12 December 1923. He had an intellectual faculty that would have surely seen him as one of the best brains of his generation. He was also a fine sportsman. We both had happy childhoods and got on very well together; he quiet, hard working, stolid and introspective; I temperamental, cheeky, physically delicate—a recipe for being a horrible young child. Apart from being born tongue-tied, I nearly died in my first month and, when in the garden in my pram, yelled ceaselessly. The next-door neighbour took his revenge by lighting a bonfire and smoking out my clean nappies as they hung on the clothesline. On being asked to site his bonfire elsewhere he said he would but I had to be stopped crying first. I can remember a stage of being slow and untidy when, in desperation and prophetically, I was told I needed a coloured man to look after me. At home it was fine but at the same school, Shrewsbury, with Cross major verging on being a genius, Cross minor was regarded as a poor edition, unable to produce even moderately good results. This was caused as much by having missed so much schooling and idleness as by what, nowadays, the charitable call "being a late starter."

Gillian, born in 1928 so three years younger than I, was very like me in temperament and looks (bad luck for which of us?), never settled down as the trained medical secretary she became, nor ever found the man of her heart. She was, however, an incredibly gifted horsewoman who broke in Arab stallions for circus and other work and became the first English woman to have her own training colours on the USA racing circuit. In fact, she loved all animals and met her death trying to save a dog on a busy American road.

Three years her junior came David. Blessed with a very retentive memory, studied agriculture and worked on the land before getting his own dairy herd in Dorset, where he put in very long hours. He found himself highly gifted musically, passing this aspect of his talents, as well as his abiding love of the countryside, to his son and daughter.

I never had any thoughts of being a soldier, certainly not before the Second World War broke out and even then I never thought that it would last long enough for me to be involved. At the tender age of fourteen any time longer than the eternity of two months' summer holiday makes no sense at all. I had no idea of what I wanted "to be when I grew up" after the engine driver and schoolmaster stages of childhood had worn off. My sheltered life and stereotypic existence was typical of the children of middle-class gentry of pre-war Britain and the confines of a classical education at public school were taken for granted. Wartime restrictions meant I was more starved of normal teenage activities than otherwise so more sheltered than normal. On the other hand, service in a wartime army would, literally in my case, make a world of difference.

Tim joined the army in 1942, having won one of the finest open scholarships to New College, Oxford, for fifty years and scoring the highest marks in the land when he took the Higher Certificate—a Sixth Form examination. He was a superb athlete as well. I was cast in less heroic mould, just scraping through my School Certificate at the second attempt and being no more than a mediocre games player, although I could sprint. I had worked as a farm laborer on grandfather's farm during the long summer holidays from 1939 and had found considerable empathy with the farm hands. This would have been unthinkable for anyone in my position pre-war. Yet, by the time I was old enough to be called up for military service— at the curious age of seventeen years, nine and a half months, an age that cut a five-year period of schooling short by over a year—I felt that I needed better to understand ordinary people before any thought of applying for a commission. My life till then had ill-prepared me for work with the "other rank element" of the Great British Public.

All able-bodied males had to register for military service when 17 years and nine and a half months of age. On the eve of that edict, on 2 April 1943, I volunteered for service in the army, the Oxfordshire and Buckinghamshire Light Infantry, feeling that my show of patriotism might enable me to join the "Regiment of my Choice" which, in turn, might shield me from one of the more perplexing organs of the Modern Army. To become an embryo infantryman would not detract from any glory there might be forthcoming and would placate an inborn aversion from, and a latent allergy to, matters technical. In any case, as I had to learn how to be a soldier myself, it made good sense to see what made the majority of my fellow countrymen tick.

The Recruiting Centre was the local Drill Hall, in Enfield, north London. I went inside and looked around. Apart from a number of others looking as lost as myself, I saw many little tables and stalls dotted about, reminiscent of a vicarage bun-fight in happier times. I was ordered to visit one and thus started a series of medical and other tests, run by brusque and impersonal men, and which included almost everything includible between head and toe. To find my way from unmarked booth to unmarked booth was a mockery of a treasure hunt for a one-way ticket to an unknown destination. I was baffled by failing to rejoin three pieces of lavatory chain and I was chastened by failing to give correct answers to a test I had felt appropriate to half-wits. I was told to strip and was embarrassed by my proximity to shivering nudity, all trying to fill glass bottles with an air of studied detachment until the problems of time and space overtook them at the very end. I was then told to put my clothes on and, after waiting some time, was called into the office. There was Authority, the Recruiting Officer, sitting amongst stained and squalid furniture, which included an overcrowded desk littered with papers. His manner betrayed an indifference bordering on the apathetic. I took a pitying dislike to him and, in the brashness of youth, felt that if I finished up my service by only being allowed to recruit people, then I could count myself a failure.

The irony of this only struck me when, 33 years later, I finished my own army service as a recruiting officer.

I was motioned to one side whilst he looked at my Enlistment Form, then studied the result of my test papers. Both were uninspiring and he remained uninspired. He sighed, shook his head, absent-mindedly picked his teeth and started asking me the questions which would make me a soldier. He mumbled and interpolated to a degree that left me confused. I thereby failed correctly to answer one question which demanded a reply other than a direct affirmative and in the ensuing verbal mix-up I was loudly and soundly castigated "a fool, like all the rest of you." Thus I earned my first rebuke literally before the ink on the paper was dry. Not an auspicious start!

I had put my occupation as "student" and, surprisingly, was asked if I wanted to finish my school year. In effect that meant I had until mid-August before I had to report for training. I could never have guessed that that four and a half month delay would completely alter my life.

In due course I received papers with my army number and an order to report to the already condemned and out-of-date cavalry barracks at Colchester where the "Regiment of my Choice" was located along with the 16 Infantry Training Centre. A train journey to the town, a bus ride to some unlovely cavalry barracks found me furtively making contact with the sentry at the gate, shyly asking directions at the Guard Room and hesitatingly looking for an Orderly Room at which to report my arrival. I eventually got to a Company Office, peeped in and saw it was empty. More to pass the time than anything else I looked at the notice board. I can well remember my surprise to see pinned up all the words to the bugle calls. Some were mandatory: "You cannot have a baby in the ITC" (the Infantry Training Centre "signature tune"). Others were cautionary: "Pioneer, Pioneer, Pioneer, dog shit on the square." Yet others were defamatory, like the Quarter Dress call: "You've got a face like a chicken's arse." I was frankly appalled by the indelicacy of it all.

My musings on the world of depravity that I had only just entered were interrupted by a gruff voice from behind me asking "what the 'ell are you doin' 'ere?" Anyone wearing plain clothes in wartime was suspect and one so dressed as I, well within the barrack precincts, was an obvious target. An Orderly Sergeant, or some such lesser godling, was nonplussed by my arrival because I was a day ahead of the rest of my draft. I reluctantly entered the barrack room I had been peremptorily shown, feeling like a condemned man. It was a large barn of a place with two-storied "bed cots" neatly arranged along two walls. There was a strong smell of carbolic soap. At one end were two normal beds and a table at which sat two men. One, a grizzled and embittered regular corporal, the other, his mercurial underling, both found me an easy target. Both of these men to my over-charged imagination loomed more than unusually large. In fact the whole barrack area had, to that time, given me the impression of an unhappy and vengeful void, dotted with sullen, sardonic, morose men whose only fault was that there was another batch of recruits to train. The minutes ticked by with unnatural slowness and terrifying deliberation, both in the Mess Hall, where, compared with the civilian standards, the food was lavish, and in the barrack room, where the comparison was merely odious. The two non-commissioned officers watched me in withering silence undress that night, for the first and last time in pink pyjamas, as I squirmed between two rough blankets on a straw-filled palliasse. I immediately realized that changing my clothes at night put me on a social class above them and so the protective value of mingling even with such a small audience as those two old soldiers was crucial to not being different. It was obvious, if only in the short-term, that a chameleon-like non-description and prosaic conformity would make life bearable.

The long-term was too remote to bother with. "Lights Out" gave a blessed seclusion seldom since encountered. Sleep was fitful. Reveille blared all too soon.

The next day the rest of the draft came and any advantage my premature arrival gave me was soon negatived by my speaking differently from most of them. I had neither the dialect nor the obscenities that seemed essential for quick assimilation at that stratum of life. During our kit issue I spoke to the storeman, another old soldier, to me a land-locked version of the Ancient Mariner. He wore two inverted stripes on his left sleeve. Although I knew the answer, I felt I had to make personal contact. I plucked up enough courage and chirruped "Excuse me, please, Corporal, but will you explain what those inverted stripes on your arm mean?" He appraised me sourly and said in a drawled monotone, tapping them with a tobacco-stained finger, "Five years, my boy, five years..." There was a reflective pause before he added, "and the first five years are the worst."

Five years, five months or five days, the time passed slowly at first but quickly gained momentum as we got into the swing of training. We were kept hard at it and I think we earned our pay (21 shillings, £1 and 5 new pence, a week and I managed to save up to 14 shillings a month). There were three other recruits who had been to a public school and we felt that we were resented by the others, who included a soldier with more than twenty years service and was still illiterate and a Welshman trying to learn English. I got used to the deadening repetition of profanities and coarse expletives, meaningless in themselves, said without thinking always and meant in any true context never. I well remember helping a Private Daley write home acknowledging a letter. We all gathered around him and one of us spelt out every word. After a good five minutes and at the third attempt, he got to the end of the first sentence: "Dear mother, thank you very much for that f***ing parcel." He asked what he had written that far to be read out and, on being told, he burst out with "it wasn't a f***ing parcel, it was a f***ing letter!" He only wanted to change the last word of the sentence. The penultimate word meant nothing to him.

The attitude between the officers and their men was interesting. Once again I found that those who should have mattered, the rank and file of the army, did not seem to matter. Was this the norm everywhere? I wondered. Personal contact and kind words were so rare that when they did occur they were a talking point. In the main we found that the higher the officer's rank, the more unforthcoming the person. Was this caused by a lack of contact with troops compounded by lack of experience and thereby of confidence? Or was it the remnants of pre-war social snobbery? Were kindness and harmony thought debilitating for recruits? Anyway, we were uncomfortable in the presence of officers and probably they in ours.

We soldiers were seldom spoken to by an officer even on parade and then seldom kindly. So unusual was it for one such to speak to us as though we were human beings with problems, or who bothered to stop and sometimes even make us laugh, that it was a talking point in the barrack room if ever it happened. Having seen how little trust or camaraderie any of them inspired, I vowed that, were I ever to be an officer myself, I would never make the mistake of taking my men for granted. The results of lack of rapport stayed with me all my thirty-nine years of service in the army, nearly thirty-eight of them in Asia, giving me a bond with the "rank and file" of all countries that never let me down.

In truth I was ignorant about life as well as matters military. But I was eager to learn, painful though at times it would obviously be. All my many brushes with fate I put down to lack of experience, laced with bad luck and, on occasions, a weak conscience. Looking back on those days I shudder at my ingenuousness, but I now regard that being naive is the prerogative of the young and sheltered. So I kept in the background and watched those around me, wise and stupid, high and humble, proven and raw. Influence, I saw, was in direct proportion to a man's sincerity and example.

After six weeks basic recruit training I graduated to advanced infantry training. Sixteen more weeks in another part of the same barracks rubbed off most of the remaining rough edges, while unending physical activity shortened our horizons to bed or the next meal. Conditions were harsh but I was surprised when only a handful of men returned after a 48-hour break mid-way through the training. Those who stayed away were duly chastised when they came back, several days late, but none repented. One man, a habitual offender, was taken in front of the Company Commander only to be told he was, according to the company clerk who had had his ear to the office door keyhole, a "lily-livered, yellow-gutted, slimy-bellied rat," at which he took one pace forward and tipped the whole contents of the Major's table over him, the ink ruining his uniform. In the event it was the Major who was punished (seven days orderly officer at the local detention centre) and not the soldier—"Case dismissed" by the Colonel.

The time I spent under training, rubbing shoulders with those I would never have wanted to speak to in peacetime, was a useful if traumatic experience. I was regarded with suspicion by them all because I spoke the King's English and had been (partially!) educated. One of the greatest benefits of being a private soldier was seeing the class of person I had to work with "from the inside." All I had to do was obey orders, not to take any initiative and to try my best. As the poet Rudyard Kipling is reputed to have put it: *Fear God; Honour the Queen; Shoot straight; Keep clean—and never volunteer!*

After finishing my recruit training and learning what it meant to be "the toad under the harrow," I was informed by the Commanding Officer that I could regard myself as a "potential officer." I said that I did not feel I was ready to train for a commission as I did not know enough about the raw material of soldiering, so I was promoted to lance corporal until I knew enough about handling men. I soon learnt, the hard way and, although it was difficult to a degree I would never have imagined, it stood me in as good stead as my time as a recruit had. I now knew much more than before what soldiers appreciated, what their thoughts were, how to get the best out of them. I lasted out until, not before time, my self-imposed apprenticeship ended ingloriously standing to attention in front of my Company Commander, the butt of his ill humour.

I underwent a Section Leader's cadre, driving instruction, and did my full whack of guard mounting and fatigue duties. I was put in command of a barrack room full of thirty hardened untamables, all bar one more than two years senior to me. I only won the soldiers' respect after I had had to resort to bare fists when I physically had to knock sense into man, a "busted" sergeant, and so angry was I that I nearly strangled him.

As far as Higher Authority was concerned I still had a long way to go but an awareness of protective colouring came to my rescue. The Company Sergeant Major held a practice drill parade one Friday evening, prior to a full-blown affair the next morning. In my hurry I forgot to take my bayonet with me but reckoned that at my normal position of rear-rank soldier I might "get away with it." Alas, I was ordered to be Right Marker and one of the first commands was "Fix bayonets." My immediate and instinctive reaction was to reach for my bayonet and, having embarked on a course of deceit, I carried on by pretending to fix it. Later I pretended to unfix it and was relieved, to say the least, when we were dismissed with nothing said. Two weeks later I asked for a 36-hour pass and was told, succinctly by the Sergeant Major, "Yes, but you wouldn't 'ave got it if you 'adn't been through the motions that day!"

By then I was well on my way to learning about men and my trade, by my own efforts and by seeing how soldiers reacted to whom and why. It was not hard to see where faults lay. Later on I analyzed it by realizing that "upper-class" Englishmen presumed they understood their "social inferiors" because of a common language and heritage—neither, in fact, true. Often the Sergeant had to explain what "the bloke" had meant. It was, I now believe, simply a case of too many officers not being commanders but military bureaucrats who had neither sympathy for, nor understanding of, the people they controlled. I did not break under the strict discipline that at times bordered on the inane: a man was charged for not eating the porridge around a dead beetle on his plate and another for not spreading the butter on his bread in the correct fashion thereby making it crumble. At other times we were treated ruthlessly by being punished for not having a full water-bottle at the end of a 48-hour exercise; being confined to barracks for three days for every missing stud from a boot after a 20-mile route march, and one man even being given seven days' detention for not picking up for scrap a rusty razor blade in a ditch. I had enough inborn wit to avoid most of it as well as having a genuine desire to find out as much as I could about "the raw material."

Even so, I knew when enough was enough after yet another example of gross pettiness, as I saw it, by my Company Commander, an elderly Major. We had been on parade for half an hour from soon after dawn when it was cancelled because of snow and slush. We went back to our barrack rooms. Without any warning we had a surprise inspection at 11 o'clock and I was told to lift up my boot where there were still traces of the morning's dirt. I was castigated in front of the others as being below standard for a lance corporal and not showing a good example. I saluted him and asked permission to speak. I reminded him of what the Commanding Officer had said about telling my Company Commander when I had enough self-confidence for officer training. "I have it now, Sir." His answer was terse: "You are no good as a lance corporal, go and try your luck as a second lieutenant." I had recently been marched up in front of him, having failed to reach the impeccable standard required at guard mounting and I expect it still rankled him. We had had a very late order to wear greatcoats when previously told to get our equipment "blancoed" ready for inspection without them.

A week later I, as Orderly Corporal, went to the office to collect the platoon's mail. I had been on a weapon training parade and so wore my steel helmet. I was stopped by the Company Sergeant Major, stood to attention in a dark passage and waited until the man inside the office marched out. "You can't wear that 'at," the CSM said as he grabbed the hat off the man who was marching out and put it on my head. Then, "Quick march, mark time, left, right, left, right, halt, right turn." The Major, not looking up as he spoke, read out my name, rank and army number. "You are charged with conduct prejudicial to good order and military discipline..."

He then did look up, his eyes dilated with horror and he asked, with vehemence, "What the bloody hell have you done with your hat?"

It was obviously not the time or place to tell him that I, personally, had done nothing. I found my right hand surreptitiously finding its way up the side of my body towards my head. It reached my hat and, horror of horrors, the CSM had clamped it on back-to-front. I quickly turned it round the right way, snapped my hand back to my side and resumed the position of attention, emulating *rigor mortis* in my fear.

I suppose I was lucky only to be "admonished" but my stock rose with my ability to make a good story out of it.

When I left Colchester in April 1944—thankful to be away from those gloomy barracks, although it had, in retrospect, been a very useful penance—there was the chance of volunteering for officer training in India instead of, as had been normal till then, in the Isle of Man and I jumped at it. Because I had deferred my actual call-up for four and a half months by then the manpower requirement for the "Second Front" in Europe had been met and reinforcements for Burma were being gathered. Until that fateful day all my thoughts had been on Europe, fighting against the Germans. When it was time for me to move on, I found that I was to be in the first draft of potential officers for reinforcements to go to India to train for a commission for the war in Burma, with the Japanese as enemy.

I was not particularly keen to go to war nor to India for any reason other than to see what I could do entirely on my own, away from the shadow of my brilliant and dearly loved elder brother. "Make or break," I told myself, as I faced the selection board of senior Indian Army officers, volunteering to be detailed. I "played" it that way as I did not want to cause any more emotional strain for mother; father was standing by to go overseas, probably to Africa, and Tim was waiting for the Second Front to take him to the continent. Mother, a part-time ambulance driver, had Gillian and David to cope with as well as her own mother to look after. To blame the army for going away so far so young relieved me of having to state the real reason for my being happy to leave England. It was one of the most fateful events of my life.

Two days after D-Day, on 8 June 1944, not yet nineteen, I found myself with a hundred and twenty others in a large draft, the first of its kind, for training in India. While waiting for our boat we had been given lectures to prepare us for our new existence. I can recall only two; one on the composition of the Indian Army and the other on health in the tropics. Once again I was shocked when the medical officer, without a trace of a smile, warned us about sex. "Don't forget, a woman for children, a boy for pleasure, but for real ecstasy, a goat."

We embarked on the antiquated troopship SS *Maloja*, the flagship of the convoy, and sailed into the Atlantic, escorted by an aircraft carrier and at least two destroyers. We swung back through the Mediterranean, passing the Gibraltar Narrows with paravanes out, feeling slightly heroic when told that we were only the second convoy to sail that way and wondering what would happen after being spotted by an enemy aircraft. We reached Port Said unscathed.

"You're going the wrong way," the troops guarding the Suez Canal shouted at us as we steamed through. "Who's king back there now?" "Send your washing back to England? this overseas service?" were some of the more printable soldierly witticisms offered in return.

The time spent in the Red Sea (with a submarine escort) was a penance: crowded, stuffy mess decks; heaving, sweaty bodies; unnatural proximity; and a heat none of us had ever imagined. The boat turned round and steamed north for one hour each evening to allow some breeze to filter below decks. Sweat from a drink of hot tea was enough to lather the face for shaving. It rained slightly—the first time in seven years we were told—as we stretched our legs in Aden.

We were taught "Roman" Urdu, the *lingua franca* of the Indian Army, by an officer whose patience proved less durable than my stupidity. I just could not make sense of its arabesque, nasal cadences, its strange-sounding vowels or the intricacies of its "soft" and "hard" consonants. However much I chanted *yih mez hai*—this is a table; *wuh kursi hai*—that is a chair, I could not relate to real tables and chairs. In short, I was such a dunce that I was banned from classes, being given the option of working in the galley or being an officer's batman. I told the "bloke" that I had elected the galley fatigues and the Sergeant Major that I would be batman. For two days I played hooky; for the last week of the voyage I scrubbed the mess decks every morning in addition to other appropriate and penitential chores. We were all relieved to get off the boat at Bombay.

Bombay! The gateway to India! How romantic it had sounded from afar but how sordid it looked and how horrible it smelt from close quarters. I gazed in fascinated horror at the crowds of teeming humanity, ever milling, scantily dressed and, for the most part, volubly gesticulating, excitably demonstrative and depressingly poor. The turbans, the beards, the dhotis, the shirts outside the trousers, the pyjamas by day could become unnoticed features of the every-day landscape. What jarred then, and still do, were the pitiful, the blind, the beggars, the wheedling children, the laden women, the scavenging dogs, the bare-ribbed horses pulling over-loaded gharries, their bulb horns honking mournfully, the old and rheumy-eyed, the young prematurely shriveled, ever eddying and swirling in kaleidoscopic patterns in the monsoon-laden, fetid air. The raucous black crows and cows wandering in the streets with an air of indifference were the only living creatures seemingly unaffected by the heat, the clamour and the squalor.

Doors on Indian railway carriages open inwards and it was fun to sit on the steps, in a cooling breeze, watching the landscape go by. The three-day rail journey north to Delhi then on up to the Indian Military Academy, the IMA, at Dehra Dun, merely enlarged the canvas. The beggars at the railway stations, maimed, blind, clothed in rags and underfed, the mangy, slinking curs, the skeletal cattle, the impoverished shacks, even using boiling water from the engine to brew tea, all jarred my senses. At dawn on the second morning the rails were so slippery that the wheels could get no traction and the train could not get up a gradient. We were ordered out to push it up! It was another world, one totally alien to me. Even the lightning on the horizon was taken for flashes from Japanese artillery fire!

I had a letter of introduction to the Viceroy, Field Marshal Lord Wavell, given to me by my great-uncle, a one-time classmate of the Highest in the Land. "Give it to Archie," had been my instructions but, even as I looked furtively at the imposing address on the envelope as we waited for our next train at Delhi station, I knew that the gap between the Viceroy and me was wider than the one between Dives and Lazarus. I never did use it and, many years later, burnt it unopened.

And so, a month after we left England, we arrived at the IMA (the "Sandhurst of India," with Gentlemen Cadets as opposed to the mere officer cadets at other training schools), our destination and home for the next five months. We were met by the officers who were going to teach us and who wore exciting new cap badges and shoulder titles. The expressions on their faces as they regarded us, travel-worn and pale, long-haired and badly turned out, the first-ever course to come *en masse* from England, showed us as much enthusiasm as we had shown for the Bombay crowds. To us, used to seeing an older generation of officer in England, they struck us as incredibly young compared with their grizzled counterparts on the Home Establishment. Not one word was spoken until a gorgeously starched wonder leisurely strolled over to us but, instead of any word of welcome, it looked down its nose and drawled, "If you want a pee, go behind that hedge there." We had arrived.

The camp was superb, set in spacious grounds made wonderfully green by the monsoon rain. After the cramped conditions on board ship, our accommodation—and being looked after by a bearer—was palatial. Here we could be, and were, happy.

Once our training had started we found what the old lags had said was true, "the scene changes, but the music never." For elementary subjects we were taken in hand by gnarled British warrant officers and sergeants who told us that "when in Rome you do as India does. Get it?" And get it we did. As we progressed with our training the officers taught us tactics and jungle warfare. Only now did those earlier lectures on the Indian Army penetrate my insular mind and begin to make sense. It was only when these different peoples were produced in the flesh that I could equate a name with a type. I don't think it ever occurred to me that by no means did all Indians speak Urdu as their first language. The majority of India's millions speak their own. I found I could get on with the local people I came into contact with. I tried out my smattering of Urdu as and how I could but it was not yet enough for a proper conversation.

One of the peoples we heard about were the Gurkhas of Nepal. We were told that Nepal was, and always had been, a sovereign Himalayan state, nothing to do with India, with entry forbidden to all outsiders; that, ever since 1815, the Gurkhas had come down from their mountain villages to join the army because they liked service under the British. It was paradoxical that neither group could visit, let alone serve in, the country of the other's birth or domicile. Wherever else did this situation pertain? We heard that they were very loyal, very brave and tractable, and that they were apt to chop their enemies' heads off with a deadly knife called a kukri. It took a long time for an outsider to be accepted by them, after which there was nothing they would not do for that person. People said that it was a great privilege to serve with the Gurkhas who were seen as superior to most, if not all Indians, and equal to the best the British Army could produce. Some went as far as to say that they were the finest soldiers in the world.

The first time I came across a group of them at close quarters was when we went on a jungle training exercise and they acted as enemy. Short men, with skins coloured brown to wheaten, shaven-pated with smooth, round faces, high cheek bones and almond eyes, they were squatting in a group during a lull, talking. I, struggling with the compulsory Roman Urdu and not managing at all, listened in awe to the staccato grunts and atonal ululations of their normal conversation. How could anyone understand, let alone speak, such a language?

They emanated a presence and showed an inner strength which fascinated me but, so overwhelmed was I at their professionalism and high standards, I told myself I would never be good enough for service with them. Despite the initial attraction, they were not for me—or was it I was not for them?

The British subalterns in the three Gurkha regimental centres in Dehra Dun, behaved arrogantly, as if they were inordinately superior to other men. I did not like them although, to be fair, I only saw them occasionally when I went out at weekends and walked around the town or when Gurkhas acted as "exercise enemy." I noticed how the Gurkhas themselves clammed up when one of their subalterns came upon them, how they answered in the brusquest of monosyllables. There seemed to be no rapport and yet, when a captain or a major spoke to them off parade, there would be mirth, a flashing of wonderful smiles, the intimacy of empathy, harmony and a common purpose. Was it a case of those subalterns not feeling as exalted as had they been with lesser soldiers? I later learnt that it was not so much the extra rank and a year or so in age but the confidence that the Gurkhas had in their more senior and proven officers and the love that those officers had for them that made such a difference. With the Gurkhas, at last, I found that those who should matter, the soldiers, did matter to their officers. I was young, immature and impressionable—and very impressed.

Six weeks or so from the end of our course, we were asked to give three regiments we would like to be commissioned into, as well as stating did we want to go to the British Army, Indian Army or be attached to an Indian regiment yet commissioned into a British regiment. I really had no idea so I sought advice from the Company Second-in-Command, a man called Griffiths who had been at school with Tim. Although I might be one of those about whom it could be said that his men would follow him if only out of curiosity, he told me to try not to go to a British unit as any experience in the Indian Army would stand me in very good stead. However, I was advised not to go into the Gurkhas as "linguistically, you're not even up to speaking Urdu," let alone my having to learn a second language, the Gurkhas' "Khaskura" (a patois hill men spoke as a second language, not the "Nepali" that educated Nepalis spoke). So I decided to join an Indian not a British unit, dismissing the idea of Gurkhas entirely.

I therefore applied, along with five others and advice from Captain Griffiths, for one of three Indian regiments. A letter was sent to the depot of our first choice with our names, and recommendations. I was number five on the list. Even though there was talk about Indian independence some time in the future, it did not mean much to us. In those days, as far as I can recall, we did not read newspapers, nor did we have access to news from a wireless. The political situation made no impression on us: we were intent on being commissioned and getting to the war, if only to prove ourselves to ourselves. However, as the future was murky (not so much as to the outcome of the war but what would happen to India and when) most of us volunteered to be commissioned into a British Army regiment and then be attached to the Indian Army. This is what I did. As I remember it, only a few of my batch were commissioned into the Indian Army.

Three weeks before we were due to be commissioned I was given a telegram. So badly written was it that I could not properly decipher it but it looked as though Tim had been awarded a decoration for bravery. Excitedly I went to the local post office and asked to see the original. I was dismayed to read that he had been killed in action. We had been so close. He had never wanted to be a soldier and hated violence. What a waste of a life of such promise. I had no details of what had happened. After so many years all that I remember very vividly is, over the next forty-eight hours, feeling an infusion of his spirit into me. I acted oddly. Certainly people would look away when I was near and, a week later, I was sharply brought back to reality by a withering rocket from one of the officers for not trying and did I want to be relegated?

In any case, I had very nearly been relegated as I had to go into hospital with "dhobi itch," a skin disease that makes walking a penance. I was promoted to Cadet Quarter Master Sergeant and made to look after the stores, riding to inescapably important field training in vehicles that took the hot meals out.

In early December we were told our future. I was to be commissioned into the British Army (not into the earlier "Regiment of my Choice") but not posted to the Indian "push" Griffiths had suggested. Only the first four on his list were selected. I found, to my consternation, that I had been posted to the First Gurkha Rifles—and that without passing my written Elementary Urdu examination, let alone my fears of inadequacy. Again, not the Regiment of my Choice.

A letter from home arrived telling me that, in essence, Tim's death had been unnecessary. Apparently a message he had been sent was capable of more than one interpretation and he acted wrongly. An Englishman, using English to another Englishman, was incapable of expressing himself clearly enough to avoid confusion and a fatality. How much more likely was I to foul up, say, an ambush situation because I could not speak the Gurkhas' language properly? I could not bear my linguistic rather than tactical incompetence causing a mother to lose her son, a wife her husband, a child its father. I saw fluency and the correct use of language not only as a tactical weapon but also as a vital, literally, element of command. With Tim's spirit now within me I henceforward found I had no trouble with learning languages. Hard work, sure, but they made sense and I enjoyed learning them. In retrospect it was almost as if God, not wishing Tim's precious talents to go wasted, had sent them on to me. Certainly, it is no exaggeration to say this gift also changed my life.

None of that dulled the thrill of having "made it." Those little pips on my shoulder were, in themselves, only small emblems of the great journey I had made till then, however great the real change in status, purpose and knowledge did they represent. From the impersonal approach during my training in England, proud though I had been to become a lance corporal, where I never felt I belonged—"belonging is sharing"—to being part of an extended family was another sort of change and one that stayed with me from that special day, 10 December 1944, for the rest of my service.

After leaving Dehra Dun a group of us spent two weeks leave in Simla. Captain Griffiths had managed to get us fixed in the Viceregal Lodge. The wonderful air of the mountains cured my skin complaint overnight and I went for long walks. One day I went up Jacko Hill, on the top of which was a Hindu temple, looked after by a man who, so rumor had it, was an unfrocked Roman Catholic priest. Rumor also had it that this man had power over the three separate groups of monkeys up there either to make them desist from any attack they were making on a person or to egg them on if he thought that the person concerned had been teasing them. On my way up I saw a European striding along the path, dressed in Indian clothes, head on chest, rapidly approaching me. I stopped until he was opposite me and greeted him, "Good afternoon, Father." He momentarily checked his pace and turned his head towards me. He looked me straight in the eyes and I saw his were a deep purple colour and twice the size of any other eyes I had ever seen. I was terrified and ran away, pausing only when I was well round the next corner. For one who had been taught how to lead men in battle this was a serious blow to morale and self-esteem. It had to be rectified.

Accordingly, next afternoon I went up again, this time with Captain Griffith's bull terrier bitch. Once there we were surrounded on three sides by monkeys who advanced threateningly towards us. Terrified we ran away, down the only open track, but were stopped by unfriendly cattle. I jumped over the side of the mountain and slithered down, in seven minutes, the distance I had previously taken over an hour to cover. At least the bitch had the advantage of not having gone though the bottom of her trousers. "Peace hath its defeats as well as war."

Whilst in Simla I met and felt happy with an English girl, Felicity Barrington, who lived with her mother. It is not always easy to remember that, during the war, air raids, reduced travel facilities and food rationing curtailed normal activities that are taken for granted in peace time. Having been to schools where there were only boys I was starved of female company—we all were. At nineteen, the euphoria at being commissioned, a fertile imagination and a brief holiday in a bracing climate were all conducive to "that rush of blood." I remembered what the old soldiers said, "If you can't be good, be careful and if you can't be careful, remember the date." It was when I discovered that she was not a well-formed nineteen but an overblown twelve that I called it a day, without ever having called it a night. I later met her in London and was glad I had been more than circumspect: it would not have been a happy liaison.

On 27 December 1944 I reached the First Gurkha Regimental Centre at Dharmsala, later to become famous as where the Dalai Lama took residence after fleeing Tibet. The narrow-gauge track down from Simla gave way to the broad-gauge railway in the plains. At one station I went to have a look at the engine and the driver saw 1 GR on my shoulders and asked if that stood for Indian Government Railways? This was not as bad as the British Service officer who thought that DOGRA on a shoulder title did not refer to the eponymically named regiment composed of Hindu Dogras from the Punjab but stood for Duke of Gloucester's Royal Artillery! Then I changed again on to another narrow-gauge line that wound its way through low hills to the railhead at the small town of Pathankot. From there it was a road journey of about fifty miles, along a gently rising valley until a steeper climb for the last 3,000 feet into the clear, crisp air, where pine and rhododendron forests vied for supremacy and Simla was a hundred miles away across the haze. The centre itself was situated at about 5,000 feet above sea level, sprawled over the hills that turned to mountains which were perpetually under snow. It had been built, temporarily, many years before and had been added to until it had spilled into some of the lower valleys. The men's lines had long been condemned but finance, that age-old bogey, stalked with deadening effect here as in so many other places in the Army of Hind. There was no electricity or running water and all conditions were rudimentary. A backlog of subalterns had been waiting, some for more than a year, for a posting to an active battalion. It seemed that I, too, would be stuck there for ages. Meanwhile, I was posted to a recruit training company to learn the rudiments of all that which is needed to be a commander of Gurkhas.

I had to come to terms with that quintessential aspect of the Indian Army, and indeed the Brigade of Gurkhas today, namely *kaida*, the proper way of doing things in a tightly knit, well-organized extended family that a good unit is. Each unit has its own *kaida*. In the regimental centre it was stiff and reeked of pre-war snobbery. Officers with "temporary commissions" were known as "temporary gentlemen" and the toast to the King Emperor on mess nights was prefaced, more than once, "Gentlemen and Temporary Officers." Contact with soldiers was mainly during parade hours. Until a new officer is accepted, he is minutely observed, much more than he realizes. Quirks and foibles are watched and, provided nothing untoward is noticed, acceptance comes sooner or later, probably with a nickname that is seldom known by the officer concerned.

In rare cases when the senior Gurkha officer, the Subedar Major, saw that a particular officer's chemistry simply was not in accordance with what the Gurkhas were used to or would accept, preventive action was taken. The commanding officer would be told that, if the officer remained, the Subedar Major could not accept responsibility for any mishap. In the British Army such events happen the other way round, any misfit only being got rid of after the "omelette had hit the fan."

At school my French master had castigated me for my abysmal ignorance and criminal disregard of the blunter, to say nothing of the finer, points of grammar. "You're no good, no good at all," he used to snort at me. "You're bottom of the class and yet, let you run free in France, you'd be better than all the rest in no time." The long-suffering man, called out of retirement for the second time, had noticed that I had a "protective brogue" and a "musical ear" that allowed me to sound genuine even if badly educated. This ability had seen me though the oral part of the Urdu exam which, despite lack of progress on the troopship, I had passed at the IMA without too much difficulty. I put that down partly to hearing the language spoken around me so not learning it in a vacuum but mainly to brother Tim's gift. The written part had been too much for me. I was not allowed to study Khaskura until I had the whole exam under my belt.

In early January 1945 14 feet of snow fell in two days. Roads were blocked for miles around and, if they remained impassable, rations would be in short supply. Recruits were formed into gangs and armed with plates, there being a woeful shortage of spades and shovels, to open the road leading up from the plains. No military work could take place. The young Gurkhas had not been away from home long enough to lose their freshness so the nearest any of us got to training for war was when one gang ambushed another with a barrage of snowballs.

Those who had had boots issued wore them, sodden, uncomfortable and very strange. Those with no boots wore sandals. The lads, none over eighteen years of age, had never worn boots before. One made the mistake, not only of putting the boots on the wrong feet, but lacing them together. The first step he tried to take saw him crashing down on the ground, bursting his nose open. He was taken to the hospital, admitted and issued with a shroud as well as pyjamas. The Irish doctor did not think he would die because of a sore nose but he had been found deficient of shrouds on the last inspection and was determined to leave nothing to chance. Every person admitted to the hospital had to sign for one—just in case. This practice had to be stopped soon afterwards as it was having a depressing effect on morale.

The two eldest soldiers worked in the band store. Both were reservists who had been considered too old for service in the Kaiser's War. Both wore the medal ribbon of the Tirah campaign of 1897, the elder having been enlisted in 1891, the younger in 1892.

When the snow cleared we settled down to the humdrum of basic training. Try hard though I might, I could not "get through" to the soldiers, chiefly because of the language barrier but also owing to only meeting them when they were on parade. On the few occasions I went to the Gurkha officers' "club" (Gurkhas only had messes after they had become part of the British Army), I had to use Urdu, which I felt was wrong. Before I could arrange to sit the written part of the Urdu exam I fell foul of the Colonel, completely by accident, but foul nonetheless. It would not have happened had we felt we "belonged."

One Saturday a British officer and his English fiancée were married in the local church of St. John in the Wilderness. We all paid a share, based on rank, for their present. That done, and not knowing the officer or the lady in question, two of us youngsters decided it would be much more fun to go for a long walk. We presumed that our absence would not be noticed, but it was. We had not been guilty of any military offence, only of a grave social solecism. We did not know how to behave as "sahibs," did not know the *kaida* and our presence was no longer required in the Regimental Centre. Although it had never occurred to us that that would be so, it was yet another twist of fate as, within a very short time my friend and I, to the envy of those who had been trying to leave for months past, found ourselves posted down to the plains of India, to a training division for the Gurkha Rifles south of Dehra Dun— from the back of beyond in the middle of winter to the middle of nowhere at the start of the hot weather.

Here, nearer the war, I felt that training had more of a purpose than was the case at the Centre in its remoteness, shadowed by those snow-covered mountains. Here we lived in the same section of the camp as the men so had plenty of chance to find out more about them. Training was based on warfare in the jungle prior to us joining an active battalion in Burma. I quickly settled down to the last touches required for the written Urdu exam, held in the rum-producing town of Saharanpur to our south, and passed it with a sigh of relief. It was now time to learn Khaskura.

I was not happy with the heat. Our accommodation was small thatched huts, with mud walls two feet high, topped by a thick rush trellis and roof made out of the same material, a haven for the tiny sand fly that gets into the eyes, bites with an itch and is a pest. Bathing facilities were rudimentary; a hipbath in an enclosed corner of the hut. Mosquitoes were in plenty and there was a squad of men whose job it was to spray every hut from time to time. I had, earlier than usual one evening, got into the hipbath when one such squad was on its rounds. The leader came into the "bath room" to spray the walls. As he left, he redirected his spray and gave me a squirt in the centre of the target. I was so flabbergasted that words failed me. By the time I had recovered my wits the squad was away and, in any case, I was hardly dressed for pursuit even had I the vocabulary to sustain a verbal barrage.

Had anyone suggested that I would voluntarily undergo any hot weathers after the war was over I would have told him not to be crazy.

Luckily for all us young officers there was, in the training headquarters, a remarkable man, Colonel Rogers, of the First Gurkhas. In 1886 his father had raised the Second Battalion and the son joined the First Battalion in 1910. He was an eccentric, a brilliant linguist, a marvelous mimic and a very good language teacher. Apart from Khaskura he spoke a number of tribal languages and, certainly to my knowledge, Punjabi and French. When he joined the regiment it was not "the done thing" to learn Khaskura because only Urdu was acceptable and the wretched man was socially a misfit for some time. A bachelor, he had been awarded a Military Cross in the First World War but was now too old to command his beloved 1/1 Gurkhas in Burma. I had the incredibly good fortune to attend one of his last-ever courses, as well as an extra week's tuition with only two others. He was vain and difficult to please but he struck a chord with me to such an extent that from the very first day of instruction I "heard" what the men were saying although I could not understand them. By the time my five weeks were over I could talk a little and felt confident that I had a solid grounding and one on which I could easily build. Although devastated, I was given a powerful incentive to greater efforts still when I got two letters from Tim during my study period. Delayed in the post, they had both been written six months earlier. I enjoyed talking to the soldiers and was stupidly pleased when they understood me. I looked forward to being posted to an active battalion before the war ended. While still under training "Victory in Europe Day," known to the Western world as VE Day, came and went: I arrived.

Celebrations for VE day included a feast in every company. I was given a drink. I was very thirsty and the light was dim. The metal tumbler I was offered seemed to contain water and I swigged a large mouthful before realizing that it was raksi, colourless country spirit. I was taken completely by surprise and the sheer violence of the stuff choked me. I asked for some water and, when more colourless liquid was poured into another glass, did a repeat performance. Here was a new sahib being tested. For the first time in my life I became gloriously drunk and found, to my delight, that I could converse fluently with the men, understanding them and being understood by them.

A regimental nautch was a replica of Hill culture where women did not dance. Young men took their place. Costumes were stylized to reflect male and female performers. Each unit had its own nautch clothing and make-up. (There was nothing homosexual about the performance. In all my service I only ever heard of two cases of a Gurkha, neither a hill man, trying to perform with a Gurkha and both were unsuccessful. Homosexuality is unknown in the hills of Nepal.) It was very much later, when I was the only British officer left, that I was inveigled to dress up as one of the dancers. I soon mastered the rhythm of the movements and found myself singing a song, the refrain of which was repetitive and pointless. The key word was "relimaiñ" and that became my nickname for many years. When it was all over, so I was told next morning, I was carefully taken to my accommodation, undressed and put to bed. I had been accepted: I now belonged.

I left India in late June 1945 to join 1/1 Gurkha Rifles in Burma. After the war ended we were posted to Cochin-China to disarm the Japanese and even to take military action against Vietnamese guerillas who were intent in impeding that task. In one engagement I found myself commanding a Japanese battalion. We returned to India in early February 1946 and were due to leave the army shortly afterwards. I had been wondering what to do after demobilization. I had no qualifications for any satisfying job or for a place at university. I dislike waste of material objects, time and talent and had, by now, learnt enough about the army to feel I could cope with peacetime soldiering. I knew enough about the Gurkhas, their language, customs, military standards, their reaction to me and mine to them, to be happy for continued service with them, a remote possibility at that uncertain time, even if it did mean more hot weathers. Lieutenant Colonel Cyril Jarvis, probably the most understanding Commanding Officer I ever had, advised me to try my luck at becoming a regular officer.

On the way back to India I stopped off at Singapore to attend a War Office Selection Board in Changi. We were billeted on the steps of the grandstand at the Bukit Timah racecourse, there being no other accommodation available. I shocked the Major General in charge when he found out that I had only served with British troops as a Private soldier. He saw that as a "bad thing," so I was joyfully surprised when I was graded "B," above average, sure of a place in the regular sun.

Back once more in India we found much more evidence of our political unpopularity than before. To relieve an Indian battalion that had mutinied, we were sent from Dehra Dun after a stay of only a couple or so weeks to the geographical epicentre of the subcontinent, near Nagpur, as the hot weather started and saw our world gradually going mad. At first we were entirely occupied with airfield defence but later we became involved, though only a little, praise be, in the city itself. The weather was rapidly becoming hotter and hotter until by mid-May heat lay everywhere like a malevolent pall. It sapped what little vitality anyone had left. The brazen sun scorched down all day out of a cloudless sky and night brought no respite. It burnt the grass, it reduced big rivers to a trickle and dried up the small ones. It took all the moisture out of the soil and wherever any vehicle moved, be it humble bullock cart along a village track or motors passing one another on the main roads, huge piles of fine, cloying dust hung effortlessly for a long time afterwards, getting into every crevice and cranny of all that passed through it. Men prayed for rain.

The countryside was arid. It lay, flat and ugly, unrelieved by any humps or bumps for many miles. Stunted runts of cattle, mangy curs and drab patches of withering trees all contrived to give an air of unsavory decrepitude. Only the birds of prey, the vultures, the kite-hawks and the crows seemed impervious to the heat. At night the jackals, ever hungry, made the place resound with their cacophonous threnody.

In Nagpur it was purgatory. A lack of any normal facility to get cool; primitive sanitation and wretched overcrowding along with chronic unemployment and abject poverty made conditions rife for political explosion. Even so the battalion played football against the "Telecoms," a Post Office team. The Gurkhas had, in the local press, been branded as "uncivilized barbarians from a foreign country" and we, their officers, were guilty of keeping our men in this savage state the better to enforce Great Britain's policy of subjugation of the subcontinent. Our Gurkha spectators all carried kukris which were shown to the crowd with chastening effect. The only incidents were when I, playing Outside Left, came haring down the wing and was tripped up in full flight by a spectator. I crashed to the ground, knocking over several of the crowd, the last of whom hit a row of stacked bicycles which all fell over like a house of cards. Unfortunately the man who tripped me took the full weight of my fall and had to be helped away with a suspected broken arm. A little later I took a corner. As I kicked the ball very hard, a small head poked itself forward five yards away from the ball which, as though drawn by a magnet, connected with such a resounding crack as to be heard all over the ground and with such force that the hapless youth was knocked out. I almost felt guilty, but was sorry that neither incident counted as a goal. The newspapers gave full and uncomplimentary coverage about "Lieutenant Cross and his tiger tactics." One unexpected result was that all the local auditors went on strike and harassed holders of newfangled peacetime accounts breathed sighs of relief. "Win some, lose some!"

Anti-British sentiments flared; Hindus and Muslims carried out sporadic acts of hate against one another. The British and the Gurkhas came in for an equal amount of vituperation; the heat and the hostile atmosphere outside the camp increased camaraderie within the unit. I remember one of many crowds that came, with a band, to demonstrate against us one Sunday afternoon. Their only tune, played over and over again, was "Will ye ne'er come back again?"

During the worst of the heat it had reached 118 degrees Fahrenheit and that was reckoned a cool year. Then, after the annual miracle of the monsoon rains, cooler weather came again. To be back in the 80s and low 90s made living much easier. Games were reintroduced and work resumed at a normal rate. Yet doubt as to our own future and that of the battalion prevailed, nagging us like a persistent toothache. We had to learn to live with it, forgetting it only when the pace of work or sport took our minds off it. The only way we found we could cope was by pretending, yes pretending, that what we were planning for and doing was to help us through the next fifty years, because, whatever our personal future, we hoped that the battalion would continue. That alone made easy and worthwhile an otherwise meaningless task.

In late 1946, after the seething heat of central India had abated, we moved to the shramming cold of Razmak, on the North-West Frontier, "tribal territory." At 6,000 feet above sea level it was the high-water mark of British-Indian imperial policy to keep the Russians away from the subcontinent and to prevent marauding Pathan bands from despoiling the fertile valleys of the Punjab. Nearby was Alexandra Post, at 8,200 feet the highest fortified point of the British Empire. The writ of the government of India only ran the width of the road and all was fair game, under tribal law, elsewhere. The Pathans, looking for a soft target and always after weapons, kept us alert when we picketed the barren, stony mountains to keep the road open until the up and down convoys that kept us in contact with Bannu in the plains below had passed us. Running up and down the mountains on road-opening days and, in the lines, squash (with excellent markers), football and once even cricket, that had to be abandoned when snow stopped play, kept us all very fit. All built at great expense, it was abandoned soon after Partition.

At that time rumor was rife and all-encompassing: rumor of Partition, rumor of India leaving the British Empire, rumor of officers' postings to the British Army, rumor of Gurkhas going to the British Army—nothing ever firm. Doubt as to the future was no new thing to live with. In the eighteen months since the end of the war we had learnt the truth of the cliché "rumor is a lying jade." None of us for a moment ever imagined we would, albeit unwittingly and unwillingly, join in the pell-mell rush to coincide with the politicians' count-down to a state of affairs which no Indian or Briton, even the most arrogant and hard-line, could ever have predicted.

Indianisation of Indian units meant their British officers pulling out, but not in our case. In Gurkha units there were no Indian officers to hand over to and we could not just leave the battalion and shove off. Abandoning men was something none of us had ever imagined but that is what was to happen. Lucky it was for the peace of mind of us all that this dreadful occurrence could not be foreseen, was therefore never envisaged.

I had started to learn the Nepali script, Devanagri, meaning "the god of the city," so revered was it originally, with the civil schoolmaster, determined to be able to read and write Nepali. I sat the wrongly named "Obligatory Nepali," it being entirely voluntary, examination, and passed in the high 90s. My brother officers told me, condescendingly, that it was a waste of time as we would never serve with Gurkhas again. It paid me very good dividends when, in the February of 1947, two of us were personally invited by His Highness, The Maharaja of Nepal, to Kathmandu for a visit. This was not quite as grand as it sounded but, even so, was unusual. We viewed the prospect with mixed feelings: we were thrilled at the thought of the visit but were dubious about travel through India with conditions so volatile.

The journey to the Nepal-Indian border started off by road, from Razmak to Bannu, thence, for the next four days through India by rail. It was slow, boring and extremely unpleasant much of the time. Still on the Indian side of the border we were met by the Legation Bungalow Overseer and a couple of uniformed orderlies. We were thankful for the peace and serenity of it all after such a long and tiresome journey. We were both very excited about the rest of the way.

Early on the morrow we went to the railway station at Raxaul to catch the train that the Nepal Government Railway operated over the Tarai, as far as Amlekhganj. There was one "up" and one "down" train every day. The one first class carriage was painted red outside and had black leather upholstering inside. The second class carriages had brown bodywork, red footsteps, silver windows, yellow lettering and green leather. We got on the train a mile south of the border and when we did reach it we were amazed to see nothing more than a ditch as the frontier. Neither the terrain nor the type of person on the Nepal side looked any different from what we had seen on the Indian side. What an anticlimax! It made our first expected view of the Himalayas and other mountains even more tantalizing.

At all the stations we were the object of great curiosity but, and this was such a contrast with India, obvious friendliness, balm to our souls after such a hectic journey. At the first station a cloth merchant who had been with us since Lucknow took us on to the platform and spoke to us in Nepali so that the bystanders could hear. The crowd quickly doubled itself and many questions were asked as to who we were and why we were travelling.

At Amlekhganj, the railhead, we were called over by someone to meet the imposing figure of the local governor who was surprised that we could speak a little Khaskura. A General, he was one of the sons of the Maharaja and he lent us his car for the journey up to the road head at Bhimphedi, a very kind gesture, while two soldiers we had with us took our baggage in a lorry. It was unfortunate that the car had a puncture soon after setting off but the driver prevailed on us not to abandon him to take the lorry as that would have been seen as cheapening the kind gesture of the governor. On this part of the journey another illusion was shattered when the first religious edifice I saw was a mosque. I was similarly surprised when I learnt that Nepal, as the arch-Hindu country of all, used Persian, the language of a Muslim country, for its official correspondence with the British in the nineteenth century.

Only when we reached the foothills were our official passes requested.

On the two-day journey we were fascinated with everything and everyone we came into contact with. This was the Nepal of our dreams and of our imagination. After a stiff climb that evening we settled into a government dak bungalow for our evening meal and the night and found great joy in being understood when we spoke to people. Next day we walked through the almost empty spaces called Kulekhani and saw two gangs of porters carrying a motor car on two large wooden platforms that had four protruding handles, long enough for twenty-five men to catch hold of. On one platform was the chassis and on the other the engine. One man carried the spare wheel and one carried the toolbox. A rope-line strung on poles ferried some goods from the Tarai to the Kathmandu Valley, otherwise all was humped by manpower. We also met some of our soldiers returning from leave. They were astonished to see us and warned us of dangers if we left the track, and to beware of bad men. Over the next mountain and there, at the top, we saw the distant Himalayas sparkling in an atmosphere clearer and cleaner than any I had seen before. The countryside was austerely beautiful. Villages of red and white, or terra-cotta coloured houses seemed to cling to the slopes or balance atop a ridge with pasture, firewood and water often hundreds of feet below. The mountain sides were terraced, with some plots so small that they had to be dug by mattock instead of a single-bladed wooden plough pulled by a pair of oxen.

We were met at Thankot by Lieutenant Colonel Sandy Macleod and were driven, in one the six cars then in the Valley, to the legation compound. Towards the end of our journey we drove along some of the one and a half miles of metalled road in Kathmandu. We thankfully relaxed for the rest of the day.

What a pleasant contrast we found Nepal was to the pulsating masses of shrilly indignant and explosive humanity we had left behind in India, constantly whipped up to a pitch of anti-British fervor generated by unscrupulous, power-hungry politicians, exacerbated by wholesale untruths and malicious acts of unpremeditated violence. Here all was clean and friendly, smiling people and we found it fascinating and exhilarating to be able to communicate with them in their own tongue. Because they were seldom seen, Europeans were an object of curiosity, not scorn. And were we curios! Large crowds gathered wherever we went and one attractive but particularly smelly Tibetan girl came over to me, pulled back my sleeve and pinched me, wondering, no doubt, if this albino monstrosity had flesh even if he had no blood. There was a magic quality to it all, helped by the romantic name of the capital, Kathmandu. Ever since then the pull of Nepal, nay the Call of Nepal, as opposed to India, has been very strong.

Colonel Sandy Macleod was one of only four members of the British Legation. He had been our first Commanding Officer up in Dharmsala and was responsible for getting our visit sanctioned. Other than these four—a diplomat, a soldier, who paid out pensions to ex-servicemen, an engineer and a forest man, and their immediate families—there were no other foreigners at all, less some Indian traders and Tibetan pilgrims. Later on that evening Sandy Macleod told us something about the country.

Monarchy has been the system of government in Nepal for the past two millennia. The present, Shah, dynasty, related to royalty in Rajputana, was once only associated with the principality of Gorkha, seventy-five miles to the west, which it captured in 1559. A later ruler is recorded as having supreme authority in matters civil and military. In those days Nepal only referred to the Valley with its three separate kingdoms: Kathmandu, Patan and Bhaktapur. "Gorkhas" were high caste Hindus, not Mongolian peasants, our future soldiers, whose heartland was known as "the Hills." It was only after the British became involved with Nepal that the Anglicized word "Gurkha" embraced these Hill men.

Over a century later, in 1768, Prithvi Narayan Shah ("The Great"), after a campaign that lasted all of twenty-five years, managed to subjugate the three kingdoms. 1768 is given as the start of modern Nepal. From then on no foreigners were allowed into the country without the express invitation of the Head of Government. In 1767 the East India Company had written to London on the possibilities of trade with Nepal. Also that year the King of Kathmandu asked for an East India Company force to help him but it did not reach Kathmandu; malaria, the rainy season, the worse of a few skirmishes and the threat of being cut off from provisions made it turn back.

At this time two strong forces were moving towards one another. In India the East India Company was expanding its territories and in Nepal, the descendants of Prithvi Narayan Shah were also bent on expanding theirs. Between 1792 and 1812 Nepal's eastward expansion caused a war with China in Tibet and the Nepalis were forced to withdraw. The "Lion of the Punjab," Ranjit Singh, also thwarted them in the west. The British, not wanting to antagonize China over the status of countries between the two spheres of influence, preferred to have a buffer region between the two powers. However, the Gorkhali government (as it was known) was determined to expand and refused to accede to the British request for diplomatic ties. A clash was inevitable; the Anglo-Nepal War lasted from 1814-1816 and Nepal finally lost after a three-pronged campaign. A treaty was signed and since then Gurkhas have served in the British Army (and, after 1947, as "Gorkhas," in the Indian Army).

The Shah dynasty ruled supreme until 1846, when it became subservient, certainly in fact though never in precedence, to the Rana family. Palace intrigues and the conflicting loyalties of the most powerful families in the Valley boiled over in September of that year when the most powerful person, Jang Bahadur Rana, ruthlessly eliminated those who stood in his way to becoming, for all intents and purposes, the ruler of Nepal. From 1847 to 1951 the Shah kings were held as virtual prisoners, being confined to their palace, and only allowed out from their palace grounds for special, mostly religious, occasions.

The Ranas (the senior of whom was Prime Minister and Maharaja, and whose power went from brother to brother, as opposed to the King, the Maharajadhiraj, whose rule of succession was father to son) ruled as despots and their power was ensured as long as the people of Nepal, especially those living in Kathmandu, acquiesced. Feudalism was the political idiom in many parts of Asia during the nineteenth century. In the first part of the twentieth century the desire of the politically minded in neighboring India to become independent from British rule had its mirror effect in Nepal where change from the autocracy of the Ranas was sought.

A number of dissatisfied Nepalis found themselves in India, by choice or because they had been exiled. One joined in the "Quit India" movement of 1942 and was jailed by the British. Some senior Indian socialist leaders tried to find asylum in the Tarai, but they were arrested and interned, only to be released by the mob. India seems to have been (and still seems to be) the mainspring of ideas not always in sympathy with Nepal's affairs of state.

A night curfew, installed in 1846, was still in force in 1947. In 1923 a Treaty of Perpetual Peace and Friendship was signed between Great Britain and Nepal. Even so, in the one hundred and fifty-one years since 1796 when regular contact between Britain and Nepal started, visitors were limited to two a year and needing approval from both the Nepalese and Indian governments.

Colonel Rogers had darkly warned us that the Gurkhas were not the same in their own country as they were in uniform, serving the under British. Cupping his right hand he had held it up to us. If the mould, the bond of trust between officer and man, was strong, that inside would also be strong. A flabby exterior only produced degraded material. Since then I have often thought of those wise words: every time relations have deteriorated has been because the outer mould was not strong enough to bear, subdue, enhance, modify or contain a myriad of separate impulses from men, normal mortals, who, despite an unusually binding chemistry of individual self-discipline, are not quite the "plaster saints in barracks" that legend might otherwise lead one to believe. Over the years I have also put these thoughts into a civilian context and, with the advantage of hindsight, I am sure this theory is correct.

An audience with the Maharaja was arranged and we toured part of the palace before being ushered into the Presence. I was amazed to see long, distorting mirrors in one large room. When the Viceroy, Lord Louis Mountbatten, paid an official visit to Nepal, those were the only mirrors he could use when he put on his full-dress uniform. Frustrated with the untoward difficulty in trying to arrange his various orders under such trying conditions, he was late for his audience and in a bad temper.

For our audience we had to observe protocol and speak in English. The Maharaja's version of this language was hesitant, full of gaps and spoiled by a verbal tic that made the two simple questions he asked us, name and where did we come from, impossible to answer without repetition. A previous Maharaja, having travelled in India where heavy vehicles have "Horn Please" and "Thank You" painted on the back, thought that combination was mandatory. A previous Viceroy on a hunting trip in Nepal, thanking the Maharaja for whatever, was baffled by the inevitable rejoinder of "Horn Please" whenever he expressed his thanks.

We toured the mint. No paper money was in use, only coins, and a sack was needed to carry any sum over a few pence. When introduced as Lieutenant Cross, the man in charge had understood that I was a holder of the Victoria Cross and was so embarrassed when he learnt of his mistake that he left abruptly, throwing down my hand which he had been shaking for quite some time, leaving us to find our own way out. I dined out on that story on many a night with my Gurkha audiences highly amused.

We had ten days in Nepal and, while we were there, received notification that we had been posted to our parent British battalions, mine being in the Canal Zone. We ignored an order to return to the battalion for onward posting immediately. To be in the "Forbidden Kingdom" was too rare an opportunity to hasten back before time. I loved every moment of my stay.

Both journeys, to and fro, involved us in an unpleasant incident every day, except when we were on Nepalese soil.

Apart from being surrounded, spat at, threatened with knives and cudgels, abused, I ran out of money and ate one banana during the last forty-eight hours. I think the experience I had in Lahore was the most frightening: with all day to wait I went shopping. Going back to the station down a very narrow lane in a tonga (a horse-drawn conveyance in which the passengers sit in the back) a crowd, shouting anti-British slogans, wormed its way towards us. I cowered as low as I could, hoping that I would not be seen, but if I was I would be considered too insignificant to be dealt with. Only as the mob passed me did they see one of the hated British and, as each one tried to turn round to wreak vengeance, he was pushed on by the ground-swell of movement behind him so never managed to do me a damage. The few squawks of defiance were swallowed up in the general noise. It was a frightening ride.

Long before we got to the station, the tonga driver told me to get down. I paid him off with the last of my money and, to my dismay, saw hundreds of women demonstrating in the courtyard. "Out with the British, Pakistan for the Moslems, India for the Hindus, a graveyard for the Gurkhas, out with the British, kill them," they were shouting. The women's mouths opened and shut with as much grace as dying fishes'. I crept around the edges but I was espied and a louder caterwauling ensued. I managed to reach the portals of the entrance in safety, when I heard a growl of throaty Urdu from somewhere above me, telling me to go away. I looked up and there was an enormous, cudgel-wielding Pathan blocking my path. So I went. I made a lunge to the entrance and the women in the middle, witnessing my discomfort, screamed the louder in gleeful mockery. I dashed, with the Pathan chasing me, on to the station platform. I dodged around the crowd, espied the lavatory and stayed inside a cubicle, quaking for half an hour, until shortly before the train was due in. And even then, on emerging, the attendant tried to get me to pay double price for having overstayed my welcome.

I was overjoyed to get back to the safety of the battalion and find that all posting orders for "British service attached" officers with Gurkhas had been cancelled. Gurkha battalions would be denuded of their officers if such postings were carried out. I could not have been more pleased.

In the isolation of the North-West Frontier, still using heliograph and semaphore, and its pre-war esoteric ritual (even down to calling "three-ton" lorries "tretons"), much of what went on in India reached us as rumor or not at all. Mail from home took six weeks and any newspapers sent out were as slow, if not slower. One top priority signal, "Operation Immediate," took six weeks to reach us from GHQ Delhi. A messenger could have brought it quicker by hand. Certainly none of us had wirelesses, yet I do not remember that the lack of news worried us. That was just as well when, two years after the event, the news reel in the local cinema showed the allied crossing of the Rhine and we only heard about a new state called Israel six months after the event. Even being used to wartime restrictions and censorship as we were, that struck us as slow.

In the spring of 1947 hordes of Pathans moved eastwards, on camels and on foot. There was no trouble but our precautions were as stringent as ever. Several weeks later they returned in one long convoy, shooting bullets in the air, laden with booty having raided Kashmir. Big trouble was brewing.

On 9 August the long-awaited details of our future were made known. Four regiments of Gurkhas were to be transferred to the British Army, the other six would remain in the Indian Army. To have non-British troops in the regular British Army was not new. The Maltese Artillery was one recent example, but to have troops from a country that had never been part of the British Empire was, had we thought about it, remarkable. Indeed, in Britain, the professional head of the British Army, Field Marshal Lord Montgomery, was adamantly and bitterly opposed to the inclusion of any Gurkhas therein. The decision was entirely due to the last Viceroy of India, Earl Mountbatten. In 1947, the Prime Minister of Britain, Mr. Clement Attlee, had visited Delhi where he had sought Mountbatten's advice about the Gurkhas. This had been given positively and accepted likewise.

At that time we knew nothing of this. However, as the First Battalion of the First King George V's Own Gurkha Rifles (The Malauñ Regiment), all of us had presumed that we would be chosen for transfer to the British Army, either as a titled regiment or because we were the 1st Battalion. Bitter indeed was our disappointment at not being chosen. We could not understand how and why we had been omitted from the list. Later on we were told that the rationale for the seemingly inexplicable decision which, basically, was financial. It was cheaper to have those three regiments that already had a battalion halfway between India and Malaya, in Burma, than to take them from India. It conveniently gave a balance between east and west that was thought to help recruiting. In the pre-war Indian Army the balance had not been two and two but two and eight. We knew that it could not have been on merit. We officers were left without positive directions so could give none. Pressure of events obscured the heartbreak. Nor was there any properly planned hand over to Indian officers. They never came till after the bitter end, and the end was bitter.

Within a week of hearing the sad and obscure news of our future on the evening of 14 August, the day before Indian and Pakistani independence, we gathered in the mess. We all dined together and, at the end of the meal, quietly but with an undercurrent of deep emotion, Mr. President arose and, tapping his request for silence, said: "Mr. Vice, for the last time, the King Emperor."

Mr. Vice, at the other end of the table, stood up, gripped his glass, lifted it for the loyal toast and said: "Gentlemen, for the last time, the King Emperor."

We all rose and, lifting our glasses in our right hands, intoned the solemn refrain to the litany of lament; "For the last time, the King Emperor."

Next day, 15 August, Independence Day was celebrated. Except for us and the Rajputana Rifles, the other four battalions in Razmak were all Muslim, destined for Pakistan. A church service was held. As the minister prayed for the peace of the two new dominions the Pathans were sniping the camp from a neighboring hill. The Rajputanas, clad in dhotis, were pelting them with 3-inch mortar bombs. It was a bad omen. Later during the brief sermon it was quiet but even this was marred by a dog that had got in behind the piano, gone to sleep and was making rude noises. Was it only God who could help all of us out of the misery and mess into which those whom some call statesmen had put us? That evening we again made a toast, "... for the first time, the King."

A celebratory parade was held. For the first time ever the Pakistani flag was unfurled over tribal territory. The local brigadier, the local political adviser and the parade commander, all British, gave three cheers. The troops jubilantly responded. After they had marched off they danced around and chanted; "We are no longer slaves, we are no longer slaves." It was all good tempered. Wherever an "I" appeared in the soldiers' cloth shoulder titles it was inked into a "P."

A letter, dated 14 August 1947 and signed by the Adjutant General of the Indian Army, had this as its last paragraph: Every single [Gurkha officer and man] is being given the choice of whether he wishes to serve under War Office, under the new Government of India, or neither, so there is no question of forcing them to serve under one or the other. Whatever they do will be of their own free will...

It was, therefore, all the harder to understand how it was that, in the event, our men had neither right to opt for British service, nor to go on discharge, with all leave indefinitely cancelled.

By then conditions in the subcontinent were volatile at best, untenable at worst. Normal army organization creaked drastically and logistical shortages of clothing, transport, equipment, fuel and rations were a commonplace and could be got used to; lack of any directions about the future was more insidious.

The weather grew colder. We were now in charge of Hindus in a religiously motivated Muslim country, a country that had become an entity on this very score. It was unsafe for our Gurkhas, being Hindus, to be alone in Muslim territory. How one driver bluffed his way out of being stopped for a forcible circumcision was a model of Gurkha subtlety and quick thinking. The battalion, despite all the uncertainties, never wavered in its discipline or its tasks but we were especially vigilant and took extra precautions when we were out of camp on the range or opening the road. For day-to-day routine we managed but when the men looked to us for future guidance we could give them none. In fact strict orders were given that we were not to give any advice at all.

All British officers were warned to return to England. I was having my tin trunk painted one Sunday morning and had just started a letter home to my parents: " ... I should be home by Christmas ... " when the bugle blew the Officers Call, at the double. I put my pen down and ran to the adjutant's office. News of our future, having taken weeks to filter through from Delhi, greeted us. We were "frozen" and ten out of the fifteen of us were posted to 1/7 Gurkha Rifles, in Rangoon, to be part of the British Army. We were due to leave in December. I went back to my room and dismissed the painter. I then remembered my letter. I continued " ... but not this year."

The Rajputanas left Razmak soon after Partition but we stayed on until early November. As ever, prior to a move, more than one destination had been announced. Calcutta we were told initially, but by the time the new frontier between Rawalpindi and Amritsar was crossed, we were given new orders, with somewhere in the state of Jammu to be our next stop.

The comparative seclusion of the frontier had allowed us not to become involved in the horrible massacres which were sparked off by Partition. Down in the Punjab, however, the grim evidence of the unbelievable turmoil, the heartlessness and the senselessness of it all, hit us hard. Myriads of men, women and children, who were of the wrong faith in the wrong country, now with homes broken, impoverished and utterly without hope, made the bewilderingly difficult journey from the Land of Penance to the Land of Promise. Millions never saw the planned end of their journey. Thousands, each morning, would refuse to get up from the side of the road. Death, that merciful releaser, would come soon enough without having the discomfort of looking for it. It was a heart-breaking task for those involved. We passed it by on the sidelines but even so were sickened by it. We saw lorries mow down whole families and the drivers drive recklessly on. With so many untold thousand already dead what were a few more deaths?

The battalion reached Gurdaspur then moved on up to somewhere near the River Ravi. The only transport was one 3-ton lorry abandoned by its rightful owners. It was a time of unnatural stress for all. Everything was of a hand-to-mouth nature, literally as to feeding, metaphorically as regards the rest. We were all due to leave the subcontinent before the end of 1947. The company I commanded was stationed five miles over the Jammu border in a village called Kathuwa. Prime Minister Attlee had forbidden British officers with the Indian and Pakistani Armies to go into Jammu and Kashmir, both war zones by then, as he did not want Briton to fight Briton, as by then it was not our quarrel. Even so I had to go to prepare what little I could for a new company commander for when he did come. I trudged the dusty five miles each way morning and evening. Folk everywhere had the jitters. I ordered latrines to be dug and this was reported within twenty-four hours by Radio Pakistan as "Indian troops digging defensive positions at Kathuwa."

Time was running out and the end was not far off. Garbled orders and incomplete messages about us leaving and Indian officers taking over never made sense. It seemed as though there was a conspiracy afoot to humble our departure even more than had appeared possible by not allowing us to hand over the soldiers to their new masters. However grandiose the idea behind the act of pulling out, where men meant more than cyphers and numbers, the way in which we at ground level had to cope with it made a mockery of every good intention in the whole operation; it would have hurt in any case and now it hurt even more. Those who have never served in as tight-knit a community as a Gurkha battalion can have little idea of the wealth of camaraderie and the warmth of human relationship that exist. But when the soldiers asked us the whys, whens, wheres and hows, we could only give general answers that had no bearing on our limited point of view. Nothing made much sense nor could anything satisfying or satisfactory be achieved. It was a forlorn, unedifying and very painful experience.

The bloodshed and the hate engendered by the over-hurried writing of history have never been measured. We living there, and through it, reckoned that three generations would be needed to heal the wounds of madness and only if there were no further exacerbating dissension during this period.

It is an old saw that England kept order by "Divide and Rule." No! The Indian Army was a living example of "Unite and Rule." Any divisiveness came from native India itself with the caste system that sees no other philosophy than that.

Seldom before had the troops' discipline and loyalties been more severely tested. It speaks volumes for what the British had done in the old Indian Army, where everybody did matter, that, during these months, virtually every unit, Indian and Gurkha, stayed true to its salt. Faith in Britain's ability to manage in a crisis, though, had been shaken and morale suffered accordingly.

In Britain the ugly and sad paradox of losing the peace having won the war was not yet apparent. The scars of the Red Fort Indian National Army trials and the mutiny of the Royal Indian Navy, to say nothing of our own Royal Air Force world-wide and a battalion of the Parachute Regiment in Malaya euphemistically "going on strike," were still so fresh we were benumbed by them; let alone by two of the gravest acts of indiscipline in Santa Cruz and Dehra Dun. In the first instance, 1/2 Gurkha Rifles declined to go over to the British and

Lieutenant General Sir Francis Tuker, himself an old Second Gurkha, had to parade the battalion and, in front of it, tell the men that the Regimental Truncheon, given to the battalion by Queen Victoria in place of a Third Colour after the Indian Mutiny, would have to be given back to her grandson, King George VI. In the event, the General won them over. On the second occasion, men on Quarter Guard duty, guarding the 9th Gurkha Rifles Regimental Centre's money, managed to run away with it.

Thankfully the vastness of India and the total personal enmeshment which all features of life demanded made these and much else pass by unrealized by many, as indeed were those appalling massacres in the Punjab: "The greatest act of British statesmanship in the twentieth century," pontificated the Premier; "Apartheid in the name of God," thought others.

We were all bound by an unusual codeword, QUIM, short for Quit India Immediately, and as soon as arrangements could be made for us, we were ordered to leave our units. Against orders, I spent the last two nights in Kathuwa with my company. There was no relief to hand over to and I hoped my talking with the men informally could tell them a little of how I saw their future, without my prejudicing what could never be easy conditions nor being disloyal to my own side. Gurkha phlegm triumphed although imponderables abounded. The senior subedar, the Company Second-in-Command, understood the difficulties. Ours was a microscopic minuscule of the whole but we felt it none the less keenly for so being. On parting tears were shed and the sorrow was genuine and hard to bear. My last view of my men (mine by proxy and mine no more) was moving out on foot and by camel on a patrol looking for Pakistani infiltrators. It went right against the grain not to be responsible for them, not knowing what they would meet as opposition, what they would do with any casualties. I was reduced to the role of an impotent, frustrated spectator.

The subedar and I sat down and, feeling that I was letting my men down by not staying with them and not leaving them in as good a way as I ought, started handing over the documents, with particular reference to the men's confidential reports. That was the least I could do.

I walked back over the border to India, indignant at the unseemly haste of having to meet an unrealistic political deadline. I felt it a shocking and grievous way of settling affairs and my heart hung heavily. We had abandoned our men, we had broken trust and, by God, it hurt. The next day most of the British officers left for Madras, bound for Burma. I did not go with them as I had had a message telling me to go to the Second Gurkhas in Dehra Dun. We had left tribal territory in October, Pakistan in November and now India in December. In January of the new year we were due to leave Burma, for Malaya. And then what? One unseemly rush with chaos all around; was this really the only way we could settle our affairs?

On my way to Dehra Dun I had to call in on army headquarters in Delhi, two hundred miles out of my way, to deliver commissioning papers for a number of our Gurkha officers. This would give them "full" officer status as opposed to their being junior to a Second Lieutenant as ex-Viceroy's Commissioned Officers, now to be known as Junior Commissioned Officers (JCOs). I went by truck, for the life of me I cannot remember where it came from or who drove it, but I do recall it taking three days and two nights. We stayed in the British Officers' Mess of the two battalions of the Ninth Gurkhas. In one we found the last three British officers engaged in target practice at the wall about the fireplace, all three almost stoned out of their minds, so traumatic was the collapse of their world. In the other battalion, which had been much chastised by some renegade Sikhs who had joined the Indian National Army (of turncoats, as we saw it), a crisis developed that night. The Indian officer who came to take over was a Sikh. In the middle of the night a Gurkha officer, hating the idea of being commanded by a Sikh, crept into his bedroom with a kukri and cut his beard off. He then went to wake the British Commanding Officer and told him to escape there and then. This he did and I met him a day or so later in Delhi.

We drove past a continuous one hundred and twenty miles of bullock carts moving nose to tail with death smelling sickly sweet the while, and that was some months after the main killings. The pitiful hordes of refugees, blanketing both sides of the road for miles in a carpet of humanity that was easy prey to marauders, the almost total breakdown of normal life, the complete lack of law and order, the dead, dying, mutilated bodies.—only kites, pi-dogs and jackals were fat—was a shocking way for a once-proud empire to go, whatever warts it had. Could even the most anti-British of the freedom fighters, hot heads, rabble rousers, unscrupulous politicians and the bloody-minded generally, ever have thought it would all turn out like this; and if so, would they have honestly wanted to have started an independent life in this manner? I could not believe anybody would want such a complete breakdown of everything people took for granted. It was all so horrific, it had to be seen to be believed.

I rehearsed those last few days over and over again, always coming back to the last remark one senior Gurkha officer made to me: "You British have been with us since 1815. Surely you can wait a few more days to hand over properly?"

I am still ashamed that the answer had to be "no."

I delivered the papers and then hitched a lift up to Dehra Dun. Only after I had been there a week did it transpire that the message sent to me about my move had been docked of its all-important last sentence which stated that I was not to go! I had to rejoin the others, still waiting for a boat to take them to Burma, so back to Delhi I, and a few other similarly misplaced, went and there we took a train to Madras, delighted to be with friends once more.

When I left the battalion, I made a resolution that, except for a family, I would never again put down my roots so deep that, when I had to leave, it was as painful as this: I had come a long, long way since joining the army, was it only three and a half years before?

I have broken that resolution more often than any other I have ever made!

2: 1948-1956

I seem to remember that there were about forty British officers who had left their Gurkha battalions in India on board the SS *Ethiopia* as she sailed from Madras for Rangoon two days before Christmas 1947, destined for one or other of the three battalions there: 1/6 Gurkha Rifles, 1/7 Gurkha Rifles or 1/10 Gurkha Rifles. The short voyage took twice its normal time as one of the two propeller shafts refused to turn. All of us were in a volatile mood and a little light-headed after the release from tensions of uncertainty and trauma, spiced by the thrill of an exciting unknown. It was a period of deflation; sadness in having left behind so many loyal friends and fine battalions in the hands of others who had never shown similar regard for them. It was a period of expectation; we were on our way to join our new units, soon to be part of the British Army. It was a period of relaxation—wasn't it Christmas?

We had a riotous time. We were too rowdy and the ship's captain begged, warned, urged, pleaded with us to make less noise, to go to bed, to stop leading his ship's officers astray. In vain! The pent-up emotions from the strains of the last months found their own outlet. By now I found that rum or beer had acquired its own evening seduction: but not whisky or gin, having inoculated myself against them by drinking them mixed, once, two years before and making myself very ill. It let me be at one with my peers but not at one with myself. It took me twelve years before I completely and irreversibly chucked the habit which, I fear, acted as a drag on my physical and mental potential.

With nine others I joined 1/7 Gurkha Rifles in Rangoon on 27 December 1947 and five days later, on 1 January 1948, the British Army Gurkhas were born. To us who had "deserted" our Indian Army Gurkha battalions the transfer was bitter-sweet. Bitter because, since leaving England, all we had ever been taught to nurture and cherish seemed to have crumbled to nothing. We were still too near in time and space to enjoy the luxury of an objective appraisal of the whole horrible and overhasty nightmare. Sweet, well that was obvious. We came as crusaders, as keen as mustard, ready to slough off the "babu-type" mentality that was such a deadening feature of Indian life, ready to be greeted and made welcome by a new unit that would revel in the blessings that the British government would undoubtedly lavish on it, confident that our main worries were over forever, secure in the knowledge that Authority would understand.

But it was not to be. A non-profit-making institution paid for out of the public purse in a modern democracy can never afford to be anything but parsimonious, especially when recruits are plentiful and have no vote, and the home country is in debt. But I would give entirely the wrong impression if it were thought we had no friends in High Places. We did have powerful friends there, but also equally powerful enemies.

In the Indian Army an officer from outside could be easily assimilated or easily discarded. We found it was not like that in the British Army. We were now in danger of being misunderstood and were very much in the minority. However eager officers on the staff were to please, they could not "feel" our problems as had been the case in India. Also it would seem to us that our men were British soldiers so long as it cost nothing extra and Gurkha soldiers if it did. For instance, as men had not been enlisted in England, they were not allowed to be issued, free, with knives, forks and spoons or combs. But on New Year's Day 1948 none of that was apparent and, whatever our feelings, we did have, at last, a new "firm base," for which we were very grateful.

After we had been in Rangoon a day or so we learnt that instructions given to those Gurkha units destined for British service concerning the "opt" (as making their choice was known) were different from those not so destined. In India, although a choice had been offered according to the first instructions we received, in practice no choice was ever allowed. Men in British Gurkha units, however, did have the choice of staying with their battalions or transferring to the Indian Army. With the Gurkhas' one-hundred-and-thirty-two-year-old British connection, an impartial observer would have been excused thinking that all concerned would opt for the British Army. But now men (and their families) were being asked, for the very first time, permanently to serve away from the land-based communications between their unit in India and home in landlocked Nepal. Unfortunately, British officers had been strictly ordered not to talk to their men about the impending opt so there was neither explanation nor guidance before nor at the fateful time of decision. This new situation was a great step into the unknown and needed definite answers to legitimate doubts before reaching a decision. Not unnaturally the soldiers assumed that their officers did not care. Certainly a Nepalese army representative was present at the opt as well as the chief clerk; I don't know who else was as I was still afloat.

If that was not bad enough, that particular chief clerk, unusually, was not a Gurkha but an Indian. He had followed the Indian Congress party line of disruptive propaganda and had been able to spread discontent, distrust and despondency among the men. Nor was that all; soldiers from Darjeeling had been further tainted by inimical, crude and adverse calumnies from the Gorkha League, a local political grouping of Indian-domiciled Nepalis.

Conditions in the battalion had not been good. The euphoria engendered by the end of hostilities had evaporated by 1947, while the end of the war, in which much hard fighting and many casualties had been sustained, merely meant chasing Burmese dacoits instead of Japanese soldiers, with poorer rice in the rations. Also being overseas, not having seen home or families for a long time, with news from the subcontinent getting worse and worse and more and more garbled, the inevitable uncertainty was not conducive either to high morale or to a happy unit. If that was not enough, the British officers, certainly in 1/7 Gurkha Rifles, were of uncertain calibre, none of them good speakers of Nepali. In fact, they were more like the officers I had met in Colchester than any I had met since.

The result of the opt was disappointing with around three hundred men electing to stay. Some of these stalwarts would have to be promoted although, in happier times, this would have been beyond them. In other words, we started off with the 2nd XI. However, our result was much better than in battalions still in India, where the number of men who volunteered for service in the British Army was in inverse proportion to the unit's distance from Delhi. Two battalions reached Malaya with fewer than fifty Gurkhas.

On 4 January 1948 Burma achieved independence. The Governor, Sir Hubert Rance, left Rangoon in HMS *Birmingham* from Pongey Street jetty with such speed that part of the jetty wall fell down. It was symbolic: Burma had never been ours in the same way as India had and, because of the Japanese War, the Burman was completely disillusioned with Britain and Empire. Men were sour but nothing worse happened than desultory shooting at night.

Meanwhile we settled down to changing over from one army's methods of pay and accounting to another's. Some of the Gurkha soldiers' tempers frayed and scenes developed that could have become ugly. So intent, and isolated, had we been in our own little world in Razmak, and so anesthetized by the subcontinent crumbling, we had given no thought to what we would find in our new battalion. We had seen Gurkhas strong in patience and fortitude, discipline and loyalty, trust and respect, showing the brighter aspects of their character. Now we were in for a nasty shock as we experienced the darker aspects of their make-up. In retrospect, my initial views on Gurkhas had undoubtedly been over-rosy and, not before time, these were now rectified. My basic approach to them never changed and my fundamental faith in them never faltered.

The men who had opted to serve in India sailed on SS *Ethiopia* on her return voyage. They left for the docks in ugly mood. They carried Indian Congress banners and spat in the Colonel's face when he went to see them off. They shouted pro-Indian and anti-British slogans and taunted those left behind. I recalled Colonel Rogers' words of wisdom: a good Gurkha cannot be bettered, but there is none worse than a bad one. With firm leadership and good officers, all Gurkhas can be good. This was the first time I had come across Nepalese nastiness and it saddened me more than a similar incident would have done had it concerned British troops, though I could not say exactly why.

Only many years later did I fully understand my feelings of that first demonstration of nastiness: the living legend that is the military mark of the Gurkhas' greatness is, to an extent, the reflection of the high calibre of British officers who have served selflessly with them for many years. The dedicated men who have been able to bring about this reputation feel lapses from a normally high standard in a most personal way. In other words, "a high standard brings its own penalties of expectation." The Nepalis themselves put it more succinctly, as I was told by one, a civilian, as I waited in Biratnagar airport some time in the late 1970s: To be tasty, radishes have to be buried; to be good, a Nepali has to be pressed.—and how!

Those men from the Seventh and Tenth Gurkhas were made into a battalion of the Eleventh Gorkhas; so bad were they that this battalion was subsequently disbanded and struck off the Order of Battle of the new Indian Army. Those from the Sixth went and joined the Fifth Gurkhas.

On 9 January we sailed, on HT *Empire Pride*, for Malaya. We were glad to be out of Rangoon, which was scruffy and hostile. Thieving had been prodigious; a spare wheel would even be taken off the back of a vehicle during a two-minute traffic jam and those who had been there for some months longed for a change. The voyage was uneventful. We were on board just long enough to teach the men pounds, shillings and pence so that they could use the canteen with their new currency before, on 13 January, changing that lot into Malayan dollars and cents. Determined to show our new masters that we were as good as tradition had us, we disembarked in military precision after docking in Penang Roads.

Oh, what a contrast to India this new country was! Things worked and things happened in an orderly fashion. A lush green everywhere, no dust, clean streets in the towns and, as we saw them, placid, happy, smiling people. What a relief, despite the damp tropical heat, to start facing the challenges of building up a depleted battalion in a new army. It was not easy as there were shortages of specialists—machine-gunners, mortarmen, signalers, cooks, drivers and medical orderlies—junior commanders, transport, accommodation, clothing and other basic requirements. So short of men were we that, once a week, I had to drive a lorry to the ration point fifty miles away in Kuala Lumpur from our camp in Seremban and help out with the loading and unloading. After a 4 a.m. start I would get back, to my first meal of the day, by mid-afternoon. Conditions were worse than they had been in Rangoon and soon there was more discontent.

For a time overt acts of indiscipline plagued us. One evening a grenade, primed and with the pin out, was rolled into the Gurkha officers' club—messes came much later—

luckily not exploding. The sergeants reacted badly to a lecture by the officiating Commanding Officer (never a tactful man at the best of times, which this certainly was not) and he might have been hurt but for the subedar Major intervening and taking control. (Names of ranks were not changed for some time later, from subedar major, subedar and jemadar to Gurkha major, Gurkha Captain and Gurkha Lieutenant.) A surprise kit check of personal belongings revealed more grenades and many rounds of ammunition. It was all a combination of a break-down of trust between officer and soldier, too many new and unknown officers posted in all at once, bad conditions, too few and yet-to-be-trained junior ranks doing too many jobs, no firm leadership at the top and, generally, the unhappiness of uncertainty. That gives weight to one of the British Army's most prized maxims: There are no bad soldiers, only bad officers.

I must not give the impression that only certain Gurkhas were at fault. In another unit one Saturday morning the battalion was lined up for the Commanding Officer's inspection. After an inexplicable delay all were appalled to see him, badly "hung-over" and still in the previous night's clothes, escorted, under arrest, across their front to his quarter by two British military policemen.

Covert and insidious attempts at disruption were further disturbing facets working against us and other battalions. This took the form of infiltration of a few clerical recruits joining up in early 1948, chosen by faceless men of the Gorkha League in Darjeeling for their communist dedication, to make trouble by causing an "implosion of indiscipline" so possibly cancelling the whole idea of British Gurkhas. Some of these men were not discovered for more than three years. Circulars from the Nepal Congress party and other exhortations of a political nature and poisonous letters of unusual (and till then unthought of) vulgarity arrived, threatening the senior King's Gurkha Officers, as Viceroy's Commissioned Officers had become known, and their families still in Nepal or north India. All were anonymous and badly written. I now knew enough Gurkhali (as Khaskura was now known) to make the translations without the clerks having a chance to read them. I had to interview men suspected of anti-British activities and opprobrium was therefore aimed at me by them.

Examples of what I translated, wrote out and sent off to the next high formation were: "The Maharaja has given his consent to four regiments to serve the British and we are very annoyed about it because if our country sells its men how can we obtain a better standard of living? ... perhaps the British atrocities will open our companions' eyes ... "; "as a result of the partition of Gurkha forces anyone who remains with our enemies the British are traitors to their country. As such they will not be allowed to return home, they will be allowed no civil job and they will not be known as Gurkhas. We will start looking for their families and we will exile them and confiscate their possessions. For this task we have enrolled ex-servicemen who will shortly start their work. Today Nepal as you knew it is no longer, nor are there any old Gurkhas left, so please come to a decision about your family. If there is any more important news I will let you know. That is all: long live India, long live Nepal, long live Gorkha."

With the end of the Cold War it is easy to forget why Malaya was so then important to the British and why the Brigade of Gurkhas had such a large part to play. Profits from rubber and tin were considered essential to Britain after a costly war and, with India no longer available as an eastern military base, Singapore, at the southern end of Malaya and "on the road to Australia," had to take over that pivotal role. How Communism, often used as a cloak for Nationalism, came to be of such a potential power to disrupt the economy and to prevent democratic self-rule for Malaya stemmed from the overwhelming initial Japanese victory against the western powers during the Second World War which had shown the frailty of the colonial masters. Communism, as the Party of Protest in Asia countries, was just as ready to take advantage of an opportunity to increase its hold over the masses as it was in Europe. Indeed, it is now open knowledge that the Soviet Union was active in formulating policies to deny the western colonial powers their former territories. At that time, though, the western powers did not understand about communist expansion.

It was certainly the case that the Soviets were meddling in the area. At one level policy was being formulated and orders given by them in Calcutta in early 1948 under the guise of an Asian Youth Congress, although "hard proof" of this was disputed until the collapse of the Soviet Union, to rid Malaya, French Indo-China and the Dutch East Indies of their colonial masters and to disrupt the Philippines. On a lower level, I clearly remember a case in Cochin-China, in late 1945, when my Gurkha unit, 1/1 Gurkha Rifles, went there to disarm the Japanese and two Japanese battalions had to be retained to keep the Viet Minh at arm's length. The Japanese brought in a Russian they had captured when he was advising the Viet Minh. The man was indeed a Russian, was dressed in khaki uniform and had hammer-and-sickle badges on the lapels of his shirt collar.

It is not easy to tell when the communists had finally worked out their revolutionary struggle and tactics; certainly Mao Ze-dong is credited by some as "updating" the tenets of communist revolutionary warfare. First there was the political or "Passive" phase. Next came low-intensity guerilla warfare or "Active" phase. Finally came full-scale war and the take-over of the target country known as the "Counter Offensive" phase. As regards the campaigns that developed in post-war colonial territories these three distinct phases merged from one to another as violence escalated. In Malaya the earliest phase started in 1928 and did not erupt into the "Active" phase until twenty years later.

Long before we could settle down properly, two major events were forced on us, making what was already a difficult task doubly so. In an effort to form an all-Gurkha Division, both battalions of Seventh Gurkha Rifles were made into Gunners. Officers of the Royal Artillery were posted in and that, whatever else it did not do, it did cement the relationship between us ex-1st Gurkhas and the battalion. 25-pounder pieces graced the lines and new ranks and trades were forced on an antipathetic battalion. No soldier in my sister battalion, 2/7 Gurkha Rifles, could speak English and the only common language with their British gunner instructors was Italian, learnt from service in Italy during the war!

The second, and greater, event was when an "emergency" was declared in June 1948, twenty years after the communists started their nefarious activities. It lasted for a decade. It is the only time that communists have been defeated militarily on ground of their own choosing. Had the Gurkhas not been in Malaya at that critical time the communists would have had the run of the country to themselves and the struggle for Malayan independence would have been very much harder and taken very much longer. It was significant that the enemy, officially "communist terrorists," were known by the soldiers as "congress." (In Nepal, thirty-six years later, I heard a senior Soviet "intellectual" boast to his Nepali audience that the Soviet Union was not only responsible for the western powers losing their colonies in Asia and Africa, but was also at the bottom of getting the British to hand over power in India in 1947. Some people will believe anything.)

We on the ground, somewhat naturally, had no idea that history was so firmly placed in our hands.

We had visitors galore. One was Major General Sir Charles Boucher, the senior British officer with the new British Army Gurkhas. He had been called to England by Field Marshal Montgomery to talk about the future of the army. General Boucher came and stayed for a Mess Night shortly after his return. He was first invited by the Gurkha officers for a drink and had enough to keep out the cold of the Malayan night, which was warm enough already. Back in the Officers' Mess he waxed violently about the Great Field Marshal this, that and the other, giving us details he might never have otherwise given had he not been "warmed up" beforehand. The crux of the matter was that the Great Field Marshal had told the Major General that no permanent commissions could be offered in a Gurkha Regiment to any British officer commissioned after 31 December 1939. That put paid to the hopes of those officers as junior as was I. Until those Gurkhas trained at and commissioned from Sandhurst were ready to take up permanent commissions in the army all British officers post-1939 would be seconded. The thought was that Gurkha units would be completely officered by Gurkhas by about 1975.

On another level I had to escort the "Queen Bee" of the Women's Voluntary Service around the newly arrived families who were still getting used to living in tents. The Gurkha Major and the Police Sergeant made up the foursome. We came up to a young maiden, comely and nubile, sitting on the ground doing some knitting. The visiting lady, who prided herself on a knowledge of Urdu, bent over her, asking to be shown the girl's work. The mother hovered nearby. Unfortunately the Urdu was badly pronounced and was misconstrued by the lass as being asked to show off her private parts, not her knitting. On the marked hesitation to show herself so publicly, further cajolery ensued. A look of resignation passed over the young girl's face. She put her knitting down, took hold of the hem of her sari and lifted it as she stood up, asking "Now or later?" A flash of silken thigh and another flash as mother's hand bore down on the upraised sari then boxed her daughter's ears. "Have you no modesty, oh shameless one?" she cackled as her daughter recoiled in bewilderment, hand to her head.

The "Queen Bee" looked on distraught, having no idea what she had asked nor why the commotion. I turned away, momentarily, to avert my gaze from the embarrassing situation and also because I could no longer keep a straight face. A gentle upbraiding by the Gurkha Major and I turned to face the inevitable question put to me.

"What's happening?" she asked in consternation. "Just a little misunderstanding," I answered truthfully but in no more detail.

Yes, service with the British Army was going to be awkward at times, and misunderstandings many.

I was involved in offensive jungle operations for a time and, to my delight, found that the soldiers from the eastern Hills, when untainted by any nastiness from Darjeeling or Delhi, were as good as and as friendly as any I had known from the western Hills, in 1/1 Gurkha Rifles. Here I found out that the eastern Gurkha is like a cat: friendship cannot be forced and the chemistry takes some time to work. The westerners are more like dogs: it was productive to make positive advances that were answered straightaway. When I knew that, faith was restored on both sides.

I was sent on leave in the autumn of 1948, five years after joining the army. I recalled what the grizzled warrior in Colchester had said to me on my second day in the army: " ... and the first five years are the worst." Now I could agree with him as I could not really believe that the next five-year period could be as abrasive, turbulent and distressing as this last one. I now saw the effect bad officers, bad faith and bad politics had on soldiers and, were I allowed to continue service with Gurkhas, I would Endeavour to make my life's work "service," in the finest sense of the word.

The month long sea journey back to England was a change and a rest from the life I had been leading and which, had I been able to see myself as my parents were about to see me, had changed me more than I realized. Strangely I did not get excited about arriving home until we were almost at Southampton. My parents, Gillian and David met me at Waterloo station. After over four years away from England, it was a traumatic experience for me and for them. I found the change from living under tension in Asia to post-war civilian England a challenge that I failed to meet. I am sure I caused worry. Certainly, having spoken to fewer than a dozen European women in all that time, I had no idea how to approach a girl without either sending violent flutters to her heart or making her recoil by my rudeness. I fear I disappointed friends and relations by my immature brashness.

I had left, in war, a boy: I returned, in peace, a man. On the boat coming back I had met a girl. I wanted to improve our acquaintance, thinking we had much in common but my parents put this down to calf love and I was dissuaded from following her up. Everything at home also now seemed much smaller than before; meat rationing was still strict and the 22-pound ham I had brought with me was one person's meat ration for more than three years.

Before I left Seremban I was told that I was expected to pay my respects to the Colonel of the Regiment, who was also Number 2 of the British Railways, ex-General Sir William Slim. On the boat we heard that the new Chief of the Imperial General Staff (CIGS) was Slim and, before we docked, that he had been promoted to Field Marshal. Nothing venture... so I contacted his staff in the War Office and arranged to meet him. I wore battle-dress as the wearing of the Sovereign's uniform in the Sovereign's country was not then frowned upon and anyway very few overseas wartime soldiers had smart enough plain clothes.

Looking back on the occasion the point that still is vividly in my memory was the difficulty in finding anywhere to park even the smallest of cars. I had never driven a car in London before, so with hours to spare I got into my 1937 "Baby" Austin 7 (a delayed 21st birthday present) and, with the aid of a map, drove up to Whitehall from North Finchley. At Marble Arch I inadvertently caused traffic chaos by stopping and getting out to see what message some metal studs in the road spelled out. I soon learnt, plus a whole host of other unsavory information. I reached the War Office building and, because I was going to see the CIGS, parked my car outside the Main Door. I was chased away by an unsympathetic doorman. I drove away, got to a large church-like building and was again moved on it being, so I was trenchantly informed, the Houses of Parliament. I eventually found a sanctuary in a cul-de-sac and got out of the car and was just locking up prior to walking back to the War Office when the large hand of an even larger policeman came down on my shoulder and an incredulous voice asked me if I knew where I was. London, as an answer, was insufficient for him as, it quickly transpired, I was parked exactly in front of Number 10, Downing Street, "the Prime Minister's 'ouse."

I took the hint and eventually I found a place outside an old building, a long way from the War Office that I afterwards learnt was the pre-war German embassy. It was lucky I had allowed myself so much spare time. Exactly at the appointed hour, 3.30 p.m., was I ushered into the Presence of Greatness. After desultory chat, during which the CIGS called for the latest situation report and learnt that a British officer, a Gurkha officer and nine men of his old battalion, 1/6 Gurkha Rifles, had been killed in north Malaya when they were caught with their pants down, literally, by bandits (the word "congress" was not on the report) when a party bathing in a river had neglected to put any sentries out. The CIGS shook his head sadly and then asked me how the morale of the men was when I left them. I explained that I thought it would be a problem in any future war to find enough specialists for such esoteric units as us Gunners. "It's not so much the men who are worried," I chirruped, "but the officers."

A growl greeted that remark. "What's wrong with the officers?"

"Well, Sir, it's like this. In 1/7 Gurkha Rifles there are very few original officers left. Most of us are ex-1/1 Gurkha Rifles. The men don't know us and we don't know them. We have had an influx of officers from the Gunners who know even less about the men than do we. If we go to our parent British Regiments we leave behind a most difficult situation. If we don't go to our units soon we can hardly be welcomed with open arms when we do eventually get there."

"Why can't you serve in the Seventh Gurkhas like you can in, say, in the West Yorkshires?"

Why indeed but who was I to say so? Emboldened I said, "I'm given to understand that the reason why we cannot is because we are looked on as such colonial forces as the East Africans, sir." Slim looked daggers at me as though I had suggested something that verged on the indecent.

"Who said that?" Another growl.

My mind flew back to that evening in Seremban with General Boucher and the "Great Field Marshal" tirade. "I'm far too junior to say, sir, but in fact I have it on very good authority that it was your predecessor." Awful visions of retribution came into my mind as I sat there, playing one field marshal off against another.

"When will they learn that Gurkhas are not East Africans?" The question was not aimed at me so I kept quiet. "Never mind." He suddenly sounded very tired. "I have not got round to that yet," and I was dismissed.

It was so sad for all of us that brother Tim was no longer at home. I found father working very hard, having been back from the army since 1945. The war had sapped his health and I remonstrated with him, saying that, were he to continue at that pace, he would be dead in six months. Having been thwarted from my shipboard romance, I became nicely attached to a childhood friend, Beryl Birt, the charming, well-behaved, red-headed daughter of the rector. I missed my chance with her as she would have married me there and then but I did not realize it. I had no idea of marriage so young (still twenty-three) and the army did not give official recognition to married officers until they were thirty. By my next leave she had married someone else.

When the Seventh Gurkhas had been made into a gunner concern I arranged to be re-gazetted into the Royal Regiment of Artillery so I could stay with them. I returned to the battalion after three months, only to find that the transfer from infantry to gunners had been cancelled and we were in the process of being made infantry once more. I found, to my horror, that I was left behind in the artillery. I determined to stay with Gurkhas until I was prised away.

Before I had been back three months, father died of overwork and I was called home on compassionate leave. I was one of the few people allowed to travel by air. It took two and a half days, having to endure night stops in Karachi and Rome. Mother, bless her, saw that I could not help by asking for a transfer away from the Gurkhas so did not press me to ask for one. Emotionally upset, I became engaged to another childhood friend, Mary Hodges, more by accident than design. Here was a classic case of my English language ability failing me at a crucial moment; the girl read more into what I said than I had intended and I had not the guts to cancel it immediately. I broke it off some time later, to her fury and my relief.

On my return from England, in 1949, I was sent, as Chief Instructor, to the recently raised Army School of Education (Gurkhas) and here my language ability and my knowledge of the Devanagri script paid great dividends. I spotted one of the recently infiltrated communist agent, Colour Sergeant Deoprakash Rai, late of the Darjeeling branch of the Gorkha League. The British major in charge of the school, who had an unhealthy attraction for him, had enlisted this man into the army. My loyalty to my immediate superior, who had deluded himself about the man's integrity and either could not or would not believe me when I "had it out" with him, was outweighed by my loyalty to the Brigade of Gurkhas, as we were now known. I also discovered other agents in other units and the methods followed to subvert people and start a rot within the Brigade itself. Even though the Major, when adjutant of 1/1 Gurkha Rifles in Cochin-China, had shielded me from highly damaging and completely inaccurate French-inspired reports which, taken at face value, could have led to me having to quit the army, I felt I had no option but to report this case without his knowledge.

The idea was that the communists should set up a cell within the school and pick likely material for their cause from among the students. These men would be indoctrinated before going back to their units where, it was hoped, they could influence other Gurkhas to be anti-British and cause as much trouble as they could, possibly ruining the name of the Gurkha in British eyes forever. By then Deoprakash Rai had been allowed local leave upcountry and had established personal links with the one rubber estate in Malaya, near Kuala Lumpur (Bhutan Estate), that had Nepali workers, brought over from the Darjeeling area at the turn of the century. He had tried to contact the Malayan communist party through sympathizers among the work force there.

It could be argued that one course of action was to close the school but that would have been an act of political folly. The Indian leader, Pandit Nehru, was ambivalent about the British continuing to have Gurkhas under their command. We had to offer as many facilities as were available in the Indian Army and that included a school for education. Do away with that and we could be accused of keeping our men ignorant. No, we had to have the establishment but it had to be purged. It is also arguable that, however nasty it was while it lasted— and it was nasty—it was only the presence of the army school, attracting the type of infiltration that it did, that brought about a situation that could be identified and rectified with minimum disturbance.

In fact Indian politicians did not like the idea of British Gurkhas and pressed Nehru to prevent them being allowed to pass through India, so effectively throttling the organization, despite the Indian government being a signatory of the Tripartite Agreement between Britain, Nepal and India for the division of the old Gurkha Brigade between India and Britain. One spurious reason was, apparently, that it distorted other countries' views on Indian neutrality. Nehru's clever answer was that he would not prevent Gurkhas being British soldiers as long as their own home conditions were below the standard found in the British Army.

(It was only when I was a civilian in Kathmandu some years later that I realized how much ignorance still exists about the status of Nepalis in the British and Indian Armies. To call Gurkhas "mercenaries" is to put a strained interpretation on that word. In 1947 it was the personal insistence of the Prime Minister of Nepal that permission to continue recruiting Nepali citizens into the British and Indian Armies depended, among other points, on such soldiers being regarded as full members of those armies so that the stigma of "mercenary" could never validly or truthfully be made. The agreed definition of mercenaries as laid down in the Geneva Convention of 1949 excludes anyone who is "a member of the Armed Forces of a party to the conflict." In 1982 the Ad Hoc Committee of the United Nations General Assembly was considering a possible draft convention against the use of mercenaries, general agreement had been given to this new definition: a mercenary:

1. Is not a member of the regular forces of a country;

2. Is paid more than the regular forces of that country;

3. Cannot be a person bound by treaties between two countries.)

At an extremely embarrassing session, my evidence outweighed the Commanding Officer's gut feeling and Deoprakash Rai was discharged, as were the others, discreetly. Only a very few people ever knew about it. He was escorted by military police from the school to the boat in Singapore, guarded at Penang while the boat docked there, likewise at Rangoon, this time by members of the British Military Mission, and finally by the Indian Police from the Calcutta docks up to Darjeeling. There, at the British depot, he was discharged from the army and set free. Soon after we got a letter from him, enclosing his discharge certificate which had not been signed by Higher Authority. His covering letter was headed

"Government House, Calcutta." He became a member of the Bengal state government and, later on, a member of the Indian parliament. Well-known for his communist views, he died of drink in the early '80s, a folk hero among many Indian-influenced Nepali students.

Deoprakash Rai was clever; he could write sonnets in English and was most useful in checking our students' Nepali, especially at teaching practices. I took over his Nepali commitments and this meant, in effect, relearning every Nepali word that I knew. It helped my pronunciation and fluency enormously as was proved in 1951 when I was the Nepali commentator for the final of the Nepal Cup, the annual inter-unit football competition. A Gurkha commentator was provided but he was awkward and faltering. After five minutes, I took the microphone from him and carried on. Reports from units (Radio Malaya's Malay and Chinese programmes were disrupted to give a frequency that allowed the soldiers to listen in on their radio sets in the jungle) were that the soldiers thought that I was the Gurkha and the Gurkha was the British officer. In all I broadcast the final of the Nepal Cup thirteen times.

In the early '50s, the "permanent cadre" of the Brigade of Gurkhas was increased to include people like myself, post-war "converts." I learnt, with a huge sigh of relief, that I was now gazetted firmly and finally into the Seventh Gurkhas. I am sure the posting people in England were glad to sort me out because, in an effort to leave the gunners, I had been taken off their list and put back on the list of the British infantry. Now I was settled for good and all, in the "Regiment of my Choice," and my heart felt much the lighter for it. I wondered how much of my temerity with Field Marshal Slim was responsible for this change of heart. Was it one of those unpremeditated actions that have a permanent bearing on life?

I had dealings with three mad men while I was at the school, itself housed in an old lunatic asylum. One, Chapalsing Rai, had hallucinations that he had to get away from everybody as his gods were calling him. Because of the guerilla insurgency, we had to carry weapons with us at all times. This man ran away, armed. It was mid-morning and we went to look for him. He was not far away on the football field. I, unluckily being the senior present, went to talk to him while a cordon approached him from behind. Six yards away he whipped his rifle up into the "on guard" position and I noted, with horror, that the rifle was cocked and ready to fire, and had the safety catch off. "Step one pace nearer and I'll kill you."

I stayed where I was and said, soothingly I hoped, "Chapalsing, it's hot out here. Let's go to the barrack room and have some tea."

The cordon behind him advanced stealthily, like some grotesque game of Grandmother's Footsteps. I continued to coax and he relented. Down came his rifle and I went towards him once more. One of those creeping up behind him spat an oath when I was two paces away. Chapalsing's eyes glazed as he heard the abuse and he lunged forward once more, his rifle inches from me. He said, with terrifying distinctness and loud enough for all to hear, "If anyone comes to try and take me, I'll shoot you."

Once again I started to tell him the joys of midday tea and, after an age it seemed, he lowered his rifle and, as he did, he was over-powered from behind. Later I spoke to him when he was under the influence of pentothal and found out his worries. A brain tumor was found and operated on. Cured, he was shocked to think he had offered violence to anyone.

The second man, also a Gurkha, escaped from the mental ward and woke me up to demand a boat passage back to India. When I could not oblige him he started threatening me before disappearing into the night. Four nights later, he had split a British Corporal's head open before coming to me to be taken to see Nehru, Churchill or the Prime Minister of Nepal. In my car I drove him to see which of those three would be able to see him but had to pass by the hospital to arrange for an injection prior to boarding an aircraft.

The third man, a Tamil from the Naval Dockyard, was a patient in the same ward where, every week, I would visit the Gurkhas, including one suffering from acute depression. After four such visits the Tamil flew into a rage when I asked him how he was.

"I'm all right," he snarled at me. "It's you who are mad. I've watched you. Every week you get out of bed from the ward opposite, put on officer's clothes and then come into this ward looking for your bed. When you can't find it, you go back to your proper ward. Get out!" he yelled, jumping out of bed and making for me. I dashed out of the ward with the utmost rapidity and never returned.

If nothing else, I learnt how to improvise at short notice, usually in Gurkhali, and this had to stand me in good stead.

One day I had to address all the Gurkhas in the large camp of which the Army School was a part to tell them that the United Kingdom had recognized the newly formed People's Republic of China. No discernible interest greeted my announcement. After all, any nation that could give away a country as large as India just having, apparently, fought a bloody and expensive war to defend it against its enemies was capable of doing anything. Only one remark was volunteered, "We did not know that Queen Victoria had promised China its independence." In the same vein, many Gurkhas could not understand why we did not let the Japanese come as far as Calcutta and stay there for a couple or so years to clean it up, then carry on and win the war!

In 1951 there was a revolution in Nepal which sent shock waves over the water to where British Gurkhas were serving. It was my job to find out about it and, once the dangers were seen, run a course for the most senior Gurkha officers from every unit, to teach them about democracy. Boring though details are, a background to the trouble is germane.

Back in January 1947 when the British were busy getting ready to leave India, Indian-domiciled Nepalis met in Calcutta and established the Nepal Congress Party, based on its Indian counterpart that was founded in 1885 by an Englishman, one A. O. Hume. The Nepalis' aim was revolution against what was seen as an undemocratic regime. I believe part of this antipathy was because, between 1945 and 1947, Muslims had "de-Hinduised" many, chiefly Calcutta-domiciled, Nepalis by forceful circumcision. The Maharaja had not sanctioned their readmission as caste Hindus; while, in Kathmandu, only certain members of society could live in houses made of stone and of more than one storey. As for the rest of Nepal, it was widely believed that people's "hands were cut off" for writing without official permission, although probably the phrase originally implied "prohibition from writing" rather than "punishment for writing." Strikes spread from India to Nepal, where they had never happened before. Mill workers went on strike in Biratnagar on 4 March 1947 and members of the Nepal Congress Party joined in. The Maharaja of that time was still Padma Shamsher Jang Bahadur (JB) Rana, whom I had met in the February, and he initiated reforms, including an assembly of elected and nominated members, an independent judicial system, a published annual budget, grants-in-aid to private schools and the establishment of consular offices in India and elsewhere. An election for Kathmandu municipality, a "provisional autonomous local council," was held in June of that year.

Students of the Sanskrit College in Kathmandu went on strike as the reforms did not go far enough. Padma acquiesced but the more conservative Ranas were hostile to such notions. Ill health forced Padma to resign but, before he went, he promulgated an act which left the positions of the Maharaja and the Maharajadhraj exactly as they had been. However, it envisaged a council of ministers, a bicameral legislature, a judiciary under a high court and a four-tier system of local government, known by the old subcontinental name as

Panchayat (*panch* = five, *ayat* = a coming together), starting at village level, then up, through districts, to the centre. They were to look after such matters as education, health, transport, bridges and public buildings.

Mohan Shamsher JB Rana became Prime Minister and decided to rule the country "in accordance with traditional usages and customs of our forefathers" and banned the Nepal Congress Party. In 1949 he annulled much of what Padma had introduced.

In October 1948 a political activist, B.P.Koirala who later became Prime Minister, left India for Kathmandu to set up a network of clandestine activities but the police found out, arrested and jailed him. He went on a 21-day hunger strike and the Nepal Congress Party decided on another round in its non-violent activities. Around this time the Government of India became worried about the Cold War and in all probability put pressure on Mohan to reform. This he did and on 22 September 1950 convened a legislative assembly, the Parliament of Nepal.

On 6 November 1950 King Tribhuvan managed to get to the Indian embassy in Kathmandu and on 10 November was flown to Delhi. The Nepal Congress Party launched its liberation struggle, brandishing leaflets and attacking places in the eastern Tarai. A Dr. K.I.Singh, noted by one Indian writer as "an obscure medical practitioner" and a one-time clerk in the Indian Army, took a group on the rampage in the western Tarai. None of this activity ceased until Pandit Nehru suggested reforms to Mohan. This resulted in the Delhi Settlement of 8 December 1950 but it satisfied neither the

Indian Government nor the Nepal Congress Party: it was neither workable nor natural in a Nepalese context. Forty Rana representatives in the Nepal Government resigned and, in February 1951, Dr. K.I.Singh restarted indiscriminate violence in the western Tarai.

On 18 February 1951 King Tribhuvan returned to Kathmandu and Rana rule ended. The state machinery set up by the Ranas had been too weak to meet the new challenges of defiance.

Some of my students who had been on leave in east Nepal at that time met a Lieutenant Colonel Deoprakash Rai who tried to force them into his "army" and not rejoin their units after their leave was over.

Two and a half years of being a schoolmaster was enough and in 1951 I was glad to go back to my battalion to take over command of a rifle company while the permanent commander was on leave. The company was deployed in the small town of Rompin, fifty miles from battalion headquarters in Seremban. The "emergency" had been a feature of life for more than three years and the old hands, experienced from Burma, had learnt to modify their tactics for this unconventional type of war. Even so, successes had not been so very common and I sensed an undercurrent of unhappiness. Six weeks after my arrival we had a run of luck. Of all the contacts we had with the enemy, whenever we were successful there was a 2 in the date. It took me some time to grasp this and, even when we had no information at all to work on, the magic of "2" pertained. I kept quiet about it outside the company; among the soldiers, however, this, and the fact that I took my full part in patrolling activities, earned me a reputation for luck, ability and determination. Equally important, the company had learnt to laugh again by the time that the permanent commander, who was never popular with Gurkha soldiers, got back from leave.

His Majesty King George VI died when we were out chasing bandits. The company signaller took the message and seemed deflated by the news. Back in Seremban one Gurkha officer, now "Queen's' not "King's", had to go to the civil hospital to see his wife. He wore a black arm-band and, waiting for transport to bring him back to the lines, had stood to attention for a minute among a crowd of jostling Chinese on the pavement to show his respect. His one sadness was that the time was not exactly at 11 o'clock when he did this but he had not wanted to be late for his transport. I felt that this indicated that all the old madness we had imported from Rangoon had left us by then.

In 1952 I had arranged to go on a trek in Nepal, with a friend in the Tenth Gurkhas, Jimmy Marks. For the first time ever a pair of foreigners were to be allowed to walk from Darjeeling across Nepal to Kathmandu, a hundred and fifty miles to the west. Before we could leave Malaya I became involved in a murder case. A Queen's Gurkha Lieutenant in 2/7 Gurkha Rifles killed a Gurkha Captain and then had attempted to take his own life. I was detailed to go to his hospital bed and translate the legal charge of murder. That made me a material witness for the prosecution and my plans to do the mammoth walk had to be shelved.

Legal proceedings were hampered by the prisoner's refusal to talk. The Gurkha Major tried, the local army psychologist, complete with interpreter, tried. Others tried; all failed—talk he would not. I, fifty miles away, was sent for. Ushered into his room I dismissed the guard, sat down in front of the silent man, tried to get him to talk to me but, after more than an hour's effort, failed. I gave up and went to report my failure. I was sent back. I started once more and suddenly sensed part of my inner strength trying to leave me. I felt weak and, looking up, saw the QGO stirring for the first time that day. He wanted to speak and his efforts pulled harder on that part of me already being tugged. He started to speak and explained why he had committed the murder and why he had tried to commit suicide. It only took a few minutes but even that strained me intolerably. Unable to continue giving of myself, I pulled back my...what? Spirit? Soul? I cannot name it but pull it back I did. I had been on the verge of collapse but recovered in time to see the man slump. I got up, unsteadily, called the sentry and went back to report my findings. My body was a dead weight and for once I had no spark on the way back home. From what I was told later, the accused men never spoke again.

By the time I was free to travel the trek had been cancelled for political reasons. I eventually discovered that there were no reasons, less that time-honoured one of it being so much easier if there are no potential problems to have to cope with. So why invite trouble by starting something new?

Instead I applied for leave to Darjeeling where I had never visited. I went by troopship and was put in charge of over a thousand Gurkhas, including women and children, and we sailed to Calcutta via Rangoon. I was put on the Chief Engineer's table with two others, a Belgian lady, Madam Bippe, and an officer in the Gurkha sappers, Tony Cronk. At the first meal he asked our names and was so underwhelmed by hearing we were called Bippe, Cronk and Cross that he broke out into guffaws of broad Scottish laughter of disbelief. We had an unpleasant week in Rangoon and I managed, but only just, to get the men off the ship and to get some films from the British Council. We were allowed on the quay to stretch our legs only between ten at night and two in the morning.

On our last day we were visited by the secretary of the Nepalese consulate and two ladies. They asked to be shown around the mess decks and the families' cabins. They invited me back to the Nepalese consulate. While there I was plied with drink but managed to remain sober. It appeared that news of our arrival in the docks had been given as a battalion that had been disgraced for turning communist, so disbanded and sent back to Nepal. I found out that the place where the "battalion" was supposed to have been stationed had not had a Gurkha battalion there, save for three weeks a month back, since 1942. This was part of a communist ploy to discredit the Gurkhas to the extent that they would be taken from Malaya, where they were winning, thus allowing the guerrillas to resuscitate and take the initiative once more. In 1985 I met the erstwhile secretary in Kathmandu and he confirmed these details.

In Calcutta, where there was a transit camp, I was told to my intense disgust that my leave was cancelled as I was wanted as the Quarter Master until the proper man arrived in three months when I was due home leave. The camp itself was about twenty miles from the centre of Calcutta, in a cantonment named Barrackpore, where the pre-partition Governor of Bengal had had a lodge. Nearby were many jute mills, an Indian Air Force base, a railway line, a main road and many jackals. The place was never quiet; the air force seemed to reserve between two and four in the mornings to test its engines.

I was requested to go to the Calcutta branch of the Reserve Bank of India to try and get a permit for a soldier going on leave to Nepal to get some gold he had legally been carrying but incorrectly documented cleared through customs. Incredibly complicated and time-consuming, it took most of three days of patience-exhausting filling in forms, visiting offices, being passed from one functionary to his next superior and waiting. The very last man whose signature would bring the proceedings to a successful conclusion was a Mr. Bugga. I had the self-control, when I met him sitting so grandly at his table, just to bid him good morning and not to ask how Mrs. Bugga and all the little Buggas were.

One day I heard the baying of a crowd outside the wire. I went as near as prudence dictated and heard once more anti-British sentiments being voiced. "Kill the British. Throw away your arms," and a new cry aimed at the Gurkhas, "Don't go back again. Stay at home." Two of the crowd furtively went to the wire on the other side of the camp to tell the Gurkha

Guard Commander they would be coming there later on that day and asking him not to shoot them when they did. The Guard Commander promised them that he would not shoot them if he did not hear them. Accordingly the crowd went a long way off, shouted in an empty field and so were not heard, while the canny Gurkha felt he had won "game, set and match" because, in fact, there were no arms in camp!

These protesters were jute mills coolies paid a few extra annas from party funds to go and shout at leave parties with the aim of persuading them not to return to their units after their leave. Not only did this fit in nicely with what I had learnt in Rangoon about the extent of communist agitation to clear Malaya of Gurkhas but also, around the same time, a move to send Gurkhas to Sarawak to prevent trouble there was started by sources that were never satisfactorily identified. The strategy was to try and prise the Gurkhas away from Malaya, northwards and southwards, while letting the centre fester till it imploded. The genesis of the communist ploy was that Gurkhas were making such an impact against the communist terrorists in Malaya that they were in danger of losing the armed struggle. Only without Gurkhas in Malaya could the guerillas resuscitate and take the initiative once more.

I did get up to Darjeeling after the permanent Quarter Master arrived and met Nepali workers on the tea gardens. They had a reputation of political unpredictability and the group I visited had only recently stopped striking. Their mood was ugly; there was a strong communist element fomenting trouble in labor relations but not against British Gurkhas as there were so few Darjeeling men still serving. Was it coincidence that most of the tea crop was sold to the Soviet Union? I approached them in a friendly fashion, made them laugh and was told by the British manager that no similar positive reaction had been seen for a very long time. Part of my euphoria was caused by the far horizons of snow-clad giants, both a magnet and an inspiration, even after only six months' jungle operations. As for being among Nepali civilians generally, I got immense enjoyment in talking to them and being with them. The difference between the Nepalis and the Indians was most marked and made a profound impression on me; the former were so much more relaxed and happy to meet . and talk to others than the latter who always seemed to be on the defensive and prone to imagine slights where none was ever intended. Was that what being a colony had meant? If so, the British had failed in maintaining adequate communications with the Indians. Yet it is arguable that, had the British not prevailed against the French nearly two hundred years before, India would have been much worse off.

I found the girls most attractive and appealing, and my male vanity led me to believe that this was mutual. I did not become involved with them because my stay was so short. The only time I have ever heard "smut" from Nepali girls was when one morning I was walking in front of three school girls who wondered out loud if my penis was longer than my nose. I turned, abruptly, and asked if they wanted to judge for themselves? Screams of feminine confusion ensued as the enormity of indiscretion and of my knowledge of their language sank in. They immediately scampered away in horror at my uncalled-for, ungentlemanly but understandable sally. Nor did they dare to go to school for the next three days!

While marriage between British officers and Asians could not be stopped, it was heavily frowned on in Gurkha units, as was the case of a similar contract being formed between a Gurkha and a European girl. Neither party was allowed to continue service in the Brigade of Gurkhas. One reason was that Gurkha family lines were designed entirely for Gurkhas and female European "intrusion" would cause so many problems that such a presence would be a great nuisance. To avoid any charge of discrimination, such rules also applied to the officers. I never did meet a Nepali woman without whom I felt life would not be worth living. I could have got myself a Nepali wife with comparative ease, but I was not prepared to have to leave the Brigade of Gurkhas and serve elsewhere or become a civilian. I was always deterred from such a marriage by the thought that my offspring would face disadvantages throughout their life as, in those days, the children of a mixed marriage would not have been accepted in either parent's community. I was not prepared to foist such a burden on anyone. In short I was not prepared to "stir the blood and blur the stud."

I crossed the border into Nepal and visited a Gurkha officer on leave. I wished I could have stayed longer as I loved it so much but, alas, that was out of the question. The troopship to take me back to England on my second leave would not wait for me.

Slowly, without realizing it, I was making the greatest mistake I could if I wanted to reach the top echelons of the army. I was entranced by my ability to get on well with

Gurkhas, on and off parade, to get the best out of them, to make them laugh, to sing songs with them and to enjoy being with them. My lack of conventional behavior was construed by Higher Authority as a narrow mindedness that the army frowns on. This also showed itself in my not appearing interested in other aspects of soldiering, "the wider picture."

By now I was being split down the middle in my regard for Gurkhas and my fellow countrymen. It was not that I disliked being with British people, far from it, but I found their parochial and material outlook depressing and their accent on "canned" humour limiting. I was allowed four months' holiday and had to attend a Company Commanders' tactics course at Warminster. No excuses; I was not so much idle as lacking enough interest to settle down and work really hard in a vacuum on freezing Salisbury Plain in January after so long for real and without any cold weather. When I did take a firm grip, I was unlucky to have an instructor who was allergic to me and everything I did. My final report graded me "E. Below average." " ... He should have tried harder as he has some intelligence and a little personality," the report ended up. Militarily I never did come of age in Europe.

That was the sort of jolt that I badly needed and I got it! None of us are as good as we think we are or would like to be and I was no exception. Comments like those hurt me and, while remaining allergic to military courses for the rest of my service, tried much harder from then on.

After that disastrous course I won back some of my self-respect. When in the Army School of Education in Singapore I had taught Nepali to British officers and soldiers and had made a note of my lessons. I had taught English to Gurkhas and my "homework" was to produce a book, working from Nepali into English, that could be dipped into by any learner. The army authorities did not accept it as it was "not produced according to recognized concepts." That was a good enough reason but I knew it was not the real one. The man who actually turned it down was, by then, the senior educationalist in the army. However, when Chief of Army Education in Singapore, he had been after the wife of my boss, whose unnerving inadequacies were so detrimental and deleterious to our work that I had to arrange for him to be posted away. As his wife went with him her potential suitor could not get to grips with his cherished but unfulfilled extra mural activities. Revenge is sweet!

I published the book privately and it went through two editions before, in 1960, being made into an official book for the individual soldier, printed by Her Majesty's Stationary Office. Not knowing whether I would be a major or captain when it was initially printed in Singapore, it came out as *English For Gurkha Soldiers* by J.P.Cross. That rankless appellation stuck and I have been known as "J. P. Cross" ever since. Old soldiers, who had studied with the help of the book, told me in the mid-1980s that they were bringing up their children on it. So much for the original official viewpoint. Of more interest, even when other writers produced pocket dictionaries and grammars with their names on them, the Gurkhas would not believe the evidence of their eyes. The publisher had printed the wrong name: no one knew as much as I did, apparently—nor did I ever budge them from that view. I do not intend to sound boastful saying that but "brand loyalty" sticks.

It took two months to produce the first draft of *English For Gurkha Soldiers*, during which time I gradually grew used to living in England, met girls and behaved more normally. I found the girl I felt I should marry and, three days after we met, went to see her as time was not really on my side. The crucial proposal misfired badly: she was sitting in a comfortable chair and I had even got on one knee to pop the question. At the critical moment, I completely forgot her name. This appeared to upset her. "You don't even know my name," she said accusingly. "How do you expect me to marry you?"

Put that bluntly it rather deflated my ego and my reply was inadequate. "Of course I know it," I said, hoping she would not call my bluff. It was sheer bad luck that, when asked to say what it was, the only name I could think of was her recently widowed mother's. That romance was short-lived—just as well, I suppose.

Then sister Gillian introduced me to a friend, Jane Pitt, whom I straightaway saw as my future wife. I felt I had to "play" her more circumspectly than I had the previous woman so I suggested we went on a motoring holiday together. At the end of it she agreed to go out to Malaya to marry me, there not being time for a wedding before I was due to return from leave. She arrived in Malaya six months after I had got back but disaster struck again. I now had a rifle company in my own right and we were sent to an area some distance away from the battalion. Until we were to be married Jane lived with Joan and

Richard Kenney, whose quarter was a stone's throw from the camp. The Commanding Officer was killed by guerillas and we all became involved on operations in the jungle chasing the gang that had ambushed him.

It was during this period that she decided that Malaya and John Cross were not for her. She wrote a letter telling me of her intentions and gave it to Richard, asking him to get it to me in the jungle in the next airdrop. Sensing something wrong, he refused and I was sent for. On the radio I was told to walk alone out of the jungle. It had taken us thirty-six hours to get where we were. I was not told the reason when I asked why. Was it promotion or a punishment, I asked? "I can't tell you," was the answer. To make matters worse I was told not to reach Seremban but to stop at milestone 3 and wait under the tree.

I refused to walk out so, very grudgingly, I was able to use the helicopter I had asked for to evacuate a sick man. This was not easily arranged in 1954. Shortly before, we had had a contact, wounding a Chinese guerilla courier. I went over to give him what first aid I could and, while I had my hands on his flesh, the death rattle sounded and he died. It was about a week later, when I was on the last lap of my journey by road in a scout car, that another kind of trouble struck me.

During the journey I felt fish-belly cold and slumped forward on to the number two gunner who was sitting forward of me. He had a muttered consultation with the driver, a shaman in his own right, and it was decided that I was possessed by an evil spirit. So I was exorcised there and then, the driver using one hand to steer around the tight bends and the other to make various signs over and on me. I then felt something pushing hard from the base of my stomach, trying to get out and when it did finally force its way through my throat, it left me as weak as the proverbial kitten and in floods of tears. What had happened was that the soul of the dead man had transferred itself to me as I had my hands on his body when he died. If my inner strength could go out to a mentally bemused Gurkha officer, there was no reason why the reverse should not hold good and I become the receptacle of another bemused soul.

I met Richard Kenney by the roadside and he told me about Jane. Back in camp, deep in thought, I changed and drove her to the coast at Port Dickson for a swim and a chat. We decided it was better for her to go to Singapore, find a job, cool off for a few months and then give it another chance, even though we had been given dispensation to get married in Lent, she had had a rehearsal at the church, and everything was fixed, including the accommodation, (and I was broke because of it).

Next day a number of officers came to see me. Those happily married were distraught on my behalf; those unhappily married were jealous, including one to whom I quoted that the world's unhappiest person was the married bachelor. He disagreed, giving me a stern rebuke that, no I was wrong, it was the married bachelor's wife. That night I went to the Kenney's to drive Jane to the station but she had changed her mind and wanted to stay and get married. However, by next morning she asked Richard to drive her to the station to catch the day train, having, unknown to us, booked herself a passage; not to England as there were no boats (and certainly no easily bookable aircraft), but to Italy then by rail, and did not want to miss it.

As one of the Gurkha officers put it; "Sahib, you have no luck. In 1952 you lost a Military Cross. In 1954 you have lost a wife." I had no answer to that either.

The next two and a half years, mostly on jungle operations, let me burn Jane out of my system. On almost every occasion when we killed or captured the enemy, there was this magic 2 in the date. If we fluffed a contact, the 2 was not there. On the odd occasion that a platoon had a successful contact when I was not there, the 2 did not pertain. During this time I had come to rely on the men, to trust them, to believe in them and have my care and affection reciprocated by them in a way that was exciting, satisfying and which gave me a sense of completion. I learnt from them always—whether a point of jungle craft or, in a camp of an evening, folklore or, for instance, when one of the soldiers asked me why and how was it that I was white, clever and a Christian and they were black, stupid and Hindus. It was very seldom that colour was mentioned and I answered that part of the question by saying that, in 1948 when we were gunners, a leave party had returned from Nepal and had to learn gun drill. By then I had not been wearing shirt and vest for some time and, when the Gurkhas stripped, all were paler than was I. Indeed they soon darkened and peeled with sunburn but at the start they were much paler. The point about cleverness and stupidity was easily dealt with by examples: was not the platoon sergeant clever to have spotted some man-made "tiger" pug marks walking backwards when the guerillas we were chasing tried to put us off the scent, and had I not been stupid to have forgotten my towel when I had gone to bathe in the river earlier on?

Christianity (thought of as an English religion) and Hinduism was harder to answer but I remembered the fable about the six blind men and the elephant: being blind none knew what it was like, except that it was big. One came to a local circus and the blind men were led to feel it. They all reached different parts of the beast and, afterwards when they were comparing notes, quarreled violently when none of their findings were the same: the trunk was a snake; the tusk a spear; the ear a fan; the body a wall, the leg a tree trunk; and the tail a rope—nothing was the same and nothing as big as each had been led to believe. We, too, were just as blind as we had not seen our god, so our ideas depended on the approach we were brought up with. Until we were dead and could see the whole "elephant" we had to be content with, say, the trunk as point of entry for the Hindus and the other points of entry for Christianity, Islam, Judaism, Buddhism and Tao.

My knowledge of the soldiers was increasing and linguistically I was becoming more and more proficient. I was gaining a reputation for tenacity over and above the stamina of the other British officers and in many cases, of the Gurkha officers. These would remonstrate with me; "Why do you always go out yourself?" they would ask. In a country where arranged marriages were still the norm, the idea of "burning out" from being jilted by hard physical work was foreign.

So much of the time we spent in the jungle was "wasted" as far as obvious and quick results were concerned. Where many a British soldier got bored too easily and so disregarded basic rules, the Gurkha was very good when properly led. Although a Gurkha is inured to having no more than basic requirements, has a limited imagination and does not need comic strips to while away the hours, so much of what he sees as important is example from above. While he will "go along with" any system that is incompetent—don't we all from time to time?—he is superb when he has individual leadership, when what he does is recognized and when he knows his commander is sincere and dedicated.

To say that, as a commander, I was a paragon of such military excellence and tactical virtue would not be true if my British seniors or peers were to pass judgment, which they did only too often. Once the Brigadier told me that my only hope of promotion was another war and I unhesitatingly answered "that makes two of us," referring to another Company Commander standing nearby. Unfortunately the Brigadier thought I was referring to him. But, regarded through the eyes of my soldiers I know I did not let them down. For me, the finest compliment my Gurkhas ever paid me was "when you are with us we know no fear." As they saw it, however, their biggest compliment to me was, "we can tell lies to the others but not to you. You understand us even to our entrails."

However, what such a long time spent "under the canopy" did produce in me was an appreciation of matters basic; a roof over my head, a dry sleep, a full belly once a day, a clean body and clean clothes, a drink of cold water or a mug of hot tea, a cool breeze after a hot and sweaty day, a view of more than a few yards, to name some of them. The converse also affected me when I joined the real world: I found too many people with too much, too easily dissatisfied and unable or unwilling properly to appreciate what they had, food being wasted, effort by others being taken for granted, a morbid fascination for "comfort and relaxation"—I tried not to show my feelings or appear a prig but it gave me an empathy with those who never had enough (is enough ever enough?) and, not grumbling, accepted it.

I went on five months' home leave in August 1956 in the knowledge that my name had again gone forward for a bravery award. It never materialized—military politics came into that one. I was tired and did little but sleep for my first six weeks. I expect I was far too jungly after so long on operations (three hundred and forty-two days in the jungle), so it was good for me to be able to get the twigs out of my ears. Besides which, that bugbear of so many officers, the Staff College, loomed and, try hard though I had at study during the latter stages of my tour, it was not even a token of what was needed. The pre-staff college course I underwent produced the comment that it would be miraculous if I passed it and rose to be a lieutenant colonel. All through my service I found I could never throw myself wholeheartedly into conventional courses with school solutions. On the other hand, whatever results I did get were when faced with problems that had no obvious answer. I never did relate to the former, only to the latter. Did this show that I only had individual, not group, creativity?

By now I was thirty-one and at the end of the morning of my life, so to speak. It was time to get married, maybe leave regimental soldiering and settle down on the staff. I was not wanting for female company, nor admirers. I took them out and tried to get to know them well enough to feel safe to get an affirmative answer when I "popped the question." Even Julia Moran—the third J and third time lucky for whom?—the major's daughter who was the dentist's secretary, could not sustain reciprocal interest. Seventeen years before, on the boat going back to Malaya in early 1949, there was Zoë Goodieve-Docker who, still under ten, had said she wanted to marry me. When I followed that up, for the life of me I could not get a small, one-sided flame from the past to kindle a passion for the present.

To help me improve my knowledge of conventional army work sufficiently to pass the all-important Staff College Entrance Examination, I worked hard on a correspondence course designed for people like me, using my brain more than I had done for years and achieving a standard that boded well enough for a positive result. I took the dreaded examination but fell sick one night, feeling miserable the next morning. When the results of the staff college entrance examination were published, I found that I had dropped points the day after my ague. I had scored 49.8 per cent, thus narrowly missing the half way mark that was needed to be considered for a nomination. I felt deflated and inadequate. In one way my luck had deserted me.

On my return to the battalion I was asked by an immensely likeable senior Gurkha officer why I had not passed. "You're not as stupid as some of those who have." "Sahib, I got ... " and I explained by how little I had failed. He looked at me, unconvinced and a little skeptically, then gave his opinion. "You did not fail. They did not pass you." My morale rose in a way it only did when something especially nice was said to me.

But luck was coming to me, in a way that I would never have expected, nor would I have believed it had I been told about it. I was not to know that in the April of that year, in the mountain village of Thuloswara, Lamjung, in far-off Nepal, a boy to be named Buddhiman Gurung, to be known as Dhampu and to be loved by many, was born. Nor was I to know for another twenty years that our destinies were to become inextricably mixed.

AFTERNOON

3: 1956-1967—1

In hindsight I can now look on the twenty years from 1956 to 1976 as the afternoon of my life. As I left England after home leave I knew I would be lucky indeed ever again to have such a demanding, challenging, fulfilling, positive and worthwhile job as my last one. Essentially active army life is early on: "the younger the person, the sharper the end," so to speak. I had yet to hear the result of the dreaded exam but knew I was in for a spell away from the battalion. Although I did not like the idea at all, I told myself not to be stupid and try never to show that I felt it was not really for the likes of me.

I could never have guessed that, except for a two-year period on the staff followed by just over two years in Hong Kong (1957-1960), I would have fifteen more years of soldiering when the physical and mental challenges would be even more demanding than in the past. These years are peripheral to this story. Not all were spent on operations with Gurkhas but, when they were, I have to say that my estimation for their extraordinary powers of perseverance had never been higher, my trust in them and theirs in me never more complete and our mutual empathy never more powerful.

I may have known the men I had commanded from 1952 to 1956 better than I had known any others but my overall knowledge of how the army, the military machine itself, worked was negligible. I was therefore sent away—banished, I felt—to the staff for two years. I hated it. It was not so much that I was the smallest cog in a very large machine after having been quite someone in the jungle with my company; it was the amorphousness of it that I disliked. I was in no way exceptional in working in the jungle, as junior commanders in the jungle ran into hundreds, but of those who sat at powerful desks only one or possibly two had ever muddied their shiny shoes on counter-insurgency operations and yet they seemed so sure of themselves. I expect a caged hawk feels the same on hearing free-range roosters crow.

My life on the staff started off in the Command Headquarters in Kuala Lumpur, in 1956. I had bought a car and, as I felt the need for Gurkha company, I made a point of visiting the men suffering from tuberculosis in the British Military Hospital at one end of the town on the Saturday and the handful of men in the leprosarium, way out on the far side of town, every Sunday. If I did miss out the patients would complain when I next went, saying that my making them laugh was powerful medicine and they needed it as well as the official stuff. (In 1992 and 1993 some of them visited me in my home in Pokhara when, remembering those days, they had come to thank me.)

Tuberculosis was a Nepalese scourge. In pre-war days no regimental depot was allowed below 2,000 feet without the personally signed dispensation of the ruler of Nepal; a requirement for those depots in Dehra Dun where they were just under the two thousand mark. In the early '50s an unacceptably high number of men contracted the disease which was only slightly checked with a 12-fold increase in the meat ration. A large civilian hospital to treat all such cases in Kuala Lumpur, the capital of Malaya, was opened by Lady Templer, the wife of the High Commissioner, and the plan was to treat Gurkhas there. Unfortunately, during one of the earlier operations, a local surgeon in a fit of absent-mindedness took the good lung out and left the bad one in, thus neatly condemning the man to an earlier death than the disease by itself would have done. As tactfully as possible, arrangements for the cure of tuberculosis patients were transferred to Britain; and, even then, I fear drugs used in their treatment rendered many deaf in later life.

The handful of Gurkha lepers had no sponsor. When I started taking an interest in them they had had no visitors for over a year. I later succeeded in official notice being taken of them but I had a battle with the Major General, Brigade of Gurkhas, before winning. I contacted the Superintendent, a nice Indian named Reddy, to get permission to visit them. On the first day he gave me his permission and took me himself to show me the one man still an in-patient. "I'm glad you've come. I want you to meet Gajendra Bahadur who hasn't eaten properly for a year."

We walked out into the hot afternoon sun and, having passed several single-storied buildings, came to one that was indistinguishable from the others, except for its number. "Note it," said Dr. Reddy, "and when you come in, never talk to the man behind the screen in the corner. He is serving a life sentence for murdering his wife. Also, touch nothing at all while you are in this ward. That way you will be safe."

I peeked in through the gap in the screen as I passed and saw a middle-aged Chinese sitting cross-legged on his bed, and noticed that he had several long red scars on his back as though he had been carefully and meticulously beaten with a switch.

I caught up with the doctor and was introduced to a listless Gurkha, who took no notice of either of us. I was gestured to a chair beside the bed and Dr. Reddy excused himself. I tried to get the Gurkha's attention and, after several minutes coaxing, had a response. My message was simple: "Try hard to get better. You will never get three "negatives" in a row as long as you are weak and will not eat properly."

I had been told about the need to be "negative" on three consecutive blood tests, without which transfer to the outpatients' quarters was not authorized.

At last I did get a reaction. The man did not know me and, till then, I had meant nothing to him. I persisted and managed to get a grudging promise that he would try. Twenty minutes after I had sat down and started talking, I felt an overwhelming fatigue. I promised to be back on the following Sunday and left to introduce myself to the outpatients.

The following week Gajendra Bahadur was sitting up, taking an interest and he seemed glad to see me. I badgered him more, talked to him about the outside world and hoped that I could imbue a sense of purpose into his still frail mind. Feeling washed out after twenty minutes, I got up and, telling him that I would be back in a week, left.

The third week he was standing by his bed, the fourth week he had walked to the toilet block, coming into the room as I did. The fifth week he was no longer there; now an outpatient, I found him happily ensconced with the other nine Gurkhas.

I continued my visits, once arranging a film show for the entire colony, borrowing films and projector from the British Council. My choice of subject was forced on me by a combination of lack of availability and lack of imagination. One of the films was all about how Eskimos make igloos. As the concept of snow was utterly foreign, bewilderment rather than interest ensued.

Some months later I received an invitation to attend the annual sports day and took part in the visitors' race. I met Dr. Reddy and asked him to describe Gajendra Bahadur's condition. I had expected to be told in clinical terms, "positive," "negative" or whatever. I was not prepared for the one-word answer.

"Miraculous!"

The hurt of being away from regimental soldiering stupidly led me to believe I liked the taste of beer better than it liked me. I gave up the habit soon after I had failed the Staff College Entrance Examination for the second and last time because of a sore head. Interestingly enough, before I started drinking beer I had learnt two languages but none during the twelve-year period of a beer in the evenings—I never took up the hard stuff. Less for the time when I was too busy to learn a language when in command of the parachutists, I learnt one a year for the next eight years, giving me nine Asian languages and one European.

When I heard the inevitable result of failure I felt a lightness of spirit that was as pleasant as it was unexpected. I recalled the legendary Irish-American policeman, Grant Taylor, who bettered the gangster Al Capone during Prohibition and taught me how to shoot a group of people in a house. "Use the Dillinger side-step and shoot, without regret, without rancor and without remorse..." Those three "withouts" came into mind as I planned my return to the battalion, about to move to Hong Kong. I had hoped to trek in the Hills of Nepal but, as my visit would have coincided with that country's first democratic elections, this was forbidden.

During the previous eleven years, since I found myself in Kathmandu, Nepalese politics had not been stationary. The Interim Government of Nepal Act, 1954, had laid the foundation for royal absolutism. Increased anti-Indian feeling was manifested and India was accused of interfering in Nepal's internal affairs.

By early 1955 King Tribhuvan was ailing and went to Europe for medical treatment. Crown Prince Mahendra, vested with all royal powers on 18 February 1955, dissolved the Council of State and took direct control of the Department of Anti-Corruption, the Central Intelligence Bureau, the Public Services Commission and the Department of Records. On Radio Nepal he made the point that four years of democracy had brought no good to the country. "Some people say democracy in Nepal is in its infancy. But infants do not indulge in bribery and corruption."

King Mahendra dissolved the Advisory Assembly on 10 June 1955 and announced a general election, which eventually took place on 18 February 1959. British Army Gurkha Signals were used to relay the results to the capital, the country not having its own telecommunications system and the British, whatever other faults they might have, could be trusted. For the record, the Nepal Congress Party won 74 seats with 37.2 per cent of the total votes. As there was a certain amount of disquiet in the country I was only allowed to make a lightening tour of two new recruiting-cum-pension-paying camps, well away from the hills, in the east and mid-west of the country.

For twelve years after independence all British recruiting and pension paying had been done in India but from now on no longer. In the west of Nepal, two hundred yards from the Indian border, a new camp was being built at a small place called Paklihawa, "the mad winds," which I visited on its very first day. I flew but not by Nepal airways. There had been six aircraft six months previously and, with an accident a month for six months, none was left. Instead, a small concern from India, Darbanga Airways, was running the schedule—more by luck than skill (the pilot of one 'plane I flew in only ever touched down on one wheel at a time)—ferrying people and stores around the place. At a short stop in Pokhara I was asked by a youth how it was that the 'plane flew without flapping its wings, ran along the ground without moving its legs and made such a noise without opening its mouth. I spent two days at Kathmandu where, as the local papers put it, "small Dakotas could land and take off in safety." From the eastern camp at Dharan I was allowed to walk around and was distressed to see many signs of the Nepal Communist Party. I learnt that its headquarters were in Dharan. I saw trouble looming on the horizon, then no bigger than the proverbial man's hand.

For my journey to India I asked for permission to visit Dharmsala, where, very conveniently my old battalion, 1/1 Gorkha Rifles, had recently been posted for the first time since before the war. This visit was one of the nicest I have ever been privileged to make. The Indian officers were courtesy personified, as were the Junior Commissioned [Gorkha] Officers. I knew the senior half of the latter. Their good manners, their natural charm and obvious loyalty to their Indian officers were impressive. What was not nearly so impressive was the state of the soldiers' equipment and training. Promotion came more easily to good games players and drama enthusiasts than to steady, serious soldiers. I compared what I saw with our own Gurkhas and I felt qualms about what would happen if India were embroiled in another war. The results of India's poor showing in the Chinese war of 1962 did not cause me any surprise, only sadness.

I also spent time with a friend in Assam and paid another visit to Darjeeling, where I met the Hero of Everest, Tensing Sherpa. I visited Kathmandu again where I met the one-time Royal Nepal Liaison Officer who had become my friend, Colonel Ghana Shamsher Jang Bahadur Rana, when, on the staff in Malaya, we had been in the same camp. He took me into the Singha Darbar and, knocking on a door, introduced me to each of the people inside sitting round a table—the

Royal Nepal Army Council, comprising all the most senior officers. I was greeted with curiosity, not suspicion, and pleasantness. I tried to picture a similar occurrence in Britain but my imagination failed me. I was given an invitation, with all the Generals, to attend a parade when King Mahendra was to review the troops. I was very impressed with the royal cavalcade.

I only need to say very little about my time in Hong Kong: the army announced that, subject to certain conditions, an officer could now serve until he was fifty-five years old. This gave me another twenty-one years of service—could they all be with Gurkhas?

I was inveigled into running 440 yards in my company team and finished up as Combined Services' champion. The evening of my victory I was offered a cold beer but my stomach rebelled at the thought of it. There and then I made the decision never to touch drink again, beer, wine or spirits, unless by so doing I hurt the feelings of those who offered me the stuff more than I was prepared to accept.

It was a decision I have never regretted. It did not take me long to appreciate that even what little I had consumed had managed to dull my capabilities to my detriment. Before I learnt that an attack of jaundice disallowed my giving blood, I gave a pint of it. That, and no alcohol, resulted in an unbelievable feeling of lightness of body and sharpness of mind that gave the resilience to face and overcome problems in a way I had never deemed possible. Just as well!

From Hong Kong I indulged in going on home leave "eastabout," spending time in Japan, Hawaii, mainland USA and the West Indies. Once in England I, along with all serving officers on leave and pensioners, was invited to meet King Mahendra at a banquet. Before the meal those above major rank were presented to His Majesty. Afterwards it was my turn. Before I approached the king I was told, in no uncertain terms by Field Marshal Sir William Slim, "Don't forget, only speak English."

The king was sitting on a chair, with no one in attendance. As I came close, he struck me as unhappy. Without thinking, I made the "namasté" salutation with my two hands joined together and said, in Nepali, "Oh dear, being king must be hard work."

The king looked at me in surprise but took no offence. "Indeed, indeed that is so. How do you know? Why do you say that?" he asked me in Nepali. I told him that I saw it in his face. He commanded me to sit down and, though I had no knowledge of how to address Nepalese royalty, I started a sincere conversation, making the king laugh and say that hearing me talk Nepali ("like a Gurung hill man") made him feel at home.

I must have had more than my ration of time or was overheard laughing with the king. I suddenly felt a hand on my shoulder. I was yanked around and there was an embarrassed and angry Field Marshal. "I said 'only English,';" he blurted out. Before I could say anything, he turned to apologies to the king. "I am very sorry, Your Majesty." Came the royal answer: "Never mind, I like it."

The next eleven years of my life were so demanding that, had I not been sustained by my Gurkha soldiers, I could not have done what I did. Bear with me briefly, please. To start with, between 1961 and 1963, I weaned the last of those Malayan aborigines away from the communist guerillas who had been plaguing the Malayan government since 1948, fourteen years previously. They had been influenced by the Malayan Peoples Anti-Japanese Army, set up with the help of Spencer Chapman, since 1942, twenty years before I came on the scene.

For over five years none of the security forces had been successful in penetrating the aborigines so had been unsuccessful in finding out about the guerillas. Living for the most part in thick, hilly jungle to the north of the country, I, with my Gurkha soldiers, found the swathe of territory the guerillas used between Thailand and the aboriginal population, which they regarded as their screen for the next big communist push against Malaya.

I managed to learn the language of the aborigines, the Temiar, becoming one of the handful of Europeans ever to be fluent in it. The chief aborigine had been a weapon-carrying friend of the chief aboriginal communist. Using a number of languages I hoodwinked him into giving me his son, his brother and his cousin to hunt for the guerillas who had not been seen by the security forces for five years. The cousin was very ill. He was also the friend, cook and guide of the chief Chinese guerilla who used to visit Malaya from Thailand every three months. I was the second European he had ever seen and

I managed to find him as he lay ill in the jungle. He was so afraid of me that when he rolled himself a local cigarette his hand shook so much he could not put it between his lips. I took him to the local military post where we tried to cure his illness. I had to escort him back to his group, during which time I won him over to my cause because "I was a good man although I had a face like a chicken's arse."

I took these three men into the jungle three times, using them as a screen as we, ten Gurkhas and I, crossed the main mountain range dividing the west of the country from the east. We carried very heavy loads and lived on an average of seven ounces of food. Our mission lasted for 52 days. We were eventually hoodwinked out of our prey by 200 yards. By then the aborigines were in two factions, one pro me and the other pro the headman who had been so elected twice, once by the communists and once by government.

I was sent back again, this time for 70 days. I carried four pounds less than my body weight but we were withdrawn just before the guerillas came down from Thailand. Special Branch felt that I had a better chance than anyone else to contact the guerillas so I was sent back for another 80 days. This time I became worn out and could not get one foot in front of the other. I lived, with my few Gurkhas, in an aboriginal graveyard and eventually won all of them over, including the pro-communist faction.

If I had never known hunger, fear, toil, sweat, dirt and utter remoteness before, I did by this time. Please note I have not mentioned loneliness. The empathy between and camaraderie among my men and me prevented that.

I was pulled out of the jungle just before contact was made as the battalion was due to go to Brunei in connection with the recent rebellion. Despite my mission being marred by personality clashes, the Malayan government appreciated what I did. The guerillas stayed away for six years. Had I known what I was up against, I would never have let myself in for the job. Even the Commanding Officer of the Special Air Service Regiment said his men would not have been up to it.

Whilst getting the leaves out of my hair back in England, I was sent for to command the Border Scouts, an auxiliary police unit in Sarawak and British North Borneo. I was as peripatetic for one year, 1963-1964, as I had been static the previous year. The Border Scouts were wrongly raised and wrongly trained. They should have been the eyes and ears of the security forces, with a sting in their tail. Their task was beyond them. They were misused. They were initially commanded by Gurkhas. I arrived too late to alter the situation immediately. I had to know what was happening all along the border, some 1,200 miles long, so I spent most of my time travelling.

It was a situation in which I was "not a pawn but a bishop." I was both a policeman in three forces and an officer in two armies. I was charged with maintenance of morale of the border peoples. I learnt another language, Iban. Once a month I was so frightened that only the dhobi and myself knew just how frightened I was. I nearly had my head chopped off by an angry Iban. I was a target of the Indonesian enemy. I saw how British, Malay and Gurkha soldiers operated. I was "a fly on the wall" as I was, to all the military, a policeman and, to the police, an army officer, so no one really minded me about the place.

The Border Scouts took a beating when, wrongly trained for the job they were given, they were mauled by the Indonesians. Their entire structure had to be completely re-thought. This I did, having re-assessed the whole situation along the border. Most dangerously I was told to do this on my own but I requested, and was given, one Gurkha to act as friend and shadow. Both of us were nearly killed in a deliberately manipulated ambush but we escaped in the nick of time. I visited places whose people had not seen a government man for seven years.

I did my assessment but it was turned down by the Inspector General of Police—why I never knew. I devised a training programme for potential native leaders so that the Gurkhas, who were involved, could be relieved of these duties.

During the year and two days I was in this job, I was never in one place for more than three days, except for one period of five days, and even then I slept in a different place every night. For ten months I was only one or two days in one place. I again found that I could not get one foot in front of the other, so worn out had I become. I was advised to resign after one year as the odds against survival were too high. I was allowed to break my contract half way, a short time after I started being paid!

It was during both these very tense, difficult and dangerous periods that I came to know three aspects of life not normally vouchsafed to others: solitude, being hunted when heavily outnumbered and nearly being killed once a month for a year. One example of the first: living in an area the size of a tennis court, with nine Gurkhas, for fifty-three days, not being able to leave. This, a time for reflection, was when certain ideas, views and feelings impressed themselves on me. Although I had been given a rough time as a private soldier by stupid officers and had seen at first hand so much nastiness in the India of 1947, it was only work in Borneo that the other two experiences gave me the indelible experience of what it means to be an "under dog," normally something my upbringing, training and subsequent activities would never have led me to.

It is this knowledge, and an ardent dislike of cruelty, stupidity and a blatant disregard for the susceptibility of others, that has shaped my life since. It has caused me to abhor the unthinking arrogance of the "top dog" whenever and wherever I have come across it, be it the minority of Stalinist communist members against the voiceless majority, be it the Hindu caste system that, when abused by a certain type of man, shallow, noisy and worthless, prevents meritocracy from flowering while allowing mediocrity, or be it British "Oxbridge-educated mandarins with firsts in greats and limitless ignorance about the world beyond Whitehall." It all makes me weep inside, silently, forlornly and helplessly. Maybe it also shows in what I write in this book.

After I finished the task of Commandant, Border Scouts, the Indonesians broadcast that their army had killed me. The Sarawak Gazette copied the story a day or so later. When I told the battalion priest, a friend of long standing, Bhimlal Sharma, about it he said that I had to live for one hundred years on account of the original announcement and had a bonus of ten more years for the subsequent one.

Nature was kind in that I forgot much of what I did, the pain and the toil being anesthetized from my mind. In both parts I was recommended for a medal (of sorts!) but politics intervened. Had I known what I was up against, I would never have let myself in for the job.

Shortly after that I was made commander of the Gurkha Independent Parachute Company from 1965 to 1968; in all I made 124 descents. In the latter part of Indonesian Confrontation with Malaysia, the company trained to operate as parachutists, special force men and conventional soldiers, all of which created problems and these had to be overcome. We went over the border into enemy territory and I used skills born of earlier days to good advantage; I was cured from a parachute injury by a "medicine man"; I had to return to Sarawak on a delicate mission ordered by the Prime Minister of the UK; I was asked to go back to Temiar territory. I went on another trek to Nepal, so back to the mainstream of the story.

By 1967, not only had Nepal opened up unlike ever before, it was now also policy to send every British officer on trek there at least once in his service. Apart from my visits to Kathmandu, almost as a pioneer, my knowledge of the country the Gurkhas came from had only been scantily reinforced when I had put a foot across the border for a day near Darjeeling (in 1951) and a "skim" visit in 1959. In other words, I had no first-hand experience of the Hills. I had six weeks at the end of 1967 to rectify that.

Since I had last set foot in Nepal there had been a significant change. The experiment with democracy had foundered and a system of non-party government introduced. On 15 December 1960 King Mahendra had ordered the arrest of the Prime Minister and some of his colleagues and, on the same day, issued a proclamation dismissing the government and dissolving Nepal's first elected parliament. The King accused his government of gross inefficiency and formed a council of ministers under his chairmanship and banned all political parties. The constitution of 1959 was suspended, less a few provisions, and a new law, called Nepal Special Arrangement Act of 1961, along with renewals of periods of emergency, saw the country through until 16 December 1962 when the *Panchayat* Constitution, was promulgated.

The system was seen as an ancient one, practiced over the millennia by previous kings. In June 1962 King Mahendra declared:

The specialty of the *Panchayat* system lies in the very fact that, by virtue of its sprouting forth from the basic life-pattern of the Nepalese people, there is no special novelty in it. This system bears the stamp of the genius of the Nepali race.

The non-party concept had come to stay, although India showed its dislike of the introduction of the *Panchayat* system by an economic blockade later that year and this caused considerable hardship in Nepal.

There were three other factors that caused worry: devaluation of the Indian rupee, to which the Nepalese rupee seemed to be tied; a land reform programme that was sending shock waves down the spine of all Nepali landowners, especially the peasantry who thought they would suffer when the officials came to measure up what there was and in whose name it had been registered; and, for the serving soldiers and their families, redundancy as a result of contraction in numbers in the British Army.

What else had I learnt of Nepal and the Gurkhas that had not been drummed into me twenty-three years ago in Dehra Dun? Nepal, an impoverished Asian third-world country, that carries a mystique few other countries do which I now knew as a land of untold contrasts, infinite variety and extremes of geography and climate. In length 520 miles, it nowhere exceeds 140 miles in breadth, normally only being between 90 and a hundred miles. With very poor communications, off the few motorable roads the main beast of burden is human and the speed of life is that of a laden person.

Beyond the flat southern part of Nepal that marches with India, the Tarai, about 300 feet above sea level, rise the foothills of the main Himalayan range, running up in ridge after ridge of steep-sloped mountains—steeper in the east than in the west—until the snows are reached, the highest not far below 30,000 feet, on the roof of the world. It is like a country on its side and, were it to be flattened out, would be about the size of France. The "Gurkha Heartland" lies between 2,500 feet and 7,500 feet, above which rice does not grow. Grazing and the search for medical herbs in the warmer months go up to about 13,000 feet. The big rivers coming down from the snows and waiting to be harnessed to hydroelectric projects, cascade through deep gorges. Nature's moods can be sudden and cruel, and a generation's husbandry destroyed in hours.

The laws, customs and way of life are slanted towards the millennia-old caste system, introduced into Nepal in 1382 AD. Hinduism, and indeed Buddhism, have produced rigidity and fatalism in its population. Nepal has as high a proportion of its people working on the land as anywhere else in the world, remorselessly tying the great majority of its citizens to a life of toil, hardship, privation, drudgery and weariness as subsistence farmers with little reward and little surplus. It is from such people, Magars and Gurungs in the west and Rais and Limbus in the east, that the Gurkhas come; men that, as soldiers, I had known since 1944.

I planned my trip with loving care, arranging to meet men of my Gurkha Para Company who would be on home leave. I arrived in Nepal on the crest of a wave of anticipation. Six weeks later I returned with very mixed views. On one level I found myself fascinated as never before as I journeyed with my friends in the Hills, west and east, finding everything new. On another level I found myself, frankly, uneasy, puzzled and disappointed.

The journey started off by flying to Calcutta by RAF Hercules. I was with Tony Kerr of the Gurkha Sappers. Tony elected to fly on to Kathmandu with the RAF, hoping later to get off when the aircraft landed at Biratnagar, in southeast Nepal. Unfortunately bad weather forced the 'plane to abort that second landing and return to Calcutta. It landed at the military air base at Dum Dum instead of the main civilian aerodrome and, without realizing it, Tony found that his passport was stamped out of India and into Nepal. In Indian Immigration's eyes, therefore, he was not in India. It also happened that he had bought some expensive items in Kathmandu and did not want to show them to Customs. Would I help him to get through Customs without opening his case and through Immigration without showing his passport?

I said I would do what I could, to stick with me and only to open his mouth when I signaled him to. At the Customs counter Tony and I leant on our cases and waited for someone to come and deal with us. Over came a lady of uncertain years and, probably, of more uncertain temper and I smiled at her as she peremptorily demanded I open my case. I told her I knew that being a Custom's officer was not her first job. Correct. I could guess her previous job. What was it? I said, with a winsome smile, it must have been a film star as she had the beauty that was so essential for such a person. Right or wrong I never did know but she immediately chalked a mark on both our unopened cases and away we went to Immigration.

Here this was harder. We had both made out our forms and I, wittingly putting English instead of British as nationality, was engaged in polemics with the sharp young man in charge. I knew that our 'plane was due to take off shortly and I kept up a friendly argument until the final call.

As I was amending my nationality for the man, Tony walked through without having to show his passport. "Never ask me to do that again, Tony," I said. "Apart from anything else, one only wins a lottery once a life time and I have not the inventive powers to do such a thing again."

For the western leg of my walk I went to the village of Luwang, which means "clove," where one of my soldiers, Bhimraj Gurung, lived. He had recently retired on pension and I had told him when I would be at Pokhara. I was surprised not to see him waiting for me at the airport. By evening I booked myself in somewhere for the night as he had not come. As I was waiting for him next morning, an American woman asked me if I could speak English as she needed help in paying her bill. Was my disguise that good? By late morning I decided not to wait any longer and, hiring a man to carry my kit, started the five-hour walk. I did not know how much to pay the man: he asked me for the equivalent of fifty new pence and I was to learn that I had been horribly overcharged!

I had wondered if my knowledge of Nepali would stand me in as good stead in the Hills as it had done with the soldiers. On that walk I was elated by the small talk I had with people as we passed by, as well as the crisp, clear and almost heady air after the muggy, clammy, stuffy atmosphere of places near the equator. The long views up to the huge snow-covered mountains, Dhaulagiri, Annapurna, and "Fish-tail," thrilled me as did the sudden sharp-edged skylines met with as a corner was turned or an incline mounted, all so excitingly different. Certain scenes etched themselves on my mind: the staggering loads carried alike by man, woman and child, who in bare feet and unharmed by sharp stones walked with shuffling gait as they picked their way with unhurried speed over the rougher patches. The small boy, no more than six years old, holding a sapling branch that would have merely tickled any tough-skinned dog, trying to urge on a large and cumbersome buffalo by swipes of the stick, shrieking shrilly and probably vilely as he did. The buffalo, unperturbed, turned its head slowly, almost gently, and gazed momentarily at its minute oppressor then plodded on, entirely of its own volition, but with the small boy triumphant.

The red and white houses, looking spick-and-span on the hillsides were, from afar, a picture. Closer to, the poverty, the improvisation and, above all, the industry of the people struck me forcibly. I was fascinated by so much; the row after row of terraced fields, draping the hills now shorn of all foliage and the product of who knows how much sweat, toil and back-ache? The long scar of a recent landslide dangerously near a village was a hazard to everyone. I saw a kite drifting lazily in the currents of air, with never so much as a flap of a wing, drop with a sudden dive on to some unsuspecting fluff of a chick below. I saw a dog dying by the side of the track with grubby-nosed children playing heedlessly around; a coarse-voiced lunatic, chained to the post of a cow-shed, stark naked except for his hat; and in another place a cow suffering from a broken leg with a jagged wound unhealed. High up on the hillside were three small girls gathering firewood and I heard the echo of their strong voices raised in song. I passed one place where small, highly coloured birds were playing hide-and-seek in a clump of bamboo.

We reached Luwang in the evening. The last half mile was steep and I followed some of the villagers who were carrying large loads of straw from an outlying field. Only strong, firm legs were visible under each load, so it was impossible to tell who was who from behind. At a stone resting-place short of the village the bales started putting themselves on the ledge set at knee height and in so doing turned into dusty and tired men. Relieved of their burdens they stood erect, wiping the sweat and dust from their faces. Another lot was behind me and I saw my friend. I shouted "Who goes there?" and lifted my walking stick into the position of "on guard." There was a delighted but surprised Bhimraj. It seems that he had gone to fetch me on the twenty-first as planned but I was not there. I had arrived on the twenty-first and he was not there. He had muddled up Nepalese months with British months: Nepal runs on the Bikram Sambat, fifty-seven years ahead of the western calendar, and has its new year in the middle of April, so is always half a month "out" as regards dates.

I was escorted up into the village, now growing obscure in the gathering dusk. The setting sun was turning the Himalayas red and, as I watched, this faded to pink then to grey before losing its colour entirely. The village was a thick cluster of houses separated by narrow, winding lanes and each with its own forecourt. By the time we got there, it was dark.

It was a happy reunion. We had known each other since we had done our basic parachute training together two years previously and, he being older than the other men, had stayed with me as batman. Mat and rug were set down and I was bidden to sit. Bhimraj collected his family and, one by one, mother, father, wife, sons and daughters were introduced. Garlands had been quickly made and I was draped with necklaces of mountain flowers.

Outside it became cold and brilliant stars pierced a jet-black night; inside was warm and cheerful. As news of a visitor spread, people came to see me, not that they knew me: but a visitor was, in those days, an event. Soon the room was full and there was a lot of laughter as small talk flowed to and fro. I noticed that the older women seemed especially pleased. I was relieved to find that I was understood and could understand what the women and children said. Shadows from two flickering lamps lit up strong, animated faces, all smiling and bright of eye. There was so much that was new and, as I asked what various things were, words I had learnt years before but had never used now vividly became real. On one shelf stood a row of very large ewers. I was told that these were used only at wedding feasts and funerals when many guests were fed and much water was needed to cook for so many. I found everybody was delighted to impart such knowledge and I looked forward to the next day when it would be light enough to see it all. After a lot more talk I was shown to a small room above the cattle shed where a bed and blankets had been made ready. I went to sleep with the buzz of excited conversation in my ears: people did not go back to their houses until well into the small hours.

Next morning I was taken to the village spring where I washed and shaved. Set in the hillside were four strongly gushing outflows of water where everyone collected to do their laundry, wash or fill up large ewers to take home. The village folk seemed quietly curious about me but I never felt anything but welcome. I had brought some basic medicines and I used them how and where I could, all appreciated greatly. One particular man, Sursing Gurung, had not been able to walk properly for more than a year and was expected to die that winter. I had no idea what the trouble was as, apart from not being trained, I was not allowed to see him. However, I told Bhimraj to fix an escort to take him over to the hospital at Dharan and I would pay for both of them, there and back (hoping I had sufficient funds with me).

After our morning meal we wandered around the village, which I presumed was typical of that area. Houses are not "homely" in the sense that they are in, say, England. They are strictly utilitarian, places to cook, eat, sleep and to store chattels. Most were two-storied with a forecourt and a buffalo shed to one side. In some places the buffaloes were tethered in the corner of the forecourt where millet is threshed, rice and pulse are dried, chickens scratch about and watchdogs lie about. Cattle normally can only pass through the narrow stone-slabbed lanes as entrances to the houses are constructed to prevent easy access. The paths near the fields are flanked by stone walls on which cactus grows. On our walk we met all of note—relatives, dignitaries, old soldiers, their families and many of less importance. Everything was relaxed and informal and of the greatest interest to me as it was all new. Kindliness was ever present because at all the houses we visited the unbreakable laws of hospitality had to be observed; a little food, a little drink, small talk and then more normal conversation. By evening I felt fit to burst and my stomach rebelled at a meal I was offered by Bhimraj's wife. I longed to get up and take some hard exercise but it was only on the third day that we got away for a week's walk.

We were three, Bhimraj and I, and a porter. I gathered porters were more expensive in the west than in the east. I relaxed when I found out that the man Bhimraj had got to come with us only wanted the equivalent of twelve-and-a-half new pence a day. We stayed in friends' houses but, as so many of them were harvesting, prolonged chats were not possible. I marveled at the way the women worked; they started the day at three a.m. grinding corn. It was then that they heard aircraft, every third night, flying high, south to north, never to fly back. I wondered what that was. On the road we saw a couple of lads wearing parachute cloth shirts and then realized that the aeroplanes were supplying Khambas in Tibet who were resisting the Chinese occupation of that country.

At dusk on the third day we had no choice of accommodation but an inn. We were tired and foot-sore. It was cold and the wind from the Himalayas was like ice. The inn was small and not much more than a large hut with mud walls and a thatch roof. Looking snug, it stood by the side of the track and in we went. It was dark in the one room and full of smoke so, for a while, it was hard to see. At least it was warm and a change from the icy-cold of outside. My two friends asked for rice-beer and I for hot tea. We also asked for our meal to be cooked.

As we warmed ourselves with the drinks near the fire we were joined by the landlord. His talk was coarse, his voice was harsh and he was plagued by a hacking cough. He looked none too clean. His wife, though plump, was ill-kempt and kept her two small boys at bay with sweeps of her arm while she cooked, brewed and stirred at the fire-place, which was made of three large stones set in the floor. Both small boys were in rags and looked ill, often in tears as if they were unhappy and had scant love shown them.

The eldest son was about twenty years of age and had been a cripple all his life, infantile paralysis, and was only able to do odd jobs around the house. He had cut his hand during the day and I bound it up as best I could. I asked if there was another inn we could reach before it was too late as I felt unhappy in such squalid surroundings. No, we had to stay put.

It was the grown-up girl who seemed to do the most work. She fetched the water, cut the wood for the fire, fetched plates, pots and pans, cleaned and stacked them, all with poise, grace and ease. With no word said, with no haste yet with due speed she did more work than the others who seemed to take her for granted. It was her face that was so sweet, so full of charm, bright yet coy. Once our eyes met and held when she came near me. We smiled and I tried to talk to her but she took no heed and went on with her chores as though I was not there. Strange, I mused. In this place where all seems ill-starred what quirk of fate has sired so fair and sweet a girl from what looks like dross? Give her a chance to get clean, dress her with good taste and she would have no par for miles around.

After our meal we talked for a while, planning our next day's journey. Feeling drowsy, we were given mats and blankets and were soon asleep, to be woken up at intervals through the night as mule trains from the far north jingled past in the moonlight.

At dawn we had some tea and were soon on our way. There was thick hoarfrost on the ground, all was calm and the sky was a rich, deep blue. We were seen off by the family, all except the girl. I saw her in the back room, at work. She looked up as we left, hands joined in front of her in the namasté greeting. We smiled briefly at each other.

On the track we did not speak until I asked Bhimraj why it was that the girl did not talk, worked so hard and yet seemed so calm? "Oh, I thought you knew," he said. "She has been deaf and dumb since birth."

We stopped by in a village where Bhimraj's elder sister lived. We had to stay while a make-shift stage was erected and, in the middle of the afternoon, the local nautch troop put on a show for me. I was at once pressed on to the stage and had to perform four times (singing and dancing) before allowed to be a spectator. Many compliments were paid: it was a most pleasant day, relaxing yet stimulating, unusual, informative and friend making.

On my next to last evening the villagers crowded into Bhimraj's house and an impromptu singsong was started. There were two madals, cylindrical wooden drums that beat out the rhythm. A man stood up and sang a song that was current in the Indian Army, the second verse, the woman's reply, falsetto;

> *I was due back from leave on the twenty-first*
>
> *It is now the twenty-fourth*

And because of you my darling
The Colonel will be wrath.

Take me if you're going to
When you go tomorrow
If you don't I'll kill myself
To everybody's sorrow.

My darling says she'll go with me
Whatever else I urge.
But I have not brought a family pass
They're bound to start a purge.

The drumbeats were quiet until the chorus was sung between every verse;

Oh stay you here and make no fuss
On service I'll not marry.
In one year's time I'll be right back
To fetch you I'll not tarry.

An old soldier leaned across to me when the laughter had subsided and told me that he had been almost stone-deaf for sixteen years and what were they singing? Putting my mouth close to one ear I told him and added; "You may be deaf but your hands and feet are still strong," as I had seen him at work earlier in the day.

He took this as an invitation to get up and join in, so, getting to his feet, in rumbustious style but quavering voice, sang a song that had been popular many long years before;

> *Oh go my darling, fry the fish*
> *And make a wholesome curry.*
> *Or otherwise I'll miss my train*
> *You'll really have to hurry.*

There were shrills of laughter as the old man had been known as a "regular card" in his younger days and all were delighted to see him performing once more. He continued;

> *A jet black goat with good crisp meat*
> *And we'll all eat a part.*
> *Yet a woman with looks however*
> *sweet*
> *Must have a golden heart.*

He paused for breath. Well over sixty, the old man had not been coaxed into song for many years.

Pure gold needs no touchstone
And a good man's heart is pure.
And if only I could raise a loan
I'd marry that girl for sure.

"Sit down, Old Man," I said. "You're short of breath. Save what's left for later on." It had not struck me that I would have to perform but as I finished talking I realized that it was my turn next. The others were all encouraging me to come into the middle of the crowd. I saw that there was no escape and that I could not get out of it without tremendous loss of face. There was nothing for it but "to roll with the punch" so, racking my brains, I got up and started;

To the village of cloves high on the hill
An English stranger came.
One night a deaf old man and he
Danced and sang with great acclaim.
On his arrival in the place
Of fluttering hand and smiling face
With flowered garlands, as of lace,
The maidens comely, one by one,
Gave him a welcome—then were gone.

J. P. Cross

Of course a second verse was requested and, after due deliberation, I remembered one I had made up years before;

> It was in the jungle that we heard them
>> Then we saw the bandit camp.
>> I fired a round but my rifle jammed
>> And away they all did scamp
>> And I realized to my sorrow
>> That my gun had played me tricks
>> Just like the type of woman
> Who leaves one in a fix.

A third verse was then inevitable and, as the audience sang the chorus several times (I had used a well-known tune to my own words), I collected my thoughts;

> Some have to stay and farm the land
> While others' fate it is to roam.
> The life you lead is in your hand
> If in the Regiment or at home.
> Despite the way of life you choose
> One thing only can you trust.
> There's one command you can't refuse

And when you're called, then go you must.

It was an evening I will never forget. On a more serious note, retired Gurkha officers I met were gloomy about the future of the British Gurkhas. There were all too few British officers of the "old school," too much emphasis was being placed on education, not on fighting. It was well known that too much education spoiled the younger men, they said, and Gurkhas never won wars by being "clever."

The night before I left Luwang I was pulled out of bed at midnight and made to perform until well into the small hours. I was told that, from the way I spoke, I could not be told from a village man if my face was not seen. The next morning, before I was escorted to the village bounds by a large crowd, head almost hidden by eight garlands, I was told that, "although we would be far away from you in body, we will not be far in mind. We will always remember you as you spread love," as nice a remark as ever I have heard. Over fifty people, many of them the older women, started me off on the next stage of my journey. One old crone pushed her way towards me and gave me a Nepalese hat, a multi-coloured cloth cone with one side higher than the other. "I'm not a Nepali so how can I wear this?" I asked her. I was told I was now one of them and any man not wearing a hat (and wearing white shoes) was taken as being bereaved.

Bimraj's mother pushed her way to the front of the crowd and, wiping the tears from her eyes, said she would not be there when I next came back. "You are my English younger son; Bhimraj is my Nepali younger son. Younger sons never fall out. Ensure your love remains strong always." I was very moved by the obvious sincerity of all: a wonderful accolade and I felt most humble.

On our way back to Pokhara we had other friends to visit. The countryside was moraine, with steep cliffs cut by glaciers æons past. I stayed at the house of one who had been a friend in my early days in Burma, over a score of years before. I took out a map to pick out the Himalayan and other features and was roughly told to hide it lest the villagers thought I was up to no good as far as the land reform programme was concerned and I would be suspect. I was introduced to some pale-eyed, long-nosed Brahmans who, listening to my speech, thought I was a half-caste. When they learnt my name they told me that they had heard of *English For Gurkha Soldiers*, which (stupidly) pleased me.

We turned up at the house of another of my men who had only recently come on leave and had just left to go to his in-laws, some hours away, to collect his wife. A messenger was sent to recall him and back he came. I was upset that he put me in a higher priority than a wife he had not seen for three years. It was in that village that the dreaded-land reform topic was raised again. A young Brahman, well versed in its implementation, dropped in and an animated, though controlled, discussion resulted. As I saw it, many of the problems of land reform were like so many other problems in emerging nations. Grandiose plans and schemes from the top but not enough middle men to get the meaning down to grass-roots level. Also, those who learn, having studied, and those who do, with gnarled hands and splayed toes, old before their time, have a large credibility gap between them and their tutors, not helped by a difference in age, environment, temperament and even language. In short, there was fear of the unknown and therefore suspicion.

And so we reached Pokhara. I wanted to send back presents with Bhimraj for his mother, aunt and wife. He suggested cloth. I asked him to help me choose three different pieces but that idea was vetoed. They all had to have exactly the same! Why? So that none could say that hers was better or not so good as the others' and there would be no quarrelling.

I wondered how western women would take to that theory!

In the large camp at Dharan I prepared for the next, the eastern leg, of my trek, my voyage of discovery. On a Saturday afternoon I saw a man hobbling up the road towards me, obviously in great pain. I saw it was Sursing, who, with his escort, had managed the long, tedious journey by rail through India. I took him to the hospital and found that there was one bed vacant. The duty doctor was unwilling to let him have it and upbraided me for making him late for a walk up to a chalet on the ridge above the camp where he was to spend the rest of the weekend with some friends. I prevailed and Sursing was admitted.

The east of the country is steeper and wilder than the west, with the villages more spaced out and many more landslide scars on the mountains. The Himalayas are farther off, there being only an outer range, unlike in the west where there is an inner, and nearer, range also. I travelled light, with no rations and no tent, relying on friends and wayside inns for food and shelter. After a week on the road, I met up with one of my soldiers due to return from leave in the district town of Bhojpur. As final preparations for leaving were being made, his mother turned to me and asked me to look after her son.

"I have never spared myself for him since his father died many years ago. I have worked myself thin to provide for him and he has never gone hungry nor have I ever been in debt. Look after him as though he were yours," and a tear rolled down her cheek. I remembered an old saying—"A mother's love for her son never dies, nor can a son ever repay his mother's milk."

A little later two brass jars were filled with water and a marigold bud was popped into each. They were set on either side of the front door. There was tension in the air and a little impatience was shown as in all imminent separations anywhere in the world with "time, so precious, unwanted." He and I were called forward and the soldier picked up his baby boy (who still regarded his father as a stranger) and, with a wonderful smile, said his own farewell in his own sweet way, the infant resisting furiously.

Then the mother to her son and the sister to me, the age-old ritual of farewell was once more enacted. A garland round the neck, a dab of rice, milk and saffron on the forehead and finally a brass bowl filled with curds, was guided to each man's lips without letting go. Four pairs of hands moved, fluttered, joined in salutation, then dropped in poise and counter-poise as the simple ceremony came to a close. The women stepped aside and in two short paces forward son, brother, husband and father bent to the brass ewers by the door. He flicked water all around as well as on his head and over his shoulders, muttering prayers as he did. I stole a glance at the three women. The mother and sister were standing and the wife was suckling her baby as she sat on the floor. All eyes were fixed on their man as they wept, silently, effortlessly and forlornly. Then it was my turn to cross the threshold and, feeling bogus, I merely bent my head and momentarily clasped my upturned hands together as I stepped outside, slightly at a loss but relieved when the tension broke as last-minute instructions were given about, of all things, a transistor radio license.

Our route led north, through harvested rice fields, now brown, bare and dusty in the winter sunshine, along a river where an otter was fishing. Up and up, until the houses were left behind and the forests were reached. Through them we walked and found ourselves on cleared land where only potatoes grew. The air was thin and cold and being so high our meal took a long time to cook. Small wisps of cloud, shaped like swallows, raced overhead.

Four days later we walked along a stream, sides thickly rimed and water a trickle under solid ice. After two hours we had to cross over a high pass and found our breath short and limbs heavy. Great banks of mist whirled and spun like smoke from a giant cauldron and, brushing the sides of the hills, leaving fresh streaks of hoarfrost. Near the top of the pass cloud was being driven in three different directions as the cold air from the snows met warmer air. The soldier picked some fern smelling of parsley and put it behind his ear. This was meant to ward off the spirits found so high up and which cause mountain sickness. I was offered a sprig and sheepishly put it in my pocket.

On the pass we saw a settlement far below us. There were three double-storied houses, a number of low shacks, few cattle but many potato fields. On two sides around the settlement were gentle slopes of rhododendron and pine forests. The third side was open, sloping down to a river beyond which rose higher mountain after high mountain up to the Himalayas. Mount Everest lay out of sight, shielded by its lower ramparts. The fourth side was a precipice.

We reached the settlement. Outside one of the houses sat an old woman sorting potatoes. Nearby was a cow, one leg broken shorter than the rest. Shelter was requested and we were shown a hut made of wattle. The house itself had two rooms on the ground floor, one the family room and the other, strewn with leaves, empty. I was invited to inspect the upstairs room. It ran the length of the house and at the far end were four resplendent Buddhas, three large gilt ones and the fourth smaller and red. They had been brought from China, long years before. Smaller statues abounded. Grain was also stored there and, in one corner, was an empty bed. Twenty people could have been fitted in that room with comfort but I was told that it caught the wind and was only used in summer.

"May we sleep in the room with the leaves?" I asked. "No, that is reserved for the cow with the injured leg. Your place is outside."

That night was very cold and very long. Next morning the soldier decided to pray. First he went to the river, totally immersing himself in the freezing water. He then fetched a bowl of clarified butter and we both went to one of the buildings. The door was opened and the sun streamed in. I was amazed to see a riot of colour. It was a monastery. At the far end was the altar. The centre piece was a large gilt Buddha, guarded by many smaller ones. Shallow cups of butter were laid out, along with many sorts of bowls and jars.

Flanking the altar was the library, fifty-four cubby holes either side, with the sacred cloth-covered scriptures peering out in yellow, red and blue symmetry. A pew ran down the centre of the room with conch, cymbals and gong within reach. The walls and ceiling garishly depicted the rise and fall of man. The fallen were shown as having their limbs torn off and eaten by ravenous demons, as being trampled on and squashed, as being burnt. The risen were sitting in the lotus position, eyes inscrutably contemplating eternity. It was very cold.

Three Lamas came in and sat cross-legged on the bench of the pew. My Gurkha friend stood in front of the altar, head bent in prayer. I sat by the wall. None wore shoes and all were hatless. A low, murmuring chant started and an acolyte came in and laid fern-like leaves in the vessels in front of the main Buddha. The soldier poured the butter into the shallow cups and the chant became louder and louder, then faded. He was told to light the lamps and this he did, his hand trembling. Again the chanting began, low, subdued and formless. It gradually rose to a crescendo and, in startling and horrific cacophony, the instruments suddenly added their discordant threnody to the ululating voices of the Lamas while the sightless, staring eyes of the Buddhas watched, blind and impassive. I shuddered and was startled when grains of maize were thrown at the altar by the Lamas and the soldier. Quiet returned and tension slowly unwound. Buttered tea was brought in and offered to all.

That night we camped in a byre near the forest. We lit a fire and I remembered I had not written up my diary for some days. And although I was warm as I sat by the log fire, I shivered when I realized it was 25 December.

After a month I was back in Dharan. I went to the hospital and found Sursing cured. He had been stricken with anal tuberculosis, enervating and painful but easy to cure. Naturally he was overjoyed, as indeed was I. He lived for over thirty years more.

4: 1967-1976 - I

On another level I was greatly disquieted. In a report I wrote, the perturbing facets were uppermost in my mind and I started; "It has been a very long 21-year honeymoon...I was surprised ... " and the report eventually came back with the Major General's comments: "I am surprised that Cross is surprised."

There is no doubt that serving men and pensioners were normally pleased to see me and to chat over regimental matters as only soldiers can. The traditional codes of hospitality were more than well observed in places where I was with particularly close friends. Yet there was an air of disquiet, not entirely due to a recently initiated land reform programme. At times I was deliberately cold-shouldered by soldiers who knew me and of me. One told his wife to set the dog on me when we asked for a place to sleep on his verandah; admittedly it was after dark. I and my companion, especially in the east, would be purposefully misled when asking the way. But why?

At one place I was nearly put into jail by the local policeman, even though I was in possession of my trekking permit, because I wore my little Nepalese hat that I had been given in Luwang the wrong way round. I did not know that if the seam was on the right side, not the left, it meant I was probably a government servant and not an ordinary person. That alerted the policeman that I was masquerading: "A person as clever as you are is up to no good," he told me. Mentally I put him in the category of the "over-educated idiot, whose knowledge outruns his common sense the day he learns to sign his name." Nevertheless, while I was wearing a Nepalese hat nobody normally took the slightest notice of me, whereas before I had always been an object of the utmost curiosity. My stature, Aryan nose and complete compatibility with a native in Nepali, made many Nepali people discard the "evidence of their eyes" for the "belief of their ears" and accept me as a Nepali. Similarly and unbelievably, the Chinese of the remoter villages in Hong Kong took me as coming from China because of what they heard rather than what they saw!

I remembered what I had been taught a score of years before, by Colonel Rogers, when he said that life in a Gurkha unit, especially as a subaltern, bore no comparison with the difficulties a subaltern in a British battalion faced. Yet, he would add darkly, "you will find that the Gurkhas are different in their own country." And how right he was!

Initially, it did not occur to me that I was behaving incorrectly as I was not brash, offensive or stupid, merely extremely happy to be where I was. I had not expected "elevated" treatment but neither had I expected to be regarded with such "sourness." I was interested in everything I saw and everybody I came across, comparing both with what I already knew or thought I knew. That immediately put me in a suspicious category: why should a person be interested in something or someone that was patently none of his business or so obviously something every sane person knew about? The more parochial the person, the more possessive is he of his patch, and this is a common phenomenon in all the Asian countries I have visited. How personal was the "sourness"? Was I regarded as a danger, a challenge, an unknown quantity and therefore to be ignored and repelled as a safety measure?

I had no answers then, but perhaps there was a clue in the fact that there are, basically, two types of Nepali. One is the Aryan, with features the same as Europeans and with whom I had, of course, come into contact in the army as each major unit has one as a religious teacher: the other is the Mongoloid, who is recognized by rounder features and epicanthic eyelids. Anthropologists will say that these crossed over the Himalayan watershed from Tibet thousands of years ago. However, in the Hindu hierarchy there are four classes. Our soldiers, from what we call the "traditional martial classes," are Mongoloid and the maps in the books that described the recruiting areas showed swathes of territory, differently coloured for each major ethnic group recruited; green, say, for Gurungs, red for Magars, yellow for Rais and brown for Limbus. Little mention was made of the many other types of people met within those areas who were very much in the majority. The picture I carried in my head as to what sort of person to find in the hills was a wrong one.

I had yet to appreciate just what it meant to live in a country that was still looking over its shoulder at its feudal past and tentatively democratic present, blithely unaware of any social implications caused by political changes. Many were wondering where their next meal was coming from, so felt resentful at one well-fed being ebullient in their midst. So much depended on patronage and many were so poor that even to tell another your name without reason was to give away something you might have cause to regret. To tell a person on a track where you had come from and where you were going was similarly giving something away that it was better to hold on to. Silence to strangers on travels and small talk for the family when in the hearing of others seemed the Nepalese norm.

There was also a "reverse superiority" syndrome. So many Nepalis, if they become well off, shun their friends from times of poverty. I was well off. I did not shun the humble, therefore I was suspect.

I was slow in realizing that, just as the pre-war King's Company of the Coldstream Guards did not represent the typical Englishman, although the soldiers might be said to typify England, so the Brigade of Gurkhas may typify the martial classes of Nepal but is far from representing typical Nepalis, or even Gurkhas. The whole ethos of a subsistence farmer on the treadmill of poverty is so different from that of a serving soldier, even though he be indistinguishable from a subsistence farmer in other, non-ethical aspects, because he is relieved from the pressures, both of poverty and of an Aryan-dominated caste system in the army, where merit counts. However, such a man normally "reverts to type" once permanently back in his home environment, if only to survive, when he finds that local pressures are often stronger than the induced standards of a military unit far, far away. I had been serving with the cream of the cream, not with "export rejects." Man, I reflected philosophically, is by nature disruptive, destructive, dishonest and disobedient. Some of those I met in the hills were also cruel and perverse, just as children can be. So why be unduly upset by seeing people as they really are? Better by far to appreciate the refined product, especially when I had helped in the refinement, than to moan about what, to the vast majority, was normal.

Another point perplexed me. Great Britain is Nepal's oldest ally. Their men had served the British for one hundred and fifty-two years yet no one outside the comparatively small circle of military men connected me with the British. Did everything we had done mean so very little to them? I concluded that that must be so. I also noticed that the word "American" was used and it took me some time to realize that the word used in the army for "fair-skinned," *gora*, was not verbal currency in the Hills. The Americans had come to Nepal in the early '60s to help establish "democracy" and had been the first white people to be exposed to Nepalese public gaze on such a scale. The British recruiting areas were only a small part of the country and the Americans swamped our image.

Back in the Gurkha Para Company the men sympathized with me; they too suffered when they went on leave in that they were seen as the lucky ones with more pay, a chance to bring home foreign goods and the benefit of having had good rations and medical facilities. They had had their turn, so to speak, and it was now up to them to help out relatives. Not only that, but the local Aryan sharks, ever with an eye to the main chance, battened on to such people and many, shamefully, were the times when false charges were brought against our men with a view to extortion. None of that I knew about. So it was not so much I as J.P. Cross who was "foreign" in their midst but, even after I had left a person's house, the owner was susceptible to pressures resulting from what I might have left or concocted with him.

In 1968 my time with the Gurkha Paras came to an end. I had known the company ever since it was raised in 1963 and later when they were deployed as Section Commanders for an auxiliary police force, the Border Scouts, stationed at intervals as long the Borneo-Indonesian border. To command the Scouts I had to become a policeman which I was for a year—lonely and hunted the while. Back once more in the army, I commanded the company and, for three and a half years, had had unlimited friendship with them, transferring them from a pedestrian and unhappy unit to one the envy of all others, on the crest of the military wave. Now redundancy was striking hard as the British Army re-shaped itself for its policy of not having troops, less in Hong Kong and in Brunei, east of Suez after 1971, so killing off living units as it contracted. Before the final pullout I was promoted to go to the British Jungle Warfare School, more loneliness, as I saw it. Soldiers will talk with a major but not with a lieutenant colonel.

I was the last Commandant of the Jungle Warfare School which trained officers and men from all five continents. We were the only unit to be retained on the Asian mainland, after the "East of Suez" policy was introduced. There was considerable political activity at the very top to try and turn the Jungle Warfare School into a five-nation Commonwealth Jungle Warfare Centre but it was fraught at every twist and turn by Malay intransigence. Even here I found myself regarded both as hero and villain of the piece, from prime minister level down to colonels on the staff.

I learnt Thai and Vietnamese during this time. I was asked to report to the Royal Thai Army Chief of Staff on the training status of his Special Forces and was an official guest of the South Vietnamese Army—both had their moments. From having been the only lieutenant colonel in the theatre left without a job to go to, on one day I was offered three jobs: an attaché to an unspecified Indo-Chinese country, a Foreign and Commonwealth Office-sponsored adviser on jungle warfare to Thailand and South Vietnam, and command of a commando battalion, having raised and trained it, for the Singapore Armed Forces. Before I had to make the decision, I was asked by the Royal Thai Army to be their jungle warfare adviser as a major general in their army.

During these three years my thoughts often turned to my trek when I found so much of a mixture and so different from "the finished product." I also started a correspondence with a widow, Christine Lorimer. She and her late husband, a friend of mine from a long time back, had kept my flat in Kuching warm when I was a policeman. I hoped that she and I could ripen our friendship enough to marry, so giving me something to look forward to after my Asian life was over.

But first I had to go and say goodbye to Nepal and farewell to the Gurkhas, believing I would never go there again. I had to know if what I had experienced in the Hills in 1967 was normal behavior. I wanted to immerse myself in such a way that either I would be glad never to return or glad that I had made the effort to say farewell in my own way. I had to see if

the old magic did work or not. Shortly before I left the Jungle
Warfare School, in December 1971, I was warned to go to Laos
as the defence attaché in late 1972. If Christine was to be with
me as my wife, I would have to get into top gear when I got
home after my trek!

I left Singapore on 4 December 1971. There was no war. I
arrived in Bangkok the same day and there was a war, in East
Pakistan. I could either stay where I was or go, not to Calcutta,
but to Bombay. This I did and waited, in Ootacamund, until
the war burnt itself out. At one point I found my way blocked
by a group of Indians who picked on me, demanding why the
South African government had such harsh racist policies.
"Colour Bar! Colour Bar! Why this colour bar?" they chanted,
not letting me move forward. Inspiration flashed: "I am
knowing where is this Malabar," I answered cravenly, "but I am
not knowing where is this Kalabar." My inquisitors were so
surprised by this utterly unexpected remark that they stepped
aside in disbelief, giving me the chance to make my escape
unscathed. I spent Christmas Day in Dharan and went on a
107-day trek. During this time King Mahendra died and people
were genuinely saddened at the news.

At a number of houses I found my framed photograph in
the place of honour, directly above the front door. There I was,
dressed in Gurkha Para Company gear or Seventh Gurkhas
ceremonial uniform, scowling down at me—giving me a most
strange feeling. In no case did the head of the household know
I was coming and the accumulated dust of ages on the

photographs was proof enough that they had not been put up specially.

There were three occasions when people dreamt that I was on my way to see them and in only one case did the man know I might turn up during the three-month period. As for the other two, one I had not met for five years, the other for ten. By the end of my trek I had met someone I knew or someone recognized me every day. I give two examples. I was on the outskirts of Bhojpur, a town in the east. A man I knew was ahead of me and I shouted something to him. Between us an old, bent woman, walking with a stick, was coming towards me. She stopped as I passed, looked up and asked in a quavering voice whether it was *Belayaté Maiñla*, a nickname I had been given to distinguish me from the Nepali original, a man, with my features and stature, who lived in Darjeeling and who had a reputation for making everybody laugh.

"Yes, Granny, it is." She looked pleased and I asked her where she lived and how did she know who I was. She told me that she lived three days' walk away and, five years before, I had spent one night in the house next door to hers. She had heard my chatter through the walls, had laughed and, with my calling out to the man in front of me, had recognized the voice!

The other example I take from the west of the country. I saw a fine, upright figure striding towards me. "Excuse me," I said as I stopped him, "but I think I know you." "What is your regiment?" he asked gruffly.

I told him and he said, no, he didn't know me. He was an ex-subedar of the Fifth Gorkhas and had been on pension a few years. I said to him, "Sahib, you were a Lance Naik in 1/5 Royal Gurkha Rifles Motor Transport Platoon when, in 1946, you came down from the Red Fort, Delhi, to Kamthi, to take over from 1/1 Gurkha Rifles. Correct?"

He nodded slowly. "You were in charge of petrol issues," I continued, "and it was I who handed over the Petrol Issue Ledger to you." It was the same man and we had last met twenty-six years before, only speaking to each other once.

My trek gave me what I wanted. I now knew that under normal circumstances I was welcome among the Nepalis. The sour, ugly mood of five years before had gone, at least from the surface. Was it only because the old magic still worked its two-way system?

In 1972, back in England, Christine and I became engaged while I was hard at my attaché studies—an average of twelve hours study every day for two months, French and Lao. I had to go over to France to complete my work. It was then time to sit the French examination prior to marriage and going out to Laos. I got back in time for a weekend course at Bristol and two nights at home before going to London for the exam.

The telephone rang and it was Christine saying that she had no intention of marrying me. So that I could not get her to change her mind, she was not ringing from home but from a secret place. I was deflated. I sat the exam in a grim frame of mind and, although the day before the oral part I had bought a

French newspaper, read only one paragraph which was the one I had to translate on the morrow, I was not surprised to learn that I had failed there also.

Halfway through my time in Laos the British government put out feelers to employ me in some linguist or advisory capacity in London after my attaché job finished in 1976, concerned with Asians. The idea of living in London did not appeal. My Asian was not a Bangladeshi fish and chip seller in Tottenham Court Road but a Gurkha shepherd playing a bamboo flute as he watched over his flocks, or even an Iban headhunter. However, I was spared from any agonizing decision in November 1974 when I got a telegram from the Gurkha headquarters in Hong Kong, inviting me to be the Deputy Recruiting Officer (West) [DRO] in November 1976. I was to signal my decision as soon as possible.

I showed it to a colleague who looked up at me quizzically. I nodded my head and he wrote something on a telegram form. It was a message to the government department who had "trawled" me for a job and it started off; "We have lost John Cross to his first love..." Indeed, being an attaché is also like being in love—it can only be done properly once!

More and more, as my time in Laos drew to a close, my thoughts turned to Nepal—that other Asian country land-locked between China and a friend of Russia, India rather than Vietnam. I had been alerted to background tension in Nepal by the Indian First Secretary who told me he had been to the USA and the USSR as a student; in the former you could talk but might not eat, in the latter you could not talk but you could eat. Before going to Laos he had been on the Nepal desk in Delhi and told me, sincerely if a little drunkenly, that, by the year 2000 AD, Nepal would be part of India for all intents and purposes. He proceeded to tell me succinct and weak points about all levels of Nepalese administration that India would rectify. Without such a remark I might have thought my task in Nepal would be routine and dull, but how wrong I was! I longed for the black and white of a "yes" or a "no," rather than the flat, muddy grey of reading meanings, hints and surmises into otherwise bland and anodyne remarks made in the code of double-speak. Such was the life of an attaché. As my Australian counterpart put it; "In, Out or Pending—boring but clean."

I had my dog put down, wept bitterly and left in February 1976 drained emotionally, but delighted to be away: first stop, Hong Kong; second stop, Nepal; third stop, England for leave.

In Hong Kong I saw a Chinese boy put his arm round a girl while waiting for a ferry and I instinctively looked round to see who was watching him, ready to take him away to a re-education centre for moral teaching, but of course no one was. Had I been under the communists for less than a year to react like that? I saw another youth choose which cassette he wanted to play in his recorder. I again looked round to see who would stop him from choosing his own tune, as had been the case once the communists had come to power in Laos, but of course no one did. Yes, I had been under the communists for less than a year. If their system could do that to me in such a short time, what did it do to those who could not escape and to those who knew no better?

I caught up with the Gurkha gossip, delighted to talk Nepali once more, feeling relaxed with so many old friends, British and Gurkha. On hearing the news of my posting as DRO, the men said that they welcomed it but were afraid that the job would be too "small" for me. I gave lectures to large audiences, British and Gurkha, about how the communists had won in Laos, bringing the flavor of one "who was there," adding a dimension of reality to and a warning of the dangers of the "threat."

I was brought up to date with current trends and problems. The one that was to concern me was mentioned, very discreetly, by the British ambassador who had come from Kathmandu to brief senior officers of the Brigade, at their annual conference, about his side of the Gurkha connection. I was told about the propensity of men going on leave and pension to fill their baggage with attractive foreign goods which they would sell back in Nepal, the itch to fill pocket, palm or purse being relentless. Indians, starved of stuff that was not shoddy, so very keen to get their hands on decent items, encouraged black market trafficking of goods from Paklihawa, where the men had to report, to India—not difficult with Paklihawa so near the border. So great was the sum involved that it eroded the agreement for duty-free transit arrangements for a landlocked country to the extent that Indian coffers were emptier than they should have been. Complaints from Delhi to Kathmandu had resulted in the Prime Minister of Nepal dropping hints to the British ambassador that, if the British could not put their house in order, those Nepalis who were inimical to the idea of British recruiting might force him to close down the western end of the business. It was to be my responsibility to stop the racket in Paklihawa and so remove the threat of a recruiting crisis.

Since I was not wanted as DRO till the October, I had been asked if I would go on a three-month trek, east and west, on behalf of the generous Canadians who had donated so much money for the enhancement of forty hill high schools. Having no ready representative of their own it was up to me to find out what forty pre-selected high schools needed, put a price and a priority on each request and, on completion, submit the list to Dharan and Paklihawa. In all I talked to the head masters and staffs of forty schools, twenty of them in the east of the country and the other twenty in the west. Except for the Hillary High School in Sola Khumbu, the best school I found in the east was not as good as the worst one I found in the west. In every case I was warmly welcomed and well looked after.

One of the problems faced by the communists in Laos was that many of their ideas, their slogans and their instructions used words alien to their newly dominated peasantry. Seminars had to be held to teach these new words and re-education programmes were introduced to ensure that the message percolated everywhere. Nepal, not being communist, had never introduced, probably never even considered, anything similar. Even so, one aspect that did strike me forcibly was, to me, a disturbing gap in the schools that I visited where the Aryans, who made up the bulk of the schoolmasters, and their pupils from the ethnic minorities.

Brought up on a verbal diet used in battalions, I often found myself at a loss aptly to describe what I wanted to, while the different pronunciations of the schoolmasters—often from areas a considerable distance from the school—made what they said hard to follow. I wondered how the pupils could absorb the teaching and how this influx of teachers from different backgrounds and ideas would affect attitudes among young men a decade later even if they did keep politics out of any teaching—which of course should have been the case?

On the other hand, I was astonished by the hard work, dedication and persistence of the very great majority of school teachers. Often walking for more than an hour to and from school at wages that hardly seemed worthwhile, they overcame enormous difficulties, not only in the poor fabric of the buildings they had to teach in and the overcrowding—some primary schools, for instance, had five classes in one room, each class sitting on one bench and reciting their lesson out loud—but also the difference in the ability to grasp any need to learn amongst many of the students from poorer backgrounds.

It was all an object lesson in how to make the best of poor conditions. I wondered how many of those in more comfortable educational jobs really did understand what it was like "on the ground."

The long walk did me good. I was particularly interested to view the country with more experienced eyes than before. I was, frankly, saddened to see what I took to be trends of torpidness in the farther-flung parts of the educational administration. Try hard though I did to avoid making comparisons with Laos, I was worried to see so much local effort either misguided or misdirected.

My journey through the eastern Hills was a voyage both of discovery and consolidation on a personal level, and of comparison with where I had come from, Laos, on another. Posters extolling Chinese communist life were in profusion—ideas from the north—and radical notions of anti-monarchical social unrest, admittedly only personally overheard once, but rumored about in many places, from an Indian engaged on teaching practice for his degree—ideas from the south.

I was fascinated to hear remarks that I had made in 1972 brought into the conversation with a chuckle, sometimes suitably embroidered, sometimes unsuitably so! I walked hard and fast, often covering twenty or more miles a day. My theory of a good night's sleep for a tired body being therapeutic for a troubled mind was again of use.

For the western Hills, I went to Paklihawa to be briefed. I had not been there since 1959, the very first day of its official existence. Since then it had been turned into an extended garden, with trees, shrubs and flowers, making it perceptibly cooler than the surrounding countryside. The local town, Bhairawa, to all intents and purposes like any town in the northeast of India, was the third hottest place in the country. It had been known to reach 120 degrees Fahrenheit in the shade. The *lu* wind that blows in April and May makes man, woman, child and beast of the fields uncomfortable if not ill.

There I found one wonderful example of how far Nepal had, in fact, developed. In 1942 a man had joined the army. He knew neither his own, his father's nor his village's name. Come the end of the war he was told he could stay on in the army provided, on his return from leave, he had found out the answers to those three points. To his delight and surprise he found that the name he had been called was only a nickname.

His son has a Diploma in Education!

Everywhere in Nepal the feeling was that the poverty and hardship were there and nowhere else. I was not pleased to discover, both east and west, that, whereas before poverty was carried silently and stoically, now it was paraded almost proudly. It was accompanied by the slightly contemptuous attitude that "if the British [or the Canadians] don't give us what we want, we'll ask someone else to provide." People were taught how to be beggars. The positive, material side of helping out poorer nations is countered by an insidious erosion of self-respect, self-help and financial probity as a once-proud people are first tempted then lured into becoming scroungers. The line between unofficial ambassadors of excellence—the traditional Gurkha face—and export rejects, like that between genius and madness, is very thin.

By the time I had ended my trek I was in a position to analyze what I had found in the country I loved. This time my wits were sharpened by the geopolitical similarities Nepal shared with Laos, having spent three-and-a-quarter years there, another similarly sized, land-locked country which also has China as its northern neighbour and where the cold war between Russian and China was being played out more obviously than in Nepal. Thus I found myself strangely but not unnaturally comparing the two cases with clinical absorption.

Facets, many-sided and interwoven, included history, geography, poverty, politics and prevailing social customs.

Nepal has a racial and cultural admixture, complicated by an original Chepang and Newar ingredient. This has shown manifestations of "dis-ease" that modern developments— education, communications and tourism have exacerbated— not a new phenomenon by any means but one that will never go away. It is present for all time, waxing or waning, to be joined or ignored but never to be beaten. The clever Aryan Nepali has the inside track but a remoteness from the outside world. The malleable Mongoloid Nepali, slower and more stolid, has enriched the world by the name Gorkha but is, sadly, strangely and unexpectedly to foreigners, without much honour and certainly has no glory in his own country.

It again crossed my mind that the reason for this is because the ethnic majority of Nepalis has done nothing to conjure its name in other men's imaginations while the small minority of Mongoloids has "stolen" the name Gorkha and made it respected world-wide as synonymous with producing results other mere mortals cannot. Also the name "Gorkha" has other meanings and other implications to the majority of Nepalis. Susceptibilities in both directions have been hurt and contrition has been offered from neither.

On my long walk I so much the more understandingly saw that the point about geography playing its part in Nepal and on the Nepalese psyche is that it is a country of contrasts, affecting temperature and temperament, humus and humours, soil and soul alike. Nepal can be thought of as a country on its side, divided into three bands. It is the middle band that was the enigma, where Aryan Nepalis and Mongoloid Nepalis rub shoulders, sometimes less than happily. In this middle band lies the "rip tide" of turbulence between the two population movements of past centuries, showing unevenly on the surface, though there are strong undercurrents of disturbance, differences and discontent—almost a subcutaneous cold war. Aberrations to the original pattern have occurred as many Mongoloids from the middle band move south to the fertile Tarai. The King of Nepal was seen as the only one recognized and highly respected factor in the country being a unified entity—of that there can be no doubt.

The contrasts I have mentioned are indelibly ingrained on the character and temperament of all hill Nepalis, not only the Gurkha of fame, fact and fiction, and are responsible for the tremendous differences discernible in the Nepalese ethos, both collectively and individually, that most of us have experienced, from the Himalayan heights of heroism and splendor to the depths of disappointing and inexplicable behavior. To offset the harshness of this indictment, it must be remembered how near so many Nepalis are to hunger and how they have learnt "to roll with the punch" to survive. It can, therefore, be understood how conventional, traditional and regimental black and white fuse into an unedifying grey when back in the mountain kingdom—hence "they are different in their own country." The sudden opening up of the country to influences that were unknown until recently after centuries of primitive feudalism was also instrumental in causing a condition of social and cultural indigestion. Hard though the comparison may sound, in many ways Nepal in 1976 was not very far off where Britain was at the start of the Industrial Revolution.

The Hindu religion also has an effect on society that will not, I believe, be found elsewhere. Its distinction of caste is obvious outside purely "religious" occasions and is seen in differing patterns of social pretension, leisure, work, marriage, family life, popular culture and attitudes to authority. This leads, among the lower reaches of Hindu society, to a "chameleon" mentality of automatically fitting in with others' interpretation of events and, at times, patterns of behavior. A hill man in the British Army serving overseas never loses these differences but they become blurred and tend to be subsumed by other facets of "getting on with life." He may well resent their intrusion when he returns to Nepal in such a way that redounds adversely against him.

On my previous visits in this middle band I was fully sensible to much of the darker side of life but ignorant of both what to look for and listen to. As I saw it now, there was a feeling of arrogance and superiority amongst the Aryans even to the point where the Mongoloid porters with me were not allowed to wash at a standpipe because "you are not proper Nepalis." In other words they were looked down on as "irritant ethnic minorities" who, despite all royal exhortations to the contrary, were not true Nepalis. There was nothing new in this, which had always led to the continuous scoring of points, the one against the other.

In the case of Gurkhas who joined the British or Indian Army, absence from home would give respite from this interminable petty struggle. For a while all, comparatively, was well and only on returning home on leave was the grim reminder brought back to them. On leaving the army the man was then and still is faced once more with these pressures. For instance, all knew that soldiers sent on redundancy were given a "bronze skull cap"—never a "golden bowler"—and most of these men were targets of Aryan cupidity or trumped up charges: I saw it myself. However, now he has a broader base from which to adjudge his ability and assess his potential. But he finds that he can neither "join them" nor "beat them" and, unless he decides to return to the old pattern, frustration, discontent and yearning for betterment all play a decisive role in his future actions. He is, therefore, out in the cold and almost everything he does from thenceforth tends to be regarded by a suspicious government as reprehensible if not treasonable, whether this was the case or not. Is the Gurkha friendliness with the British more one of reaction against the system in his native land than one of convenience, where merit can rise to the forefront? Not a comforting thought to the British "myth-makers."

I, in the comfort of my Regimental Fortress in Welfare-State Britain, clicked my tongue and frowned at such unregimental behavior but did not myself ever have to face such social pressures. In the land of my birth the government had made a "safety net" of welfare benefits under the poor so that, according to those who thought they knew, social ills and constraints would be eliminated. Many saw such benefits as flying in the face of nature with the survival of the unfittest as they offered two cheers for democracy.

Be that as it may, those with whom I and some other very privileged British citizens had spent more than thirty years of our adult life and with whom we had served with so much affection and trust had accrued an unfair amount of opprobrium in the body politic of Nepal—tinder for the Mischief Makers. Thinking about this I remembered and extrapolated what the Chinese Assistant Military Attaché in Laos had said to me, in answer to my question "What can any one man do?" "Given the correct conditions," he said, quoting Helmsman Mao, "one spark can start a forest fire."

It was this sad state of affairs that, amongst others, posed a threat to Nepal, albeit latent, and particularly so when viewed in the context of the struggle for power and influence in Asia between China and the Soviet Union which had a long way to go. Nepal was important to both countries: to China, more prophylactically than aggressively; to the Soviets, through India, more aggressively than otherwise. It thus seemed inevitable that increased pressure from both sides, in one guise or another, would be a feature of life (and most probably death also) for many years and to an extent then unseen. In the middle band the threat of the "Party" was very near the surface of everyday life, although it was a moot point whether the party referred to was Communist, Congress or a figment of public imagination. It was fear of being dubbed a "Party Man" that caused averted heads and whispers lest Authority came to hear of it and the person, haplessly innocent in all probability, went to a fetid and soul-destroying jail for an indefinite length of time, thus exacerbating matters further. Often "Party" only meant any aspect of political indiscipline in the eyes of officialdom. It needed no communist backing at all but it was a situation that those trained to aggravate tensions could take advantage of. This was the more obvious in the east than in the west; with more Chinese literature than any other type of similar material around it could be argued that indeed China was in the lead, especially if the presumption that as the Chinese Information Office in Kathmandu seemed to be used more than was its Soviet counterpart was correct. This was not necessarily so.

I was looking for the true "Nepal-ness" of Nepal so I took as my starting point the word "pedigree," which comes from the old French for "crane's foot," the one time three-toed sign, used for showing linear descent. In the context that I was using it, it stood for the main stream of Nepalese life, the leg, before branching out along one of the crane's toes; to me the intriguing question was whether the country had enough internal cohesion to go along the middle Nepalese toe or whether external pressures would force it to go along the Russian/Indian toe or the Chinese toe. The gloomy thought at the end of my trek was that, before Nepal could be saved from Indian or Chinese hegemony, it had to be saved from itself.

On the surface, however, life continued normally. During my sixty days in the Hills if I got whiffs of trouble it was because I was often taken as some sort of Aryan Nepali by the Aryans themselves. I was the subject, and object! of intense curiosity as I was able to talk to them in a way that most of them said they had never come across before from a foreigner. Almost without exception I was both pressed to stay longer and to return later on. My trek was a wonderful reconnaissance in depth for the new job. However, sixty days of hard walking were not long enough to fathom trends except in matters about which I was concerned; recruiting, pension paying and welfare. The last thing I wanted to happen was for official Nepal to think I was "snooping," but I loved the country enough to have this as a very slight risk.

Even so, seeing the same type of mistake being made by petty authority in Nepal as the vanquished had once made in Laos, hearing the same kind of small talk of discontent, with the forced smile, the lowered voice and darting eyes, made me ineffably sad. The cloud at last had left the horizon, and, now looming, was much bigger than any man's hand.

I went on leave to England after my long walk. It was nice being back there; no revolution, no poverty, cool weather, gentle slopes and contours, pastel shades, an ordered tempo of life with reliable telephones, reliable mail, potable tap water and no need for mosquito nets. All were a pleasant contrast from what I had been living with and through. On the other hand, I was struck by the negative side of life: the discernible lack of purpose in many matters; the slowness of getting things done; too many people over-weight, over-indulgent—too much meat and drink—and under-exercised; young people behaving as though they had invented sex; the casual and materialistic attitude of so many towards so much that so many elsewhere had to do without all made me feel that my fellow countrymen were blind to the need of hard work and took too much for granted.

As usual I was in a minority and when I looked around the seamier side of life I felt it would merely be priggish to question if all that I had done over the past thirty-three years was "just for that." Yes, it was and, as the Gurkhas say, I had been "singing by a river and working at night." Who really cared what I had done? Only myself, as I looked into the mirror every morning when shaving!

In a quiet Dorset village I met Sally Walton, then nursing her mother in a terminal illness. She gave me thoughts, as I gave them to her, that, come the magical age of fifty-five when my services would be wanted no more by the army, if not before, they could be for her.

My sister Gillian came over from America where she was busy with racehorses. She was still unwed and we had had thoughts of looking after each other in our dotage. Certainly the home in Dorset, so lovingly tended by a green-fingered mother, was a powerful magnet to retire to England. But now the Sally factor gave the future a new dimension.

It was decided that I would go by myself to Nepal in October 1976 and, when it was suitable for Sally to come out, she would join me there. I did warn her that it was not a family station and the wrong time of year but that, where matters to come to pass as I expected them to, I could shorten my two-year tour so return to England for good and all.

Recruiting was in full swing when I arrived in Paklihawa. The system was, in one respect, different from the recruitment of British soldiers in that it was geared to reject men, not to accept them, with so many trying for so few vacancies. So keen was competition to get into the British Army that people went to unethical (by British standards) lengths to try and be enlisted. There seemed to be a mystique about recruiting, rather like the old assumption that only British pilots could navigate ships in the Suez Canal. Certainly the recruiting processing in Paklihawa, however dedicatedly applied, was woefully inadequate. I resolved to change it.

It was now that I had another insight into the Nepalese character. Family ties, nuclear, extended or fictional, are of paramount importance. Until a personal relationship is established, scant interest is shown. A stranger slipping on a banana skin is regarded as a jape of the gods to relieve the boredom of the onlooker. In the way two dogs will sniff at first meeting, so a Nepali will spend the first part of any talk with a new acquaintance in finding out what, if anything, they have in common. This is reflected in the proverb about a "buffalo-selling" relationship: if an event such as that can be traced between the one's family and the other's, the bond of mutual help is established. I was walking behind the out-going DRO when a man, followed by a youth, came up to me. I could not place him and, before I could ask him who he was, he introduced his son to me, and told me that I had to enlist him in his old regiment, the Gurkha Signals. The "had to" part jarred but I told him that I was not yet the DRO, so had no power to enlist anybody. "Ah, but you and I played football together in 1954 so we know each other," came the surprising rejoinder.

Then there was my one-time Gurkha Para Company driver who had brought me his son, having taken him away from school in far-off Dehra Dun. It was my second day in camp and he bounced into my room with the news that he had brought his son to me and the boy was waiting outside. The father said that the lad was mine, to do anything I wanted, clean my boots, water the flowers or send to the Singapore police. The boy looked abashed; I felt put upon. "Can I do anything with this lad?" I asked, "really anything?" I was told indeed that was so. "In that case," I said, turning to the father, "I give him back to you."

There are three English words that are used by the Nepalis when they talk about how to get on in life: force, source, course. "Force" is the power of money; "source" is personal contact that carries an implied bond so it is incumbent on the more powerful to help the weaker; and "course," a poor third, is when a personal qualification overrides the other two. Thinking about how this affected our men, serving and pensioners, I changed my clothes and went for my daily jog.

I had noticed many people who seemed to have no particular job to do but it was not up to me, then, to take any action to control numbers. I met a short, strong, good-looking man—why was he not with the lot that were being processed for recruits? He seemed just the type—so I stopped him and asked him his name.

He answered directly, with no trace of servility, "Buddhiman Gurung."

5: 1956-76: II

In late July 1969, towards the end of the monsoon, an impoverished Nepali peasant named Tanka Bahadur Gurung, Tanké for short, died in his mountain village. Aged forty-four, not tall enough to be a soldier in either the British or Indian Army, he had been a very strong, very honest, impetuous and hard-working man. His eldest daughter was married and lived two days' walk away. Five others, two boys and three girls, were at home. His eldest son, Buddhiman, was thirteen at the time and remembers it. Putting his story together, it runs like this:

My family home is in a village called Thuloswara, in the district of Lamjung, in central Nepal, near the top of a steep mountain. It was never hot and often very cold. Farming land was an hour's walk downhill, where it is always much warmer.

As a young man, my grandfather, named Thuné, decided to go far away to Darjeeling in India, a long, uncomfortable, difficult and sometimes dangerous journey in those days. He took his wife with him and worked in the tea gardens, where he married a local girl for a second wife. He came back in 1939, 1997 in our Nepalese calendar, with my pregnant grandmother, a boy of four, Tanké, and a girl two years his younger; these were my future father and aunt. Thuné's father, my great-grandfather, Aas Bahadur, had, by then, moved from the main house at the top of the village and built a much smaller place to live in near his fields, at the bottom of the mountain.

As Thuné's family approached the village the boy Tanké became ill, losing his speech. Thuné called on his father, an animist priest, to see what was wrong. Going into a trance, Aas Bahadur called a god from Darjeeling to come and cure the sick child. This god said it would make the lad well but had to stay nearby and for food, once a year, needed nine eggs and nine flowers, with prayers. So, about a hundred yards to the north of the house, a hole for it was dug in a bank. Prayers were said, a flat stone was put in the hole to keep the god there and, for protection, a large rock was placed over the hole. As soon as that had been done, the ill child was able to speak again. Four months later Thuné walked out of the house by himself and was never heard of again. The family never forgave him.

Great-grandfather worshipped the "god from the east," as it was called, every year and taught my father also. The rock was dragged away, prayers were said, and nine eggs and nine flowers were placed on the flat stone in the hole for the god. The rock was then dragged back and placed in front of the hole but, how strange, every year during the night after the act of worship it was always two paces away the next morning, leaving the god's hole open.

Even though people waited up all night to see how this happened, for no wild animal could have moved it, nothing was ever seen although the boulder's movement was heard.

I was born in the house at the bottom of the hill when father was twenty, in April 1956. It was small, not much more than four walls, a roof and a mud floor. We had no furniture. We sat and slept on rush mats. Years later my mother told me how hard it had been to bring up the family, so poor were we. Father made simple ploughs from the trees in the forest which was only yards from the house. He sold them for what now seems almost nothing. I was scared of the forest. Wild animals, deer and monkeys, lived there, as did leopards that slept in caves. We could hear them calling to their mates. The deer came out of the forest at night to nibble at the crops, while the monkeys and birds tried to feed on them by day. The leopards tried to catch the deer and the goats. If we found any freshly killed animal, we would bring it back to the house, cook it and eat it. I was afraid when sent to collect firewood from the forest and was always ready to run back as fast as I could. Only wood and water were enough for us, nothing else was.

I was also afraid for another reason; the gods and ghosts in the forest were fearful and had to be respected. Below our house was a small shrine of the god of Sundays. As we passed by we always had to put a piece of sacred *duba* grass on it. Any stranger who seemed to be on his way to the forest to get rid of nature was warned off that place. A short way from the river where we bathed and fished for little fish was a waterfall. Although the lush grass that grew near it was suitable for cattle fodder, we feared to approach it as it was haunted by some kind of ghost. Everywhere in our kingdom are such places; sometimes they are sacred only to animists but, even then, it is better for Buddhists and Hindus to respect them. I learnt that at a very early age.

Let me give you an example of a neighbour, Mandhoj Gurung, that happened maybe forty years before I was born. Everybody knows it to be true. Mandhoj was ordinary. By the age of nine he was already good mannered and hard working, like so many other boys. He lived with his parents.

Early one morning he went out of the house and had not returned by the evening. He did not come back the next day. He was not at the house of a neighbour. It was not the recruiting season when he might have been tempted to run away, without telling his parents, to join the army.

The local animist priest, the shaman, was called in to see if he could help. When the moment was right this man went into a trance and, shaking, called on the deities and spirits of the surrounding forest to let him know where young Mandhoj had disappeared. The answer was that the lad was safe and unharmed, with a spirit of the forests, a *ban jhañkri*, and would return home. With that the parents had to be satisfied.

Next morning Mandhoj did come back, happy, smiling, well fed. He had left the house as normal but was not sure what happened. He must have gone to sleep, instead of going back home, and had woken up in a cave somewhere in the forest, warm, comfortable and very, very happy. He had been well looked after, quite by who or what he was unable to say, and had been fed with delicious food, but again quite what it was he could not describe. But he had been taught how to read the future luck [divinations], how to communicate with the...and here he was not sure whether they were spirits of the dead or of the unborn.

Ever since then he has had the power of prophecy, proved time and time again. He himself became an ordinary soldier in the Assam Regiment and married my aunt on his first leave. Now he is completely deaf. His foot stuck in a stirrup as he was getting off a horse and it ran away, dragging him for a mile. He must have broken both eardrums. He was lucky not to lose his life.

The power that the gods have over a person's life is unbelievably strong. The "writing" on the inside of the forehead shows it. None can see it until after death and, even when the skull can be seen, it is not understood. Nothing can change it and it is all-powerful. This "writing" is responsible for a person's successes and failures. Hindu priests have an amazing ability to see into the future: every year they produce a calendar that tells what the weather will be and if there will be earthquakes, drought or even civil unrest. They are seldom wrong! I wish I knew how they found out such things.

We were always dressed in rags and went bare-footed. Father wore the Gurung "kilt" and, over a shirt, the square cloth that we people tie at opposite corners and wear over our shoulders. This forms a large pocket. He would always carry a sickle except when he went up the mountain to the main village. Then he would put a kukri in the front of his waistband.

We would be scared of the rough people from the north, Tibetan Lamas. Four of them visited us when I was still small and asked for me to go with them to be taught how to be a monk. As soon as I saw them coming I hid behind a large box set in a hollow behind the cooking place. I heard all their talk, how they would persuade me to go with them, how they would allow me back after a year and a lot more. I could not be found that day so they said they would return next day. I crept out to sleep with my mother when it was dark and told everybody I would not go. Studying to be a monk was, I knew even at that age, very hard work. A boy had to sit still in the same place for up to six months at a time, except once a day for nature reasons. When he was successful his topknot would suddenly sprout out of his shaven skull. The skull would be combed and that, too, hurt. He would have to start from the beginning if he were unsuccessful. No, I did not want that. I can remember us children playing, borrowing a small cushion from the house, putting it on my head, and pretending I was a Lama.

Food was always a problem, with only enough land for us to grow our own for three months of the year. The crops were maize, which we ate even before the cobs were ripe, first boiling them, millet and mustard plants. The other nine months of the year we were hungry. Looking back on it, it seems that life was one long struggle against hunger. Father did as best he could, doing odd jobs for some rice as repayment, borrowing a little money—people did not lend him much as he could not easily repay it—and eating what we could find ourselves. We all took a hand at that. I can remember, as a small child, not being sure which sort of leaf mother had told me to collect in my little back-basket, woven especially small for me by father. There was nothing in the house except a bit of flour, so I had to collect as much as I could. I filled my basket up and took it back. Mother had to wash and boil all the leaves very carefully as some of what I'd brought back was bitter and could have been harmful if eaten raw. Quite often my parents would go hungry so we children could have what little there was.

Because food was so short we often had gruel, which I did not like. My grandmother scolded me when I grumbled. One day when I was still small, a pot of gruel was bubbling on the hearth and I and my eldest sister tried to see which of us could blow on the fire to make it hotter, using a tube of hollow wood. In the struggle sister pushed me and I put my hand into the boiling gruel. It was very painful and I screamed. Grandmother hurriedly prepared a covering of salt that hurt even more. Once was enough! I had a herbal remedy applied daily to prevent scarring and a piece of thread was drawn between my fingers morning and evening to prevent the skin joining. Every week an uncle, who was a great hunter, shot a whistling thrush, a black and dark blue bird that lives in ravines beside water, so that I could eat its meat, a known cure for burns. Other sorts of meat only made burns worse. It was all most painful but I bore the pain because I knew that no man could join the army if he had a scar such as mine would have been. Six months later I was back to normal, my skin clear. My sister, who had been slapped and scolded at first, nursed me very tenderly and helped me get up in the morning, go to bed, wash and everything else.

Father was part owner of a few buffaloes and a flock of goats. We knew if the leopards had killed a buffalo by the swarm of vultures that came to eat the dead body. What is so strange is that no bird of prey will eat any dead cattle if the head is pointing directly to the north. Move it away from due north and it will be eaten up in no time! As part-owner father looked after the animals, gave a goat to the owner once a year and shared out the kids. I was kept healthy by buffaloes' milk and by being rubbed all over in heated mustard seed oil. This makes inside the body warm. Meat we had about six times a year, when a chicken or a goat, ours or a neighbor's, was eaten. Rice was a luxury we seldom had but, even so, I was a strong lad. I was like my father, small but strong. I grew up more patient than dad but seemed to have his ability to control anger and make many friends. Everybody was friendly with my father.

Once a year father would walk down to India to collect salt. It took him a week to get there and about ten days to return. His back would be raw by the time he returned as the salt soaked through his sweaty clothes, even though he put large leaves between the sack and his clothes to prevent this.

Only a few people lived in our part of the mountain. In those days all travel was difficult and very slow. There were practically no roads in the country, so I later learnt, except in the capital, Kathmandu, and maybe some dirt tracks in the flat south of the country, next to India. Kathmandu is a week's hard walk away to the east and people only went there to join the Nepalese army or to try and have an audience with an important person. No one would go far without others as it was dangerous to leave the local area without another person. India is also a week's walk away. Once India was reached, due south from where we lived, travel became quicker with roads and railways, though the Indians laughed when they saw Nepalis, calling out, "There go the hill men!" as an insult. People said how difficult was travel in India, as the place was full of beggars, thieves and crowds, with heat and dust everywhere. Our fresh mountain air and cool water were so wonderful after the plains of India.

In the last twenty years travel in Nepal has been become much easier. India and Kathmandu can be reached in a day and small roads are being built and will soon reach into the mountains.

Our people, the Gurungs, have been famous soldiers for a very long time, formerly in the days of the *raj* and since what the old soldiers call the inding-pinding of India and Pakistan [in 1947], in India with the Indian Army or overseas with the British Army. The British were more popular than the Indians were—better pay and conditions of service, overseas travel, the soldiers could buy goods that were not duplicate [shoddy] and much more. I came only slowly to learn all that from what the pensioners always talked about. At any get-together conversation was always about army days. Service in the army was our one way to a better life and so was very popular.

Father was too short to be a soldier but my uncle Jamansing, his younger brother, joined the Indian Army. On his first furlough two years later, he brought enough money, all in coin because we did not use paper money then, to buy some land on the other side of the valley, on a steep slope. Before any cultivation could start, we had to prepare the land by digging it with mattocks—what a backbreaking job that was when the soil was hard! First of all we had to make a rough shelter to save us going back to the house every night. It was still standing there when I visited the place with my English "father" in 1987.

The land was ready for sloughing after a few weeks. The shelter came in useful then, not that the distance was so great, but the sloughing animals, the plough, the yoke and other paraphernalia had to be got ready and, once on the move, the two oxen, one of which we had to borrow, moved slowly, eating the forest greenery as they went. We had to cross a small river and the oxen always took time to have a drink. By the time we had climbed the steep slope to the land, it would be the middle of the day.

My main job was to collect fodder for the oxen. Some of the best was in the most difficult place near a steep waterfall, not the one where the ghosts were, you may be sure of that! It was tough work but I became proud of my skill. I learnt how to swim, broadcast maize and play with a rough wooden bat and ball, rather like hockey. Once I killed a hog that had strayed from another village and was eating the maize. I took it home and said it was a hare. Did they laugh at me! In truth I did not know either animal. In the monsoons we would have to go and bang tins to keep the monkeys away from the maize. I was very ashamed once when I went to sleep. When I awoke the monkeys had eaten much of the crop. It could be very cold when out with the cattle up the mountain and we would take chilis with us, munching them to keep ourselves warm.

When there was no work my grandmother thought I should go to the village school and learn to read and write. I even had my own slate. Father opposed my going to school, saying that he had never been there so why should his son? He never agreed with grandmother insisting I went. In later years I blessed what granny did for me; it gave me a basis I could not have done without. School was an hour's climb up the mountain. It was fun meeting other boys and girls. Down in our corner of the village we kept very much to ourselves. I was about eight when I first went to school and can well remember the other boys making fun of me because I was small for my age. I used to put a stone on my head and cover it with my hat so when the masters hit me it would not hurt. Schooling was free for those like me who were too poor to pay fees. In such cases a gift of grain was expected to be made to the two teachers instead.

One great-uncle was a bully and, when I was slow in learning the alphabet, on three nights, from evening till midnight, he tied my topknot to the hanging shelf which every house has where goods are stored and made me sit on my heels as a punishment. That was extraordinarily painful.

When I was ten the government began land reform. This made it harder for the poor people. Now father was forbidden to cut any more trees to make ploughs so there was even less money than before, and that had been little enough. We managed to increase our food by scattering a tiny, fast-growing seed, the size of mustard seed, in the parts of the forest where the undergrowth had been burnt. The taste is good but the cooking must be exact. The monkeys and the birds find it difficult to eat as the seed pods stick in their mouths, so not much of the crop is lost.

On uncle's second leave he married and his wife made space even tighter than it had been although another helper was welcome. Father-in-law was a powerful man in the district and there were a number of brothers-in-law, most of them army men. The eldest was called Birkha Raj Gurung, a man whose knowledge of the scriptures was equal to that of the professional priests, both Hindu and Buddhist. I liked him and he seemed to be amused by me. When we met he would talk about what it was like in the army in Malaya. It thrilled me to think of a life where the *sarkar* provided everything—food and money, clothes and medical care, interesting work and a pension at the end of it, which I understood as being paid for doing nothing—and wondered if such a life would ever be for me.

One method of farming land in Nepal is that the landowner gets someone else to cultivate the land and the crop is divided between owner and worker in two equal shares. Father worked for one whose land was a day's journey away, on the other side of the mountain across the valley. The new plot was the other side of a village, Nalma, and we all went there, including grandmother. We worked it for two years but it was a great effort and too much trouble.

By the time uncle had four children there was no room for all of us in the house and no place to be alone. Uncle said strongly that the house should only be for him and his family. We were not wanted. Father, the elder, was much poorer and was forced to move out. About twenty paces below the house was the shed with the animals and we shared it with them. For some time the two men were not so happy together but they never became enemies. Uncle had given us some money on his return on one leave, a lot then but not so much these days [±£70] and that might have been the price of our having to move out. Father paid his debts. Life was even harder from that time on; harder, poorer, dirtier and hungrier. School was out of the question. Father was ashamed that there had never been enough money to buy other than clay cooking pots. Living so poorly made father keep away from other people even more than in the past.

Many of the villagers said that I should aim to be a soldier. What good that could do before I was old enough to try my luck, I never did learn. I had heard from the many old pensioners around the place that after passing the physical tests, all that was needed to join the army was write one's name in the roman script and count to fifteen. If that was so, fine, but my fear was that I would be too short.

Up in the mountain villages it was easy to see who the villagers thought were certain to be soldiers. The good lads, those who were big, strong and had no physical defects, were not allowed to go to the difficult places to get fodder for the cattle lest they slip and fall, breaking a leg or worse and so spoiling their chances. In my part of the country almost every lad wanted to be a soldier and I was no exception.

One day, about three months after we had moved out of the house, father was finishing off some sloughing on our small plot. Somehow or other the buffalo managed to get away from where it was tied and went running off towards the forest. Father went mad with rage; he stopped what he was doing, picked up a stick and chased it. He trod on the spike of a bamboo shoot and it went deep into his foot. There it stayed, very painful.

During the rainy season, the monsoon, the damp and the heat and the mud and the sweat make it very difficult to keep clean, no matter how hard a person tries. We had no basic facilities, so refuse from the house and peoples' dirt were never far away attracting flies. Small cuts and sores quickly become infected and poisonous overnight. Under these conditions, father never stood a chance, especially as he always went bare-footed. An old razor blade was found and the wound was cut open. The piece of bamboo was pulled out. After that father became very ill, with a high temperature and fever.

Proper medical treatment was also a problem. We relied on herbs and spells from *jhañkris*. Each community had some to call upon and, when such people were genuine, it was surprising what they could cure. We all firmly believed in them, not only for curing illnesses but for the correct death ceremonies.

The neighbors always gather after the day's work during any serious illness. Father was still in the cattle shed, which he never left. Sometimes he seemed to be aware of what was happening, at other times not. Mother and I were worried, she especially. The little ones were still too young to understand what it was all about. My eldest sister was sent for but only her husband managed to reach us in time to meet father.

On the fifth or sixth day of his illness father seemed to get better. He demanded a drink of rice beer, *jañr*, and drank much too much. In those days, apart from home-brewed *raksi* [spirit chiefly distilled from millet], there was only water to drink. Tea was something soldiers returning on leave occasionally brought with them. It could be drunk with pepper, ginger or with the juice of cane sugar. In our house we had none and, even if we had had any, I'm sure father would not have drunk it!

That evening more people came than normal. Father's end was near. It was late, around midnight. All of us had gone to sleep. I dreamt that a child came to call me and I saw its head was half-shaven. As I was called so I awoke and I went to my father, who just had time to tell me to take over the burden of the family before breathing his last. The others woke up in time to hear his death rattle.

His corpse was covered. There was not enough money to buy the *pitambar* [saffron coloured cloth for corpses], but we found enough money to buy a token strip from the nearest shop, two hours' hard walk away. The neighbors always help the family of a dead person and stay until the body is under the ground or burnt. We have two types of Buddhist priests, Lamas and Gyabrings. The villagers sent for Gyabrings and three came before dawn. Two wore the traditional clothes used for death ceremonies: a scarf, with a long tail of it hanging down behind; a crown, with six or seven leaf-shaped pieces, big enough for a picture of the seated Buddha; white cloaks, with blue and red round the body lines, reaching halfway down the body, with trousers of the same colours. The third was dressed in what I call village homespun. All three played horns which sounded notes like a sad cow in trouble, making me want to weep.

It is most important that the spirit of the dead person is sent on its journey speedily and with the correct ceremony. If not, it will stay around the place, doing neither itself nor others any good. In our community a white cloth and a pound of rice have to be placed near the head. All relatives must come for prayers if possible. For us people from twenty-four houses came. Everybody had a meal after the corpse was buried. Ceremonial dancing always takes place to make the departing spirit happy for its onward journey.

I had to have my head shaved. The eldest son is ritually unclean for thirteen days, but other relatives only until the dead body has been buried or burnt. Father was buried the next day, deep enough to keep the smell of decay in. When my grandmother died in 1987 I was glad to be able to take full part in burying her beside him. Being older, I could understand much better just how hard a life both of them had led and how much I owed to their love and care.

As I was so young I only had three days of it. I was not allowed into the house, or to eat salt, or touch a dog or a cat. I had to wash all my body in a stream daily and wear a white loincloth, *dhoti*. The more high caste a person is, the stricter are the rules. I felt sad, lonely and afraid. My future was to be from day to day only.

I did what I could for my family. I ploughed land for three other people, although I found the ploughs too heavy to carry, earning meals and sometimes money. There were so many of us who were poor but I think I was worse off than most. It was difficult not to eat everything that mother could scrape together, knowing that the young ones were also hungry. Occasionally I was sent to Pokhara to get a load of rice. It was a four-day task. Pokhara opened my eyes to what seemed to be wealth and ease. As a reward I was given enough to feed me for the time away and some of the rice I'd carried back. I never had enough and no one would lend me even one rupee.

Mother became seriously ill and was taken over the valley to her elder brother's house. He was then a soldier in the Nepalese army. Another woman took care of my youngest brother, Hom Bahadur. Even so, both mother and brother nearly died. I fear that one of my two younger sisters did take sick and die. She was the best of us all. She died in my lap as I was comforting her, only eleven years old, the most beautiful person I have ever seen. Mother took more than a year to recover. Hom Bahadur's health also suffered and he grew up thin and with his thoughts inside him.

I tried my hand at making baskets and managed to earn a few coins. It was miserable work as bamboos and similar grasses have to be soaked. My hands were damp most of the time, almost as damp as my spirits. I would only go to the top end of the village when there were feasts for weddings or religious celebrations. I'd be sent for to be a servant, preparing the place, serving the food and washing the dishes. I was old enough to talk and joke with the girls but they would not speak with a lad dressed in rags and who could not even give them a cigarette from the ones for the party unseen by others. Some of my equal-aged friends were married but, for me, marriage was out of the question.

There was one incident that led to a marriage in an unusual way. One day a group of us, young men and girls, went to collect firewood. One lad, Santa Bahadur, an expert at going up trees, climbed to the top of a very big and tall tree. There he started swaying backwards and forwards to such an extent that two of the girls shouted up an exciting challenge to him; if he could jump from that tree into the branches of the next one, both would marry him there and then. That made us all excited. The boys said that, of course he could jump such a distance weren't boys superior to girls? Santa Bahadur shouted down, "if I jump, miss my footing and die, are you prepared to mourn me as a wife should mourn a husband?" That made the girls taunt him even more, because they thought too afraid to make such a leap. That made Santa Bahadur carefree and he started swaying in the branches to get as much swing as he could to make what was a dangerous jump. We fell quiet as we watched him. After he had got the branches to sway as much as he could, he let go and jumped. In the air his body turned and he started coming down headfirst. Were we scared! We were even more scared when he tried to hold on to a branch but missed. Luckily he was able to catch onto another branch some way down the trees and climbed down safely. Did those two girls look foolish! Back we went home with our bundles of firewood, chattering about it.

That evening the parents of all of us knew about it and gave all of us a very big scolding. It was the talk of the village for a while but gradually people forgot it.

Or seemed to forgot, I should say. Santa Bahadur joined the Indian Army and, on his first leave, went to the house of one of the girls who had given him the challenge and slapped her face! Naturally she asked him what he thought he was doing. His answer was that, because she had said she would marry him, he looked on her as a wife, so could do what he liked—and marry him she did. As the other girl had already married another of the lads who went gathering firewood that time, Santa Bahadur did not have the problem of which one to choose.

I am glad to say there is one way that poor boys can meet girls. In each village is a house set aside—the *rodi* house—were the youth of the village can meet on equal terms. In the evenings, after their meal, boys and girls gather under the strictest supervision. Mind you, those who have their hearts set on each other slip away! There are songs and dances. The boys sat on one side of the room and the girls on the other and the songs were in the form of a competition. Each group has its leader who sends the group's message in the form of a short song, the rest of the group joining in the chorus. That has to be answered and the songs would continue until one of the groups cannot think of what to sing in return, so losing the competition. This can take all night.

The lamp that lit the room was not bright so it did not matter what clothes were worn. I had learnt to dance and sing when it was decided by the two eldest in the village that I should be part of the cultural group for the traditional dances. Young boys dress up as girls, *maruni*, and my first time I found it most odd but the women showed me what to do; elder boys act as the male leader of the dance. I was one of those after three years as a *maruni* and enjoyed the singing, the dancing and the flute playing. We were all happy and forgot our sorrows for a while.

Sometimes bands of young men would come to our village as guests and we would go to theirs. Those were great fun. In the Hills we hold our *ijjat*, our good name in the community, in such high regard that anyone who tried to misbehave during those occasions was treated like an outcast.

At village social gatherings the "old and bold" would soon start talking about army service and the lads would sit near enough to hear, listening carefully. Pensioners told me that I looked the sort of lad who would find it easy to join, but they always added that I was too short so I'd only half listen in, feeling it was not for me, although the one thing I desperately wanted was to join the army. How else could I live a man's life, how else could I get a wife, how else could I look after my other family members? I was so short that I knew in the heart of my heart I could never be a soldier.

I did hear one story that gave me some heart. When the British were fighting the Japanese a father and his son went to join the army. The father was much too old, the son too young and too short. First it was the father's turn for inspection. That morning he had shaved in hot water so looked young enough and was made a soldier. The son had been told by his father to stand on his toes when the person measuring him looked at the height that was marked at the top of the pole, above his head. This he did and so was just tall enough. The fact that he stood on his toes was never discovered. Both fought against the Japanese.

Another story made me sad. Two young men were married not long before they went to the war. Janga Bahadur Gurung, the richer, had fallen in love with his wife and had a more expensive marriage than the other, Debi Bahadur Gurung, who was not so rich and did not love his new wife. The musicians for this wedding had been paid less than for the other so were jealous. They decided to put a curse on the instruments of the other band which had been paid more. The curse is only effective on one day of the year, Nepalese New Year's Day. In our year 2000 [mid-April 1943 AD.], seven musicians gathered round a *chautara*, the stone squares built for resting heavy loads or gossiping villagers and on which two sacred trees are planted. They watched the leaves fluttering and, when a gust of wind shook one from either of the trees and it dropped, they tried to place themselves underneath it and catch it in their mouths. If they were successful, it showed that a curse had been put on the instruments of the other band. A record five leaves were caught.

The rumor was that both men were dead when in fact they were still alive. Letters, with red thread in the left hand corner of the envelope and written on red paper—a sure sign of death—had reached their homes with the news. So, despite no official confirmation, ceremonial mourning took place. They were dead and their wives were widows. When the two men returned, although alive in body and spirit, they were dead as far as the villagers were concerned.

Janga Bahadur was stopped outside the village bounds, halfway up the hill and was allowed no farther. He did not exist so he was not there. In spite of that, food and blankets were taken out to him that evening while the elders sat in council, considering how to solve this difficult problem: a dead man alive, his wife a widow. The solution was that Janga Bahadur would have to be reborn.

A large hole, seen as the womb of Mother Earth, was dug and Janga Bahadur had to live there for ten days, each day representing one of the ten lunar months of baby carrying. Being unborn he needed no food but every night food was secretly taken out to him.

The ceremonies of birth, cutting the cord and taking solid food six months later, were shortened into six days when the village band played at the weaning ceremony. That was when the curse put on by the other band worked: three drums split and the two wind instruments broke. That was seen as the gods not allowing Janga Bahadur to remarry his wife because it would be adultery. He was ordered out of the village. That night he was joined by his wife, they still loved each other, and they ran away, never to return.

As for Debi Bahadur, he knew he was dead as a man although he was alive, so he decided that, as he was named after a goddess, Debi, he could only stay alive by wearing woman's clothing. He and his wife had never loved each other and she had already gone with another and, after the horrors of war and his tragic homecoming, he became half-brained. He wandered away to India to near where he had done his training during the war, near the River Ghaté. In his village he is still known as "the daughter of the River Ghaté."

Our gods can indeed be cruel, although when I was young I really had no idea of any religion. My mother never had—she still thinks all priests a danger!

I remember one day when the conversation was exciting. The talk had got on to the cleverness of the British. One man, recently returned to the village on pension, told the most extraordinary story about men getting to the moon. Everybody was thrilled and then one old fellow said he knew all about it. "These fair-skinned ones, as cunning and as hairy as the monkey god, Hanuman, used to live somewhere up in the heavens, probably on the moon. They were strictly told not to eat the flesh of cows but they did eat it. So they were punished by having to live on earth with other men. They were told that they would only get back to the moon by effort and luck. Now, thousands of years later, they've done it!" All the others slowly nodded in agreement.

Much of the time the talk was on local matters, farming, politics, village history and family affairs. From the top of the village I could see the snows and far away mountains, much higher than ours. The highest in our district is at Purankot, where there had once been a fort belonging to the local ruler. It is in ruins now, but when it was built hundreds of years ago, the whole district was called the "twenty-two *raj*" [principalities]. There were two branches of that ruling family, the senior with its roots in Thuloswara. Not far from where the old men used to gossip was a large stone, the *Sinduré* stone, so named because he who was appointed to be the king of Lamjung in olden times sat there while red lead powder, *sindur*, was put on his forehead. My family was responsible for arranging a king from another state to be king of Lamjung and one of the three brothers that one king had moved east to Gorkha and became the present royal family. The king was fetched about five hundred years ago and the Gorkha branch was established about fifty years later. The old men of the village are very proud of that connection—proud, too, that one of the local swings appeared on the back of an issue of the one rupee note.

Swings are part of village life, especially after the rainy season. There are six seasons: rainy, autumn, dewy, winter, spring and summer, each of two months. The new year starts at the end of the spring, has twelve months, each with from twenty-nine to thirty-two days, but, as they are never the same from year to year, we have to wait for the new calendar to tell us how many days any month has. The swings are of two types, one where the person swings backwards and forwards, called a *lingé ping* and the other that goes round and round, called a *roté ping*. They are used to celebrate the biggest of our religious festivals, Dashera and Diwali. Children and grownups love having a go on the swings, shrieking with delight and fear as they turn or swing faster and faster.

Dashera lasts for ten days and involves much praying, happiness, drinking and visiting friends. All parents try to give their children new clothes and, even in our poor family, father would put himself into debt to buy each of us a new piece of homespun cloth. Usually our clothes were old and much patched. I never wore a new set of clothes until I was twenty years old. Towards the end of Dashera a buffalo's head is cut off, with one blow of the sacrificial kukri, in the village temple. The pensioners would tell how all the weapons in the battalion are put together in one place and blessed when the buffalo has its head cut off. If the man detailed could not do it in one stroke, bad luck would follow during the year and the man would be in disgrace. In Kathmandu, so I was told, it became the custom to bless the cars and motor cycles used in government offices in like manner. My English "father" said probably that was all the maintenance some of the transport ever got!

How it all started is lost in time but what I do know is that, when Shiva was lord of all the deities, a demon used to torment the minor deities—there seemed to be no end of them—and wise men so much that they all went to Shiva to ask him to get rid of the demon. This was done by a goddess, the beautiful Durga Devi, who killed it. There was another battle many thousands of years later, this time when Indra was king of the gods and there was more trouble with demons. I only learnt the full story much later but I understood that the yearly head cutting of the buffalo is a token of evil being defeated in that battle.

Dashera begins on the day of the new moon at the start of the cold weather. At the next new moon the other important festival, Diwali or Tiwar, is held, lasting five days. This celebrates one of the victories of the goddess Laxmi and on one night every family makes many lights to guide her back home. Gambling is allowed during this festival. All families make a great effort to meet up, especially brothers and sisters. One day dogs are worshipped, on another, cows, and on yet another, crows.

Every spring, at the rebirth of the year, is a fertility ceremony, Holi, which is the season of marriages. Red powder, to look like blood, is thrown everywhere. We children loved it and would come home red all over and could not get it out of our hair for days afterwards!

There are, in fact, two Dasheras in a year, the first taking place in the spring. It is the last time people from other villages can travel in safety before the monsoon. Swollen rivers, landslides and muddy paths, as well as leeches, make travel dangerous. We would go to the next village, Turlungkot, even higher up the mountain, for a two-day fair. There are competitions of stone- and rock-throwing. Many young men from miles around come and try their luck, showing off in front of the girls as heroes. A lot of *jañr* is drunk and maybe a fight or two breaks out. There are stalls selling sweetmeats and unleavened bread, beads, bangles, cloth and other goods. Years later when I took my English "father" there was a video and a charging engine, complete with fuel, that had been carried up the steep slopes. People then drank tea as they knew the "colonel sahib" was visiting and the old men were warned not to drink too much *jañr* because they would lose their *ijjat* if they were seen drunk.

Since the political troubles of 1990 our Gurungs have wanted less and less to do with either Hinduism or Buddhism, saying it is time to get back to our original animist roots.

I loved the walk to the fair above Turlungkot with my family, joining in with friends, and having a quiet word with some of the pretty girls when I got the chance. Up and up we climbed, past an old stone trap where a goat was tied to trick a tiger into where it could not turn round or get out again, past a sacred stone that had come out of the ground in living memory, and the place where the princes and princesses of olden times would pitch their tents, now turned into a football ground by the village committee. Just below is a small well that always has some sweet, cool water in it in the driest of dry seasons. On up the mountain, through the rhododendron forests we went and, at last, in a cool breeze, reached the top where the crowds were already gathered. Compared with our quiet corner of the village it was like a small town.

There is a temple on the top of the mountain and there I saw for the first time the Aryan Nepalis, the priestly class called Bahun. Long-nosed, thin-legged, hairy and talking loudly, they are so different from us Gurungs. Clever, quick-witted, inquisitive and with much knowledge, it is not easy to make them firm friends. Once I saw the *hom* sacrifice, the burning of grain in holy flames, that takes place only sometimes. A pit, covered by flat stones, had been dug in front of the temple; several Bahuns sat around it and the leader, reading aloud from the scriptures, made a signal when grain had to be thrown onto the flames at the bottom of the pit. It took me some time to compare this act of worship and sacrifice with our own hunger.

We Gurungs plan our lives on a 12-year cycle, called *barga*. Each year is named after an animal or bird, some of which agree and some which do not. Men and women can only marry if the two *barga*s agree. For instance, I am of the "monkey" year and I could marry a girl of most of the other years, but not with one of the "dog," "tiger" and "boar." The holy books also decide Nepalese marriages and it is the Bahuns who know where to look in them for these. When I was young I did not know how the Bahun Hindu influence matched the Buddhist teachings. The old men of the village would talk about all that, but much of it was above my head.

Nepali babies are one when born, and we Gurungs become a year older on the day when the *barga* changes. This gives us two ages, the actual age we are, which does not count and the one we use, which makes us two years older than we are! Many British officers have been puzzled by that.

In 1967, after the party held for the change of *barga* was over, I stayed to listen to the old men gossiping. There were always tales of fighting against the enemy, of *bahaduris* [bravery awards], of "how I got the better of him," of "what I said to the 'Kornel' [Colonel] sahib," and of foreign countries with exciting names. Then the talk turned to people. First were the Gurkha officers. Then the British officers, who were good or who were bad and their strange habits and wild customs. In the group was a cousin of mine, a corporal from the Gurkha Engineers, Dharmasing Gurung, on his last leave before pension. He turned to me and said that my only hope was to get to know an officer called J.P. Cross. "Why, he likes us more than he does his own kind, is envied by his own people and should have been made a general by now. He knows all about us. He speaks our language just the same as we do. He tries so hard at everything. When he was young he loved his cold beer after games, inviting everybody to join in before he went to change. Now he has given up drinking beer; he never did like raksi or smoking. He asks the men what the 'white stuff' drifting up from the end of their cigarettes is and, when they say 'smoke' he shows mock surprise and says he thought it was their money they were burning. And the songs he sings at

Dashera. The soldiers always laugh loudly and the British sahibs laugh because the Gurkhas laugh. If he were to go to Paklihawa, down almost on the Indian border, as the DRO sahib it would be good news for all of us."

All agreed and somebody said that one called Langlands sahib was also very good news for Gurkhas. But that talk was not for me as I was too short for the British army.

By then I had managed seven long, hard years on my own and had often thought of leaving home, of moving down to the south of the country, to the Tarai. For a small sum of money the landless are allowed to buy land there. If I could set myself up, I would be able to bring my mother and the others down to live together, but I did not have enough money for the journey, so how could I buy any land? I could not borrow any as, with my youth and lack of a paying job, nobody thought I would be able to pay the interest. Rates of borrowing are high, often 36 per cent a year. Debt is a Nepalese curse and is handed on from generation to generation until repaid. When it is eventually cleared off, the amount of interest that has been paid is often many times more that the original sum. Hunger doesn't stand still either.

The talk that day made up my mind for me. Moving south to the Tarai was not possible but I had to get away. There was not enough food for us at home. I was now old enough, at nineteen, to look after myself. I had learnt that someone smaller than I went to India and managed to be a soldier so why not see if I could do the same? That must mean that the Indians took people the British did not. I looked young for my age, so I would try hard, if only once, to join the Indian army.

On the other hand, I could not go to India because a young man from Nepal had to be taken there by his father and only if he was an Indian Army Gorkha. However, a recruiting officer from the Recruiting Depôt at Kuñraghat, sixty miles south of the Nepalese border, visited the village looking for recruits. I told him I wanted to be a boy soldier. He was ready to take me if I could show him my father's discharge certificate. That I could not do as he had never joined the army. Uncle Jamansing, now on pension and sonless, said that I could say I was his son, but one of the villagers told the recruiter that I was not the son of the man I claimed as my father but his nephew. Indian recruiting authorities only accept the sons of Indian army soldiers so I was not taken. My future became even blacker.

There is a festival for the women, *Tij*, towards the end of the wet season. By then it was known that I had thoughts of going to try my luck in the south. During the songs in the *rodi* house, the girls sang messages about my going. They were sad; I had to remember them when far away; I had to come back safely. By the time Dashera came round and we had cleaned the village and assembled the swings, we again gathered in the *rodi* house and this time the messages of the girls were even more loving.

In the spring of 1976, when I was twenty years old, there was nothing I could do, except be as a slave to others. I could not help my family. There was, however, one hope. My uncle, Birkha Raj Gurung, had just been promoted to the very high rank of GM [Gurkha Major], at the British camp in Paklihawa. Dharmasing, back on a few days leave before his resettlement course in Paklihawa, said that when he met Birkha Raj he would tell him that I, and another poor lad, ought to be helped. His idea was that we should be put to work in one of the cookhouses, where, if nothing else, we would be fed.

On his return from the course Dharmasing reported that the GM said we could go but by then I did not want to. I was too short and others would scorn me as below standard so they would not accept me as an equal. Why bother others? Why lose my self-respect? I'd rather "hide" at home and, in any case, I could not afford to go to Paklihawa.

Dharmasing persuaded me to go and gave me a loan of a hundred rupees [±£5]. Even if I did not have a hero's farewell, I had said goodbye to too many people to be able to return without success. And what had a distant relative once said to me? "Those lucky enough could even find a potato growing in their hair!"

Before I left there was a farewell in the *rodi* house. Then I went home and said goodbye to my mother and grandmother. They wept, thinking they would never see me again. I thought very highly of both ladies. Mother had a motto: "Never get angry with people. If you feel like that, be angry with your arms with a mattock or hoe." I can recall when she was not able to sleep at night with worry getting up in the small hours and, especially if there was a moon, putting in a couple of hours work in the fields. It tired her out and calmed her down. My! Our hill women's work is never at an end. I put on a brave face, telling them that I would come back when I had made good. At the edge of the village the young girls were waiting for me with keepsakes, a handkerchief, a flower, a kind word.

I walked to Pokhara, then went by bus a hundred miles south. This was the first time I had done the journey and everything was new and of great interest. I was scared by the narrow twisty roads, the cliffs below we might fall down and the cliffs above with rocks that could fall on the bus. I recalled what the old soldiers said about how many people had been killed in the war when trucks had turned over. By halfway, at a place called Tansen, I had seen so many huts and hovels with so many other poor people that I realized I was not alone in wanting to find work and that competition for any job would be intense. I wanted to cry but I kept my tears back. I think it was a mixture of the unknown and the uselessness of all I had tried to do till then that made me heavy with sadness.

When the bus reached the plains I felt I was in a different country and in the town near Paklihawa, Bhairawa, I knew it. The crowds of Indians, always making a noise, were foreign. They would stay up half the night talking loudly: the mosquitoes were just as troublesome. The old men in the village had warned me twice, never to trust an Indian, as he will do you down as often as he can, and against malaria from the mosquitoes. In Bhairawa both scared me.

At Paklihawa I went to the camp but could not get in as recruiting was taking place. I stayed in the nearby *"paltan bajar"* [army-sponsored shopping place] for three days, washing up dirty glasses. Birkha Raj, the GM, and another Gurkha officer came round and told the owner to give me work but the man took no notice. It was hotter than I had ever imagined, my money was gone and, mentally beaten, I went into the camp. I found out where the GM had his quarter and told him, frankly, that without his help, I and the other lad with me were finished.

Officially there was nothing that the GM could do. There were no vacancies in the camp and, as I learnt later, there was a waiting list of hundreds of ex-servicemen wanting jobs. A person, as we say, may warm himself by his own fireside. However Birkha Raj understood our problem and arranged that we each work in a cookhouse, one in the Queen's Gurkha Officers' Mess and one in the Sergeants' Mess. I got the sergeants'.

What a place that camp was, despite the heat. I had never seen such order and tidiness and cleanliness. It was beyond anything I had imagined, even from the descriptions of the pensioners in the village. There were separate places to wash, launder clothes, eat, cook, sit, sleep and two toilet rooms. I remembered what the old soldiers had talked about: creases in trousers, rolled up sleeves with the turn-up exactly so much, the saluting, the smartness and the way the British worshipped time. Now I could see it all for myself! I could now understand what the old soldiers had meant when they said, "A woman has to leave home and go to the house of another, a man must wear the *sindur* [red fortune mark put in the parting of the hair of a woman after marriage] of the *sarkar* before he knows how best to behave in life."

The colonel was very strict and would not have allowed us in camp if he knew about it so our orders were to hide the one time in the day that he walked around the lines, inspecting everything everywhere. He never came out after that so it was safe to move about. Our hours of work were very long, from 5 in the morning to around 10 at night. I was afraid that people might think I was a thief when they saw me walking about like one. The dear old head cook loved me. He would keep a watch out and, always in time before the daily camp inspection, tell me to hide in the small latrine nearby. I was never discovered. He had been a prisoner of war in Japanese hands and had wonderful self-discipline.

One day we had to cook for a big party, to say farewell to the colonel sahib, the head cook said. I was happy; no colonel sahib, no hiding. I said as much and was told not to be so stupid; there was always a colonel sahib. The old one was going and a new one was coming.

Sometime that afternoon I was walking in the camp and an elderly British officer I had not seen before, dressed to play games, come running in my direction. He was smaller and thinner than the others I had seen—always from a safe distance. He was almost our size. I had no time to hide. He stopped me, asked me what I was doing, where I lived, how old I was, was I married and much more. He spoke in fluent Nepali, with a smile, and seemed so happy. I answered normally, though he was the first British officer I had ever spoken to and my heart felt it was about to burst. I feared I had been found out so would have to leave the camp and start again to worry about where my next meal was coming from. In great sadness I went back to the head cook and told him my unexpected bad luck. His answer surprised me.

He smiled and said, "Oh, that"s the new colonel sahib. Have no worries about him. He always talks to people like that. He is a good man who never turns away the poor and needy. His name is J.P. Cross."

EVENING

6: 1976-1979

In early November 1976 I started my last army job and one that I had been looking forward to for two years, being in charge of British Army interests in west Nepal. Based on Paklihawa, a mere 200 yards from the international border, I was responsible for recruiting half of the requirement for the Brigade of Gurkhas as well as for paying pensions to the ten thousand odd ex-servicemen scattered over much of western Nepal. To help look after these old soldiers and their dependants, as well as being the link between serving soldiers and their homes, there were twelve offices, called Area Welfare Centres, staffed by ex-servicemen. These were scattered around the countryside, collocated with the district capital. Few people not connected with the Brigade have any conception of just how great a part this organization plays in investigating and relieving individual hardship and welfare cases, as well as monitoring welfare sponsored community projects. Those old soldiers from the pre-partition Indian Army who have British welfare pensions survive to an average age of seventy-four, far outlasting Nepali average life expectancy.

In camp men staging on leave, the camp staff and their families had to be looked after. A farm and a workshop had been established to help "resettle" those about to leave the army by running courses at both. Over and above all that, an extensive system for the administration of all that had to be done, including the maintenance of welfare funds, was my responsibility.

It was a salutary reminder of how little the Brigade of Gurkhas meant to some Nepalis when I told a subordinate to open an account for "Gurkha" welfare in the bank in the district capital of Lamjung. It would be a slow process as it took several days to walk there and back but, even so, it took much longer than expected. I wondered at the delay and a month later I learnt that the bank manager had refused my request. It transpired that the bank manager had insisted that no account with the word "Gurkha," however spelt, could be opened in his district. "Gurkha" could only apply to Gorkha district, so the new account had to be in the name of "Lamjung" welfare. Eventually we prevailed. The delay had caused unnecessary hardship for those in need of speedy financial help.

It was most important that I kept contact with officials of the Nepalese administration in five zones and thirty districts that comprised my area, around twenty-five thousand square miles of territory. Partly "political courtesy," it was also obligatory because, without Nepalese government permission at district level, no welfare project money for schools, irrigation or small suspension bridges could be processed. All this gave me ample scope to get out and about so meeting some very interesting and nice people whom I would never have otherwise met. Although it saddened me I appreciated the advice of one Chief District Officer (CDO) who told me never to trust a Nepali official's word until what he had said was in writing and officially stamped. Unless that is so does a person say what he means and mean what he says? Probably not; it is not prudent always to be stark in speech and much, in Nepal, is said by leaving so much unsaid, with hint, inference and gesture carrying much weight.

Most CDOs were men of high calibre with whom it was a pleasure to come into contact. Some had less imagination than others. I remember asking one if he would be amenable if I could arrange for a school for the deaf and dumb being established in his area? He considered my suggestion and said, no, he didn't think deaf and dumb was correct. "How about dumb and blind?"

Until 1959 Paklihawa camp had only been a staging post for young men on their way down to the recruiting depot in India. Ten years after the decision to include Gurkhas in the British Army, India had at last got round to telling the British that they had to recruit their Gurkhas on Nepalese soil and this, in turn, led to Paklihawa being enlarged, with a headquarters and a much larger camp for eastern Gurkhas being built over in Dharan. There the camp was pseudo-Britain, the British were natives and the Nepalis foreigners. Had it not been for the military hospital in Dharan and the dedicated work done by British doctors and nurses to "non-entitled" patients, the presence of the camp would probably not have been tolerated. This was because Dharan was, then, the centre of the communist movement. The authorities in Kathmandu, eager not to be the target of communist vituperation, neatly turned a potentially embarrassing situation from themselves to one positively so against the British. The site would never have been chosen by the British as there was a water problem and no access road. In every other place looked at by the British reconnaissance group "civil unrest" made it move away until the most unsuitable site of all, Dharan, was "offered" a few days before the group would have had to report their mission unsuccessful.

Paklihawa, and later Pokhara, were the opposite, the British were foreigners and the Nepalis natives. As there was no campus in those days, only a large presence of pensioners, all was relatively peaceful. Even so, gangs from the Indian border town of Sonauli (two miles away) and from the neighboring town of Bhairawa, and groups of soldiers had been involved in fighting. The Indians and Nepalis wanted to attack one another and the camp at Paklihawa was as convenient a place as any for the gangs to vent their spleen; the soldiers joined in as they tried to protect the place and their property.

Now, seventeen years later in 1976, policy had led to Paklihawa camp being transferred to Pokhara where there was already a small pension-paying detachment and the announcement of this had led to feelings of grievance. As more trouble was feared, mine was seen as the most sensitive unit in the Brigade of Gurkhas. Added to that, the very day I became DRO I found another grave scandal, this time about recruiting. A sick Queen's Gurkha Officer, thinking he was about to die when he was in the military hospital, called in the Brigadier and gave him what is known as a "death-bed" confession—and then recovered.

To understand what happened it is worth giving some background to recruiting as, regrettably, more nonsense is talked concerning it, both by Nepalis and non-Nepalis, than any other aspect of the Brigade of Gurkhas. In those days, the recruiting staff consisted of the Brigadier in Dharan, his deputies in the east and the west, and a handful of retired Queen's Gurkha Officers of the highest calibre, known as Area Retired Officers, AROs. For initial work in the Hills, retired rank and file, known as Recruiters, or Galla Wallas, were employed.

Annual requirements were divided into general duties men, clerks and non-obligated specialists: cook, tailors, armoires and equipment repairers. It was up to me to determine which areas to tap to produce the specified numbers of men. Training, in those days, was done in Hong Kong and, once dates of flights were known, I worked back for fixing my own target dates so letting the recruiters plan the dates for their own initial selection. With the vagaries of the postal system, this meant a minimum of six but preferably eight months' notice of key dates was required for me to have sufficient time to do the job properly.

By the time I took over it had become apparent that, unfortunately, there were some flaws in the system that a few unscrupulous and greedy men were taking advantage of. One recruiter illegally amassed more than one hundred thousand rupees (big money in those days) although he was only responsible for bringing in ten men. I therefore decided to tighten up procedures to the extent that it would be virtually impossible for bribes to be accepted at either of the two lower levels, the common allegation, or, if they were, to be kept secret from me. There were twenty-five recruiters and I increased my total to forty. As each one had about two thousand hopefuls approach him, an impossible eighty thousand men had to be processed for the amount required, usually around the two hundred mark.

Even then I had not reckoned on the extraordinary amount of loose talk, much of it malicious, that, on occasions, accused even me of "only enlisting my own friends" and accepting ten thousand rupees for each man I enlisted. Had that been the case, I must have had 2,148 friends (my final total in the five and a half years I spent in the job) and would have been 21,480,000 rupees the richer!

Initially I did not realize the extent of the damage caused by these vicious rumors, despite their origins lying in certain malpractices. Nevertheless, I did realize that, for the system to be above suspicion, I would have to include sterner and more effective measures than hitherto had been the case.

In this instance the Queen's Gurkha Officer who thought he was going to die revealed gross breaches of conduct of one ARO and his associated recruiters. Matters came to a head when, in Kathmandu, the Prime Minister again spoke to the ambassador, with a warning that, if the British did not clean up their act, the future of western recruiting would be in jeopardy. The Inspector General of Police (IGP), Khadkajit Baral, first spoke with the British defence attaché and ordered his deputy in the western region, Lok Bahadur Rana, to talk to me. He said that if I thought it worthwhile, he would get his plain clothes men to investigate. This I asked him to do and, much later, he read out part of the report he had submitted; *...the taint of corruption was with all twenty-five of the* *recruiters, but it would not be possible to bring charges that stuck in a court of law.*

Some time later I met Khadkajit Baral, whom I already knew, from when the western Police Training Centre in Butwal opened. Through small talk I found out that, over thirty years before, I had played football with one of his elder brothers, an unexpected link. It was now that I was warned never to treat an Aryan Nepali as though he were a Gurkha soldier, as this would be much resented. That I had realized but, even so, I thanked him for his advice.

One of the many difficulties of Paklihawa was the mail. There was a British Forces Post Office that operated through Dharan and that was steady though slow, two weeks being par for the course for mail from Britain. The local Nepalese postal system was not efficient and the quickest way was to use the Indian post office, a few miles over the border, at Nautanwa. That meant a vehicle had to go to and fro several times a week. A side effect of that arrangement was that the drivers had to have an Indian as well as a Nepalese driving license. All went well until, to the drivers' unqualified dismay, they discovered they would have to be emasculated if they had more than two children before any renewal of their Indian license could be authorized. By now we only had one driver we could send over the border. This Draconian order was in force for as long as the Congress party, under Indira Gandhi, was in power.

Before I allowed myself to start learning about so large a swathe of territory, I had to get to grips with the work in the camp, which included sorting out the grave problem of financial malpractices among the recruiters. I also had to start thinking about moving the unit up to Pokhara, a hundred and five miles to the north. This was due to take place in 1982 but, on my third day in camp, I was told we had to be out of Paklihawa by the end of 1978, long before the new camp would be ready. This completely changed all previous planning. We would have to close our hospital, pension-paying facilities and, later, a school for our Gurkhas' children.

Another early task was to find out about the black market traffic in goods that the ambassador had warned me about. My Gurkha Major, Birkha Raj Gurung, was one man I would trust under all circumstances. He knew that the out-going GM was the leader of the racket and had been for a long time. He also knew that his fellow countrymen can be vindictive and that the campaign, not to have the unit moved to Pokhara, was masterminded by the same man who did not want to see his easy source of income spoiled. Birkha Raj had nearly been reduced to tears with frustration when he had tried to bring matters to a head with the previous DRO (who had not believed, or not understood, a word of it) but he knew he could achieve nothing in isolation.

We had a long talk to try and work out a plan to combat both corrupt practices, the black market menace and the recruiting problem. Equally important was the camp security, the hordes of unauthorized people who seemed always with us. There was a Hindu temple in the camp where the locals had worshipped for many a long year and they could not be kept out. Unbelievably, no pass system existed so petty thieving was rampant. At the end of our talk I asked him about the lad I had seen my first day, Buddhiman Gurung.

It appeared that there were two such lads in camp, both dirt poor and both from the GM's village. Until either was lucky enough to find a paying job, he had allowed them to keep body and soul together in camp, this despite the previous DRO, an unsympathetic and inarticulate man, who would have ordered them out of the camp had he found out about them. The two lads had had to hide during the morning inspections but could wander around after that as the DRO never moved more than between his office and his room. I sighed inwardly, was even Birkha Raj going to prove unable to resist such pressures?

I did not probe but asked what would happen if both young men were told to leave? We were not a rest camp for Nepali paupers, however much people might think we were.

"Saheb, they have nothing. I did not want them to starve or go to India without hope of anything positive." He spoke with great dignity and my heart warmed to him. "I was going to tell you about them."

I considered the problem. There was nearly always food left over in the cookhouses, either to be thrown away or "stolen." Willing labor was always at a premium. I, too, knew how hunger gnawed a person's inside. I thought I knew a good man when I saw one. The wistful look on Buddhiman's face let me know that here was no scrounger. I made my mind up and told the GM they could stay and join some other young hopefuls (employed as office runners), so live openly. However, they would have to go back home during the "closed," non-transit season.

Meanwhile the news of the camp's premature closure disturbed a faction of pensioners who had already tried to reverse the decision to move the camp. Now it was to be moved even earlier we could expect trouble. If matters turned sour I could have an unwelcome trinational problem on my hands. During the previous two decades many military hill men had migrated south to this flatter, richer land, often near the camp where the rudiments of comfort—electricity, potable tap water and schooling—were now to be found in some places. They were also attracted by our camp "cottage" hospital, the ease of being paid their pensions (the Nepalese banking system was, by comparison, cumbersome) and the ability to keep contact with friends. But there was a small element of troublemakers, led by a former pupil of mine at the Army School of Education. They had, the previous year, forwarded a petition against the move to the British government and had been openly hostile to my predecessor. I was warned I was to be a target of their vituperation.

I called a meeting. Birkha Raj was, initially, not keen on having one so far ahead of our move but I pointed out that it was much better to let them blow off steam sooner than later. I decided to have it at 8 o'clock on a Saturday morning. An unusual time, my reasons were that Saturday was a holiday, so there was no excuse for people not coming; that, so early in the morning the crapulently inclined should still be sober; and that, before we had gone on all that long, they would be hungry, so want to go and eat. It was a wise decision.

I took an added precaution of telling my audience that I was going to make a recording of the proceedings. After a while the ringleader rose to his feet, adjusted his spectacles and started sonorously to read out a prepared statement, the previous year's remonstrations against the move. I stopped him, reminding him that I had not asked them to discuss the decision that had already been taken by the two governments but to tell them how I was intending to implement it now that the move had been brought forward.

The upshot was that most of the pensioners took what I had to say in good heart, although they were sad about it. I thought that that was the end of the affair but, as so many times in the past, I was wrong.

Two weeks later, during a visit to where we paid out pensions in Pokhara, I was shown a cutting from a Nepalese newspaper, saying that I had not allowed the ex-servicemen to talk at the meeting in Paklihawa. It worried me as ex-servicemen had their own place under the constitution and any foreigner suppressing them would be in ill odor. I heard later that, on the day it was published, the Soviet attaché rang his British counterpart to ask if I were the same J.P. Cross who had been in Laos. Letting me know that they were watching me!

I went to "explain my case" to the Gandaki Zonal Commissioner, Ram Chandra Bahadur Singh. I found him a big man in stature and authority, pleasant, personable and friendly. I took the offending cutting with me and explained that it was indeed exactly as written, except that one word was missing, "politics," which, in Nepalese terms, implies self-seeking, deviatory and possibly underhand tactics when going about any business. I did not, I explained, allow the pensioners to talk politics but only details of the move. That was just what was needed on my part: the British embassy sounded out the reactions of various ministries but no one was particularly interested. Even so, I feel sure the incident was noted down.

Back in Paklihawa there had been a reaction and the authorities there had need to check on me. A meeting was arranged between me and a Public Relations Officer for the Saturday and it so happened that I gave a dinner party for the Lumbini Zonal Commissioner, the Chief District Officer, the local Police Chief and the local Battalion Commander on the Friday. I brought the conversation round to the matter, casually, and noticed the interest taken. I explained how the incident arose and was relieved to see nods of assent all round. And, on the morrow, no one came. The matter had been understood and buried.

That did not stop Birkha Raj and myself receiving odious letters, some of which threatened us with death and other unpleasantnesses. In the event I only had a couple of men speak to me in the language of the gutter.

Around that time Sally came out from England to marry me. This was the fourth or fifth time I had been on the verge of getting married, not to her every time, let me hasten to add. Never too late, 'tis said. Yet she behaved most queerly, showing unaccustomed temper where I would have hoped for, if not exactly expected, unsubdued passion. She left me, having come to the conclusion, I presume, that she would be better off without me. I say "presume" guardedly as women's minds have more gears than have men's so it is always very hard for men to fathom which way a woman's mind is moving. I accepted fate's decision remembering that "a good wife is a harbor in a storm but a bad wife is a storm in a harbor." Another old tag I had learnt in a French lesson when at school came to mind. Translated it runs, "between a woman's yes and no, there's no room for a pin to go." I started to pick up the pieces and once more think about the future. I wrote to sister Gillian in America with tentative plans for us to live together when pensioned off in 1980. Time was running out with a vengeance.

In late 1977, when I had been DRO a year, there was an incident on our resettlement farm, situated on the border of India and Nepal. The spoiled son of the local land owner in India had taken his cow buffalo, on heat, past the bull buffalo belonging to our farm, only yards away, with the cow in India and the bull in Nepal. The maddened bull had broken loose, chased the cow and been shot by the landowner's son, being wounded in the body and blinded in one eye.

The Indian witnesses, perjured to a man, vowed that the son was away undergoing medical treatment at the time of the incident; indeed the man produced a doctor's certificate to that effect. It seemed that we could do nothing to bring the man to justice or to prevent him from repeating the performance; wasn't he in a foreign country?

Shortly afterwards I was visited by the local police chief, who asked me if I wanted help in ensuring that the land owner's son did not make any more trouble until the camp had been moved to Pokhara the following year? "How long did I want him put in jail for?" Of course I wanted help but I demurred at getting tangled with a convoluted legal process. His price for peace and quiet was a wheeled chair for his grown-up son, who sadly could not walk. I managed to provide one and there was no more trouble from over the border. Nor did I ever make enquiries as to the actual fate of the landowner's son.

A couple days later, on my afternoon jog, I heard the honking tones and heavy rustling wings of the demoiselle cranes migrating south. They would slowly circle, as though getting their bearings, often above a Hindu temple and I wondered what there was about such places that attracted people to build there to a god and for birds to use as a marker. I stared up at the sky to see them better and noticed, for the first time, that I could not see clearly at long range. Although I did not give it much thought, presuming it was dust blurring my vision, I had, in fact, started to go blind.

I replaced all the recruiters with men I personally vetted and indoctrinated them in my new, drastically changed, system. It was most satisfactory to be told, by both the doctors and later the trainers, that from then on a much higher standard of man had been brought in for selection than ever before—they in their morning and I in my evening.

My first recruiting period was a tiring experience. It soon became clear that most young Gurkha aspirants do not believe a British officer can know more about Nepalis than they themselves know. This trait is offset by the trust a hill man will place in a foreigner, especially one not enmeshed in an extended family web, that he will not place in another Nepali.

A "good question" is what manner of man is required for service in the British Army? The DRO is told that the Tripartite Agreement allowing recruiting to take place stipulates recruitment is open to "all martial classes." As far as I was concerned that meant I had to continue with more of the same, the type of men who had been my comrades in arms for more than thirty-two years. In fact not all members of the martial classes are necessarily suitable for enlistment. One of the common and erroneous beliefs is that only the sons of present or one-time members of the British Army are accepted or, indeed, the type of man that is needed: alas, very often the reverse is true, despite what the proud parent may insist to the contrary. This is because many a lad, brought up away from Nepal in his formative years, may turn out to be an excellent technician because he has enjoyed a high standard of education in the army schools but he very often loses the quintessential requirement of a Gurkha soldier. This is very difficult to define but is blazingly obvious when seen. What, in effect happens, is that he loses a dimension of a traditional Hill Gurkha that lessens his suitability for high standard army service. Nevertheless, if all points and aspects between two potential recruits are equal, the rule I followed was that the one who was the son of a British Army man was selected.

However, it would be wrong to say that only those brought up in sight of the eternal snows are the required material. Alas, those who live along any of the tourist trails often pick up many undesirable traits even if they have similar potential to those whose parents have moved to an area in the Tarai where back-breaking work cultivating virgin soil has enhanced the ancient virtues of hard work and family discipline, when no snowy mountains can be seen. In any event, even by the time I was doing my first recruiting in 1977, Nepal had started to change irrevocably. The towns were filling up and I had yet to realize many of the implications of what it meant that many hill men had not adapted to town life nor did the young know how to while away idle hours. After all, it was but a short time in the history of development that a sheep drover had become a Jeep driver.

But on to the question of what makes a good soldier; what does a DRO look for? As I saw them then, and still see them now, the basic qualities of a good soldier consist of an indeterminate mix of self-confidence, determination, motivation, correct temperament, character, self-discipline and appearance. Added to that was my personal, subjective "gut feeling" of the man as, after spending so many years with Gurkhas, I had acquired a "diagnostic fluency" in my dealings with them, almost always successfully. I had to try and assess whether a man was "deep" or "shallow," genuine or a bluffer, a tight-corner man or unreliable.

Personal knowledge of each man being out of the question, a face-to-face interview was probably as good a way as any to judge what manner of man was the aspirant. I well remember the very first interview I undertook when there were six hundred and sixty young men to be processed. I felt overwhelmed at the task; at eighty interviews a day, weekends included, it was a formidable proposition, lasting for more than eight days. At ten minutes each, without any pauses for meals or a break, meant more than thirteen hours a day and, of course, having to draw out some of the more diffident men meant that, in fact, interviews could be longer than ten minutes. To repeat myself six hundred and sixty times over a nine-day period and remain sane was a mental task of considerable magnitude, yet without talking to each man myself meant that the overall basic standard could not be properly adjudged. I had to decide which questions over a ten-minute period would give a representative picture of the man and allow him to show his true mettle, so that I could make the all-important decisions of whom to accept and whom to reject.

It was a cold day when my first-ever man to be interviewed came into my office. He was a young Gurung, full of confidence, but shivering. He looked around then came up to me and said, "Cousin, this is a big room for one man." I realized that to "pull rank" would be counter-productive as the young man was being entirely natural and, with such a friendly remark, to have snubbed him would have merely meant that he would have retired into his shell and, apart from it being difficult to draw him out again, would not have given me such a good idea of his potential. "You're cold," I said. "Warm your hands by this fire for a moment while I sort out my paperwork." He went over to the small electric fire, held out his hands and grinned. On the spur of the moment I asked him a Nepalese riddle: "Which is better, fire or water?" Another impish grin, "Right now, it is fire, but I've known times when it was water."

And then an idea struck me—I suppose eggheads would call it lateral thinking—and I asked him two more questions that had no fixed answer as I explored the possibilities of this approach: "Which do you value more, the eyes or the mouth?" and was thrilled when he gave the reason for "eyes" being the more useful: "You have to keep a watch out for your enemies, even when you are eating." "Which do you value more, the ears or the nose?" "The ears" had it because "a person can always breathe through the mouth but one can't wear spectacles if there are no ears to fasten them on to."

With a thrill I realized that the lad was thinking out his answers, was reacting constructively to an unexpected situation and was using his brain. I knew I was on the right track and had to think out less ludicrous questions. Over the next few hours I improved and perfected a set of questions about farming, making baskets, schooling, social pressures, Dame Fortune, religion, mostly in rhyming couplets, using no erudite, so unknown, words. This method proved most effective as it allowed me an insight as to a candidate's mental process, his personality and his potential; it kept the man at ease because he was intrigued, interested and willing to show off his knowledge. Relations never became strained and, as I learnt much later, the interview acted as a bond between us, whether the potential recruit was successful or not—and it had the additional merit of keeping me alert all day!

I found another interesting and significant factor from this type of interview. There was an inverse ratio between a candidate being nearer to Class 10 when a student sat the all-important School Leaving Certificate and his ability to think laterally. It created an impression that never left them, dimmed though it may have become in time. I put this down partly to the rote system of learning that requires only fixed answers to be given in every case, so depriving a student of any ability for original thinking, and partly to the low standard of teaching to be found in many of the poorer rural districts. Despite a state-run education system, there seems, sadly, to be little wisdom attached to it, especially when work in primary schools, where a high calibre of teacher is required, does not attract such men. I was amazed when I found three Pokhara-based lads I took as porters on a trek did not know that "that white stuff on the mountains, called snow," was cold and wet!

(At the other end of the academic spectrum slavish adherence to the rote system results in an inability to take what might appear simple decisions. The British Government gave the relevant authority some money to have a First Aid handbook for use in remoter areas. Five years later nothing had been produced. And why? The idea of printing anything in the "degraded" Nepali that is understood at village level was anathema to those in whose hands the decision to publish lay because that was not the language normally used in government publications. Not quite the same, I am told that drafters of laws use a language that is vague enough for more than one interpretation of the text to be made. The rote system can be held responsible for its adherents seldom having any original ideas.)

It was during these interviews that certain characteristics were shown. For instance, if there was a lack of self-confidence I detected it by the continual asking for the last statement to be repeated, "echoing" as it is known; the inability to look the questioner in the eye; inconsistency of answer; shallow, unthinking "parrot-like" replies designed to please rather than convey the real opinion of the speaker—I blame the unadulterated rote system of education for this failing. All these told me that that person was not who was wanted. The "chemistry" was not correct. Ignorance is excusable: stupidity is not. Without self-confidence a man is likely to be a disadvantage if not a danger to himself and to others, possibly fatally so, when the going gets really tough.

Other facets of a good soldier appeared in other tests. Determination; it was not easy for the aspirant to do all that was asked in the physical tests but border-line cases showed by the amount of effort put into the "last few yards of the mile." This showed whether the man was or was not likely to persevere when faced with tough situations when it will not be the "last few yards of the mile" but the "last few yards" leading up to an enemy position.

Motivation was hard to fathom but a man with an obsession for money to the extent of having an unbalanced approach to it is not what is wanted either. That having been said, financial pressure to join is intense and competition fierce. During my time the ratio of success to lack of it was one in four hundred aspirants. I believe that six people benefit from the enlistment of one man. My putative figures, therefore, for 2,148 successful men meant 857,052 were unsuccessful and so 5,142,312 people "went without." No wonder the darker, not lighter, side of the hill men's character came to the fore when it did.

Back to the point of the disbelief that I, an Englishman, could know enough or more about Nepali humanity, certainly in an army context, than the potential recruit did: a man who has not been brought up under hard conditions is more likely to crack when, on active service, he finds himself cold, tired, wet, hungry, afraid, out-numbered by the enemy and far from base. Will he give of his best although the audience is of the smallest? As a person who has himself experience of all these in full measure, and seen men crack under the strain, I knew what to look for, albeit an exact or even adequate description is very difficult. My definition of "high morale" is "the ability and willingness to give of the best when the audience is of the smallest."

A fair question is what makes a British officer a judge of all these characteristics in a Nepali? As a young officer on joining his battalion he will set out to learn as much as he can about all aspects of his men in the knowledge that he is ignorant. Because of an initial language difficulty he realizes the limitations of his knowledge whereas an officer in a British battalion, or any indigenous officer of any indigenous army, takes his knowledge for granted and so does not realize the limitations of his ignorance. "The spectator sees more of the game than does the referee" gives another clue: many years serving with Gurkhas gives the British officer as good a background as any, with experience playing a very great part. Of course mistakes are made during initial assessment and, even when, in the great majority of cases mistakes are not made, men change as they develop. However, it must never be forgotten that the DRO is not asked to spot future Gurkha Majors. His task is to see if a potential recruit is of the required calibre who, if enlisted, will not sully the fair names of Nepal and the British Army, and what his potential is amongst his peers.

So what is success in recruiting? There are two sides to this: one, that the regiment to which a man goes will benefit by his presence; the other, that, when the DRO meets a rejected man or his family in the hills, he is greeted as an individual who puts service before popularity, who is completely fair, unbiased and above personal pettiness.

I did any amount of jobs in my rising-forty years' army service, difficult, unusual and challenging but, on reflection, probably the hardest one of all was as DRO—also one of the most rewarding. I think this also shows up the uniqueness of the relationship between the two kingdoms that has intrigued, puzzled and fascinated many, and infuriated a few, for many years. What is it that the British, their army and its tradition, its system and its mystique, do to a Nepali that realizes such potential for military excellence that the world admires, fears and regards the "Gurkha" so highly even if, such is the ignorance of many, often without realizing that there is a connection with "Nepal."

There is, of course, no one answer, no one reason, no one unsolved mystery. Rather there is an amalgam, a syndrome, a catalyst of many factors: as the British officer sees him—or would it be more correct to say that the eulogistic regimental histories that the young and inexperienced British officer reads tell him? The Gurkha embodies so much that is good that he is an instant attraction. In the Gurkha, simple hill man or honoured veteran, the British somehow convince themselves that they see all they admire on the moral high ground of a military man: uncomplicated simplicity, basic honesty, unstinted devotion, strict self- and corporate discipline, sincere trust, genuine affection, sustained dedication, outstanding loyalty, heroic bravery, unquestioning obedience, unbelievable smartness and unequalled stamina, both mental and physical—so many good attributes that a myth has grown up which feeds on itself to such an extent that is dissolves into frustration, recrimination and disenchantment when either human frailties pertain or when realities of the real world prove too heavy. But now he has the prospect of status at home and a repayment of debts. He is a "man," in the only honourable profession normally open to him.

For the first time in his life he finds himself in a position where "the man"—his training, his welfare, his comfort, his problems, his very livelihood—is the concern of a dedicated band of highly motivated, trained and talented individuals, whose cause is service not self-interest, and whose bedrock of faith is trust. He finds himself in a traditional but forward-looking society with a stricter code of conduct than he has ever known before, where patrimony, partiality and the familiarity that breeds contempt or provides for subtler social pressures are all absent, despite what a disillusioned, small, but sadly vociferous minority of those "who know best" like to believe to the contrary and who have a self-inspired, semi-divine right of selective reporting to suit their personal failures. It is these "invincibly ignorant" people who are the spreaders of pernicious, unfounded and often malicious rumors that can cause so much damage. As so aptly put, "a lie is half way round the world before truth gets its boots on."

His British officers recognize that all men in the British Army are rational, conscious individuals with any amount of potential and are determined to develop each man as much as circumstances permit. And the man responds. He is now someone in his own right and his opportunities for advancement depend on him, on his own showing, his own ability, his own performance and not on the whim of another: this is heady wine.

Not every society, though, can fully please everybody all the time. A high standard brings its own penalties of expectation. But the strength of the Brigade of Gurkhas, indeed of all military Gurkhas since 1815, lies in the warp and weft of its fashioning, the steady and unspectacular application of the dull, uninspiring but important tasks done properly, without which the foundations for successful action in an emergency would not be strong enough to bear the burden or the consequences. That the Gurkha has stood the test of time is self-evident; that he will continue thus is a tenet of British faith.

Although it is wrong, stupid and unrealistic to consider all Gurkhas "supermen," "heroes," "ten feet tall," there can be no doubt that there is an unusual bond of empathy between the British and the Nepalis, showing mostly in the Brigade of Gurkhas, which heightens their appeal and tends to hide mistakes. Likewise, just as the Gurkha's first impression of British officers' integrity, impartiality and cleverness will probably be tempered by reality, close contact and experience as the years pass, here too, the basic core trust is very seldom lost. Gurkhas are intensely human people, with strengths and weaknesses like everyone else. The Gurkha's strengths are the ones the British Army needs and his weaknesses not so intrusive to be an encumbrance or a liability. I am sure that the extraordinarily successful results of the Gurkha presence in the British Army stem from his strengths and weaknesses being nicely balanced with the British soldier's weaknesses and strengths. The Gurkha soldier and his British counterpart complement one another to an amazing degree.

So what is the final verdict on this undoubtedly unique relationship as British and Gurkha serve side by side? The Gurkha sees the British, and all that a military life with them means, as the one traditional way of bettering himself in a fair and friendly climate where merit counts and trust is paramount: and the British see the Gurkha as epitomizing and providing the type of soldier they need, with the Hat Felt Gurkha seldom slipping from its correct angle and with sufficient "spit and polish" in peacetime and enough camouflage in war to cover what warts there are. This was certainly true during my time.

Equally true is it that if the British Army Gurkhas were without the reputation and standing in matters military they have, and had not the friends they have, then, in the harsh economic climate since the early 1980s in Britain, a governmental flick of the fingers, followed by a stroke of the ministerial pen, would have disbanded it to allow out-of-work Britons to take their place.

Maybe the fact that this has not happened is the accolade of acceptability.

In my first season I did not recruit from where the worst of the recruiting scandals had been perpetrated, Ghandrung, the third largest village in the Gurkha Heartland. It had, unfortunately, provided more recruits and had bred more Gurkha Majors than any other single village in the west. I expected trouble and, months later, I got it. By then, as I later learnt, the Prime Minister had told those representatives of the national *panchayat*, parliament, who had recruiting areas in their constituencies, to go and find out "how dirty the British were" this time. This they did and found not one jot nor tittle wrong. The Prime Minister, the Zonal Commissioner and the DIG held a meeting in Pokhara and that year's recruiting was a topic of conversation. As quoted to me the question was asked; "What is it that J.P. Cross can do to Nepalis which they cannot do to themselves?"

My Brigadier reported on me that I had "tackled the recruiting problems with the zeal of a Victorian missionary." I think the remark was meant to be damning with faint praise: I took it as a great compliment.

I had never expected that first year would be the unhappiest in my career. More regimental gilt had worn off the ex-serviceman gingerbread than I could have imagined. I had found scandals in every department of my little unit that no decent commander should have countenanced; I had found unhappiness in the military and civilian staff, and I hated the disdain in which the name of the British was held outside the camp—the result of "the slow defeat of never doing anything properly" ever since Paklihawa started. I had failed yet again to get married. Win some, lose some: in March 1978 I was told that I could stay until I retired in 1980 if I so wanted, to have three and a half years as DRO rather than the two originally planned. I agreed.

By then I had watched Buddhiman for over a year and had been most impressed. I had been moved by his having to leave home because of hunger and, despite an unthinking "throw-away" remark one Dashera that I would enlist him if he danced well, as happened in the Indian Army before 1962. I found out that he was under the required height so, being too small and over-age I could not be tempted to enlist him so bring on my own head the accusations of partiality and favoritism that I had been trying to stamp out. But I had spoken and the hill men felt that when a British officer spoke he meant what he said. I had to do something to make up for my "throw-away" remark. I needed a new batman and asked Birkha Raj if he thought Buddhiman would be suitable. Yes, he would be. He would be told to report to me at my bungalow and that I would pay him three hundred rupees a month.

He came and I bade him sit down on the grass by my chair. "Has the GM sahib told you why I have called you?"

Yes, he had.

"I want you to be my batman. I have about two more years to do before I go home. I have told the GM that I would offer you three hundred rupees a month, but I have changed my mind." The last thing that I planned to do was become so involved in any aspect of my job that my roots went too deep when I had to leave. I had therefore decided to set him up so that he would not go hungry again. That way I could make a clean break when the time came; yet I was being pulled in another direction by the inchoate desire for a son such as he, that I had never had and probably never would.

A look of concern played over his features as I told him that I would not pay him as previously announced yet I would clothe, shelter, feed and give him pocket money. Instead of pay I would give him money to buy enough land to support him, a wife and two children. I paused to see how he was taking it in. He was silent, absorbing the import of my offer.

He said he would accept and I went on to ask what I should call him. Without any hesitation he said; "Son. We are now father and son."

In the forests below the snow line the rhododendron trees were flowering white, unlike the red of the lower reaches. Above them the broad uplands were covered with sheep, watched over by a man and his son, self-sufficient for months at a time. A powerfully fierce dog, capable of putting leopards to flight, was straining at its chain, mouthing its fury at our approach. On the skyline a curved, jagged, snow-covered mountain barred our way. Our destination lay beyond it. My heart sank at the distance, height and difficulties involved. This was a Nepal I did not yet know.

We were six and had walked over two hundred miles from where we left the road, two weeks earlier. One porter had decided the journey was too hard and another had been so idle we were behind time. I had sent both back and found a couple of willing lads in a remote village where I hoped to find material for recruits. Most were illiterate, all were tough, inured to privation and unaffected by the spread of questionable attitudes resulting from the influx of tourists, the spread of education and the pervasive weakening of moral fibre due to the presence of so many Indians in Nepal out for gain.

We were cooking our evening meal and six yaks, five black and one red, were led in by their herdsmen. They tried to reach the water before their loads could be taken off, so thirsty were they. Loads were stacked in a heap, the yaks were watered and allowed to graze. After darkness had fallen the herdsmen huddled with the animals, covering themselves with the long hair of the yaks' belly, shielded from the intense cold.

Walking against the grain of the country we started to climb the mountain so steep that the feet of the man in front were above the head of the man following him. When it leveled out at the top of the pass, at about 15,000 feet above sea level, flurries of snow and sleet obscured our vision as we picked our cautious and tired way over the rough, rocky surface.

Movement down the mountain relieved our aching heads and shortness of breath but was slow as we had to move carefully through steep snowfields until we passed below the snow line and could see where we were treading. At 8,000 feet we came across villages, Tibetan in character with fluttering prayer flags, minuscule fields and people who knew how to brave the elements, hacking a life out of virtually nothing. Everything was too far from base to consider getting soldiers from such places and the pass we had crossed was closed for much of the year. We moved back down to more accessible areas.

That was not easy either. Our path lay along a Himalayan river, sometimes at the water's edge, sometimes on a cliff face so narrow that two people could not pass. How the porters managed with their loads was a source of amazement. Down, down, down, over rickety bridges and along narrow tracks, the weather becoming hotter and hotter. We had to acclimatize, so great was the difference.

We continued west for another hundred miles or so then south, once more against the grain of the country. I paid courtesy calls on the far-flung posts of the administration, the first DRO to go to many of the places I visited. All of us suffered sunburn on the left as we moved west and on the right on our way back, travelling east but many miles farther to the south. In these lower valleys it was stinkingly hot. My admiration for those who scraped a living from that soil, and who could still smile, was indeed great.

The monsoon had begun when, seven weeks and seven hundred miles later, we got back to Paklihawa. Most of us had lost a little weight, I had gained a greater insight into the land of contrasts I now had to work in. I had set up a great rapport with Buddhiman, enjoyed being in his company and, as he had a fount of knowledge, had learnt much new about folklore, customs and family life.

It was during these talks that I learnt how he had reacted to the promise of a new life since he had met me. Three days after our first meeting he had been called to the GM's office. Until then he had kept hidden, just in case, and, at nights, he had lain awake for a long time wondering what was in store. The head cook had been so sure all would be well but he was terribly worried. And then the call came, an official one. It could only to be told to leave camp, despite the head cook's assurances that the new DRO would not throw out a poor lad.

He went, very scared, and was overwhelmed when informed that he could stay. He was ordered to report to the doctor, who was to check that he was fit to help cook! Would you believe it? He had never seen a doctor before but had been warned by the "old and bold" that he would have to strip in front of him. That worried him as he could never show anyone what was regarded as such a private thing. A bell rang and it was his turn. He was inspected all over and the doctor had something that looked like two pieces of rubber with a bit of metal in the middle. He put the two ends into his ears and the little round end bit all over Buddhiman's body. It was ticklish but he bore it. When told to strip he asked the doctor how could he expect him to do that. But strip he had to and, when waiting to be X-rayed, the very idea of it gave him the giggles and he was abruptly told to keep quiet.

He was given three hundred rupees pocket money, a small fortune to him [then about £12]. So the head cook was right, the Colonel sahib did look after the poor. As soon as possible he had gone to Bhairawa and bought the first new clothes, except the yearly homespun when a child, he had ever worn. It was grand to be allowed out in the open after so many weeks hiding and he tried, for the first time ever, to play football. He knew nothing about it as there was never anywhere flat enough to play in the village. He got on well with the others but at times life was hard when there was not enough food left over and the head cook would not get any more rations out for him. At other times he would eat till he almost burst and the tea! Hot, sweet and very good. The head cook told him that he would get worms if he drank too much but that didn't stop him!

To let him earn some more pocket money I had sent him out as a porter with a trekker from Hong Kong. He described it: "By that time I was not in practice and the load was very heavy. I ached all over, that second day, and my feet hurt. It was not easy to wash during that trek and I stank. I wanted to fold up and weep but of course that would never do. The other lad with me looked as if he would weep but I told him to be a man. I told myself that I had to make a job of that trek and, from the present of money at the end of it, the British officer must have been pleased. With the money I earned I bought some proper metal cooking pots, rather than our old clay ones, and got someone to drop them off at home."

With no chance for enlistment and the camp closure looming, where could he go then? "I was unhappy and worried about my future. I had no money to return home and, even if I went back, what would they say? The shame would be intolerable. Why not die? Why was I born? I abused the gods for their letting me be born and, having done that, for making me so small."

He knew he was liked by the sergeants and was good at his job. He thought that if he could get some practice in cooking he could get work in a hotel. He knew how to sing and dance so he might get a job with the troupe in Pokhara run by an ex-Gurkha Captain. He also practiced his handwriting. Other than that there was no point in staying on. In the Dashera of 1977 he had danced in front of me and I had said that if he could perform properly in the "plate dance" I would consider him as a soldier. He had practiced hard just in case he did grow taller and broken a number of plates and made people laugh. He could see that I liked him. "You talked with everyone and everyone seemed to know you." In his wilder moments he had wondered if he could work for me.

Buddhiman had something to say about the trek we did with Sally: how nice it was to be back with his own hills and rivers, the cool water and the fresh air after the flatness of the plains and the overcrowded towns. On the way back, at the bottom of the Nalma hill, he was told that she had decided not to marry me but to go home to England. Certainly we had talked and walked together but he could see my heart was, by then, not in it. Back in camp he had heard Birkha Raj say that she should not have decided to go back to England as she would never get such a good man again.

As for when I had called him to talk about the future, once again his heart was in his mouth when told I wanted to talk to him and would probably take him on as my batman. With three hundred rupees a month he had worked out that that would be just enough to settle the family in the Tarai.

So he had gone to the bungalow, heart thumping, trying to look cool. I had calmed him as we watched a squirrel come and take an apple core I had lodged in the bark of a large tree. He had listened very intently to what I had to say and, when told that I would never allow him to go hungry again and, as he was too small for the army, I would look after him, he thought of his dead father, and, as he then told me, "I wept inside." He had asked himself why such love should be shown to him, nobody but a penniless and fatherless lad? Who was I to do this to him? How could he ever, in this lifetime, repay me? "I had always been afraid of big men but here were you offering me a cup of tea and speaking so nicely to me. I lost my fear. And then you asked me what you were to call me and, out it came, so obvious really, "Son." That's what we are, father and son. And it is like that. I was deliciously happy and vowed to work as hard as I could but I knew that I could never repay such kindness."

In the fullness of time I went to Ghandrung to try and sort out the recruiting scandal and later learnt that, on our way there, Buddhiman had been so worried for my safety he had suggested to the others that they take it in turn to act as sentry at night. He had said he would taste anything given to me to eat lest it be poisoned. "Were I to die it would be in the service of one who had helped me and that would be an act of great religious merit."

After the coolest reception ever I addressed a large group of villagers. I did not need them to tell me how to do my job; I did not go into their homes and order their wives to cook me a meal. Who did they think they were to try and tell me what to do? I was punishing the village, did they say? Punishment? My writ and jurisdiction lay within the barbed wire of Paklihawa and Pokhara camps, nowhere else in the country. Who had mentioned punishment? Not I. If they had thought they were doing wrong, that was up to them. If there was a taker of favors, there must also be a giver. also be a giver of them. I invented a Nepali word when I asked them if they were hill men or fools—Gorkhali or "Murkhali"? (A play on the word "murkha," a fool.)

If the community were to accept whatever I said about the conditions for recruiting I would consider reopening it next season. If I heard so much as a mouse squeak out of place I would close the area again. I sat down and waited for a reaction.

The senior man, the local representative on the district council, stood up and welcomed what I had said. "As the Colonel sahib has said, if there is a taker, there must be a giver. I am guilty of giving; I am guilty of corruption." The next senior official arose and made the same confession. I had never heard such openness before and I doubt I'll ever hear it again.

There were also two servicemen on leave. Both talked big about what they would do to this new DRO who came from an eastern regiment. When Birkha Raj asked them what they thought of what I had said, one had to admit that he had decided to visit his fields that day; the other said that he sat at the back where he could not be recognized as a serving soldier. "We had never been talked to like that; we had no idea that any foreigner could talk Nepali like that. He dried our mouths for us and we had no answer."

That was such a contrast to Luwang where, by my having helped cure Sursing in 1967, the two names taught in the village school were the King of Nepal's and mine. Men would come to me with bowed head for my blessing. I was welcome in every house and so much empathy was there with Sursing's widow, whose dying husband (never a soldier) I had told that his family would not starve, would always dream of my arrival in the village, once even before I had planned it.

At the end of 1978 the agronomist campus of Tribhuvan University started their move in to Paklihawa camp and I was ordered to do the recruiting in Pokhara where there were neither cookhouse nor latrines, let alone any camp protection. Because all my staff had to be re-allocated elsewhere or sent on redundancy, recruiting at Pokhara was impossible. I was also told that I could not allow civilians into the camp at Paklihawa, despite this having happened all through the twenty years of the camp's life and the campus staff moving in. I refused both orders. It was then that it was discovered that parliament in England had not given its consent to release the camp free of charge, so that had to be put right. We held our breath for a week and were allowed to carry on as planned. In any case we could not have warned the six hundred and sixty young men and their recruiters to change the venue from Paklihawa to Pokhara in time.

There was a severe fuel shortage because of trouble in the Assam oilfields, so the recruits could not reach Kathmandu in time to reach Hong Kong for training as flight timings could not be changed. (Aircraft could refuel in Bangkok.) I was on the point of arranging a fleet of trishaws to be ridden, turn and turn about by one recruit with two sitting in the back, when luckily stocks of fuel improved enough for normal arrangements. Even so, we had to use the recruits to load up the transport for Pokhara but, until the authorities in Hong Kong authorized us payment of men to unload the vehicles, the stuff had to stay loaded, as there was, literally, no one to unload it.

The situation up in Pokhara was untenable. My three senior staff were new. There were no soldiers, only a few civilians, virtually no medical facilities. We did not yet own the land where the medical inspection room was to be built. There was no paymaster, although a million pounds sterling went through our books annually we were told that we "didn't need one"! Nowhere was ready to put any of the unloaded kit—financial authority to hire casual labor to unload it took a couple of days—and scores of pensioners milled around every day, wanting pensions, welfare moneys or medicines. There was nothing to stop the world and his wife from using the camp as a pleasure park. There was a store for a British-aided project and mules in profusion milled about. My boss in Dharan told me that my camp was not an army camp! Everywhere was hideous with the noise and dust of camp construction. The approach to the camp was over the narrowest of road bridges spanning a spectacular gorge, easily blocked or ambushed, then through a rural slum that spread to the very edge of the camp. Protection against the type of person no army would want to enlist had to be asked for from the local police.

There were, most unusually, three lots of recruiting that year and two the next. The first lot was almost impossible; the problems of aspirants under canvas, a rudimentary catering service, too few latrines and with nothing to do in their spare time could have been coped with. The extra British medical staff "wanting a few days leave in Kathmandu" before coming our way was the proverbial last straw. I made bitter complaints; our programme was finely tuned and intermeshed. It was too inflexible to pander to the doctors. What the recruits thought about the much-vaunted British method of doing things I do not know. Gurkhas are philosophical people and could see that, on the ground, we were trying our best.

Manage we did, although the second lot clashed with Pokhara being cut off by road for over a week: more than a hundred landslides on the southbound road and two bridges down on the Kathmandu road. Despite all difficulties, our results were better than they had been the year before. All smell of corruption had vanished, although the concept of no money needing to change hands for recruiting is foreign to most Nepalis. Indeed, on more than one occasion, I was regaled with lurid tales of how even the Colonel sahib took bribes. I would let my traducer, once even a woman, finish before asking him if he would like to meet this villain. "Yes." I would then let the man know who I was. This always had the gratifying effect of him making a very quick exit, one even jumping onto a horse, the faster and farther to escape my lashing tongue. It would have been funny if it had not been annoying but it was fascinating to see how the accusers could not credit any other system working. Favors are seen as commodities to be bought and sold rather than as "bribery."

The habit has been exacerbated as more and more foreign aid money is pumped into the country; failure or not being up to standard was not attributable to any personal weaknesses but to money not changing hands—but who ever saw it? This gut feeling was as prevalent as was witchcraft in medieval Britain. In both cases failure could be ascribed, by the unfortunate, to circumstances beyond their control.

The terraced fields climbing the steep slopes, harvested of their winter crop, lying dusty and barren waiting for the spring rains, were on every side. Deforestation and soil erosion, sure signs of pressure from overpopulation, were making Syangja, the large district to the south of Pokhara, into a dust bowl. Along with the whole middle band of Nepal, the world's next desert was in the making, according to United Nations experts as far back as 1974.

I was on trek, visiting schools to which British money had gone, calling on eminent pensioners and generally keeping my finger on the pulse of affairs that were my concern. A referendum about the future political structure of the country was in the offing and Buddhiman was concerned about possible trouble. He felt we should make camp in a secluded spot lest some of the local rowdies make a nuisance. That evening he came into my tent for a chat.

I asked him about his financial affairs and whether he had enough land. He said that he had bought land in the valley below the village which should be worth a lot in the future. There were plans to dig an irrigation canal so be able to have two or even three crops a year instead of the one at present. I told him that, as my son, I did not want our love for each other to be ephemeral, nor want the relationship to wither after I had gone on pension in 1980. We could spend time together if and when I came to Nepal as a tourist for three months of any one year. I would give him enough money so that he could enhance himself sufficiently to lead a positive life. I also told him that I would pay for his marriage and let him go in search of a bride. He was happy with what I had offered and, on our return to the camp, I set about arranging for funds to be transferred to a bank account in his name.

Buddhiman asked me how he could repay me. I said that there was no need to think about it. "If you were to forget me after you've got married, that is another thing," I said. His answer was that he would rather die than forget me and would return all I had given him rather than let me down.

I suggested we set up house together after I retired. I had tentative plans to build a house in Nepal, after retirement, and come out as a tourist. Nothing would please him more. He told me that everyone in the village would also be happy: I had already asked the village elders if I could regard him as my own son and they had been pleased to say yes. He told me he would give me to eat what he ate and his house would be mine. When we became as father and son in 1977 he had asked Birkha Raj if he could marry one of his many daughters. Birkha Raj was astonished at the request, even though he could now look after her properly.

Apparently his daughters had been born away from the Hills and been brought up in army quarters, so had never known a tough life. Marriage with a hill man would not work out.

Buddhiman had already tried four places and was refused in each. All parents want their daughters to be as comfortable as possible and the better off the male suitor, the better off his wife. He had yet to buy any land then so was regarded as a pauper. Because no foreigner had ever been allowed to settle in Nepal and act as head of family without first becoming a Nepalese citizen—a process that could take over twenty years—the idea of Buddhiman ever being regarded as a well-off person was just not acceptable. Eventually the only thing he could do was to claim, by right of custom, his eldest maternal uncle's eldest daughter. She was too young to wed but in any case he had to wait a couple of years before the divinations of the almanac were propitious.

On my next journey I found myself uncommunicative, edgy and not my usual self. I sensed that somewhere something was not right. I got back to the camp and Captain John Rogers, my chief assistant, hedged when I talked to him.

He gave me a telegram, asking me to read it before I said anything else. It was short and to the point; sister Gillian had been killed in a motor accident in America. My future stared me bleakly in the face.

That, and the increasing difficulties of being unable to see properly, were great burdens. There was nothing I could do about my sister; I did not know that anything could be done about the eyes. Looking into sunlight was a penance, so was walking where shadows dappled the ground. I was determined not to give in but it was not easy. Buddhiman sensed that I was in trouble and, as the months passed, he was always half a pace behind my left-hand side, giving me instructions as to obstacles in my path and obstructions to be avoided. He was wonderfully patient, always giving me encouragement, never letting me become bothered by the curious when he had to lead me through difficult places. I could not have coped without him and my affection and regard for him grew daily. He carried an umbrella, handle close to my ribs, ready to catch on to my pack straps if I stumbled or fell. He was not always successful and at times, on slopes, I would tread where there was no path, putting a foot over the edge and so falling over.

I went exploring part of the Far Western region that had been neglected. The area was so remote that, when I got to the recruiter's village, I was the first foreigner ever to visit it. The people were most friendly and interested in me and my four porters, as Buddhiman and I needed to be self-contained so as to avoid food and accommodation problems. Distances were great and we covered around twenty hilly miles a day. (I had a zeroed pedometer so could say with confidence that I walked over a thousand miles on trek every year.) The map was not always accurate and, for our next stage over some 10,000 foot mountains, we had a guide. There had been a storm the night before and the rivers had swollen. We had to cross one that was in spate after a storm, the bridge a stout plank, narrow and with no handrails. It was dangerous; a slip could have been fatal. The porters edged across. I steeled myself to cross when Buddhiman came back over and said he would carry me. I refused. He persisted.

"No. I'll cross by myself. No point in two of us drowning."

"No point in my staying alive if you die. If one has to go, let both of us go."

I could still see enough to know that the porters were watching anxiously and, as I shuffled across, hating every moment, I felt that all I needed to make it a theatrical performance or a circus act was a roll of drums! But the roar of the river would have drowned the noise.

One of my official visitors was a very old friend from India and Malaya days, John Whitehead, now the Brigadier in charge of all Gurkha matters in Hong Kong. He asked me why I had quarreled with the medical staff during the previous recruiting. It did me no good, especially as the Major General felt I was taking too much into my own hands. There were moves afoot to have my service extended by two unprecedented years, until 1982 when I would be fifty-seven, and it would be foolish of me to jeopardize that. Besides, what was I to do in the future? He thought that teaching English as a foreign language would be apposite for any future job in Nepal but I had to have academic qualifications to start training and he knew that I had none. He had been talking with the educational authorities about me and their suggestion was that I study for the Final Diploma of the Institute of Linguists, equating to a "good Honours degree," in Nepali. The only snag was that a candidate had to be a qualified interpreter. I was not but, if I was interested, a strong recommendation, based on my qualifications in nine Asian languages and French, would be made to the Institute.

After the monsoon of 1979 there was more recruiting and one particularly fine man was rejected on spurious medical grounds. Army doctors spent five minutes with each Gurkha potential recruit and an hour with a Briton—not quite a true comparison as some of our men's tests had been done beforehand. "We rather cut corners, I'm afraid. Not really ethical," said the senior British doctor. The man in question came from the village above Ghandrung and I recalled him to be re-examined by a Nepali doctor. I did this for two reasons: I wanted to right a wrong and I wanted to show the Ghandrung area that the recruiting organization was not faceless but cared for individuals. To have detected a mistake among so many and to put it right was evidence of efficiency and compassion.

As expected the man was completely fit. I told him that, in January 1980, I would send him to the Gurkha Contingent of the Singapore Police where the Chinese doctors would be less likely to make mistakes of diagnosis. He was to go home, tell his father (who had served with me in India) and mother, come back and go on trek with me. It was time for my annual inspection of the Far Western welfare centres and Buddhiman was due to go to his village to get married so could not go with me. "Of repayment, I want none, but to vindicate my actions, I want you to be the champion recruit." And he was!

Much of the time I spent in studying Nepali pending the exam which I planned to take in England when on a short leave in the summer of 1980. I made out memory cards for the more esoteric vocabulary I needed. I could still manage to read under certain conditions.

J. P. CROSS

On this journey over wild country walking proved difficult and halfway through our journey I had to cease looking at my memory cards on the move. I had taped four hours of vocabulary and that would be my evening staple.

At Salyan I called on the local policeman to show him my trek permit and, as we already knew each other, to chat. He was full of news that Pokhara camp had had a major nastiness but he did not know any details. I put it down to no more than a fracas caused by a drunken pensioner but, when I did get back, I learnt that it was more serious.

On a visit of the Foreign Minister of the People's Republic of China to Pokhara many admirers of the system he represented gathered at the airfield to welcome him, follow him about and bid him farewell. Some three hundred fans returned to their homes in a group, going along the road up which lay our camp. On an impulse they went up the approach road to the camp instead of going on home.

It was then that all my requests for camp protection became obvious. There was no gate, only a piece of string between two walls. The man where the gate should have been was a civilian who lived outside the camp. Susceptible to pressures he was unable to stem the tide. A policeman in plain clothes, monitoring the march, slipped into the stores and begged refuge behind a pile of blankets. Captain Rogers, who came out of his room to see what all the noise was about, received more than his fair share of abuse. Only one window was broken and some flowers uprooted but the implications for our future were serious. Apart from Pokhara being the opposite of Dharan in a cultural context, it was different in another important aspect. In Dharan, the camp was there before the campus; in Pokhara it was the other way round, so much more of a magnet to volatile students. An Indian professor from Patna university, a founder member of the campus, was a communist for whom the urge to embarrass Kathmandu and London must have proved irresistible. For the first time in the history of Nepal uniformed representatives of a foreign army, whose officers had no diplomatic status, were in the epicentre of Nepal. However friendly were our relations with Nepal, the communists saw that here was a situation that was ripe for exploiting: but it should not have taken so many of us by surprise.

I had timed my arrival back to go to Thuloswara for Buddhiman's wedding, the marriage of the Colonel sahib's "son" being a big social occasion. I was greeted by the news that I had to have a report about the situation ready for the Brigadier on the day after the wedding thereby, sadly, not giving me enough time to get there and back. The ambassador was most concerned, as were Hong Kong and London. The world press had got hold of the story and blown it out of proportion and people were worried. I wrote a letter to Buddhiman explaining my predicament to bolster his morale and sent it with two people he knew well.

I set about finding out the mood of the students. Not a breakfast eater, I would often go for a jog when that meal was taken, between 9 and 10 o'clock. I ran up the road which the students walked to their lessons on the campus, classes starting at 10. None seemed hostile and many asked me where

I had been over the past few weeks. I did this for three days and concluded that there was no overt hostility, at least to me.

I had talks with senior members of the administration and the police. I also made contact with the Royal Nepal Army. All were most embarrassed but none thought we should move outside the town. Despite the awkward bridge police or army reinforcements could more easily be sent to us where we were in Pokhara than farther out. In fact the authorities did build a new bridge; there was money for only one and although there was another in greater need of widening, "ours," the lesser used of the two, was given priority.

The Brigadier came over from Dharan to discuss the situation. I had long advocated a green belt around the camp and I now managed to convince him how necessary it was. The way the situation had so quickly got out of hand was proof that I needed Gurkha soldiers for gate duty—that I needed a gate!—to escort money from the bank and other duties; I also needed a cookhouse, more latrines, an approach road away from the rural slum and a green belt. The Brigadier reported our mutual concern and the local authorities' reaction to the ambassador who unusually forwarded the plan to London on a Saturday. Although there were no more large attacks on the camp stones were thrown at lights on several occasions, posters against recruiting were put up and the recruiters, in the hills near Pokhara, were threatened.

All that I had requested was eventually provided but not without much bother. Not only had the British government to find the money to buy the land for the green belt, once it had been paid in to the local officials and we were told it was now ours, it never arrived in the Nepal government's coffers. We were then told that the land was not ours until the money was "found"—which it was several months later.

Buddhiman had expected me to officiate at his wedding as any father would and was bitterly disappointed when I could not go. On his return to camp with his bride he told me all about it. He had missed me very much. His uncle acted the part but it wasn't quite the same.

"Our weddings take a long time and are full of ritual and tradition. The groom, his father and a helper sit together while relations and friends of the family daub saffron-coloured rice on their foreheads, bind strips of white cloth round their heads and insert low value rupee notes as an offering. A band of local musicians arrives then everybody, surrounding the bridegroom and his two supporters, move towards the house of the bride, instruments blaring to let them know of the arrival.

"A large feast will have been prepared. The bride's guests eat first, then those of the groom's procession and nobody can eat until the groom touches his food. Finally the bride's family eats. The groom and the bride may never have seen one another before but, in my case, I had known my wife to be, Bhim Kumari, for some time. The groom and bride meet with the family. The woman's face is always heavily shadowed and she keeps her head down, with her gaze fixed on the floor in front of her. Bride and groom place their hands together, his at the bottom, then hers then his, hers again, topped by father's and mother's. Holy water is poured onto a silver coin that is in the topmost hand and that is passed down to the bottom hand of all, the groom's. The red *Sindur* paste is put in the bride's hair parting by the groom. From then on she is his. Curds are offered and such unpleasant things as goats' entrails are hidden in the liquid and, once they have been found, boisterous play ensues as bride, groom and attendants try to rub them in others' faces. The guests also try to make the newly-weds speak as, until then, they have not opened their mouths in front of each other. A hookah is offered to the groom either too high or too low for him easily to smoke it. This is all very good-natured and done to try and get the newly-weds to talk. That takes the rest of the night and it is dawn before the next stage starts.

"The bride's family now have to put a tika on the betrothed couple. The bride is carried into the room on the shoulders of one of the family. She weeps, sobs, cries and makes a lot of noise. This is expected. Were she not to weep, were she to go with a glad heart, it would show disrespect to her parents and the guests might think that she was not the virgin everybody assumed she was.

"The procession goes back to the groom's house, groom and bride separately, taking not the slightest notice of each other. In the procession, complete with band, will be clothing, bedding, utensils and maybe a bed for the couple, all carried on men's backs. It is then the turn of the groom's family to give a feast to the bride's procession; the groom and his two supporters sit and have saffron rice plastered on their foreheads while the bride, sobbing separately, stays with a woman from her household.

"There is a lot more to it, visiting in-laws, returning to the bride's house for a specified time, but the couple will not talk to each other until at least the fifth day after they have been married. I was lucky with my Bhim; she was too young really but, apart from anything else, mother needed another pair of hands in the house.

"I told my wife not to be afraid of me. I would wait until her blood was warm; there was no hurry."

No one in the hills believed that I would look after Buddhiman as my son when I was away from Nepal. The richer the husband, the easier it is to get a wife. Buddhiman's quest was disappointing. One, a particular girl friend, was refused because, both man and woman being small, their sons would also be too small to join the British Army. His wife was too young to be married, according to the law of the land but, as the Nepalis say; "The king does not ask the stones questions and they don't tell him."

Buddhiman brought his bride to make obeisance to me, as her father-in-law. I could not easily see her features. She was more than modest; so shy that she turned her face away and did not answer when I spoke to her. I found it hard to recognize her when we met again up in the village and it was only because she came shyly to welcome me that I knew it could be no other, because, like everything else by that time, her features were a blur.

I tried not to let the worry about my eyes spill over on to others. I had devised a shade that gave me limited but clear vision. It was an empty frame, covered by masking tape which had a minute hole pricked out in the middle of each side, both eyes being shaded by a metal piece, clipped on to the frame. It provoked much comment, people under the very mistaken impression that I was wearing such a contraption for fun. I found this unthinking attitude a burden but normally gave a quiet answer when asked what it was all about.

In fact, recognizing people was becoming more and more difficult. I made many mistakes, cursing myself as I did. I welcomed folk as not having met them for many years when they had left my office only ten minutes previously and vice versa. I continued jogging around the road in camp, seven times round to the mile, fourteen times one way, fourteen times the other, as the circuit was simple and had no encumbrances. One day I saw a stout fellow wearing a floral waistcoat, standing to one side of the road. As he was still there when I passed him again, I called out that his waistcoat suited a woman more than a man. No answer. Offended? I jogged on. Next time round, he was still there and I went up to him to apologies. It was only when I got close to the "man" did I realize that I had been talking to a flowering shrub!

So ended 1979, in its way a very difficult year, as apart from my eye sight progressively getting worse, the impending referendum boded no good for 1980, to say nothing about a very bleak personal future.

7: 1980-1982

By January 1980 morale was low. Away from all my domestic recruiting and eye problems, all of us were worried about the phenomenon of Tarai- and town-grown ground swell of measurably increased political dissatisfaction against the partyless form of government that bore "the stamp of the genius of the Nepalese race." Any consent of respect for the system had changed to consent of indifference and even this snapped, somewhat incongruously motivated by the death of Z.A.Bhutto in Pakistan, and posed such a serious challenge to law and order that a referendum was announced to see whether a multi- or non-party system was the preferred choice of government. By that time almost everybody who could have gone on strike had done so and there had been occasions when cruel and senseless violence had flared. Human reasoning is not hereditary.

In any depressed area of the world emotions and attitudes become exaggerated. Change only comes from the dissatisfied. People complained about the government being corrupt. As has been observed by others "corruption springs more from the climate of society and state control of the economy than from any parliamentary arrangements. Most government in India is corrupt within weeks of taking office. The African minister who is not corrupt, by British standards, is acting very oddly. British eighteenth century standards were similar; not to help one's friends, or oneself, is, like elective democracy, a recent north European curiosity of human behavior."

Because Nepal was not an open society it was hard to keep tabs on the situation but it only periodically affected us, unlike the Assam dispute with the Indian government in Delhi that had drastically cut our fuel supplies and which we did know all about. Our generator supplies of oil were often down to a few hours' running with never more than two days' supply and vehicle fuel hard to come by. We coped—just, but on mature reflection, I could not say quite how.

My illusions of Nepalese harmony had been shattered by two cases, both concerning ex-servicemen. One man had been chased by a bear and had tried to escape by climbing a tree which, unfortunately, was where the bear also wanted to go to eat its fruit. The man hit the bear as it slashed at him, losing much of the flesh of his right thigh. He managed to escape by jumping out of the tree but had fallen over a precipice. Luckily he had lodged only a few feet below the lip. He was not rescued for over two days. He was carried to Pokhara hospital, another two-day journey, so was in a very poor condition by the time he asked to be admitted. This he was refused because, having been a British Gurkha, he had had his good luck so would not be treated now. He was turned away and made his painful journey down to Paklihawa where we had looked after him in our camp hospital for three months while he made a very slow recovery. The other, a much older man who had badly broken his leg when he fell off a horse, was refused hospital admission because he said he favored the non-party system and it seemed that those who could have mended his leg favored the multi-party system. I arranged for this man's recovery in the military hospital in Dharan.

Such clever and normally such rational people who work in hospitals—and elsewhere—have no right to be so stupid.

As far as going blind was concerned I was still comparatively young and strong but I had no idea if I could be cured. The hospital in Dharan did not cater for eyes so I had visited a Nepali eye surgeon in Kathmandu who had talked about cataracts "ripening" and mine not ripe. How long did that take? What were the chances of any operation being successful? The answers were unconvincing. I kept my worries bottled up, wrote cheerful letters home and slowly came to a decision: rather than be blind or semi-blind for the rest of my life, far better to end it. Buddhiman had left his wife at home and devoted his attention to me. I forget what it was that had hit me that day; whatever it was it crystallized my thoughts. Sitting in my chair, I said to Buddhiman; "Son, what have I got left in this world? Father is dead, my wonderful elder brother is dead, my sister is dead, my mother is old and my younger brother and his family say they would help but I would not want to burden them. I have tried so many times to get married but so much of my service has been spent in the jungle I have never managed to get myself a wife. All I am fit for is to be a burden to others and that I am not prepared to be. Better to end it all with a jump over the cliff." I hated giving people trouble and was not prepared to be a burden to others for the rest of my life.

Buddhiman dropped to his knees in front of me and took my hand. "Never say that again," he said passionately and with the utmost conviction. "I am yours and you are mine for as long as we live. I'll look after you. I'll give you to eat what I eat; we'll share everything. Please don't worry."

I was humbled by such a spontaneous display of love and, voice not quite my own, thanked him most sincerely, promising not to do anything stupid and feeling ashamed of my self-pity and lack of resolution. If ever anyone repaid a debt of gratitude by personal love, it was Buddhiman's wonderful and unremitting care and concern to and for me during those long months of increasing darkness and difficulty.

Luck came my way, to an extent that I would later see as crucial to my future peace of mind: in April 1980 I received a letter to say that I had been retained in the army for a further two years. I was delighted; not only did it put off the day of fending for myself but it allowed me to sit for my language exam and have the eyes looked at within the system. The news spread through the camp and the most senior civilian clerk came into my office. "I have just heard that you have an extension. Is it true?"

"Yes," I answered and was most touched when he went on to say that he wanted to be the first to congratulate me and that, once a week for the past year, he had been to the temple to pray that this might happen, even though he well knew that it had never happened before. That struck me as an act of faith as unprecedented as the extension of service.

One morning during the run-up to the referendum Buddhiman rushed into my room with a piece of paper. "Look at this! Look at this!" he said. It was a manifesto, violently anti-government, and, as I remembered it, word for word as the first secretary in the Indian embassy in Laos had told me in 1974. All that was missing was the year 2000. He told me he had visited a friend in the campus and had been given it there. To me it was proof that the agitation was being orchestrated by Soviet and Indian money and agents. In the event, the hill men were strongly against any change. Indeed, by the time of the referendum, so many people were fed up with disruption to an already creaky system and were so fearful of more trouble of a similar nature if multi-party democracy was voted in, that the non-party method was retained.

The protracted process of hill recruiting had been harassed to an unacceptable degree by something I never thought possible, by Nepali communists. I was getting worried about reports that the young men in the villages around Pokhara were being intimidated from offering their services to the British. That and minor disturbances at night, coupled with a poster campaign, worried me. Having no legal authority outside the confines of my camp, I was hard put to rectify this problem. However, I thought up a scheme. One of the unusual features of being my own boss was that I could choose my date to celebrate the Queen's birthday. That was due to the vagaries of the weather in a place that could not hold more than a few people under cover. That year I decided to hold two parties, one for Gurkha officer pensioners and the other for senior Nepali civilians.

After the pensioners had had their meal I stood up and begged for silence. I explained what was happening and said that I was ashamed that so many honoured and experienced men in front of me allowed the situation to get out of hand.

Indeed, it had been rumored that some members of the gangs were their sons. "If I had been the DRO when you were trying to get enlisted, not one of you would have been a choice," I taunted them. "What's wrong with you? Either you want your sons to have a chance or you don't. If you want them to be enlisted, it is entirely in your hands because I'll cancel this year's allocation for this area if you don't get to grips with it."

It worked: the gang which was responsible for the intimidation was rounded up—there were not nearly as many men as thought—and brought in front of a committee of the "old and bold." They groveled, whined and repented, saying that if they did not do what they were told by the communists they would be beaten up and if they did, they could expect a similar fate from frustrated ex-servicemen. The phrase "willing to wound but afraid to strike" occurred to me as did the paradox that the country which produces such wonderful soldiers also breeds a frame of mind that makes them the antithesis of soldierly material. In truth, the basic qualities of both Anglo-Saxon and hill man seem to be the same: both peoples are fierce, obstinate and untamable and both peoples need special handling to get the best out of them. As soldiers, I believe the hill men are "the first in the world" but, when they are badly behaved civilians, they are very bad: "the worst in the fold." How much of this is because caste restrictions lead to frustration?

More and more I put this down to individual chemistry reacting adversely when empathy is absent so producing a volatility that is hard to counter. "A Gurkha's blood does not heat up but when it does it cannot be measured" is a significant proverb.

I had learnt that the four hardest things to do in Nepal are: to arrange a marriage without a hitch; to buy land without becoming involved in a dispute; to find the right person in the chain of authority to have enough clout to get a positive outcome; and to have people satisfied with, understand and accept a decision.

Those Aryan, non-"Gurkha," Nepalis who had been responsible for "invading" the camp had gone to the Zonal Commissioner with a grievance. Why did the British not enlist their ethnic groups? The Zonal Commissioner's answer, so he told me, was that they were not good enough. "The British do not discriminate; they will take you if you are good enough." He was not to know that the people complaining were not of the "traditional martial classes." As laid down in the then still secret Tripartite Agreement of 1947, these people were not eligible for enlistment. Experience has proved this to be a correct and wise decision. Recruiting for clerks was done by advertisement so any who cared to apply could do so.

Feelings ran so high against those who were spoiling the one avenue for advancement for the "traditional martial classes" that "Gurkha" students in the campus turned on the two ringleaders responsible for organizing the anti-British sentiment and beat them up severely. One of them was in hospital for a month and the other for two weeks before leaving for the Tarai; one has been elected as the district representative in the central government every election since!

Despite my urgent plea through the ambassador for recruiting to be postponed, it went ahead. As the young men walked through the town to be processed the campaign reached its peak with one side fighting the other. For most of them it was the first time they had seen a bloody corpse. I was afraid, such were the feelings and tensions, that our whole British/Gurkha connection was in jeopardy. It was deft handling our end and a very large slice of luck that enabled us to beat the political dangers.

One of the doctors who had come from Hong Kong to help with the workload of recruiting came to see me. "I hear you have a problem with your eyes," he said. "Let's go to your room and I'll have a look."

Yes, an operation would cure me. Hadn't his father-in-law had the same trouble? He had had the operation and now could write so small that his family complained that their eyes weren't good enough to read it!

It seemed to be a case of "grinning hard and bearing it," waiting for both eyes to be ready for polishing, yet no one could say how long that would be. The relief and the joy that flooded through me were enough to bring a broad smile on to my face and I thanked the doctor for his message of hope as fervently as I had thanked Buddhiman for his love.

Because of my extra two years in the army I had a month's home leave. I drove to Kathmandu with Buddhiman and on the way he opened his heart. He said that I had let on only to him that I was unhappy and discouraged. He could see the effort I put into being as normal as possible but I was worried at losing my sight permanently. He reminded me how one day we had to cross nothing more than a stream but the sun was so bright I had tried to crawl across, like an actor looking for something on the stage. He had told me he'd carry me but I had declined. Not taking no for an answer he had carried me over but I had known that a group of young people saw this and sniggered, making disparaging remarks about how weak foreigners were. Buddhiman told them that I was without much sight in both eyes and, until they had any experience of blindness, they could not understand. I recalled the incident and my answer that God would have observed their conduct.

Many unthinking people presumed that the blackened frame I wore was worse than a circus joker and that I was trying to be funny. Buddhiman would tell anyone I had roughly spoken to not to be concerned at any intemperate outburst. What I had not known was that sometimes people talked behind my back about my inability to see and therefore I could not pick the right man to be a soldier. With atropine in the eyes to make the pupils larger I could not face bright light. One day one of the retired Gurkha officers, who should have known better, made a foolish remark about fair-skinned people only seeing nasty things, so their eyes had to be covered. I had answered with great dignity. The other Gurkhas didn't know where to look at such a tactless remark.

Buddhiman recounted one incident that I only vaguely remembered. "There is a Hindu temple on the hill just behind the camp and we went up there one day to talk. I told you I was praying for your recovery and that modern medicines were strong and could cure many illnesses that used not to be curable. You then took some playing cards, little ones, out of your pocket and, in the temple precincts, proceeded to play by yourself. The way they turned up excited you and you said, 'Son, the divinations are being kind to me and I have a good chance of success.' To have forgotten that shows how concerned you were."

I went to England by way of Hong Kong, where the eye specialist looked at me, told me to continue with atropine and that I had to wait for a good while longer before any operation.

Without Buddhiman I "felt" my way home, being helped by kind air hostesses and by asking porters on the railway stations which platform I was on. I tried to get my eyes operated on by an expert in Harley Street but, no, they were not ready. I jogged on the roads at dawn, not wanting to be in cotton wool all the time. I could cower into the hedge when I heard any vehicle coming my way. On my fifty-fifth birthday I felt how lucky I was, in so many ways, yet on that morning jog, the thought kept on at me; why have I been through so much and still have to bear with this latest affliction? This thought will have plagued people from the very start of time!

With my curious eye shields I could read, putting spectacles under the masking tape. I went to London to sit for the Final Diploma of the Institute of Linguists, four written papers and an oral. I walked the five miles from my accommodation to the exam centre, asking people to read the street names for me. I found out that I was the first ever to sit Nepali since the Institute had opened in 1910—a world record! I was asked what my "specialist subject for the long essay" was;

it should have been submitted, along with any five unrelated topics, six months before. I had not done this and told the secretary I would bring my choice of subject and topics on the morrow. Of the half dozen offered, I chose "modern history and politics" and, that evening, produced the five topics, not an easy thing to do. The one that was chosen for me was "Mongolian versus Aryan: The Nepalese Dilemma." I was allowed twenty extra minutes to compensate for when my eyes had to be given a rest. A professor from the School of Oriental and African Studies set the papers and took me for my oral, Nepali being one, but not the best, of his languages. The standard of the exam was higher than I ever imagined and I had grave doubts about one of the written papers that I knew was beyond me. So, despite being given a distinction for my oral, I set up my second world record—the first person ever to fail the Final Diploma in Nepali.

In December 1980 HRH The Prince of Wales paid an official visit to Nepal. In his capacity of Honorary Colonel-in-Chief of the Second Goorkhas he went on a trek in the west then paid us a visit. We sent out invitations to those we thought the prince would like to meet, especially holders of the Victoria Cross and the George Cross. We included the only Gurkha to be awarded the Order of Patriotic War, 1st Class, Russian Revolution, won in Burma by a subedar in the Third Gurkhas, also those who had been Queen's Gurkha Orderly Officers and all those of honorary commissioned rank, as well as our senior staff from the welfare centres. One turned up in December 1981, his letter having taken more than a year to reach him. There were camp staff too and those pensioners who happened to be in camp that day. Security was as tight as we could achieve. By then I was not seeing at all well and, before the royal motorcade reached us, I announced to the assembled pensioners that they would have to tell the prince their names as I presented them. Even if I did know their names, I could not be sure who I was talking to.

I put in a double dose of atropine and wore a peaked hat, drawn well over the eyes. The ambassador, John Denson, came the night before—we held a party and a cultural show for the "old and bold"—and it was agreed I should open the door of the prince's car, be presented and then take him off. It was in the nick of time that I saw I was about to open the chauffeur's door instead of the prince's, but I don't think that was generally noticed.

The Prince was fascinated by the first group I took him to. There were three holders of the Victoria Cross, presented by his grandfather or great-uncle, and one of the George Cross, awarded when it was the Empire Gallantry Medal, a rarity.

The prince leant over the chair where Nandalal Thapa, GC, a frail old man, was sitting. "Where and how did you get your award?" he queried. I translated. "In Quetta, in the 1935 earthquake. I saved twelve men but the citation only said I had rescued ten." "Poor old man," the prince said in an aside to me. "Still upset about it, forty-five years later."

Halfway through the prince looked up and saw how many there were still to be spoken to. "This may be hard work for you, Sir," I said, "but it is not making their day, it is making their year." An old man dressed in peasant clothes leant on a stick, legs slightly apart, glaring at the prince. The photographers saw a picture coming and got their cameras ready. The prince held out his hand and asked the man which his regiment had been. The old man did not take the proffered hand, nor answer the question. I asked again, in a louder voice. Still no reaction. I put my face close to his ear and bellowed; "What is your regiment?" The cameras clicked and the man said; "I was never a soldier," and relapsed into silence. The prince was intrigued; here was someone who had slipped through our security cordon.

"Why have you come here if you weren't a soldier?"

"I have come to see you."

"How did you know I was going to be here?"

"We all know about your coming here."

The prince asked him how long it had taken to get to Pokhara and was told; four days down, one day here and four days back, nine days in all. That impressed the prince as much as anything during that visit. The reason the old man had not shaken hands was that the gesture was foreign to him. Later one woman's magazine captioned the photo of me trying to get through to him and the prince watching as "one of the holders of the Victoria Cross being presented ... "

At the end The Prince of Wales turned and thanked me, offering me his hand. He asked me what I was thinking of doing after I left the army and I told him that I had no idea. He asked me a second time and I gave the same reply; "I really have no idea, Sir."

"In that case, I'll have to find you a job," were his parting words.

Buddhiman had been in one of the groups the prince spoke to and I had allowed his wife into my room overlooking the parade. Both were thrilled. He had shaken hands with the prince.

"How soft it was, as soft as the way he spoke so nicely to us! I had never dreamt that I would shake the hand of the man who would be the King of England. Our royal family does not shake hands and I did not know that the English Crown Prince did. I was thrilled and for at least three days afterwards, I'd look at my right hand and shake my head in wonderment. I gave thanks to my mother for bringing me into a world where I could shake hands with a prince."

To try and remedy the weakness that resulted in failing the exam paper that contained such erudite language I started studying Nepali with a professor at the university and had soon increased my vocabulary by another 3,000 words. I wrote out many new "memory cards" and taped them, another four-hour programme. Ordinary reading was too difficult for more than short periods so listening to the recording was not the bore it might have been.

After recruiting in January 1981 I signaled the hospital in Dharan about the chances of being operated on. "I can't be optimistic if I have a misty optic," I japed, remembering a Christmas cracker joke from schoolboy days.

I had to go to Dharan for a conference and went to see the doctor about my eyes. There was no point in my being impatient, I was told. The next morning the left eye ceased to be of any value but there was just a tiny bit I could see out of the right, so patient I was. One of the British wives told me that she wondered why the army had let me stay on two extra years when I was so unfit.

I had driven to Dharan and, on the way back, we had permission to use a feeder road that was being made, cutting many miles off our journey. Our permit had to be surrendered halfway yet, at the end of the road, we were not allowed forward without producing the same permit. I remonstrated but to no avail. It was still chilly and the man who was stopping us, a thin creature, was dressed in a green jersey. I suggested that we go to see his boss in the office, a furlong away, on the main road. He agreed to this and moved ahead quickly. I soon lost him. I could not read the sign boards so was unable to tell which office was which but, luckily, I did find the man. He had not gone to the office; he was sitting, sunning himself. He looked fatter than before and he was opening his coat, so I thought, to get the sun to his belly. I called to him and angrily asked what he was doing, only to be greeted with giggles from the people near me. I was talking to a green rain tub.

One thing to take the mind off a problem is to give it a harder one. I had to visit the two northern districts of Manang and Mustang to talk to the Chief District Officers about the "Proof of Citizenship" certificate that each soldier now had to have. To go to the district capitals, lying on different rivers

317

with part of the Himalayas in between, one by one, meant a longer journey than were I to go from the one to the other, over a pass of about 18,000 feet. The thoughtless remark about my being unfit rankled, so I decided to visit the two places using the shorter but harder route over the pass. For porters I took two lads who desperately wanted to be enlisted. As a spur, I told them that, if they managed to get me across the mountains in time and in safety, I would let them start the selection process at the last, not the first hurdle.

We had never been in those parts before and I was surprised that even in the remote areas we passed through there were people who knew me, some only from my voice; administrators, policemen, passers-by on the track. The night before we reached the snow line we heard an avalanche. I managed until we reached the snow line. Here the glare was too much even wearing dark glasses. I had to be led; Buddhiman put one hand out behind him and I clasped it, putting the other on his pack. On one ledge crossing a very steep slope we could hear the shale sliding down. I shuffled like an old man, slowly, oh so slowly. The one night we spent in the snow saw us all with mountain sickness and with Buddhiman in a bad way. I told him to get into his sleeping bag in the tent and I crawled into mine later. In the middle of the night I awoke and could not hear him breathing. It was all I could do not to shake him to ask him if he were dead! By then my dependence on him was total.

No journey we did together was so hard. Next morning we struggled to the pass, I wanting to lie down and get my breath every five minutes but Buddhiman urged, coaxed and cajoled me to keep going. What the band of healthy young tourists thought I was doing did not concern me; I was only dimly aware that we were not alone.

On the way down the mountain I slipped, skidded and fell innumerable times, treading on Buddhiman's heels and bumping into him. Never, by word or gesture, did he show any annoyance and my love for him welled within me. At 12,500 feet we came to Muktinath, one of the holiest of Hinduism's places of worship, and he went to where a flame burns under the spring water that makes the Ganges sacred and prayed for my eye sight to be restored.

It was my bad luck that the Chief District Officer was out when we got to Jomoson, the district capital. He had gone to Baglung, many miles to the south. Although we walked more than twenty-five miles a day to get there, we never met up with him.

I got back to camp tired, having averaged over twenty miles a day for some two hundred miles. Only days later, in the middle of recruiting—I could still just see with a tiny window in the right eye, in dim light—I was handed a message ordering me to Hong Kong for an operation, leaving Kathmandu on the coming Tuesday. I rearranged the programme, conducting a hundred interviews a day and, at 2 o'clock on the Sunday, had completed my list of successful recruits. By 4 o'clock my other eye was also useless. I was desperately tired but content to think I had managed to work until two hours before the eyes "packed up" after a 30-month "countdown." I could now understand how it is that Indian peasant women always seem to prefer their faces to be hidden by their sari. That is the only privacy they can have. I had been living in a world that was not dissimilar and felt cut off from my fellow men.

I went by road to Kathmandu, leaving at 4 o'clock in the morning and getting to the airport by 9 o'clock. Buddhiman went back in the vehicle and I was on my own. I needed help for everything I did and missed my son like an ache. At Bangkok, where I had to wait for three hours, my ticket was mislaid and I was stuck in the transit area. Even though I had such difficulty in seeing, my eyes looked normal. The Thai authorities thought that I was up to something by my unusual behavior. I spoke to them in Thai and help me they did.

There was a further six-hour delay which gave time for my ticket to be found. I was "rescued" by a French-Canadian Buddhist girl, Nicole Couture, on her way back to Hong Kong from having been in retreat in a monastery in Nepal. She helped me reach the hospital and handed me over to the man on duty. I was shown my room, next to the gynecological ward, reputedly the quietest so good for eyes, at dawn. The duty sister upbraided me for being late!

At the medical inspection, when I signed my willingness to be operated on, I was asked why I had not reported in five months earlier when I was expected. The hospital had sent the doctor at Dharan a letter sending for me the previous December. Even though I had asked him what instructions there were for me, he had told me "to be patient": I had been blind for five months longer than I need have been. I suppose he had not forgotten how I had complained about the flawed medical support he supplied during recruiting. As the formalities came to an end the doctor gave me a warning. "One trouble with your sort of eyes is that, if you get a hit on the head, you could be blind for life."

Both operations were successful. The surgeon told me the left eye had been "copy book," what doctors dreamt about. I was overjoyed. My first day out of hospital I telephoned my mother. She later said that my voice throbbed into her ear; "... I can see, I can see, and in colour ... "

I had to wait a month or so for the right eye to be operated on and I stayed with the Gurkha Transport Regiment, a few minutes' walk from the hospital. There I was looked after by people, some of whom I had enlisted, with kindness, love and sympathy.

I had been out of hospital for nearly a week when I was fixed up with a rough pair of tunnel vision spectacles. The very next day the one paper I had to re-take for the Final Diploma Nepali examination arrived. I sat in my room to tackle it. It was not easy but I was confident that I could deal with it. I had covered the right eye against too much light and held a small magnifying glass in front of the left, converting it from a distance lens into one for reading. That was fine, until I came to the middle of the page I was writing on and found that it was a physical impossibility to see the bottom half, due to the restrictions of tunnel vision. I wondered how I was going to finish the exam and hit on the idea of balancing the magnifying glass upside down on my cheek bone and holding my head at an angle so that it neither fell through nor over the top of my spectacles. In this way I could steady the paper with my left hand, having lowered my head the distance required to see the bottom half of the paper. I gave myself the same twenty minutes extra that I had been allowed the year before and just finished in time, sweating from exertion.

With my script I wrote a letter to the secretary of the Institute of Linguists, explaining why my writing might have been bad. I offered no excuses for a poor performance. I knew that I was bound to set up a third world record: either be the first person to pass the Nepali or to be the first person to fail it twice!

After the right eye had been polished (I was told it nearly burst and I am extraordinarily lucky to have any sight in it) I learnt how to walk again by myself. Using a stick, I would wait until someone wanted to cross a road and tag on. The glasses were half as powerful as standard binoculars and I now noticed that expressions on the faces of people who walked alone were inwardly withdrawn. I put this down to a manifestation of the avoidance of contact and involvement when in crowded places. It was only when two people were talking to one another were the expressions on their faces "alive." I wept when I saw the stars for the first time in over a year.

On my way back to Nepal I had a night in Bangkok. I wanted to visit the Gurkhas of the embassy guard, some of whom I had sent and all of whom I knew from my visits there when I was in Vientiane. Crossing the main road was an adventure in its own right. Halfway across I stopped and laughed with the sheer joy of being able to do it by myself.

At Pokhara airport I was met by a radiant Buddhiman, who had been told that I was on my way back, cured. He had wept with joy at the thought of meeting me again and ran to embrace me. The others watched, smiling, before they too came up to greet me. Buddhiman told me that he saw from the look in my eyes that he still meant so much to me and that, now I was cured, I would not go back on what I had said about living together as a family. Some of the pensioners said that I would but Buddhiman had never doubted that I had meant what I said. He could see I was much weaker than ever before.

I had to learn how to walk up and down slopes in my thick tunnel-vision spectacles but, so overjoyed was I to be able to see again, it was a happy challenge. In Hong Kong I had been to the hospital church and offered my thanks to all my Christian friends for their prayers. In Pokhara I asked Birkha Raj, now working in the camp as a retired officer, if he could arrange that I hold a puja for all my Hindu friends who had prayed for my recovery.

He and Buddhiman got permission from the senior priest of the most famous temple to perform a sacrifice on my behalf. A goat was bought and, on the morning of the appointed day, I had to have a bath before sprinkling it with water; this was to make it shake itself, a sure sign that the god had entered into it, rendering it holy, so worthy to be sacrificed. That evening, in accordance with Hindu custom, pieces of its meat were given to all the camp staff. News that I, a Christian, had done such a thing in honour of my Hindu friends spread everywhere fast and I think it was the most popular gesture I ever made.

Some months later I had to return to Hong Kong to have the stitches removed, be fixed up with new glasses now that the eyes had regained their original shapes and fit myself with contact lenses. I had to learn how to balance using them but the difference they made was magical. Each time I put them on it was like the Lord kissing my eyes. On my first trek in contact lenses I told Buddhiman what "freedom" meant to me; "to be able to walk fast down a stony track in the half light of dawn, without having to be led."

My time in the army was running out and I told Buddhiman that we needed to get out and visit old haunts again. We went to the south of Pokhara, in the mountains of Syangja. There water is scarce, especially in the period before the monsoon. No views of the Himalayas greet the villagers; horizons are restricted. It is hotter, being farther south. It is a hard place to live comfortably but, even so, the rules of hospitality and the ties of the family are ever strong.

The village was small, compact and clean. The chief family had service connections over many years. Our host and Buddhiman's great-great-grandfathers were brothers; they were of one family, we were likewise of one family.

Our visit had been planned, we had not arrived unexpectedly. I was made comfortable in the guestroom across a courtyard from the house. That evening I was called into the house, a large, clean place, with many metal pots and pans glittering in the light of the lamps. The women of the house were gathered in front of a mat, the menfolk busy with something I could not see. I was invited to sit on the mat.

One of the brothers came up to me, tied two yellow ribbons round my neck, sprinkled some water on my head and muttered something that sounded like *syah syah*. I noticed, through my thick spectacles, that, until then, the expressions on the women's faces were withdrawn but, on the incantation of those magical words, it was as though a light was switched on inside every one. I was offered a glass of milk, not taking it in my own hands but having it fed to me by one of the elder women.

I am now part of that family. I can now go into the house and demand food to be cooked and work to be done in the strict social family order by being "father" to Buddhiman. I was most touched by such a gesture that had only once before been made to me by Buddhiman's own family. I unthinkingly addressed one of the women by the courtesy relationship I had used before, based on our relative ages more than anything else, but was gently upbraided for not knowing which particular cousin, or niece, or aunt, she now was. That pitfall of relationships stays with me still, exacerbated by terms of kinship not having a constant meaning in Nepal and poor eyesight.

The memory of the doctor's warning, that I could go blind for life if I were to hit my head, haunted me. Rather than end my days in an impersonal institution in the land of my birth, I would much prefer Buddhiman to look after me with love, were the unthinkable to happen. But how was I to go about living in Nepal without the annual requirement of a non-tourist visa, long enough to clock up the time necessary for being considered a citizen? I was told that there was an 18-year waiting period for citizenship, far too long for me to be in limbo. I did not want to lose my British passport if only because I might need to go to England in a hurry for the eyes and it was a lengthy, time-consuming and cumbersome process getting a Nepalese passport, which then only lasted for one year. Buddhiman and I talked at length about it but came to no conclusion, save the one that I had to come back after pension and see if a way of us three living together as a family could be found.

One morning I was given an envelope, with the logo of the Institute of Linguists, and I hesitated to open it, knowing it was my exam result. Taking a deep breath, I tore it open and, to my relief and joy, saw that my third world record was being the first ever to pass in Nepali.

At the end of 1981 I went to the Tarai to visit the welfare centre based on Chitwan. I was invited to the house of a pensioner and, while there, a schoolmaster saw my vehicle and came into the house to solicit aid for his school.

He knew of me and during the course of conversation he said that scholars were highly regarded in Nepal and, with my qualification (I had become a Member of the Institute) I could write a thesis in Nepali. He even suggested research on "Intellectual Variance," a thought that left me cooler rather than warmer. He would write to a friend of his in the university in Kathmandu and when I passed through in April I must go and see him. He was bound to help me. I took a note of his name and address, wrote to him on my return and, in the traumatic weeks at the end of my service as DRO, forgot all about the idea.

The Chinese have a proverb that a journey of a thousand miles starts with but a single step. Nothing is said about the chances of arriving. In those last few days, as I pondered what to say when I was given my last party, my thoughts turned back to my very early army days when I only wanted to see if I could manage tolerably well on my own. During my service I seldom had my eyes on the promotion stars but neither was I always watching where I was putting my military feet. There are four "Ds" as to why full military service is not attained: death, dishonour, disability and disillusion. None pertained to me. I had walked those thousand miles and only waited to see what was round that last bend.

I was given a party in the Gurkha officers' mess and had to make a speech. I told them that I would assuredly cry if I did not make us all laugh and went on to do just that. I reminded them of the black market and recruiting scandals and how, as a team, we had overcome the threats both had posed; that our name stood very high (here I quoted the Nepalese proverb "Pure gold needs no touchstone and a good man no adornment"); that the local agitators had not prevailed; that we had made the future secure by our policy of impartiality and lack of discrimination; and I thanked them with all my heart, especially for bearing with me during the months of my going blind. I reminded them of the two most precious gifts possible; not riches, though they certainly helped, but good health and peace of mind. With those two, everything else fell into place.

I said that, of all the many things that had scared me during my service, that which scared me most was the way time slipped by without my noticing it and I reminded them of the Nepali song that proved my point:

> *Dashera is over, Diwali is near*
> *The marigolds are all in bloom,*
> *On the village swing sits a maiden*
> *fair*
> *But alas for me there is no room.*
> *The prime of life for me is past*
> *Long may that maiden's pleasures*
> *last,*

and in a loud aside,

> *"but never let her know!"*

The next morning, in a daze, I was driven round the camp road in a bedecked Land Rover, with the people from outside as well as the camp staff lining the sides. Many people came to see me off, the sweepers we left behind when we moved from Paklihawa, the limbless, the poor and the humble—all people I had helped in their hour of need. Bhim Kumari was brought down from the village to say goodbye. The sentry on the gate had his time cut out to know who to let in and who not to, all demanding to be allowed to say farewell. I was proffered drinks of milk, little bits of rice cake, flowers by people as I passed them: at the quarter guard, heavily garlanded, I inspected the soldiers and saluted the flag. In the vehicle once more, I drove out of the camp, the crowd waving.

I had given away my military clothes to those who I knew were short of things to wear. Buddhiman had told me to keep them but I said that if I did retain them my mind would not let me leave the army and it would be hard enough as it was; why make it harder? I left some boxes of civilian clothes and books behind in the stores. When Buddhiman took them to Birkha Raj's house and told him he was sad that father had gone, the answer was "He will come back. If ever you let him down, next incarnation you will be less than a dung beetle."

A little distance away another Land Rover, with Buddhiman and my kit, ready for the road, waited for me. I got in and drove away, heart so heavy it was ready to burst. I called in at the welfare centre at Damauli, thirty-two miles down the Kathmandu road, and thanked the staff for their work. The Gurkhas say so much by leaving so much unsaid. We spent the night at the welfare centre in Gorkha where an old friend of Gurkha Para days was in charge. I was not in the mood for small talk. I felt drained, almost as if I wanted to sleep for a long, long time and wake up finding it was all a dream. But I knew that was nonsense!

I had met many interesting and friendly people of all stripes, far too many to remember, let alone to name. I had kept close contact with officials in thirty districts, from the Tarai to above the snow line. I was never made to feel unwelcome; my admiration for the manner in which they overcame the intricacies, pressures and difficulties they had to work under increased during that time. The cleanest people I ever came across were Tharus in the Tarai. I had been instrumental in persuading the British ambassador to persuade London to divert a Hercules aircraft and many tons of rice, already destined for Cambodia, to drop supplies where there was a famine in the Far Western areas centred around Dailekh. I had managed to get financial aid properly to places where it could do most good to most people. I had managed to clean up the recruiting and the black-market scandals. I was honoured when one senior Nepali official told my direct military superior that he should let me stay for a total of ten years. I had done my best to foster good relations between the Nepalis and the British. I think I left the organization in a healthier state than it was when I arrived. Now it was time to hand over to someone younger, pack my bags and go. "Something attempted, something done ... "

In Kathmandu, at the transit camp, I found a letter waiting for me: come to supper that evening, in the professors' quarters of the university. The name meant nothing to me and to be sociable was the last thing I wanted. Buddhiman urged me to go.

I was very warmly welcomed by a smiling man and introduced to his wife and father-in-law. Children from the other quarters thronged in and, concentrating on the present, I kept them all in fits of laughter for half an hour, still having no idea who anyone was but luckily I am skilled in the art of not letting on to folk when I do not know them!

A meal was served, deliciously cooked. The professor started talking about the need Nepal had for people like me and I should meet the vice-chancellor. I quailed at that idea. No, I had to go; he would tell the vice-chancellor to expect a call. Still not connecting my host with the letter I had written four months before, I thanked him and his wife for a great evening and left.

At 1 o'clock on Sunday, a working day in Nepal, 18 April 1982, Buddhiman and I drove to the vice-chancellor's office. The great man came out of his office to welcome me. Against all expectations, I knew him: Ram Chandra Bahadur Singh, the one-time Zonal Commissioner I had met in Pokhara and who knew all about the recruiting scandals. He stretched out his hand and led me into his office. We sat down and he said; "Colonel sahib, as soon as I was told you wanted to see me, I knew I had to ask you to join the staff of the university."

This was completely unexpected. I thanked him and said that I would be delighted to work under him for Nepal. I would do it for nothing. "No, we will do it properly and make you a full member of the staff."

Coffee was produced and I asked him when he wanted me to be ready. "Any time convenient to you, three months, six months, a year. Go home, enjoy your leave and come back when you are ready." He glanced at his watch. "I am going to the palace in a few minutes, I will tell them about my offer."

Palace was synonymous with the king who was the Chancellor of the University. I took my leave and went outside. Buddhiman saw my grin from ear to ear. "Son, I have been offered a job. If all goes well, I'll be back here in a few months and together we can face the future."

8: 1982-1984

Going on pension is like being detribalized. An adult lifetime's military habits and procedures have to be placed in a civilian context; the longer the army service, the harder this becomes. I had long ago realized that the world was not flat and there was no stepping off it when no longer a soldier. This is especially so for one like myself.

For my mandatory, month-long, end-of-service resettlement course the army authorities responsible had advised Teaching English as a Foreign Language—and some of my friends would say that that was a little too near the truth for comfort! This would be of great importance to me for work in the university at Kathmandu. While still in Pokhara I had been told that a civilian concern in Piccadilly would instruct me, so it was a bitter shock when a young woman on their staff told me I was unsuitable student material so would not be accepted. No reasons were given. This decision also embarrassed the army authorities so much that they let me sit in on the army's own language school at Beaconsfield, in Buckinghamshire, where English was being taught to non-English students, including Gurkhas. It was a poor substitute for a properly slanted course.

The Falklands crisis erupted and my old battalion, 1/7 Gurkha Rifles, was part of the re-occupation forces. I found it hard to watch pictures of their embarkation. I did get to Southampton docks to meet them on their return and to travel with them as far as Fleet, in Hampshire, where they marched through the town. Their spontaneously enthusiastic welcome, their popularity and the esteem in which they were so obviously held, their soldierly bearing and the sense of occasion all brought a lump to my throat. Tears were not far away.

I also managed to pay a visit to the legendary Sanskrit and Nepali scholar, Professor Sir Ralph Turner, then in his ninety-third year. Arguably one of the finest British linguistic scholars of the twentieth century, he had produced, after sixteen years, a dictionary of Nepali, a model of its kind. Published in 1931, it was now out of date. I had wanted to see him to obtain his approval and permission to update it. His current work was finishing off another large linguistic project that had already taken him sixty years.

We chatted in his book-lined study; he was full of charm, kindness, wisdom and warmth. He seemed pleased at my suggestion and gave me his blessing for it. In his written confirmation of the project he listed certain conditions, one that the new edition be published as the Turner-Cross dictionary. The School of Oriental and African Studies (SOAS), in London, gave me their written encouragement for the project.

I spent my last day in the army, 20 June 1982, back in Beaconsfield, helping to brief a group of Rotheram Adventure Scouts for a job they were going to undertake in Nepal during their long school holidays—the installation of a supply of drinking water for a village just above the camp at Pokhara. It gave me a fitting sense of completion to have worked that very last day and it gave me an even greater longing to get back to

Nepal and surrogate son, Buddhiman. And so, on my fifty-seventh birthday, and after thirty-nine years and eighty days army service with nearly thirty-eight years of them spent in Asia, I became a civilian. I expected the first five years of my new incarnation to be harder than any military service ever was!

As I jogged along the lanes near Child Okeford in Dorset that first civilian morning, I mused about my changed status. I was no longer part of the British Army, that demanding, turbulent, disruptive organization which, in turn, could be so helpful, so understanding and so protective. Over-protective, too, for I was virtually helpless by myself, so long had I been looked after—and spoiled. I was now on my own, with no one owing me a living except the statutory limits set by the welfare state and my army pension (and that taxed as unearned income and lower than the previous year's!). What were seen as my eccentricities—interest in languages, fascination with the raw material of soldiering, years in the east and an urge to "go one step farther"—had done my career no good. The British Army, like the Royal Academy, desires docility in its children and even originality has to be stereotyped. Nevertheless I had had a rewarding, challenging and positive life in the army. I was profoundly grateful for the opportunities that had come my way. I could look, once more, in the mirror and meet my own gaze with equanimity. Some of my more perspicacious Gurkha friends told me later that I should never have stayed in the army had I wanted to achieve my full potential. Others told me I would have risen much higher had I not put my men first and had learnt to toady to my British superiors.

On my flight from Kathmandu to Hong Kong, on the first leg of my "return ticket" back home, a Nepali air hostess had sat next to me after the cabin lights had been turned off. She told me she was a single woman. With my heart as heavy as it was I was split in two whether to explore the possibility of marriage with her or throw away what seemed to be a golden opportunity. I knew I was not myself. I knew I could only trust myself after I had regained my equilibrium. In the heart of my heart I knew that my money and status were the attraction for her and, were my eyes to pack up on me, she would probably do likewise. If I were to go blind, it would only be love that would nurse me, not opportunism. It had to be Buddhiman and his family. It could be no one else.

Nepal owed me nothing but I had to go back to Kathmandu to see the university vice-chancellor, to be accepted or rejected, not for any academic experience as I had none; but for who I was and what I could do with and for Nepalis. I had complete faith in Buddhiman; although there was nothing in writing to say that we were "father" and "son," the psychological need for and dependence on one another were stronger by far than any paper transaction.

I wrote letters to the vice-chancellor and to the registrar, if only to keep contact. I told them that I was now able to join them and asked if there was any aspect of a future task that I could be preparing for. With no reply after two months I wrote to Colonel Mike Allen, the defence attaché in Kathmandu, asking him if he could find out anything. His reply was ominous; no one knew anything nor seemed to want to know about me.

In deciding how to react to such unwelcome news I fell back on the three principles I had used as a soldier: a firm base, an alternative and a reserve. This meant holding on to my base in Britain as long as Nepal was indeterminate and keeping enough money both to meet all reasonable needs in Nepal, and to keep me "in pocket" if I had to return to live in England. To that end I booked myself a flight with some two months of my visa still valid. I wanted to see what the ominous silence was all about. In the very worst case, I would merely be treating myself to a winter holiday. Choice of dates was important. I did not want to be in England so long that affairs "cooled down," nor did I want to forego the pleasure of living at home with mother for a longer period than when a boy, forty-six years before.

Once a year Nepalis try and join up as a family. During the Tiwar ceremony, held in late October or early November, it is the religious duty of brothers to go to their sisters to have a *tika*, a sectarian or orthodox mark, daubed on their foreheads. Fictitious relationships play a large part in Nepal. Buddhiman's aunt by marriage was therefore my sister, so it would be most appropriate for me to be daubed on the day of *Bhai* (brother) *Tika*, especially as I had told her the year before that that was what I intended doing. That meant arriving in Nepal a few days before 17 November.

I remembered the significance that the numeral "2" had in those early days in Malaya. Quite unplanned, I left home on 12 November (11th month, 1+1=2) in 1982 (1+9+8+2=20=2+0=2). Also it was raining when I left the house for my jog that last morning. That I immediately noticed. Whenever a draft of reinforcements during the war went to their battalions and it rained that morning, the omens were good. Here was I, getting similarly soaked, at the outset of one of the most unlikely journeys I had ever undertaken; all very heathen in its way but quite amusing and, secretly, rather comforting. Nor was that the only time that 2s played their part before I got a final answer to my quest!

All went smoothly until I reached Delhi, surely nobody's favorite place. The Kathmandu connection cannot be confirmed until Delhi is reached and is often over-booked. At 5 o'clock in the morning my good omens seemed to have deserted me. I made my way over to a portly official who looked at me disdainfully when I asked him to help me. I made the mistake of talking to him in Hindi. Before 1947, certainly among British officers of my generation, we considered it bad form to speak to Indian functionaries in English because it showed we had not related properly to them. Indeed, we took it as slightly humiliating to be spoken to in English by such people if only because we thought it showed they had not related to us.

I was answered in English, with gesticulating arms, a wringing of hands and a lop-sided shake of the head: "Just I am not knowing." Nor did he seem the slightest interested. I smiled and broke into a vernacular song that had been popular in the anti-British disturbances in the early '40s: "Forward, young men. Do not flag in your endeavors. Fight with purpose." The other passengers turned to stare in bewilderment. The official's nonchalance dissolved in good humour and I received a triple accolade: being personally taken to the domestic terminal, not being allowed to pay for portering my baggage and getting a seat to Kathmandu.

As I stepped out of the aeroplane the familiar feel of my surroundings enveloped me as comfortably as a warm rug on a cold day. I felt a surge of love as I saw Buddhiman and Mike Allen waiting for me. Immigration and Customs were perfunctory, being waved through by smiling officials who knew me.

It was a joyous yet subdued reunion. Nepalis do not show their feelings in public but we had more than enough time to talk at our leisure. When we were alone I told Buddhiman that I had made a new will and that he was the major beneficiary. Instead of showing his pleasure he rebuked me, telling me not to talk about when I was dead. The affinity and empathy between us is subtle and unusual to many Europeans.

There was no going to see the vice-chancellor because all government offices were closed as the Soviet leader had just died. Neither gloom nor rejoicing, a holiday was normal government policy. Next stop Pokhara.

I was still getting used to doing everything for myself. A Nepalese facet to this painful process was the inevitable exposure that resulted from no longer being shielded by having an official status. To Kathmandu Nepalis, especially to those of high caste, an unofficial European is very low in the social scale and, unless clearly he is rich or well known, he finds himself thrust to the back of the throng, queues not yet being the fashion. The crush outside the ticket counter at the bus station, with so many wanting to get home for Tiwar, the pushing and shoving, were familiar yet challengingly different. I found myself yet again relying on Buddhiman for fixing all local details.

The bus journey from Kathmandu to Pokhara, a hundred and twenty-five miles, takes from seven to eight hours. Conditions are cramped with legroom severely limited and hard, narrow seats. It soon becomes tedious—but it only cost £1 pound and 59 new pence! Buddhiman and I sat together, he telling me how his last journey had been on 20 April, the day after I left. He had found himself weeping as he passed places we had walked together when on trek, nostalgia often getting the better of him. It had taken him a week to get used to being on his own again. The thought of the boxes stored in Birkha Raj's house raised his morale and was proof that I would come back. So we reminisced happily as the bus bumped, jolted and swayed, content to be in one another's company again. We also talked about the future, but in more guarded terms, both of us well aware of the tenuous and unchartered path ahead.

Glad to leave the bus and stretch our legs, we walked the half mile to where Birkha Raj lived. As we opened the gate he came out of the house, all smiles and happiness. "I knew you'd be here about now," he said, "I was waiting for you."

"But you did not even know that I had arrived in the country, let alone that it was only yesterday we decided to come today," I protested.

"Ah, but a bus driver bound for Pokhara saw you at the ticket counter and told us about it when he got here."

Like so many other Gurkhas, Birkha Raj had saved enough money to build a house in or near a town. Not only were schooling facilities better than in the villages but also conveniences such as water and electricity, however erratic, enhanced the quality of life. Other relatives would live in the villages and the town-dweller would regularly visit them. Land, that most useful of assets, still had to be managed.

The Hindu faith has many rituals that need strict observance but the actual ceremonies always seem less co-ordinated than in many other religions. People come and go as they please, carry on conversations and regard it all as a happy occasion. There are so many temples, shrines and wayside gods dotted about and in houses that Hindus do not feel members of any one "church." Thus, the daubing ceremony took place in an atmosphere of relaxed informality. A cloth had been spread on the verandah on which were little pannikins, each with a different coloured paste, a sprig of duba grass and a pot of water. "Sister" and I sat cross-legged with the cloth between us. Mumbling the age-old mantras of propitiation and adding her own kind words of good wishes for the future and a welcome in the house always, I had water sprinkled around me with the sprig of duba grass before having upright coloured lines drawn on my forehead and a new Nepalese hat placed on my head. Before I creaked to my feet and put my shoes on, I gave my "sister" a ceremonial gift of money.

Buddhiman had delicately probed my intentions and, on learning that we had a few days before we need go back to Kathmandu, had sent a message to his village elders—at their behest and I strictly in the dark. I was only told that I was expected in Thuloswara, a day's hard walk away from the road head.

On our way to the village I insisted on making a detour to visit a man who had lost the use of his legs. Years back he had made the journey to Paklihawa to try and enlist but had been taken ill on the way. His legs had withered and he had been bedridden ever since. When I was DRO I had helped him with funds given by the Hong Kong-based philanthropist, Sir Horace Kadoorie. This allowed him to buy back some land that had been kept until his late father's debts had been settled, and some creature comforts, such as bedding, books and a transistor radio. I had also suggested that he might be better off if his legs, now useless, were amputated so that he could push himself about using his arms and a pad to sit on, rather than having to rely on being carried if he wanted to move. Primitive but effective. The actual cutting would not have been so much of a problem. Getting him down to be inspected had involved being portered, a slow, cumbersome and, at times, painful mode of transport. Expensive, too, as it involved two other people whose time, away from their farming, had to be compensated.

The man, Kamansing Gurung, would have been most upset if I had not visited him and, once there, Buddhiman kept urging me not to dally. We moved on, the air crisp and the snows visible from the higher ground. We were due at the top end of Thuloswara and, as we turned the last corner, I saw the village elders gathered near a red banner, with *swagatam*, "welcome," picked out in white. A band of atonal horns and drums wailed its thumping threnody, garlands were proffered and I was led to the local temple. All this had been kept a secret and, thanks to my ignorance, we were later than expected. My arrival should have coincided with the arrival of a goddess, brought down by half the elders from a temple in the mountains, to be installed in the village temple. The rest of the elders had been the welcoming committee. No wonder Buddhiman had urged me to hurry and, in the way it all happens in Nepal, my lateness was excused.

This was the first time I had been at the installation of an idol, so did not know what to expect. It had never occurred to me that I would be called on to participate. I tried not to show bewilderment when, bidden to take my shoes off, I was led to a wooden sacrificial post in the temple precincts where there was a tethered goat and given a *lota*, brass pot, of water. I was told that I had to sprinkle some water on the goat prior to its sacrifice. This I had done once before. The trick is to make the beast shiver and shake itself, so showing its divine possession, before the water is finished. I was more skilled than when I first tried to do this after my eye operation. As prayers were chanted I was taken to a chair placed hard by the hapless beast, which was then deftly decapitated with one strong kukri stroke. Blood splashed me.

The headless corpse was dragged round the sacrificial post, thus ringing it with blood and making the temple precincts ready for the new deity. I had to stand by the temple door, as a guardian, but against what remained unspecified. I took up my position, feeling slightly sheepish. The goddess, still in the open, was picked up and placed inside for perpetual

343

entombment in the most propitious spot. As this was being calculated, more prayers were said. I was taken away to the village high school, a few minutes' walk away.

A couple of years earlier I had caused a stone resting place, a chautara, to be built near the school so that the pupils had somewhere to sit when relaxing. A chautara has a semi-religious significance, especially when two trees are planted side by side on the top of it, a banyan (*Ficus indica*) and a peepul (*Ficus religiosa*). When two such trees are planted they later have to be married, a protracted and expensive business. In this case there was only one tree, a *Fraximus floribunda*, that grows to a great height, has a pleasing scent and gives good shade. My task was to plant it. All the spadework had been done and the tree was ready for planting in the hole dug in the middle of the square, knapped stones. I put it in and tamped it. Masters and pupils watched my every move with great concern and a touch of seriousness. As I stood up I was rewarded with a ripple of applause. I was escorted back to the temple area for the next part of the programme.

A shelter had been rigged up near the temple and benches placed underneath. At one end was a chair and I was invited to sit down with the village elders. A leaf plate with pieces of the slaughtered goat was handed to each one of us. It was the Hindu equivalent of the host at Christian Holy Communion and, having been hastily cooked and tough on the teeth, I could only swallow it whole. Many other villagers squatted outside, joining in the proceedings and greatly enjoying the occasion.

Speeches were now the order of the day. I was welcomed and, having been reminded about what I had done for them during my time as DRO, was told that the village was mine, to be visited or lived in whenever I wanted to. I felt deeply touched at such a gesture of love and trust—a European Christian so intimately involved in an Asian Hindu ceremony and community. When it was my turn to give tongue, I said so. "As for the freedom of the village, what more could I want?" I concluded.

At that, an old, much decorated warrior called out; "All the mothers want to see your children playing with theirs. What about it?" Tremendous applause, no ripple now, greeted this sally, with gales of laughter from the men and suppressed giggles from the women, mouths covered to hide their smiles. Everybody expected a worthy riposte, piquant yet not overstepping time-honoured social norms. All I could think of was challenging my questioner by asking him why only when I had retired was he bringing up the topic I'd been expecting for so long. If he really meant what he said, "Line up the virgins, here and now, for the divinations to be matched."

If not quite game, set and match, it was enough, satisfying the dictates of the occasion with an overblown reputation for repartee. It also showed that, if home is where you're not turned away at any time of the day or night, I was there.

On my return to Kathmandu I had an interview with the vice-chancellor. He thanked me for my letter and, with a twinkle in his eye, asked me if I ever got his reply. I said that sometimes letters were very slow and quoted as an example one that took forty-four years to reach Kathmandu from Calcutta.

Yes, he did have a job for me, he told me. I felt an inward surge of relief but said nothing while he wrote the magic piece of paper that unlocks so many doors of officialdom. I found that I was to work in the Research Centre for Nepal and Asian Studies, "CNAS" (pronounced "see-nas"), established by the late King Mahendra himself and seen, by some, as the jewel in the crown of Nepalese academe. The interview was friendly and soon over. I expressed my heartfelt thanks.

All official procedures are labyrinthine and I found the Nepalese system particularly so. I was handicapped by not knowing the "chain of command" of a university so being in constant danger of being lost in the maze. From my earliest brushes with Nepalese officialdom I knew how convoluted matters would be and how no junior functionary had been trained to take decisions that could conceivably be construed as being in the province of a superior. I decided that my safest bet was to approach all people and all problems with due respect, chafing nether at slowness nor inefficiency, showing willingness to satisfy the primordial, inevitable and never-ending curiosity about me with a joke and a smile. Any show of temper would generate resentment, so immediately downgrade any standing I had in the eyes of others. By imagining I had "snail's eyes" out on stalks, I probed my way forward, slowly, surely and successfully.

One difficulty was, so I gathered, that no foreigner had ever been asked for by name before and that, even with the king's blessing, paperwork was essential. The registrar forgot to process me for some days, so keeping Buddhiman and me on tenterhooks, but it gave us time to settle into a ground-floor flat in Patan, Kathmandu's sister town. Our living arrangements were basic and I kept our household purchases to the bare minimum. Our flat was the ground floor of a house very close to the zoo, overlooking the deer and the one elephant. Jackals, peacocks and caged tigers, ever unhappy at being permanently confined, made the night hideous with their noise. Yapping curs and cooped up poultry added to the cacophony and broke our sleep.

My first day in CNAS was a bit nerve-wracking; it had been a long time since I was a recruit. I found all my colleagues more than eager to meet "this son of an Englishman," to see how I reacted and to test the extent of my knowledge of Nepali. Gone were the stolid hill men who fill the ranks of the Brigade of Gurkhas whom I knew so well. Gone were the epicanthic eyelids, gone the wispy moustaches, the steady calm gazes and the wonderful smiles. Instead were aquiline noses of the Aryan Nepalis, hirsute faces, many of them bearded, a more quizzical attitude and much harder to get to know well. I had just signed the attendance register when a busload of them was disgorged and, finding escape impossible, was engulfed where I stood. I was bombarded with questions and I managed to give a quick, apposite reply in each case that had all of them intrigued and most of them laughing. Any remaining ice was broken when I answered the question, "What shall we call you?" I remembered the schoolboy retort, "Call me anything you like but don't call me late for dinner." From their mirth I could tell that local wit was not at degree level and that I'd been accepted as a person if not as an academic. One said how young I looked as I had few wrinkles, "no strinkles, no prinkles" as he engagingly put it.

It was forty years since I had matriculated. Apart from handling men, what I had learnt in the army, more than useful in its own sphere, was too far removed from the meridians of Nepalese higher learning to have any bearing on subjects needing research. However, I felt that my recently acquired membership of the Institute of Linguists, backed up both by SOAS and Professor Turner's interest in re-writing his dictionary, would result in just that. But no. Along with that earnest of Nepalese sincerity, a non-tourist visa, I was given a year's contract as an assistant lecturer, as an historian, not a linguist. My research project was "The Nepalese Contribution to the British Army."

I had learnt that academic prowess could be rewarded by the granting of honorary degrees and, with suitable recommendations, certain privileges under the constitution which made living in Nepal the easier. It seemed a pity that I could not work in a subject I was happy in rather than one that had never interested me. I had never thought of myself as an historian.

But a year's contract I had, signed by the head of CNAS. I was to be paid 1,235 rupees a month, at that time some £56, which covered the rent of the flat. I was also allowed leave: 30 days home, 15 days sick, 9 days casual and 3 days for holy festivals. We worked a six-day week but had twenty-five annual public holidays, ranging from celebrating the monarch's birthday to paying regards to eclipses. We also had the day off when the king or any head of state went on, arrived or returned from a state visit.

I was, in fact, delighted to have been accepted at all. Even so, I had remonstrated as to subject matter to be researched. Apart from there being no research material easily available, surely the subject should be the other way round, "The British Army's Contribution to Nepal"? No, the contract meant what it said and, to my surprise, rather than the director of CNAS elucidating his chosen theme, I had to produce a project and defend it at a meeting of the National History Compilation Committee.

This was easier said than done. The material thought to be available from the British embassy did not exist, so causing me concern for a few days. Recalling the planner's maxim "define your aim," I had the brain wave of rewriting the theme, giving it an exactness the original had lacked, as well as knowing where to find material for such a proposal. Accordingly I proposed that I write on the long-winded title; "The Brigade of Gurkhas in the British Army; Operational, Administrative and Personnel Aspects Relating to the British Army and Nepal, 1948 to 1982." I then listed all the relevant details, wrote them out in as simple a way as I could and submitted them for the scrutiny of the historians.

My efforts had a rough passage at the meeting as the committee was under the impression that "British Army Gurkhas" covered service under the East India Company from 1815 until 1858, then under the Viceroy of India until 1947, and in the British Army proper since 1 January 1948. I won my point but had to include potted histories of individual units pre-1947 and details of recruiting, and terms and conditions of service before my proposal was accepted. The one item the committee really wanted from me was the still secret Tripartite Agreement and that was not possible.

My place of work was situated in the main university campus in open, rolling country to the west of Kathmandu. The campus grounds are spacious and extensive, being dominated by the hill feature and village of Kirtipur. Now placid, its villagers suffered badly in the dynastic struggles of the mid-eighteenth century. From my flat it was a pleasant 40-minute walk to work, along a footpath. Scores of folk walked to work from outlying villages into Kathmandu and I was one of the very few who walked against that tide. The way by road, which I took when on my bicycle, was longer and less fun. Both ways, I was the object of great interest and not a little speculation for some weeks.

Work in Nepal starts at 10 o'clock. This practice stems, in part, from the fact that most journeys to work are still made on foot, some from a considerable distance, sometimes as much as two hours away. In part it also stems from the many household and domestic chores, including feeding and watering livestock, that have to be done in the early morning. Most people prefer to eat at home, it being cheaper and more convenient.

Being used to a half past 7 start, I took slowly to the new regime but was grateful for the time when I could work on my own interests, still fresh after an early jog. Punctuality was movable and depended on the seniority of the person concerned. There was a break of thirty minutes during the day, with work stopping at 5 o'clock for nine months of the year and at 4 o'clock in winter. I found it a long day, especially that last hour, even had I not had to do all my own typing, the only method I had of producing my project on paper. Never very good at sitting for long periods, that walk back in the evening was pure joy.

Buddhiman went back to school after thirteen years. Class 5 in his village, he now passed into Class 8, showing how much he had learnt in the meantime. We were joined by his young wife who, shyness personified, had never been away from home before and found life in the city more than strange. I arranged for her to learn how to operate a knitting machine, buying her one when she qualified, and English-style cooking. We had mixed success with such tantalizing dishes as curried potatoes in porridge and cake with cabbage.

People I had managed to help when DRO would come to see me, some even claiming a fictitious relationship that was nothing more than an eye to the main chance. I physically had to push one man out of the house. The son of a regimental friend told me how he held down three government jobs at one time. Two were not far apart in Kathmandu but one was out in Bhaktapur, so he spent his day calling in on each, signing the attendance register, telling his superior that he had work to do elsewhere and disappearing. He contrived to visit all his desks twice a day—and to draw three salaries!

Another particularly unpleasant man threatened Buddhiman with a trumped-up charge to prevent him staying in Kathmandu. "I warn you," this man had said. "I am educated, you are not. I am of the town, you are of the village."

I only heard about that much later and it upset me. Luckily Buddhiman did not need that threat as a spur to studying.

The cultural reasons for such an attitude set me thinking. I had served in the country of a Christian king when a young soldier, a Muslim king in Malaysia, a Buddhist king in Laos and now here I was in a Hindu kingdom. Asians "live" their religion more than is so in the west. Hinduism and Buddhism are the official religions of the kingdom, while Islam, and to a small degree Sikhism, also flourish. Christianity was suppressed in 1768 and proselytizing forbidden.

Mythology and religion are inextricably mixed on the subcontinent. The home of both Hinduism and Buddhism, India's religious influence has long penetrated other parts of Asia, while many ideas alien to both philosophies have been absorbed within its culture. Sadly, however, since the eleventh century when Muslim conquerors started to enslave and convert many Hindus, tensions have often surfaced with fatal and fateful consequences, resulting in many thousands of deaths over nearly a thousand years and the birth of Pakistan in 1947.

A Hindu was originally not a member of any particular religious faith but a member of the society living around the River Indus. Hinduism, with no formal religious hierarchy, has always been essentially static, inward looking and self-centered. Core Hinduism is much more easily understandable by Christians as it did not have any caste system as practiced today. Buddhism, by contrast, was neither tied to local and household deities nor to particular locations, so satisfied the religious instincts and demands of travelers.

The Hindu caste, or colour, system was designed with a political rigidity not unlike the bishop-clergy-laity syndrome that kept the early Christian church intact. Fear of unquantifiable, unknown and assertive elements of a fanciful cosmic world was so strong that basic survival needs could be given a religious, therefore a not-to-be-questioned, authority. Had cattle in those very early days been slaughtered to extinction, where would milk products, ploughers, leather and manure have come from? Similarly, centuries later in the harsh, arid, dusty, hot world where Islam took root, how could rabies and intestinal worms have been controlled had dogs and pigs not been placed under religious discrimination? Even today, certain swathes of forest in Nepal are preserved only by a religiously inspired fear: merely to pick up firewood is to invite divine retribution in the form of hail to flatten the crops. No ugly landslide scars that disfigure so many deforested hills elsewhere mar the areas so protected.

King Prithvi Narayan Shah declared that Nepal was the true "Hindu-stan." The constitution of Nepal declares that the country is the only Hindu state in the world. Some see its royal ruler as semi-divine. After 1950, with the emergence of Nepal from behind tightly closed borders, the need to define distinct national values, from political philosophy to dress and language, was felt because of Nepal's desire to keep aloof from what was seen as Indian political hegemony.

The declaration of a Hindu state in the constitution compelled the policy makers to define these values in relation to Hindu ideals and primarily high-caste Hindu values, all intimately and continuously influenced by the pantheon of

353

countless Hindu gods and goddesses seeing all aspects of man's nature, good and bad, portrayed on a cosmic scale. Time, too, is seen as cosmic or otherwise and only the former is strictly adhered to; normal time is never more than an approximation; take it or leave it. Love and hate, sincerity and treachery, good deeds and sinful action are all aspects of the gods' own behavior, which can uplift man or bedevil him with destructive relentlessness. If the whim of the gods manifests itself adversely and cruelly by an individual not having paid due attention to making all the necessary oblations and sacrifices—however trite and trivial these be—it is the fault of the individual. Placating, warding off wrath and spite, and acting as a god's slave are constants: they whom the gods have made their heirs, the twice-born Brahmans, view those below them as the gods view mankind—an attitude that feeds on people's bigotry, superstition and callousness.

There is continuous tension between all aspects of malevolence and benevolence. Never really knowing which side of the coin may be revealed and with an eye to the main chance, toadying, flattery, fawning and a subservient approach to one's seniors ward off calamities more effectively than do accountability and a moral imperative. This is still found in the ancient and time-honoured system of *chakri*, which a dictionary will only define as a vapid and shallow translation of "service," "domestic service," "duty" or "attendance." Sure, but much more also: it is calculated acts of servitude, generally menial, designed to reward the doer with worldly advantage.

It is still practiced. One of the office runners at CNAS was a case in point. Every Saturday for six months he went to the house of the man senior enough to give him a job. There he worked in the garden for no pay. Finally he was rewarded by being given a place on the staff of CNAS.

A corollary to *chakri* is the "crab culture." A crab will see another crab climbing up a bank and will fasten itself on to a limb, thus preventing the climber from going any higher. If an advantage can be accrued by stopping another's enhancement, it will be taken with, best of all, the stopper making use of what the stopped might have made use of. This is not seen as unfair, nor do personal relationships normally enter into the equation.

Two basic and fundamental differences of belief in, perception of and relationships between Hinduism and Christianity shape, colour and influence to a lesser or greater degree all the thoughts and actions of believers of both faiths, consciously or otherwise, throughout their lives. In essence, Brahmans will say "I am god" whereas Christians will say "I and God": for the former it matters who you are, not what you do; for the latter it matters what you do, not who you are. All other religious and cultural differences stem from these two. A Hindu's religion is influenced by two facets: *karma*, the position into which one is born, the points one has to score for the next world and any aspects of a past life that have to be paid for in this incarnation; *dharma*, acts, functions and observances that have to be followed to ensure enhancement. My own definition of religion, especially under such circumstances, is "behavior focused on salvation."

On the surface the many similarities, not diversities, between Brahmans and those from amongst humbler Hindus may mask degrees of emphasis rather than basic differences. Brahmans find it difficult to come to a decision and abhor confrontational situations. This leads to grey areas of accommodations rather than the black and white of absolutes, discourages any sense of accountability, public conscience, ethical censorship and, outside one's family, normal moral imperatives, so causing a straightforward and simple matter to become convoluted in the extreme. This affects standards of comparable probity to the extent that undue intransigence, lying and false witness are apt to be a defence against hostile consequences of too hasty a resolution of a problem. This is the approach used by functionaries, including the police, who thereby put themselves above the law as we, not they, see it. Conscience is not inconvenienced. A Brahman's religious views and priorities affect his conception both of the civil administration and of politics, so all three are apt to become entwined. The sadness of the Brahmans is that they can believe no truth that does not paint the world in their colours—nor, for that matter, can Christian missionaries.

A parallel in the Western world would be looked on as unsavory political opportunism. However, as far as a Nepali is concerned, unless there is a signed and authenticated piece of paper as proof, does a person say what he means and mean what he says? Probably not: it is not prudent always to be stark in speech and much, in Nepal, is said by leaving so much unsaid, with hint, inference and gesture carrying much weight.

The Hindu "code of ethics" is based on the Laws of Manu, reputedly the eldest of the twelve sons of Brahma. These lay down that those born within the Himalayan region, our

Gurkhas, are of the lowest caste whose touch does not pollute water. So it is that, however good such a person is, he is proscribed by his low status from full fruits of any intrinsic worth. No wonder there is continuous stress. Rabindranath Tagore puts this from a Brahman's point of view: *Hindu India had originally accepted the bonds of her social system in order to transcend society, as the rider puts reins on his horse and stirrups on his own feet in order to ensure greater speed towards his goal.* Fine, except when the non-Brahman Gurkha is the horse with stirrups digging into him. There has yet to be a Hindu Calvin or Luther.

Also laid down are the Brahman's four basic "rights" in life: religion, worldly goods, sex and salvation, in that order. All need to be satisfied. In brief: religion is the strict retention of the caste system; what the Western world looks at as bribery, sticky fingers or financial improbity come under the heading of worldly goods; sex covers not loose morals but rather full enjoyment of a male-dominated society; and fourthly, no matter how much human laws have been transgressed on earth, salvation for onward and upward progression is assured. Fatalism, induced and imbued by centuries of a rigid society riveted to unfathomable whims, is unbelievably strong. The high caste man who threatened Buddhiman looked down on him culturally and objected to the opportunities now open to him.

The power that the gods have over any person's life is "written" on the inside of the forehead. That, not the person, is responsible for success or failure. This should induce modesty for the former and does induce an attitude of non-

357

responsibility for the latter. Most of what I have put here I only learnt after I joined CNAS. No wonder I had not understood so much during my earlier times in Nepal.

I had shown my project to the British ambassador, John Denson, when it was still in draft. We got on well together and I felt free to ask him his advice on such matters as British government policy as it affected the armed forces and the South Atlantic crisis as viewed from his Kathmandu vantage point. He read it and warmly congratulated me on what I had achieved. I was so pleased that I very foolishly started counting my long-term chickens, imagining the award of honorary degrees and complimentary diplomas.

Eight months after I began work on my history I handed it in. Four hundred and twenty-eight pages long, I had typed all five copies myself and made many maps. It was a great relief to have finished it. I waited to be called in by the director of CNAS to discuss it. Nothing ensued and, after a few weeks, I had the feeling that a one-handed clap would have made a bigger impact. When we did meet it was a perfunctory affair. I was told that finding assessors would be a problem and, until that was arranged, I could work on anything private so long as I signed in every morning. I decided to write about the year I spent with the Malaysian aborigines and the one after it when I was commandant of the Border Scouts in Borneo during Confrontation.

My eyes reminded me why I was trying so hard to be allowed to live with Buddhiman. I developed grit under the eyelids which, on one occasion, refused to open. I could not wear contact lenses. Petrol and diesel fumes made vehicular travel purgatory and riding a bicycle in tunnel-vision spectacles was out of the question. My 40-minute walks twice a day now took twice as long as formerly and a banking problem resulted in my having to wait forty-seven days to cash a cheque for my pension in one branch bank. I had to write an application to the manager of the head bank to correct an error in my account number. I wrote it in Nepali, gave it to the messenger and waited. When the man returned he told me that the manager had refused to accept my request "because foreigners don't know how to write in Nepali." I felt that I could not move on to the next square until I threw a "double six." I was taken to the manager who quizzed me. He seemed surprised that I spoke Nepal when I explained my circumstances. He grinned and signed my application.

For the week it took to sort this out I would walk to CNAS, sign in, walk the three miles to the first bank, argue the toss there, go on the two miles to the second bank and then, by the time I had walked the three miles back to the flat, it would be late afternoon. Handicapped by wearing thick tunnel-vision spectacles, it was very tiring and slow.

By now I was part of the scene on my daily walks to and from Kirtipur. Small children, maybe as many as two dozen a journey, barred my way until I had made their heads squeak, wobbled my knees, put my finger up my nose or taken one of my eyes out. These acts were loved—anything for a laugh. I also made friends with several dogs which I fed. My walk was taking me longer and longer, even when the eyes were not troubling me.

One evening, as I was slowly making my way back after a difficult day at CNAS, I was stopped on the path by a man with his small daughter. We chatted for a few moments when the man, looking left and right, said; "You went to the [name given] hotel for a drink once, didn't you?" I thought back, several years, when I had gone into the bar of that hotel and, waiting for a friend, had ordered a soft drink. "Yes." "You told me the following jokes ... " he added, as I marveled at his memory. He looked around to see who was in earshot then, *sotto voce*, "I am not only a barman, I am a police informer. I am one of those who watch over foreigners."

Before I could give any suitable reply, he continued; "Don't worry! We all know you and like the way you play with the children. Bad men don't do that. We regard you as one of us." I felt elated at that little incident, morale rising because of it. However, it was Buddhiman's love and concern that really kept me going.

I learnt that the Densons were leaving sometime in September 1983 and early on the 12th (that magic 2 again!) I rang him to ask when I could come and say farewell. We met at noon; he told me his final audience with the king had been postponed at short notice the day before and he was standing by to go to the palace that day. Would I like him to mention my case to His Majesty? Would I!

Soon afterwards I was rewarded with a letter from Mr. Denson stating that he had indeed mentioned my sight and my work to the king who had turned to his Principal Private Secretary (PPS), Narayan Prasad Shrestha, and told him to make a note of my case. This the PPS did. The ambassador had also spoken to the Head of Protocol, the Foreign Minister, an old acquaintance of mine, and the Vice-Chancellor on the same subject during his final talk with them. It was very kind of him.

Stupidly I sat back and waited for something to happen. Nothing did. It was then time for the two-week Dashera holiday. Buddhiman sent his wife back to the village a few days before we locked the front door and went for a 190-mile walk through the mountains, visiting friends. We collected Bhim Kumari from the village and went to Pokhara. Buoyed by my name having been noted, we searched for and found a plot of land, almost an acre in size and, after much discussion, decided to buy it. Lying to the south of the town, in a quiet area, it was large enough for Buddhiman to sustain a cottage industry—we thought of bees and honey, mulberry and silk worms or poultry—to keep him busy at home. If the gift of staying permanently were bestowed it would become my base. In any case, if the original dire predictions about my eyes—the unthinkable—occurred Buddhiman would be on hand most of the time. The house we built there would be in his social and ethnic area, while being the centre of my circle of friends. If the king did not authorize my permanent stay in Nepal, I as a tourist for three months every year would use it as my second home. We bought the land for £12,500, a good buy as it was worth over seven times that when we finished building on it in 1985.

Back in Kathmandu I realized that the initiative for residence had to be taken by me, writing a petition to the Head of State. I had never had to do that before so I sat down and concentrated hard, not so much on what to say but how to say it. I started off: "Your Majesty, I most humbly submit this petition to Your Majesty for Your Majesty's kind and compassionate consideration. I am requesting I be granted Permanent Residential Status in Nepal..." I went on to say why I was submitting a petition direct to the throne rather than applying for citizenship, the period for which was eighteen years on a non-tourist visa. It was two pages long and it took many drafts to get it to a standard that was neither groveling nor presumptuous. It was not easy.

I fixed a meeting with the Head of Protocol to ask him to vet my draft and took it round to his office in the Foreign Ministry. I felt I ought to do it in style, so put on my university "uniform," a chocolate-coloured coat over jodhpurs and a long-tailed shirt tied on one side by ribbons and worn outside, but I was not allowed into the ministry grounds by the man at the entrance. I told him that I had an appointment but to no avail. "If you telephone for permission, you can get in, otherwise you cannot."

Politely I asked him to let me use his telephone for confirmation of my appointment and should not have been surprised to learn that there was no telephone there. I fished out a copy of my CNAS contract, which I always carried with me for occasions like this and, glowering at him, flashed it under his nose, thereby impressing him so much that I got in without having to subsidies his wage packet.

After a bit more hassle I did meet the Head of Protocol, a charming, courteous elderly gentleman, who was inundated with details of the king's impending visit to the USA. He only needed to correct the salutation and ending and I was told to hand the revised version to the office outside the palace gates.

I re-typed the petition, fingers trembling with suppressed anxiety—it was the irrevocability of my action that caused it—and had it ready by the following Tuesday. Was it coincidence that I handed it into the office at the palace gate at two minutes past two on the 22nd of November, with all three traffic lights I passed shining green?

One day two members of the Soviet Academy of Sciences arrived for a talk programme in CNAS. It appeared that five hundred experts were working on various but related aspects of the Indian subcontinent, three hundred of them in Moscow, the rest in India. However, a handful had learnt Nepali and were, even then, preparing a history of Nepal from a communist viewpoint, finding out who had suffered under government repression and compiling a list of such people. "When the next revolution comes," intoned the lecturer in heavy English, "we want to ensure it is left-wing and not right-wing." I, the only foreigner and sitting at the back, saw the forty or so Nepalis in the audience sit up as though an electric current had struck them in a very sensitive place. The lecturer was, I saw, embarrassed by the thrill of expectancy that reverberated around the room and tried to play down his remarks. "I don't say that there will be a revolution ... " he began lamely, but the damage had been done.

The cloud I had seen over the years was now covering the whole Nepalese sky and had a momentum of its very own. Its centre was over Kathmandu.

While I was finishing off my own story there was a change of director in CNAS; Kumar Kharga Bikram Shah, a brother-in-law of the king, took over. The announcement of such an august personality as director had an electrifying effect on the staff and, on the first day of his tenure, there were more of CNAS's researchers to meet him than I knew existed. I viewed his arrival with mixed feelings. His links to the very top would put me in the shop window when recommendations regarding my work came to be made in any final analysis.

I soon learnt that the new director was a man who was more decisive and energetic than his predecessor, and that meant that I could expect action where before there had been drift. On our first meeting he told me to make sure my history was quickly processed and to prepare a proposal to update Professor Turner's dictionary. (The Great Man had died on 22 April 1983.) I made out a seven-year proposal and submitted it. My quest for assessors was unsuccessful.

I do not know who vetted the two stalwarts who were eventually found, eight months after submitting my work. One was a geographer who had a marked bias against the Brigade of Gurkhas and a degree from the University of Auburn in Alabama about American history; the other, only slightly less virulent, had a degree from an Indian university on demography. Taken in isolation, neither seemed suitable for assessing my project, eight long months after I had so expectantly handed it in. I was completely taken aback when it was adjudged as being without value and in no way suitable for the university. As I read the report a small, cold worm turned in my stomach.

A meeting was called. There were four others; the present and past directors and the two assessors. I was told to state my case and say why I had produced what I had in such a form as to merit condemnation. I explained, clearly and succinctly, that I had not only done exactly what the National History Compilation Committee had approved and in the form I had outlined but also that I had made three-monthly reports to the ex-director, who stayed silent in toad-like immobility from start to finish. I ended with a saying often used by Gurkha soldiers when blame is unfairly laid: "As every soldier knows, the only hard thing to do is to obey orders correctly." While taking the tension out of the meeting, the future of the history was in no way resolved. I fumed inside when I found out that the worthies on the committee charged with the compilation of the nation's history did not have it in their gift to authorize such a subject.

A couple of days later, still smarting from the way I had been treated, it was the turn of my dictionary proposal to be put under scrutiny pending its approval or rejection. I had every hope that no snag would crop up. Hadn't both chancellor and vice-chancellor of the Royal Nepal Academy sent their congratulations when they heard about it, as well as had a significant number of scholars? So I was not prepared when he who headed the handling of proposals came into my room and calmly told me that my proposal was not to be sanctioned as he was unwilling to waste Nepali tax payers' money on it or me. I did not answer immediately: the choice between honour and survival is not an easy one and, anyway, I was counting up to ten before replying. I was particularly incensed at the remark about tax payers' money as the person making it had spent three years in Britain on a British Council scholarship and claimed to have been converted to communism when studying in Edinburgh.

By then my "snail's eyes" were fully extended. My natural inclinations had to be kept firmly in check. I said as little as necessary and, after he had left, sat back in thought. It was plain that politics rather than scholarship or personalities was involved. I had already learnt that the politics of my two assessors differed from my own views. I had noticed how they favorably reacted when Russian scholars came to give us the benefit of their wisdom and unfavorably when the Americans came to give of theirs. I concluded that, even though there was an element of "crab culture" in their thinking, they were probably closet "Rouble Bahadurs," so wasn't I an obvious target?

The director sent for me and told me that my proposal had indeed been turned down. I asked him why and was given three reasons, all of which had been foreseen, in writing and attached to the proposal, by the late Professor Turner, who had said that they really did not matter. After I had invited the director's attention to them there was an uneasy silence. I was not giving up without a struggle.

"So what do I do now, Sir?" I asked. It seemed that I could well have no further part to play in CNAS, at which I said, with a rare show of indignation; "I have come to Nepal on two counts. I was invited by the vice-chancellor to work here, to give what I could for the enhancement of Nepalese learning. His Majesty has seen fit to confirm this. I have also come here as I have an eye problem. Without the one, the other is nothing. You might just as well kill me here and now and throw my corpse out of the window." And slap my wrist, I added to myself.

The number two of CNAS, sitting to one side and silent till then, now spoke up; "Go away and think out a new proposal. Come back with your answer tomorrow. There may just be time to process it."

"You expect me to think up a major proposal overnight?" I demanded, feeling like a recalcitrant Private soldier in the Company Commander's office being given a second chance to go on a sanitary duties course. I swallowed my anger, took a grip of myself and politely took my leave. Anger, let off its leash, is dangerous as it makes its owner's self-control vulnerable and puts self-respect in jeopardy.

My walk home was with heavy heart and I was very near despair. There are more subtle versions of dishonesty, cruelty and perversity than those so brashly manifested by children but they are just as hard to counter. A low standard of work was one thing but prostitution of scholarship by politically orientated opportunists was another. It was not even a case of what the sergeant major said to the new recruit; "You should not have joined if you haven't got a sense of humour."

Buddhiman let me in and saw the look on my face. "What's wrong, Father, what's wrong?" he asked with concern.

We went into my room and sat down. Over a cup of tea I said, "Son, tonight you and I must pray hard to as many of our respective gods as possible. I am in trouble. Listen ... " and I told him all.

Pray we both did and, during the night, I awoke with an inspiration: why not compare the Nepali of Turner's time, using his dictionary, with modern Nepali, using a Nepali-Nepali dictionary that had just been produced by the Royal Nepal Academy? I turned over and fell into a dreamless sleep.

Back next morning in CNAS I approached the main characters in this little drama with my idea and it was immediately accepted in principle. I worked on it in detail in my room (which had a view of one hundred miles of the Himalayas), during which time five colleagues came to see me, one by one. They all said how upset they were at such treatment. I was not to take it as any personal failure on my part but the chemistry of my antagonists made them bitter and scheming. Nepalis in the universities as far off as Allahabad and Poona also heard about both times I was thwarted.

Unknown to me, three other members of CNAS went to the director and said that I had to stay as long as they were working there. After some discussion, it was decided that I be asked to consider myself the "appointed adviser to the International Affairs Section [of CNAS] to assist it in assessing the military and intelligence aspects of the strategic balance of power between the Soviet Union and the People's Republic of China in east, south and south-east Asia."

I accepted. I felt sure I could find my way around any snag this unexpected bonus might produce and that I had emerged unscathed after a very tense week.

9: 1984-1986

By 22 November 1984, despite asking about my petition, I had heard nothing. During the Dashera holiday in the October, on the way to Buddhiman's village, something had burst in my right eye while I was climbing a steep slope in strong sunlight. I was badly frightened. I decided that I had to find out what was happening. My linguistic project was ahead of schedule and clearly of interest. The director was happy with my work—no trouble on that score. The only person who could tell me what was happening was the king's PPS. I could either go and see him before work, at home, or write him a letter and give it in at the palace office. I did not like the idea of dropping in unannounced, a common Nepalese habit, so I wrote to him, explaining my problem, hoping that such a move did not offend any code of conduct of which I was still unaware. My "snail's eyes" could not probe so far into the unknown. Dated 29 November 1984, this is what I wrote:

It is a year ago that I submitted a petition, for permanent residential status in Nepal, through your office, for favor of placing before His Majesty. I am heartened to believe that His Majesty knows about me already in that royal permission has been granted to let me work in Tribhuvan University as a Nepali; a rare, if not unique honour, and one of which I am deeply sensible.

The reasons for this, possibly unusual, request were rehearsed in the petition I gave in to a member of your staff on

22 November 1983, having first learnt that His Excellency, the British Ambassador, during his final audience with His Majesty on 22 September 1983, had made mention of my name, with His Majesty instructing you to make a note thereof and, subsequently, I myself asked the Head of Protocol, Mr. B.P. Rimal, on 17 November 1983, to check that the draft of what I intended to request to be placed before His Majesty was, in fact, in accordance with the required style and practice.

After ringing your office a number of times to enquire about the progress of my petition I was asked to submit a further copy; this I did on 2 March 1984 and for which I hold a receipt.

The aim of this letter is to try and ascertain when my petition will be placed before His Majesty for His Majesty's consideration and decision. The main, and pressing, reason for my wanting a decision (one way or the other) is that, on 4 October 1984, a blood vessel in one of my eyes burst, thus reminding me how near to blindness I am, and that I could arrange my residence in Nepal—were His Majesty's decision to be favorable—before indeed I did go blind. A further reason for asking you about my case is that I am being pressed for a decision, in England, for the disposal or retention of property there and I feel I cannot give this until I have clearer ideas of my future.

I do not want to be a nuisance or an imposition to anyone and I fully realize that the pressing nature of state business precludes such a request as mine from being given any priority whatsoever. Nevertheless, were my own circumstances not as threatening as they are, I would never have written to you to ask you, humbly, sincerely and urgently, to let me know how this matter stands, for my own peace of mind, to say nothing of the planning that I have to do whichever way His Majesty's decision is made.

If you were to wish to question me on any aspect of this I am ready to meet you at any time you mention, be it at your office or your residence.

I hoped that I had achieved the correct tone in the letter. Nepal did not owe me a living but, even so, as the Nepalis had let me into their midst thus far, in a comparatively short time, I had no doubt as to their sincerity. However, personal wishes and official channels are not easily reconciled. I felt that, provided whatever I wrote and said was motivated by and combined with "face" and respect, a similar cordial reaction would be forthcoming.

Westerners use a direct approach to matters. This is seen in confrontation politics and by such phrases as the common and unthinkingly uttered "you know" with which the speaker tries to involve the listener more, maybe, than the listener wants to be involved. Such an approach is anathema to most Nepalis; indeed, it is seen as the height of bad manners in Nepalese society to show impatience at an out-stayed welcome or to appear to be busy, even when hard pressed. So, when one of my friends at CNAS asked me what I had done to try and resolve my query, I told him. He said that I should use the Nepalese approach and go and see the PPS at his house before he went to work. I told him that I would only use such a method if invited or taken by a mutual friend. I also felt that not to wait until the letter had been processed would show a degree of impatience that would not be welcome.

The professor who worked in the next room but one from mine was a very old friend of the PPS. He was a personable, much-travelled and well-read man, and was on friendly terms with me. We would always greet each other and spend a few minutes chatting. I was told that he was my obvious conduit for personal contact. Worth a try, I thought.

I chose my time carefully and was on the point of broaching the topic when two others, trawling the rooms for gossip, joined us. It was pointless waiting till they went—I had not an hour to spare—so I told all three my problem and asked the professor if he would help me. To my delight, the other two thought that a good idea and said so. The reaction was sympathetic but vague and, seeds of my request sown, I went back to my room.

Instead of greeting me jovially during the next two weeks, the professor turned his head away and passed by silently. Then, on a Friday morning, he entered my room. With unusual directness he came to the point and, not without embarrassment, said; "I'm afraid I can't help you. Although the PPS lives only three minutes' walk away, I can't go across to his house before work starts as the many people who congregate there in the hope of favors will all wonder what I'm on the scrounge for and that would go against me. If I were to ring him with only your request for an introduction and interview, it would not help me and would get you nowhere."

He glanced out of the window, grim-faced, then turned back to me. I held his gaze and said; "Thank you for letting me know why you can't help me. I understand your position." So that was that.

Buddhiman was most upset at the turn of events but there was little either of us could do except cluck our tongues. Next day, being our weekly day off, we went for our usual walk. We were in hilly paddy-field country. Inevitably we started talking about the future; the unsatisfactory position of knowing nothing whatsoever about how my petition was faring, nor how long the recently delivered letter would take to percolate—another year? I knew cases of people who were in their seventh year of waiting to hear about their application for citizenship and in no way could I wait for anything like that long for an answer. Buddhiman reckoned that I ought to give it another two weeks before making any final decision to keep on with my quest to stay in Nepal or to withdraw gracefully.

Our attention was caught by a fight between a large bird of prey, a black kite, and a python on the far side of the valley. The snake was probably sunning itself when it was spotted. I could just make out a shiny, writhing ripple under the bobbing bird. Claw and beak were too strong for the snake, which took a long time dying. No matter who or what, the struggle for survival is a constant.

So it was back to work on the morrow, with a 14-day countdown. As usual I was early and was surprised when the professor also got in before time. He came into my room and sat down opposite me.

"Colonel sahib," he began. "I have met the PPS and had a long talk with him about you. He says that he is angry with you."

Oh Lord! Surely my reminder had been tactfully worded? I'd spent enough time on it.

"He is angry with you," continued the professor before I had time for more introspection, "because he wants to help you but cannot as what you have asked for does not exist. He has told me to tell you to ring him at his house at 10 o'clock tomorrow."

I did not ask the professor how or why he had had a change of heart. I was only too glad to think I was taking a definite step forward in my quest, whatever the end result. All that day I was haunted by the words "angry with you," "wants to help you," "what you have asked for does not exist." Buddhiman's reaction was as surprised as was mine. We both could only hope for the best. Those phrases were still ringing in my head when I dropped off to sleep that night.

On 4 December 1984 (was I stretching the omens by seeing 4 as 2x2?) I went to see the PPS at his house, as fixed by my telephone call. A short, friendly man with an air of authority, he met me in the garden and led me to a couple of chairs. Once seated, he told me his difficulty was that what I had asked the king for did not exist and, therefore, my petition could not be laid before him. Unexpectedly and very sweetly, he turned to me and asked; "What do you suggest?"

"Honorary citizenship," I answered in a flash and, even as the words were coming out of my mouth, I knew that I had none of the necessary qualifications for such a status. However, the PPS was less worried than I and said that he would add a recommendation on humanitarian grounds. I was told to submit a new petition.

The PPS also gave me his office telephone number, telling me to ring him in three months to see what was happening. I thanked him sincerely for giving me so much attention and went on to the university for a normal day's work.

By 8 December I had written my second petition and, together with a covering letter to the PPS, deposited them in a large envelope at the office by the palace gate. By then the functionaries knew me well enough to make the getting of a receipt easy, although they all gathered round, ready for their ration of laughter. I had been advised that, in this petition, I needed to spell out in greater detail that which I had contributed to Nepal as well as that which I wanted than in the one I had originally submitted, which had never got as far as the king. Accordingly I wrote this to His Majesty:

I most humbly submit this petition to Your Majesty for Your Majesty's kind and compassionate consideration: quite simply I am supplicating Your Majesty to allow me to spend the rest of my days in Your Majesty's kingdom. Briefly the reasons why I am asking that this petition be placed before Your Majesty are twofold:

First, having spent forty years with Your Majesty's subjects, thirty-eight of them in the Brigade of Gurkhas, I have developed an enduring affection and a profound admiration for Your Majesty's kingdom and Your Majesty's subjects. I have gained much from knowing the Nepalese as well as I do; in wisdom and understanding, in good nature and tolerance, in fortitude and pertinacity. Over the years I have tried to express my deep love for Your Majesty's subjects in deeds as well as in words. I have given at least [figures given] from my own pocket to alleviate distress—and I have been told that Radio Nepal has broadcast this fact twice, albeit at a higher figure. Furthermore, I have already obligated a significant proportion of my final estate in my will especially for those with no parents or a mother only, to be administered through the British Army's pension-paying organization. Additionally, I believe that, among Your Majesty's subjects who are serving in or who have served in the British Army, I am probably the best known British officer, serving or retired, and, during my five and a half years as the Deputy Recruiting Officer (West), I was able to play a not insignificant role in lowering tensions that existed, to give but one example; during the move of the camp at Paklihawa and the subsequent establishment of the present camp in Pokhara, to say nothing of advice I gave to Your Majesty's subjects, both from the east and west of Your Majesty's kingdom, in adjusting themselves peaceably, properly and purposefully, as they came back on pension.

When His Royal Highness, The Prince of Wales, visited Pokhara on 12 December 1980, he personally told me that he would find me employment after I left the army but, before I could pursue that unprecedented offer, I was invited by the Vice-Chancellor of Tribhuvan University to serve on his staff and the realization that I could continue to work with and for Your Majesty's subjects transcended even that which had been offered me by my own Prince. As Your Majesty may recall,

Your Majesty has allowed me to become a fully-fledged member of the university in the Centre for Nepal and Asian Studies, working on Nepalese terms of service and pay, and I am given to understand that, in the twenty-five years of university life, I am the first foreigner to be asked for by name on such terms. I regard this as an exceptional and signal honour and I am wholly sensible to the amount of trust shown by Your Majesty and Your Majesty's advisers for this unique privilege to have been sanctioned. I am bilingual in Nepali and have an Honours degree therein. The late Professor Turner made me his successor to update his famous dictionary and the Department of Indology of the School of Oriental and African Studies in London regards me as their "link" man between London and Kathmandu as regards the Nepali language. I am currently engaged on a 2-year project in comparing the Nepali of fifty years ago with modern Nepali. I have also been appointed as adviser to the International Affairs Section of the Centre due to my considerable experience of many parts of Asia.

The second reason for my petition to Your Majesty is because I need physical help. Between 1978 and 1981 I went blind. For the last fifteen months in this condition I had to be guided wherever I went. Even though I had the utmost difficulty in completing my routine tasks, I still managed to cover about 1,500 miles on foot, liaising with Your Majesty's officials in thirty districts. My guide was a Nepalese orphan, one Buddhiman Gurung, of Thuloswara, Lamjung, who looked after me as a son would his father. Indeed, I had already "adopted" him to the extent that he need never suffer the privations and poverty that had driven him hungry from home by paying for sufficient land to maintain a family of four. Sixty years old and a bachelor, I regard Buddhiman as a father would his son and he is a major beneficiary in my will.

Even after the successful removal of the damaged lens in both my eyes, without contact lens or spectacles I have to be guided everywhere I go. Indeed, except locally by day, I never dare venture out alone. Nor is this all: I have been warned by expert medical advice that, if I am hit on the head, there is a strong possibility that both retinas will become detached and I will be permanently and completely blind for the rest of my life. If this were to happen, the only person in the whole world whom I know would look after me with love and care is my "son" Buddhiman Gurung. Rather than spend my years of blindness in an impersonal institution in England, I am petitioning Your Majesty to allow me to be looked after, with peace of mind, by Buddhiman Gurung and his wife, in the midst of friends, in the land I love, namely Your Majesty's kingdom. Last September I suffered a rupture in one eye, thus all too grimly reminding me how near to blindness I am, so adding urgency to my plea.

I am not petitioning Your Majesty for the privilege of full Nepalese citizenship because, by the laws of Your Majesty's kingdom, insufficient time has elapsed for this to be allowed and I dread having to wait the full period before applying for this status. I had hoped that, academically, I might be drawn to Your Majesty's attention as being considered sufficiently distinguished for the constitution to allow me to be gauged as worthy of being a citizen in Your Majesty's kingdom. But time is also against that course of action, so I am petitioning Your

Majesty graciously to consider, on humanitarian grounds, that I be granted Honorary Citizenship. My especial problem is that, if I do not retain my British passport, I will not be able to return to Britain for treatment at the very earliest opportunity were anything to go drastically wrong with my eyes, as might happen at any time, thereby making the unthinkable even more likely than otherwise. If Your Majesty were to grant me this most rare and exceptional privilege, I would be able to settle my affairs while I still have my sight. In England all I have is an 86-year old mother so, in this respect also, time is not on my side to settle my affairs expeditiously.

Were Your Majesty to look favorably on my petition then, with my home in Nepal, I would have a sanctuary for the rest of my days and there could be none happier nor more loyal than I.

I most humbly and sincerely hope and pray that Your Majesty will look sympathetically on this petition.

Your Majesty's most humble servant.

and signed it. I checked it three times against any spelling mistakes!

What I wrote may not have been "deathless prose" but it most certainly came from the heart, unbearably stilted and ponderous though the style was. There was nothing that I wanted more than a firm decision on which to plan the rest of my life. After more than six years of uncertainty was this to lead to a final answer? I translated what I had written to Buddhiman. He was awed by his name being mentioned to the monarch and queried the amount of detail I had included. I did not like putting so much about myself but, as I discovered later, it was the correct approach to have adopted.

By now Buddhiman was studying in an English language medium school that started at 6 o'clock in the morning. This meant a 5 o'clock rise for us all. Financially we found that the three of us, including guests, could live off £200 a month, all in.

Apart from a few outside distractions, such as presenting a paper to the Linguistic Society of Nepal and writing a formidable-sounding article in my "adviser" role ("China's Strategic Process: Considerations for Policy and Strategy in South Asia"), I worked hard at my comparative study of Nepali. It was a wearisome and painstaking task, demanding continuous concentration. Every time I was interrupted I found that I made a mistake. My Nepali colleagues learnt that I was not available for their daily dose of gossip. I arrived early, was at work when the others arrived and was at my desk all day without pause. I used a bookshelf as a standing desk to relieve tired limbs and earned myself an undeserved reputation not so much for hard work as for great academic talent.

The process I adopted meant that I had to work through every entry of Turner's Nepali-English dictionary three times. At the end of it, I felt like that Scottish lady of legend who had done precisely the same with an English language dictionary, apparently thinking it was a novel. She said that she found "the plot verra interesting but a wee bit concentrated." I expect the story of the same lady and her reading through a telephone directory is similarly libelous, with her still finding it "verra interesting" but that there were "too many characters in the plot." Some of the entries I had to unravel were abstruse, others banal. I had already learnt that *jangal*, rather than meaning "jungle," originally meant "a place bereft of trees," but I found myself frankly ignorant on ganglions affected by yoga, invisible rings round the navel and which lunar mansions are auspicious. Words of Sanskrit origin, modified for Nepali, were almost beyond redemption. How was I to choose between "raven," "snake," "boar," "potter" and "hell" for the one correct meaning, or between "colour," "redness," "love," "joy," "anger," "song" and "musical harmony" for another? Or between "white," "black" and "the third fold of skin of an elephant's left buttock"? Not that all entries to be dealt with were so complex and perplexing. Despite learning something new every day (which I remember senior army officers saying is a "good thing"), I did wonder what use would be made of all my efforts. My findings could well end up like the British Army's definition of a hovercraft—"a solution looking for a problem."

Eight months after my history had been condemned one of the assessors came into my room. I had shown him a condensed version of what I had written that was an introduction to a photographic book, *Gurkhas*, with a foreword written by HRH The Prince of Wales. I had also shown him the dust jacket of *In Gurkha Company*, an abridged version of my history project published in England. In both cases I said that others had not found what I had written was valueless. Now he sat down opposite me and sighed audibly. He said that his heart was troubled and I agreed with him, saying that, at times, a heart could indeed be troublesome. I waited for him to come to the point. He did.

"My heart is heavy, Colonel sahib, because I would not have written what I did about the history project if I had understood what it was all about."

I stared at him for a long moment. Silence was the best and safest answer.

The other assessor also came into my room that week and asked if he could borrow a copy of the failed project. I fished it out and gave it to him, telling him to be sure to return it. This he did a few days later and I asked him what he thought of it. "Excellent, excellent. The best book on Gurkhas I have yet read." A pause, then, "It is excellent as a reference book."

I held his gaze and, mustering what dignity I could, coldly told him that the brief given to me by the National History Compilation Committee had been precisely that.

Sunday, the first working day of the Nepalese week, starts this cloud-laden monsoon morning as on any other—cocks crowing from 4 o'clock, dogs barking and, in the zoo, the tigers roaring their sad threnody of caged despair. By 5 o'clock it is fully light and the valley wakes up.

The valley is ringed by hills that stand some 3,000 feet higher at around the 7,500-foot mark. Nestling in their lee are villages where people who have migrated from the Hills live, all of whom have long since forgotten their tribal languages. They live as elsewhere in Nepal, houses separate from one another and surrounded by patches of cultivation chiefly, at this time of year, rice. Below them, on the flat ground, are villages peopled by the original valley dwellers, the Newars, and later arrivals, Chhetris and Bahuns, of a completely different character being heavily concentrated, with narrow, angled streets, and houses of three stories, all joined together. Hindu idols and shrines are fitted into odd corners, daubed and dabbed saffron and red in respect of their holiness, and are also imprinted on some of the paving stones with which the streets are built. There will be a main temple in a small durbar square and a slabbed-stone tank of filthy water. Standpipes are now a feature of these villages and, at the end of the monsoon, there is no shortage of water like there was for the period leading up to the arrival of the rains. At these standpipes the women bring their copper vessels and queue for their turn to fill them with good water to cook the morning meal so that the man of the house can go to work, and the children to school, having fed. Later on in the day, if the sun comes out, the dry-dugged gammers will wash as there was too much of a scrimmage on the previous day, the one day off in the week, the Saturday, when the men who go to work during the week had time off for their ablutions.

These villages are mute witness to the violent history of the valley: compact and secure, housing more than a thousand able-bodied men, they are built on ground overlooking the fields, strongly built against enemies fighting dynastic wars or just looking for plunder. Their angled streets would prevent an easy rush through and would be useful for blocking purposes or mounting counter-attacks. They also have the great advantage of leaving maximum space for cultivation. Now the scene is one of a large green sea of growing paddy with villages on the higher ground standing sentinel. However, as land prices soar beyond belief, plots near feeder and main roads are being sold for building, thus eroding the old pattern.

Nearer in is the Ring Road, built in the 1970s by the Chinese. This neatly encircles the two towns of Kathmandu and Patan, divided by that very holy river, the Bagmati. Two generations ago the townsfolk would drink the river water but nowadays this is impossible due to heavy pollution.

The low cloud, with its patches of drizzle, has lifted slightly by 6 o'clock. On the side roads and in the gulleys it is muddily splashy. Small children and dogs start on their daily routine of recycling nature. On the Ring Road a few early morning travelers, dressed in some sort of raincoat or with the almost universal umbrella, go about their business: a relief for an overnight watchman; votive offerings of flowers being taken to a shrine; a couple of grave-faced, shaven-pated Buddhist monks robed in maroon and amber, in earnest discussion; two spindly-legged, dhoti-clad Indian plainsmen, pushing a flat-topped cart of fruit to their chosen selling place; people waiting for the delivery of dairy milk; and the occasional taxi. Some Royal Nepal Army recruits double along with a non-commissioned officer. When it is dry the squad will form up by the side of the road and lie down to do various exercises, but today, in the all-pervading dampness, running is enough for them. Other soldiers, in a large lorry and a small Soviet-made vehicle, are out practicing driving. Some stalwarts are jogging, a few of them from the Tibetan refugee camp, and the occasional older man, probably a retired army officer, takes his morning constitutional. Near the perennial springs the large daily wash, often hotels' linen, starts. It may even dry.

By 7 o'clock the first news broadcast of the day can be heard. The flat-toned, monotonous voice of the reader drones out from many of the houses, following a passer-by so closely that he can hear the entire bulletin as he goes on his way.

There is a wide swathe of grass on both sides of the Ring Road, with warning notices proclaiming to the general public that no building is permitted within a specified distance, a copy of one of the last laws the British passed in India. Cattle, untethered and untended, graze there happily now that the days of parched fodder, or no fodder at all, are at an end. Some have a heavy piece of wood hanging from their neck to impede movement, a type of hobbling device. A few are disconsolately lonely and it could be those that have been let loose as a propitiation when a Brahman dies. All look much sleeker than before. Little knots of goats and sheep also crop the short grass. Leeches are not the pest they are in the rest of the country.

Sun peeps through the dispersing mist, revealing the many greens of the crops, varying from a golden green, to a rich velvet green and then to darker browny and moss greens. In places the smoothness is broken by clumps of eight-foot tall maize, the long leaves now sere with the pods ripening. The old Buddhist shrine of Shyambunath, perched on top of its own sanctuary-like hill, glints ethereally. It, to the south of the valley, and Bodhnath to the north, both command a good view of the fields. In olden days no animal could plough within sight of these two shrines. Even now sloughing is seldom done by animals. Heavy-handed mattocks, bent backs and strong arms are still all important.

In the town the day starts later than in the villages. Shops are open until late and many do not open again till 10 o'clock. Street sweepers do what they can against the mud and filth, mendicants beg for food at house doors, stray dogs scavenge and children start to play in the streets. There are many Indian merchants in Kathmandu. One carries a flat tray of mangoes on his head as he passes a temple, the very temporal home for some not very spiritual monkeys. One animal sidles up, warily eyeing both vendor and fruit, its intentions obvious. The vendor tries to move away quickly but his load is such that haste is imprudent. The monkey paces him, tensing its muscles. The Indian puts his free hand up over the rim of the tray and picks out the first mango that comes to his fingers. He hurls it back over the monkey which lollops after it, so letting the vendor escape by an act of self-protection that can also be counted as a holy gesture.

By 9 o'clock a stream of workers and school children from the outlying villages pick their way round the dirtier patches on the narrow paths as they move into Kathmandu. The clouds have dispersed and a hot sun is blazing down. Many may still have a petal or two on their heads, showing that they have paid their religious respects for the day.

An hour later the main roads are blocked with traffic. The police on point duty valiantly try to cope with the onslaught, waving arms and blowing whistles, as those better endowed than the villagers go to work. Clouds of dirty exhaust pollute the air. Motor cyclists weave their way in and around the vehicles, as do many on pushbikes, defying or merely courting death. By half past 10 most of the staff have joined up with their desks and maybe even the man with the keys has come so that anything locked up overnight can be got out. Little groups of men form and disperse, only to reform, gossiping to their hearts' content, for isn't important work only done between twelve and two?

Inside the bank a gaggle of new-world, low-budget travelers turn the pages of the book in which the arrival of remitted money is written. None understands the inevitable two-week time lag between date expected and date announced. They are a motley crowd, not expecting either the heat or the dampness of monsoon conditions. They give off an aura of unwashed sadness that may belie their normal habits. The bank staff regard them with a tolerance born of familiarity. Some of them are very shabbily dressed, draggle-bearded and unkempt. They are a permanent target of small boys' ribaldry. Where these foreigners go on leaving the bank is a mystery—like flies in winter.

By noon all the very important people are busy, ensconced in lordly isolation in upstairs offices, all aware of the heavy responsibilities which they are entrusted with and all keeping a fine balance between prospect, probity and policy. In outer offices deferential subordinates diligently apply themselves, ready in an instant to answer the desk-bell that rings when higher authority demands their presence. The tempo is kept up till 2 o'clock when the important go to meetings with other important ones and the lesser minions revitalize their severely depleted vitality with glasses of over-sweet and luke-warm tea.

Life unwinds gradually until 5 o'clock when the rush begins in the other direction. The sun has gone in, the clouds hang low and menacing and it starts to drizzle. The women toilers have returned from the fields, tired and wet, to prepare the evening meal for their ever-hungry family. The bread-winner gets home and relaxes. After being fed, the children huddle up to a lamp and do their homework and men gather out of the rain in twos and threes to gossip. The women are just thankful that yet another day, when so much has to be packed in to keep the minimum momentum needed to sustain life, is nearing its end.

Then it is bedtime and, for those who live near the zoo, the roar of the tigers—driven to distraction in their small cages by a daylong, inquisitive, teasing crowd of onlookers—joins the shrill and never-ending barking of the dogs. However tired people are, they are forcibly reminded that, even though another day is over, the night is still young.

The months ticked by and, at long last, it was time for me to ring the PPS in his office in the palace. Conversations on the telephone in my place of work were audible to all who were in the vicinity of the main office. However much I desired privacy, I was not to have any. I described how I made the telephone call in a letter home:

...I told you on the telephone that I thought my future would be decided in the near future. I had rung the palace and spoken to the PPS, who told me to ring in some fifteen days' time. I rang you on the 4th and was due to get hold of the palace on the 8th, the following Monday. It was a strange sensation, the countdown so to speak, wondering whether my unusual quest would be met or not. Some of my pals in the university came in to ask how I was faring. The day before there was an uneasy calm as I plodded through my work. Buddhiman wished me well as he left for school on the Monday morning. I told him that I need not tell him if I had been lucky or unlucky when I came back as he would see from the look on my face. I once more plodded my way through the morning and, feeling rather like a prep school boy going in to see the headmaster, I made my way down the stairs into the PA's office, where I found the telephone was not in use and, indeed, the PA not there. I picked up the receiver and dialed: thoughts assailed me as I waited for the dial tone: so far, I had done all I could to influence events in a situation that really had no form, no shape, nothing ever cut and nothing dried...and yet, was there anything I should have done, over the months, that, with hindsight, I could have played better? For some nights before I had rethought all that Buddhiman and I had been through from the very start. I "counted sheep" with the officials with whom I had spoken, with influential men I had met and dropped hints to, with chance remarks I had made in the general direction of power. The dial tone rang and my heart thumped. I had tightened myself into a position to hear the worst news—failure. I was not prepared to hear an unfamiliar voice at the other end of the telephone querying who I was, obviously not knowing the name. The man on the other end said that the PPS had left the country for treatment and, no, he had not put my petition before His Majesty, no, he did not know when he would be back and, no, he did not know how severe the [PPS's] complaint was. I thanked him and, feeling flat, replaced the receiver and went back to my room to work...

It was a great disappointment. My esoteric word-worrying palled during the next two weeks. I felt punctured and did not ring until I learnt that the PPS was back, nearly a month later, hands ever sweaty! Apparently the man answering instead of the PPS had thought I was a Nepali imposter so was very suspicious. I was told that my petition had come back to the PPS from the "security" major general in the palace only the previous day. The PPS was very hopeful that my case would be successful and he would try all he could. I was to ring back in fourteen days' time—until then fingers had to be very firmly crossed.

After two slow weeks: "Thank you very much for ringing, Colonel sahib, wait a minute." A pause, a rustling of papers, a thumping heart. "Hello! Are you still there?" I said I was. "I have placed your petition in front of His Majesty and he says that honorary citizenship is out of the question."

I had known all along, in the heart of my heart, that it had to be so and the PPS had tried his best. So that was that. It had been a brave attempt and a hopeless gamble, with much heartache on the way. Ah well...

"Hello! Are you still there?" Stupidly I had made no answer and hurriedly made amends, trying to sound as though my heart was not in my boots.

"His Majesty has ordered that your petition should be sent to the Ministry of Law and Justice," the PPS continued, "to see if you are a suitable person legally to be allowed to stay on a long-term basis." My heart looped the loop, or something similar, as I struggled to grasp the implications of this unexpected piece of information. A long pause, then, "You can find out the answer from them." Could I? Visions of traipsing to yet another ministry, of polite but nebulous meetings with those (even presuming they were in when I called) not used to such requests, of having to explain to every link in the chain until he who was senior enough to give an answer was eventually reached, of time, effort and patience required, of... "Wait! Hold on!"

I heard rustling and, with the receiver barely muffled, a semi-audible voice asking a subordinate a question. I smiled vaguely at a man wanting to use the telephone, shaking my head to tell him that I had yet to finish my conversation. The voice came on the line again.

"Hello! Colonel sahib! I have the ministry's answer in front of me. They say that there is no legal objection as far as the constitution is concerned."

"Thank you very much indeed for all the trouble you are taking on my behalf," I managed to say, as much in reflex as with reason. "Can you tell me what happens now?"

"Yes, now your petition will go the King's Council. Ring me back in two weeks when there may be a definite answer."

Buddhiman and I talked this over that evening, cautiously excited, but not daring to take the outcome for granted. However, it was clear that the tide of events was running in my favor: patience was needed and it was pointless fretting— though very hard not to.

It so happened that one of the King's Council—the king's eight wise men—was an ex-subedar, Purna Bahadur Gurung, of the First Gurkhas. Two of his younger brothers had been in a company I commanded in 1/1 Gurkha Rifles in 1947 and, after a lapse of thirty-six years, I had met them when Buddhiman and I were on our 190-mile walk in the autumn of 1983. It is such contacts as these that act as the subcontinent's "old boy net." Buddhiman and I decided to go and see him in his Kathmandu flat.

Next Saturday we walked through the mediæval city, with its narrow lanes, open shops and jostling crowds, past many temples and meandering cattle. Purna Bahadur lived in part of a house backing on to the compound that caters for the Indian Army's Gorkha pensioners. A fine-looking man in his sixties, he greeted us affably and bade us sit down. Small talk was the order of the day until tea and a fried egg each had been offered and consumed. It was then time to broach the reason for our visit. Purna Bahadur seemed surprised that the King's Council should be involved as "it has never happened before, so why should it start now?" However, he did say that he would ask the secretary and, having noted our telephone number, let us know what resulted. The point I made was not that I was angling for him to suggest any special "treatment" for me but rather that Purna Bahadur, being a man of the same district, Lamjung, as Buddhiman, could vouch for the probity of the Nepali citizen closest to me. Fears of my being "turned" or adversely influenced by a person hostile to prevalent conditions was understandable. In any case that aspect of being processed was looked after by the relevant branch of the police, as was bound to be the case, for both of us.

Purna Bahadur rang as promised. The secretary knew nothing of my case nor had he had to deal with anything like it in the past. As I had no idea of what channels such processing had to take, I could not start to guess the reasons for nothing being known.

It was about this time that I met my director as I was leaving after a day's work. I had asked him a couple of times if he knew what was happening. He had never committed himself, how could he? He had been in the habit of suddenly appearing in my room to see what I was doing but he had ceased checking up on me by then. "I learnt today that your petition is being worked on," he said, smiling as he did. I made a suitable rejoinder, thanking him for any help he could give me.

A few days later an office runner came into my room and told me that he had just answered a telephone call from the university central office. He had been told to tell the chief administrator in CNAS to prepare a curriculum vitae for the "Kornel sahib" and send it in as soon as he could. The runner was sworn to secrecy not to tell me but, having helped him out with some financial problems after his father died, he now regarded me as his dad. "Please do not let on that you know about it when you are asked for details," he begged.

Sure enough, the next day I was asked to give my life history. I said that I had done that when I joined CNAS but, were another wanted, of course I would oblige. I could see that the chief administrator was glad I had not asked why these details were wanted.

When I next rang the palace the PPS told me that the paperwork had now to go to the cabinet of ministers "and I have asked them to hurry up and told them that you are a good man," he added with an uncharacteristic chuckle. I was also told that an underling would take charge of my case from then on; the implication surely being that the processing was proceeding smoothly?

The underling was a nice man to talk to on the phone and was an old schoolmate of the university vice-registrar, by then a friend of mine. Although it was maddening not to be allowed to have a chat face to face in the office, it being hard for any individual such as myself to get into the palace grounds where the offices were, tenuous contact could be made through the underling's chum. This was a benefit I had not expected. However, after my case had gone to the cabinet, on 20 June 1985, bombs exploded in Kathmandu and elsewhere in Nepal. I imagined that the cabinet would have little time for such matters as my petition. I continued to ring the palace as stated, sometimes to find that my contact was away—illness, then the death of his father requiring a statuary mourning period at home slowed things up—always to be asked to ring back in a week to ten days. I tried never to show impatience, being fortified by hints from my contact and the assertion that, if the Nepalis would not help an Englishman who had spent over forty years with them, whom would they?

It may be wondered why, with all seeming so hopeful, I still felt uneasy as to the outcome. I had learnt that unknown whims, unforeseen snags and unaccountable pressures in the system had been bedeviling features of state matters since the earliest times, dashing the most optimistic hopes at the very last moment. There was often disappointment before that talisman of Nepalese authority, the written word, was in the hands of the supplicant.

I was due to go to England in mid-July, at the start of the new financial year when new annual contracts started, and shortly before then I rang the palace yet again. My contact was embarrassed at the delay; my petition was now with the Home Ministry, known to be slow, having been dealt with by the cabinet. There was still nothing definite but it appeared that the paperwork for the final decision to be taken by the king, that is to say for the Royal Seal to be affixed or not, was all that was left. That had to take its own course. I told my contact, to his evident relief, that I would ring back as soon as I returned from England, about six weeks later.

Again, rather shamefacedly, I returned to the world of omens. Before having my eye operations, I would occasionally play patience, a kind that might "come out" once every twenty-five times. That time I had had two consecutive hands from different packs that "came out" as soon as I started playing, something I had never previously experienced. I "knew" that my eye operations would be successful so ceased to worry about it all. This time, in "wondering mood," I told myself that the first hands I played would be significant. To my utter amazement, I had an unprecedented initial run of three consecutive hands "coming out." Telling not a soul of my heathen idiosyncrasies, I went on leave in good spirits.

On 24 September 1985, two days after my return, I rang the palace. Still nothing definite but I was to ring in ten days' time.

By now I was more confident of a successful outcome. Had nothing been forthcoming I would have been told very early on—it was details I wanted—but I had learnt never to take anything for granted, so allowed myself only that one constant pipe dream.

On the day before I was next due to ring the palace an excited office runner came into my room and told me that I was wanted on the telephone and that the royal palace was calling. The look of subdued awe on the lad's face was proof, were any needed, of the power that those living inside it have on those living outside. Keeping my voice as steady as I could, I identified myself. "Could you please bring a photograph of yourself round to the palace, now?"

One thing I have learnt is always to carry several passport-sized photos with me. It was unlucky that I had not ridden to work that morning and the urgency with which the photo was wanted put walking, or even going by bus, out of the question. I had told my contact that I'd be round within half an hour and, keeping my fingers crossed, asked to be allowed the use of the office car. Granted!—a minor triumph—and I was at the palace gates just as a dapperly dressed official walked down the road to await my arrival. We exchanged greetings and pleasantries, the sentry obviously having a hard time not to laugh and to face his front. Back in the office everybody thought that the asking for a photograph was a positive sign, so did Buddhiman that evening.

The very next morning, Friday, the 4th—that 2x2 once more!—of October 1985, I rang the palace for the tenth time and was told that all I had to do now was to go to the Ministry of Home Affairs and get the paperwork sorted out. "What actually has been allowed?" I gasped, only half believing what was being said to me. Even then there was no definite answer. "What if the ministry won't go along with what you say?" I asked.

The answer was a rebuke. Did I really think that anyone anywhere in Nepal would query what had been ordered from the throne?

"Of course not. How silly of me to ask that," was my groveling reply. What I did not know then was that the king has to give his consent before any such petition can be processed and, once given, only royal command cancels it. It is then the responsibility of the various departments to sort the matter out. Had I known that I would have been spared more mental turmoil than I care to remember. Despite it being so time-consuming for one so busy as a Head of State, His Majesty devoted every Friday afternoon to such matters.

Interest among my colleagues was intense. When I said that I now had Royal Assent congratulations were many and sincere, some with handshakes, others with bear hugs. I trod air, as the saying has it, and such matters as rings round the navel and folds in the skin of an elephant's behind, to say nothing of any disappointment with my history, now ranked as trivial and appearing to have been put in my path as a penance. Even so, I waited till closing time before going back to the flat with my good news.

I was greeted at the front door by a worried and expectant Buddhiman who had been watching the road. "What's happened, Father, what's happened?"

"His Majesty has given the order that I can stay..." I started to say when Buddhiman put his arms round me and, calling his wife, tried to pour out his heart. He was, in fact, almost speechless. "How wonderful, how wonderful," he repeated as Bhim Kumari, heavily pregnant, joined us and hugged me from the other side. I think I counted Buddhiman's "how wonderful" twenty-two times before he broke into tears.

After we had dried our eyes I looked at my diary and saw that it was ten months to the very day that I had had my interview with the PPS. The Nepalis count pregnancies as lasting ten, not nine, months and it was almost too much of a coincidence for me to have become a "new Nepali" in exactly that time.

Next day was a holiday and we decided to go to the most famous temple in Nepal, Pasupati Nath, where Buddhiman would thank the deities to whom he had prayed so often for listening to him. Not being allowed inside the sacred precincts—as a beef-eating Christian I was eternally barred—I was bidden to walk round the temple complex. I waited for Buddhiman to join me when I was halfway round, opposite the most sacred shrine, with platoons of monkeys walking round and past, taking no notice of me.

I went to the ministry and made contact with the section officer in whose charge were citizenship—and shotguns! It took a week for the paperwork to come from the palace and it was only then that what had happened hit me. During the four days it took to get the necessary pieces of paper produced my euphoria penetrated that dark, dusty and rustling office. I had a glimpse of their photostat copy of my petition and was interested to see lines drawn in the margin against the positive aspects of what I had done for Nepalis, with a "goose's egg" around the bit about being offered a job by The Prince of Wales.

As I was leaving the ministry after one of my visits I was hailed by a large, jovial Nepali who came up to me. He was obviously a senior official.

"Do you recognize me, Colonel sahib?" he asked.

I dread that question, asked all too often. I made a guess, unfortunately wrong, and was corrected.

"No, I was the Chief District Officer in Pokhara when you were in charge of the British camp. Your eyes were giving you much trouble then." Near blindness excused me of any discourtesy.

Having told me that he had been promoted to a senior post in the Ministry of Home Affairs, he congratulated me on being allowed to stay in Nepal. "Your paperwork came to me for certain recommendations. I remembered that you had made that puja in Pokhara for your Nepali friends after your successful eye operation, so I "pushed" your case forward quickly!"

He smiled and I thanked him, never having thought that the ripples of my act of appreciation would have lapped to such a far shore.

The infinitely more relaxed attitude shown to me in CNAS on being so favored was evident here also, as well as wherever the news spread. None of them had given me any chance of success, despite what they had said to me from time to time.

The paperwork took its own time to complete. As nothing like this, so I was told, had ever been known to have happened before, there was no precedent on which to work. I was treated as a Nepali and had to be identified on the final forms as whose grandson and son I was. Eight drafts were produced before the two forms—one the certificate of authority and the other spelling out various conditions—were ready for my photograph, both thumb prints, my signature in Nepali and English and, most important, the Home Ministry Principal Secretary's signature adorning the ministry's seal.

What I had been granted was permanent residential status in any part of the kingdom; the retention of my British passport; and the right to buy property and one house in my own name. The conditions I had to sign were that I would observe all the laws of the land, I would have to have a visa and that, with or without any reasons given, I could have these privileges withdrawn. When I asked why this last I was told with a smile that such a condition, written or not, applied to all Nepalis; whereas for them behavior of an adverse nature could result in a long jail sentence, for me it would mean expulsion—"but you still have a valid British passport!"

I was taken to see the secretary who signed all the copies of the certificate. He congratulated me, shook my hand and told me that what I had been granted was unique in the history of the country.

"Sir," I said, with ill-concealed emotion, "I couldn't be happier."

His Majesty, the King of Nepal, then set above the constitution, is a very understanding person. To show my appreciation of what he had granted me, I wrote to thank him:

I humbly request that I may be allowed to express to Your Majesty my deepest sense of profound gratitude at Your Majesty's munificence in allowing me to spend the rest of my days in Your Majesty's kingdom.

I am most sensible to the unique privilege and honour that Your Majesty has bestowed upon me, thus not only answering my innermost prayer and most heartfelt desire but also allowing me even closer ties with Nepal, a land I have long loved and in which I can now make my refuge and my home in peace of mind and joy of heart.

I am so overjoyed with what has befallen me that words of thanks and expressions of appreciation, while utterly sincere, are all too inadequate to reveal my true feelings. I doubt there be any happier person in Your Majesty's kingdom.

I would further like it brought to Your Majesty's notice that I fully accept my new status with total conviction, undying love for Nepal and unswerving loyalty to Your Majesty.

In conclusion, may I reiterate my continued devotion, loyalty and respect to Your Majesty.

At the end of October, I received a letter, headed Royal Palace, Nepal. It was from His Majesty's Principal Private Secretary and stated:

I have had the honour to submit your letter of October 18, 1985, to the gracious attention of His Majesty the King and I am commanded to thank you for your thoughtfulness in writing. I do hope that your stay in Nepal will be rewarded with joy, peace and creativity that you so much look forward to finding in our land.

This was particularly pleasing and I reflected that, while His Majesty the King may indeed be semi-divine, he is also an old Etonian.

In November the six nations of what was soon to become the South Asian Area for Regional Cooperation (SAARC) held a four-day preparatory seminar in Kathmandu, attended by very high-grade people of Bangladesh, Bhutan, India, the Maldives, Nepal, Pakistan and Sri Lanka. This was organized by CNAS and I was one of a number of people who were invited as observers. On the third afternoon we were late in starting. A roly-poly European, walking with great determination, thrust himself into a group of Nepalis demanding to know why the delay. As he lacked all normal courtesies he was ignored. I was nearby, wearing university fig, the national dress. When I answered this blustering individual in faultless English, he could scarcely believe his ears.

Who was I? was the first of a series of questions about my credentials and my answers increased his disbelief. He slipped me his card and asked me to contact him. I saw he was Albert I. Bannov, the First Secretary of the Soviet embassy, who transpired to be half-Azerbaijani, half-Russian—and, I later learnt, a member of the Soviet Army's intelligence network, GRU. Euphoria allowed me to do just that and when I rang him a week later I really did think his excited reaction was one of having easily won over an agent in place, if not a defector. I went round to see him. Unusually he lived outside the main compound and I found his house without much difficulty. After being introduced to his very nice wife—"her name is Alla, not the god Alla but the Ukrainian Alla"—I was invited to sit down in a darkened corner. Banov switched on the taped music, which all communist representatives inevitable do when talking to people unofficially. Alcohol was produced and declined, with Alla giving him what sounded like a rocket for trying to force me to drink when I obviously did not want to.

Slightly chastened, he demanded that food be bought. A tray of assorted goodies was put in front of me. "Eat!" I was ordered. I was wearing dark contact lens and could not see any utensils. I hesitated. "Eat!" I was ordered a second time. Presuming it to be finger-dry stuff in the various little compartments on the tray, I dipped into the nearest. A damp stickiness clung to my fingers and, feeling it easier to lick the offending substance clean before wiping my hands, put the mess into my mouth and instantly choked on some very hot mustard.

I was later asked to find out what the British embassy files held about the Chinese and, by inference, the Nepalese armies. I declined, remonstrating, and explained my position, how I had recently had royal approval to stay in the country, how I was dependent on Buddhiman, how, in turn, I was looking after Buddhiman and his family, and how they would fare if I found myself not wanted by the Nepalese authorities. Bannov replied that I was more communist than he was as his only idea was to make as much money as possible and find himself a nice house in a nice district in Moscow, but he would look after Buddhiman for life if I was caught working for him and was kicked out.

I left as soon as I could but he somehow tracked me down and asked to speak to Buddhiman. He offered him a five-year scholarship in the Soviet Union, there and then, and was puzzled by a firm, polite yet very definite refusal.

American watchers of Bannov's residence reported me to the British embassy the very next day.

Much more pleasant was when, in early January 1986, we held a seminar to discuss Britain-Nepal relations in advance of the state visit of Queen Elizabeth II and Prince Philip in February. That visit was wonderful; more people thronged the streets than ever in living memory and, at a presentation of selected pensioned Gurkha officers to Their Majesties in the British embassy garden, there were five Gurkha holders of the Victoria Cross. I was in charge of one group whom I introduced, first to the Queen, then to the Duke of Edinburgh, "leading from the rear," and finally to Sir Geoffrey Howe, the Foreign Minister. Two Gurkhas, commissioned from Sandhurst, presented their fathers to Their Majesties. Two other Gurkhas arrived from the east having heard that the queen of England had come to do the recruiting herself. It was a day none of us would ever forget.

The rest of my time at CNAS was a bit of an anti-climax. Hom Bahadur, Buddhiman's younger brother, came to look after me and, for the first time in his life, had a man he could turn to as a father. It took him some time to settle down. He learnt to distinguish the difference between the front door bell and the telephone bell before the others left, Buddhiman to Pokhara to oversee the house being built, his wife and baby daughter to spend time in the village until it was ready. Hom Bahadur went to school, ran the house and learnt how to ride a bike. It all brought him out of his shell. I finished my linguistic project and submitted it. With 26,000 headwords examined for changes of meaning and spelling I had found 48,521 such had taken place in the sixty years spanned by the two dictionaries. It was accepted as being a major contribution to Nepalese learning. We had a meeting: members of the Royal Nepal Academy, the English language faculty and the Central Office attended, as well as a strong contingent from CNAS. A seminar was felt appropriate to let linguists, teachers and journalists know how the language had changed and the implication of such changes. Two weeks later I was asked by the archivist why I had not submitted my work. I told him I had but had not asked for a receipt. He had hidden it so successfully it was not found for eight years—a wonderful example of "crab" culture.

My landlord arranged for a word processor to be bought for me from Hong Kong by the senior air hostess of the King's Flight. Unfortunately my initials were recorded as P.J. not J.P., so that entailed a maze-like tour of exploration around the customs offices. We also found that Amstrad details, for customs, were not at the airport, so had to go to the main office and there—pause for breath—we made out an application for an assessment to be given. Paper and stamp were needed: we had neither so had to get both. There were four grades of functionary in the department. No 2 signed the application. Then to No 4 for another letter, to No 3, to No 4, to No 2, to No 1, to No 3, to No 4, to a typist for five copies of the answer. Then to No 4 to sign the No 5 copy, to No 3 to sign the No 4 copy, to No 2 to sign the other copies, to No 3 to initial the signatures, to No 4 to initial all the copies, to the clerk to put one copy in an envelope and to enter that fact in a ledger. Then back to the airport office, where another round of musical chairs took place to change P.J. into J.P. before I became the proud possessor of a word processor. Exhausting. In fact, although it took us four hours, we were, in golfing terms, "eagle" for the course...

Our house in Pokhara was not ready when my contract came to an end so I went to England for a holiday. The thrill I felt when I entered the house for the first time on my return was only equaled by my pride at a vision fulfilled when I look at the name of the house on the stone gate. This I had carved in marble while still in Kathmandu and kept as a secret: Dhampu Niwas [residence]. As I walked up to the front door I turned to Buddhiman and said that I could die happily in such a place. It is twenty minutes' walk from Birkha Raj's house. Initially, he wanted us to live nearer him, so that he could keep an eye on me and ensure that I was all right. I would have liked to live near him and his family but there was no plot in that vicinity that was large enough to sustain Buddhiman and a decent-sized plot, for vegetables, poultry and pigs or any other venture.

The house, a large two-storied building of knapped stone, high ceilings and large rooms took a year to build. The foundations are very strong and, as they were being made, the locals averred that they would last a thousand years. We designed it ourselves and there is none other in Pokhara like it. It has attracted much complimentary comment. The view is superb with six peaks of over 25,000 feet and at least ten others of over 20,000. I am much happier here in Pokhara than ever I could be anywhere else, in Kathmandu or in England.

I am asked why I need such a big house and my answer is that, apart from it being a long-term investment, as the family grows we will not feel cramped. Added to that, I most sincerely hope that Buddhiman's children and grandchildren can keep up the liaison with my brother David's children and grandchildren, started and welded so strongly by us two. It would be a grievous pity, I feel, if the love already engendered cannot be maintained for generations. I also say that, with such an extraordinary and unique privilege, I must live in a place that reflects such a status. This is expected and accepted by all.

It has been a long time and I have come a long way since those far-off days, over forty years ago, when, immature and irresponsible, I embarked on SS *Maloja* on 8 June 1944. Even as I write that date, I can see as fine and propitious a crop of 2s to start off such a long journey with, for a foreign land in time of war, so ignorant I now blush when I think of it. I only wish father and Tim could share my joy.

The sheltered lives and stereotyped existence of the children of middle-class gentry of pre-war Britain and the confines of a classical education at public school were, for most of us, taken for granted as utterly normal and our non-plebeian birthright. God still wore spats and had a fob watch in his waistcoat pocket. The squire in the manor still had his shoots and the keeper still lived in a cottage on the estate. Overseas service was, for many, still the mark of the black sheep. From that time on, change has seldom been so fast.

Another question often put to me is how can I cope with the cultural differences of East and West. I reply that, when faced with a problem that would send an oriental crazy, I regard it as an occidental would and it does not affect me. Likewise, when faced with a problem that would give an occidental ulcers or a heart attack, I regard it as an oriental would and I can laugh it off.

A third question put to me is have the other religions of the world that I have met in the east affected me. I reply that I am a baptized Christian and carry my Christian God with me in my head. When pressed I admit that I have mixed with too many other religions to have the arrogance that Christianity can be the only way to approach the Great Life Force that is the wellspring of all religious thought. I regard the religion of my upbringing rather like the regiment of my choice; both are where I feel the most comfortable. Just because I had a commission in a Gurkha regiment and would not want to be anywhere else, that in no way implies I think any less of people in any other regiment or other branch of service. Similarly is it with religion; both can inspire an equal devotion through a basic discipline—the camp and the cloister, the bugle and the bell. I have discovered that I have, therefore, a deist, not a theist, outlook to religions which I see as being only one of several alternative methods of conducting one's private spiritual affairs to one's private satisfaction.

An interviewer on BBC Radio 4 asked me if I could be comfortable in Nepal. To that I said that physical comfort depended on the furniture but, with peace of mind, one could be comfortable anywhere. While there are flies in the ointment, mail, banking, bureaucratic inefficiency and medical facilities being the most encountered, no country anywhere is free from some sort of frustration.

In Nepal, a closed country ruled by despots for over a century, the very idea of seeing a foreign face in the Hills, let alone there being a meeting of minds and interweaving of destinies such as mine and Buddhiman's, was beyond comprehension. In these last forty years, conditions have altered almost beyond recognition.

If overcoming affliction, challenges and temptations purifies the soul, if religion is doing to others as one would be done by, if love be the flame that welds two destinies, if faith be the touchstone of our actions, then, by the grace of God, we have both come home, Buddhiman at midday and I at dusk.

AT THE VERY END OF THE DAY

1986-1992

Ankle-biters and anarchists—an unlikely pair!—were a constant backdrop to our life from then on. Both became part of the scene and, as far as the little ones were concerned, I found it fascinating and enjoyable to a degree only previously imagined. As any grandparent will agree when kids get fractious, it is the privilege of age to hand back the little lovelies to their parents. Regarding the political scene, the country was once more as apprehensive and as brooding as I had known since twenty years before during the Land Reform programme. However, I was determined to enjoy the fruits of my previous labors in peace, so did not let that which did not concern me unduly worry me: although a very privileged guest, Nepal was not my country so it was not up to me to suggest what I thought would be a better way of running affairs.

On my return from visiting England I first of all decided to pay a series of protocol calls on all those who might conceivably have an interest in me, or should I sound less egotistical and say my presence, remembering my unique status. There were three groups of people; administrators, police officials and army men, both the Royal Nepal Army and the senior officer in the Indian Embassy Pension Paying Office. That took a few weeks.

I opened a bank account but was dismayed when it took one hundred and eleven days for my money to come from my Kathmandu bank. When I went to Kathmandu and remonstrated about the delay I was smiled at disarmingly and told that the money had not been sent because it was thought I had not meant what I said. After all, who would want to go to Pokhara when established, as I had been, in Kathmandu? And yet, I could not grumble at dilatoriness when a bank statement from England took eighty-two days to reach me. The banking system is complex; a token is given when the cheque is presented and the bank passbook is scrutinized. A delay of up to two hours ensues as many clerks with many ledgers process the cheque until the senior man signs that the money can be drawn. Even then there are two people to pay out the money, one to count it once and the other to count it again. Eventually I was given an accolade of sorts: once I had presented my cheque, I would be invited in behind the grill, offered a chair and all would stop work. I would have to "perform," that is to say, tell a joke or two, sing a verse or so, or chat them up generally. On the other side of the grill queues would lengthen but none grumbled outwardly. That over with, my money would be ready in twenty minutes. Some time later I made the account into a joint one so that Buddhiman could cash cheques.

Next it was time to try and get hold of a telephone. I knew some spare lines were available and could be given to people when permission was granted by the Zonal Commissioner. I visited this gentleman, one of the Tarai community who, I felt, still found life strange in Pokhara, and put my case to him. CNAS still alleged high hopes of continuing with some linguist research and other projects. All I got in return was the "come-back-when-I-have-thought-it-out" type remark. I was visited by a powerful man, a member of the national non-party parliament. I had known him a long time and he said that, as he knew I was worthy enough to have a telephone, he would talk with the Zonal Commissioner and "fix it." We went around to this man's house before office hours and, as the two Nepalis were arguing the toss, I stayed in the background. I was called over and the proposition was starkly presented. Get the Zonal Commissioner's gardener's third, and illiterate, son into the British Army and a telephone would be mine. In fact I had already enlisted both elder brothers and the present hopeful had been turned down the previous year as illiterate. No matter: that was not relevant. I stared at this official a long second, asked to be excused and left, inwardly seething.

I learnt that the telephone exchange people had a call from "the office" to say that I was not to be allowed to "buy" any of the yet-to-be-allocated lines. Angry I was, I was determined not to show any resentment. It would do me no good. It comes hard to have to say it, but Nepalis can be as vicious as they are normally charming. They are seldom wantonly cruel, often wantonly thoughtless, and, as in any organization anywhere, a problem is much easier to deal with if it does not exist. In the prevailing political turmoil that was seething under the surface, I am sure Authority unconsciously echoed the words of one Henri Queuille: "in politics, it is not a question of solving problems but of silencing those who raise them."

More pleasant and much better both for body and soul, I started jogging in the early mornings. During the days, stung by being branded by one embryo author as the tenth of ten eccentric Englishmen in Asia, spurred by the thought that people might be interested in my story and sustained by being asked to write a book on jungle warfare, I found myself arguing with my Amstrad computer as I settled down to "work something out." I was also asked, by no less an august personage than the Chief Of Army Staff of the Royal Nepal Army himself, in the late winter of 1987, to become the official historian of his army. Come one, come all.

Birkha Raj was very keen that I be integrated into local society. He knew that my best defence against any whims of those who were still suspicious of my status was for me to be "part of the furniture," accepted by all and sundry. I was approached on two flanks, Hindu and Buddhist. I was very happy for this as, despite being a baptized Christian, I am aware that local gods had need to know me and recognize me as friendly as I had to be accepted by them. I saw no clash.

The Hindu bit came first. A new temple to the goddess Kali was to be built and Birkha Raj was the main organizer; land, money, shrine and goddess. He called in one morning and asked me to be at the stone-laying ceremony. He would be there also and would tell me what to do and where to do it.

I went as bidden and sat at the back of the rows of chairs to one side of the large square stone chautara in front of which proceedings were to take place. I was called forward to sit with the senior guests. I saw that a subscription was inevitable and, mindful of living on a restricted budget while waiting for life assurances and Old Age Pension to mature, felt a thousand rupees would be about right. That would make it about £30. Birkha Raj, sitting next to me, asked how much I was willing to give and I sensed he was uneasy when I told him. He went away to register my amount and came back looking grim. Leaning over he quietly asked if I was sure I wanted to give a thousand rupees. Knowing I would not be taken advantage of if I gave him the decision to make I asked him how much he felt I should give. A thousand and one, came the unexpected reply.

My name was read out and I was asked to step forward and make a speech. This I had not expected but felt I could not refuse. I explained how I had lost my sight and how I had given thanks religiously to those Hindus who had prayed for my eyesight to get better (applause) and how the king had given me a unique status so I could enjoy life with them (more applause), and sat down. Back home, Buddhiman explained that an offering ending in an odd number was luckier than one ending in an even number: one goes out, the other comes in. Oh!

Some two weeks later I was approached for the next stage, the installation of the goddess. I had tentatively planned to be in Kathmandu over that period and said so. No worry, their date would be changed. I didn't suppose I would be wanted to talk at this session, but I was wrong. I had no knowledge of what to say under such circumstances but that did not seem to matter. On my morning jogs I tried to seek inspiration as, on the flatter parts of the road, I glanced to see the rising sun striking the Himalayas. It was to be a useless exercise as the main speaker happened on the same theme as I had chosen. When it came to my turn I declined to rise to the occasion.

My audience of about three hundred did not take no for an answer so I plunged into my poor second choice. Religion had come to stay and here was an example of the power of the goddess Kali... I cribbed and embellished the story (of Eduard de Bono's lateral thinking) of how a bad man slipped two black stones into a bag when he had said that there would be a black stone and a white one, and then challenged a hapless woman to accept the verdict of whichever of the two stones she picked out, black against her and white in her favor, there being no choice but she not knowing so. I had my audience on the edge of their chairs as I told my story but had a twinge of atavistic conscience when later several people told me they had had their knowledge of Hinduism greatly increased by my mastery of the scriptures.

I was first speaker for the opening ceremony, the last stage, and played safe. My talk, aimed at the children, was about the blind men and the elephant, well known by all adults and safe from misinterpretation. Later proceedings were held up when a lorry bearing a recently shot man-eating tigress was driven past so all could see that the creature, responsible for over a dozen deaths, all Brahman women, over the past months, was finally dead.

The Buddhist side of integration took the form of paying for a guest room for visiting abbots at the local crematorium. I had no money to spare for a year and many pensioners gave a share of the money without asking for interest. Even such a mundane project was heavily and suspiciously scrutinized by government agents fearful of something happening that was not straightforward. The same Zonal Commissioner was invited to the dedication ceremony, arrived an hour late and was in a hurry to move on. He told me not to go ahead with what I had planned to say when invited to speak as this would make him later still. We all felt deflated.

Buddhiman went to Kathmandu to finalize his School Leaving Exam and thrilled us all by getting a place in the Second Division. The result came during the monsoon, which is regarded as an unspoken benison of the gods and a curse. Without the rains nature will dry up and life become unsupportable: when too much and too violent, generations of labor will be washed away as hillsides crumble and crash into the valleys. Death and destruction are ever-present threats. Hill people do not expect to travel in the monsoon, when there will be days of drizzle, of heavy rain, of mud, of leeches, of cloud and of blazing sunshine, hotter than before the rains now that the haze and dust of the drier months have been washed away.

As normal, after the first rains had softened the soil sufficiently, sloughing took place. That year people had just discovered that there was such a thing as a curved blade that put the soil on to one side, so making a better, quicker and easier plough for both man and beast. Some farmers started to use only one bullock, a revolution, indeed, in its own fashion. Others said that the strain was too much for one animal, so still used two. Rice seedlings were planted in nurseries. It is a matter of nice judgment when to start transplanting them: fields have to be flooded and the soil made into the correct muddy consistency before groups of villagers take to the fields, helping each other out on a rota basis. The menfolk are responsible for coaxing the oxen to flatten the soil with wooden rollers. Planting is the job of the womenfolk and mighty weary they feel at the end of a long day, with back aching, feet and legs caked in mud and hands tired. The prettiness of the scene is only in the eye of the beholder.

The first day of the monsoon is the equivalent of St. Swithin's Day in Britain except that it needs to rain both morning and evening for the monsoon to be heralded as a good one. The Pokhara valley has the highest rainfall in the kingdom. Unlike many other places, the pre-monsoon heat is often alleviated by fierce storms that lash the landscape: almost horizontal winds hit houses and often rip off roofs that have not been weighted down by large stones. "The mountains make their own weather," it is said and, with the Himalayas seemingly almost near enough to put the hand out to touch, those living in the valley are at their mercy.

By the middle of the monsoon the rice sowing had all but been completed. The sickly yellow wisps would soon be that loveliest of colours, the deep emerald green of growing rice. I always find the extra dimension of seeing the sky and the mountains reflected in the paddy fields (no relation of the Irishman of the same name) particularly attractive. There are four rivers near us of which three are only fordable in the dry season. By now we had two dogs and, instead of jogging, Buddhiman and I took them for long walks each morning. We explored the countryside together and found it like a split-level maze. Moraine country, there are deep gorges and cliffs of a hundred or so feet that make walking hazardous. It took us quite a time to learn about the tiny paths up and down that, at first sight, do not exist. As the ground softens, chunks of rock and shale crash or slither away, to the eternal discomfort of any man or beast happening to be there then.

We came across monkeys, jackals, pine martens, mongooses, vultures and some eccentric pigeons that swim in the ice-cold river water to keep cool. One evening, when the rains had left off, I took the dogs for a walk and saw an animal which I did not recognize. I asked the locals and some said it was a hare, yet others said it was a jackal. I discovered it was a Burmese ferret badger (there is a Chinese variety of a lighter colour) which lived in burrows on flat ground, was nocturnal and fed on grubs. It looked like a half-grown Alsatian dog but had a much wider and bushier tail. The dogs go mad when they find one. They also love chasing the monkeys which, at this time of year, are great predators, not having had much food during the period before the monsoon. Maize is what they like. They sidle up to the fields, sending out sentries to see if there are any enemies before the main flock comes up behind them. Around most of the fields small boys and girls sit disconsolately in the rain with, if they are lucky, a home-made umbrella of plaited grasses. At the rear of any flock of monkeys come the mothers and babies. All are most adept at hiding over the lip of any precipice where they know they are safe.

Taking dogs for walks is not a Nepalese habit and we are often asked where we are taking them and why. Educated Nepalis use the English "morning walk": indeed they also use the English for "love marriage" and "half brain." Any connection? Certainly Hom Bahadur fell in love with a girl called Devi, from the same village and, luckily, the divinations agreed so that his threat of elopement if they were not allowed to get wed did not materialize. This was when I came across Mandhoj Gurung, the now-deaf man with the gift of prophesy, at work, so to speak, as opposed to purely socially on my visits to the village.

Many years ago when Birkha Raj was an illiterate boy, Mandhoj had told him that he would do well if he joined the British Gurkhas, still almost a novelty, and would become a high-ranking officer and, although against the odds of late promotion at every rank, he achieved the highest rank possible for a Queen's Gurkha Officer, Honorary Captain, and was the senior Gurkha officer in the western recruiting set-up besides being made an MBE. Devi's father, Singa Bahadur Gurung, at an equally young age, was told he would only have trouble if he went overseas as, for him, British water was "cloudy." He was selected for the Gurkha Police Contingent in Singapore but fell ill as he got on the boat in Calcutta and got worse and worse after he reached Singapore so that he was boarded out and returned to Nepal. As soon as he stepped ashore once more he started to recover his health and, by the time he got back home, he was sound in wind and limb—his illness never diagnosed.

He asked Mandhoj what would happen if he were to join the Indian Army and was told he would have two great crises during his service, one in the army and one at home, and would only get half his pension. So, with trepidation for the future overlaid with the challenges of the moment, he joined the 5th Gorkha Rifles. In the early '60s he was nearly killed in action. Shortly afterwards he was successful in capturing a Pakistani spy, a major masquerading as an apple seller. Then he had to go home to help bury an elder brother who had died without any previous signs of illness. Just before he was due out on pension as a subedar, he was promoted to Honorary Captain, which he still is, but, for some reason best known to

others, was only allowed an Honorary Lieutenant's pension—
so it was he left the army "with half a pension."

Several months before Devi was married she became ill
and Mandhoj was sent for. There was nothing evil to be afraid
of, it was her marriage divinations making themselves felt. She
was an unlucky girl in that she had been born on the night of a
new moon and these divinations needed most careful
reckoning. Her future husband could only come from the east
but one within the family would die: if he came from
elsewhere she would have a very unhappy life but there would
not be a sudden death in the family. Her father was faced with
the problem; daughter or whom? Hom Bahadur lived directly
to their east. Singa Bahadur decided that it would probably be
his own father who was in his second childhood and three
weeks after the wedding, the old man died.

I went up to do what a father has to do for his son at his
wedding, which was as Buddhiman had described his own
wedding when I was not there. Afterwards they came to live
with us in Pokhara for a year or so.

Buddhiman had enrolled in the local campus as an arts
student but found the student unions almost unmanageable.
There were separate Soviet and Chinese communist factions,
an Indian-style Congress group and, hated by all the others,
those students in favor of the current non-party political
system. The campus was off-limits to local police so the
students felt strong enough to "manage affairs" themselves.
Classes suffered badly: Buddhiman discontinued studying
because of the "mumbling and grumbling."

Early in 1988 I went to see the police to ask how safe it was for me to wander around as I did. I was told that, for me, there was no danger at all. Heartened, I was walking back home when a wizened old man stopped in front of me, saluted and said that he too had been in 1/1 Gurkha Rifles. By then I had been away from the battalion for over forty years, less for a few days spent with it in 1959. I looked at him and felt an odd sensation. When we were together we were both fresh-faced youths. Now, an old man, wrinkled, a little bent, losing his hair and his teeth, I felt I was looking in a mirror at the myself of yesteryear and realizing how much time had passed. I asked him his army number and he told me the one he had been given after we left. No, no, the one you had when we were together. It took him a moment or so to dredge it up: 2493. It rang a bell and I remembered his name and that he had been a driver. He did not react much when I got it right. After all, a Gurkha regiment is an extended family and we had been together for a year or so!

We invested in a plot of land to the north of the Kathmandu Valley. It had been very quietly suggested to me that I be put in charge of what was described as the Boys' Campus of the Royal Nepal Army, in Bhaktapore, and that had drawn our thoughts to having our own place in that area. The site was above the smog line, faced south and was at the top of a small slope down to a river, across which was the range of hills that enclosed the valley.

Over in the east of the country the large base at Dharan was due to close and there was much talk among the old soldiers and others in the eastern hills that the British were no longer interested in them. I was asked to go and talk to them as I was known and, as an ex-serviceman myself, we could "take off our masks" when we met. As I had moved the western equivalent from Paklihawa to Pokhara in 1979, the worries and anxieties of those affected by such a traumatic event were very real to them. In that case we in the west could fall back on Dharan for certain facilities, such as the hospital and resettlement courses. Capping the wellsprings of discontent was hard enough then: now it would be harder still to calm fears of abandonment at worst, disenchantment at best. The camp at Dharan had outlived its original rationale, namely to be at the end of the Indian railhead in a country without any roads or air facilities. Thirty years ago the Tarai had been the area to aim for: now Kathmandu and the use of the new road network (still to be developed in the east) made a large camp in the east redundant.

I had last wandered the eastern hills twelve years before and found the whole area much more relaxed than I had known it, on and off, since 1967. News of the closure of the camp in Dharan had reverberated around the villages, causing many people, ex-servicemen and civilians, to wonder what it was all about and whether the British were abandoning them, thus ending many years of British connection.

The weather was the worst I had ever come across in my ten thousand miles in all-weather walking in Nepal. We were in cloud, mist or rain for twenty-six out of thirty-four days. It was on the morning of the tenth day of our walk that the earthquake, predicted for the morrow by the almanac, struck. We were to spend the night by the side of a large river, half a mile wide, and the porters had suggested we make camp on the flat ground by it. Buddhiman had vetoed that suggestion and we were in a house up a twenty-foot bank. Early in the morning all were awoken by a loud, grating, stuttering noise. Our beds shook and we bolted outside, I being dragged. Luckily nothing in that vicinity fell down, although there were cracks in the older houses. The wide river was momentarily hurled off course and six feet into the air. We would have been swept away we not been in the house. I met far more folk than I would otherwise have done as they came in to the welfare offices to report damage to property and livestock. I therefore had a much wider audience than expected and could spread my reassuring message that, despite their fears and rumors to the contrary, the British were not abandoning the east.

The glamour and vainglory of regimental soldiering over the years of four decades had long faded. Nevertheless the magic of camaraderie then formed, dormant for so long, instantly and without hesitation rose to the surface everywhere I went. At eight welfare centres we visited names and numbers, in the main, sprang to the mind and almost everybody had his own anecdote about the times we had spent together—some true and flattering, some untrue and flattering, but never neutral! Looking at the men's animated faces and shining eyes was once more like looking into a mirror in reverse: once smooth-faced, clean-limbed, upright lads were scarcely recognized now that they had become shriven, wrinkled, toothless and grey-haired or bald. I, too, after so much time, was one of that large army of "those who fade away." In all I suppose I spoke to about ten per cent of the pensioners and I got the firm impression that everybody with whom I spoke accepted what I told them wholeheartedly.

But that aside it was the reactions of one ill man and one old woman I had gone to meet that held the attention of the serving soldier who was with us and Buddhiman, for whom this journey filled in much detail of my earlier service as the old men gossiped. The man lived in Bagsila, where I had made a detour to visit the widow of an old friend whose two sons I had helped over the years. I was told he was ill and, from behind his house, I called his regimental number, rank and name. I found him sitting forlornly on a wooden bed in the front of his house, clutching a stool to keep himself upright. His face was puffy, he coughed and wheezed and was obviously very unhappy and very ill.

He did not grumble at his fate nor did he bewail the effects on his family but told me his troubles as though he were reporting how he had been on patrol in yesteryear. I reminded him of our time together in the early '50s on operations in the jungle in Malaya. That started him off. For over an hour he was back in time, reliving old actions, quoting old remarks, even singing an old song as the years rolled back and his illness forgotten. He clutched a sickle in his hands, twisting the handle vigorously as bandit after bandit was met and dispatched. He needed no prompting. His wife and daughter, sitting on the floor nearby, stared at him in wonder and delight.

"Never did I think we would meet again. I can now die happy," he said as I left and slumped over the stool once more as loneliness and heartache overtook him once again. He was dead a few months later.

The old woman was the mother of a friend I had served with in the Gurkha Parachute Company and with whom I had walked the eastern hills twenty-three years before. He was the man who worshipped at the monastery after washing in ice-cold water. I had stayed with her in Bhojpur, she a widow even then, and had met her again seven years later when she had started to go blind. Her son, pensioned, had gone to Kathmandu several times to try and find me but had failed. He had suddenly died of a heart attack eighteen months before and his mother was still bereft.

She was sleeping when I went to see her. I woke her up. "Mother, the English friend of your eldest son has come to meet you," I called. She bade me sit down beside her and then she poured her heart out, weeping copiously as she did. I held her hand and muttered soothing words but could not stop the flow. I then had an idea to take her mind off her sadness.

"Mother, was it in 1959 or 1958 that you made that journey to Kathmandu by yourself?"

"Neither, it was in 1957 and I took my youngest with me ..."

For ninety minutes the old lady gave me chapter and verse as she retraced all her footsteps, giving me graphic accounts of the hardships of the journey—how she once went for five days with only water to drink, how she was ignored, misled, how folk tried to rob her—but she had prevailed and been successful, even if her people hardly recognized her when she got back home, months later, so thin and weary was she. For sheer pluck and guts I had seldom heard such a story and wished I had thought of making a recording of it. She did not need any prompting: she sat bolt upright, eyes dry, a clarity in her diction and a hardness in her voice that belied her frail body. She went on and on and on.

It was time to go. Gently I told her it was getting dark and I had to leave. At that she came back from the past into the present, slumped and started to weep. Can I accept her invitation to come again and stay?

By the first week in September the rains had slackened and we had three days of sunshine, even seeing the Himalayas for the first time, if only for five minutes. Perversely, it rained all that night and at least two complete hillsides collapsed, softened by endless rain and jolted by the earthquake and the tremors that came for fourteen days afterwards. Overnight rivers were filled with soil, turning their approaches into mud that, thigh-deep, was glutinous enough to entrap a single traveler. The grit and stones in the black, evil-looking water made the river roar when normally there would have been a happy ripple. The intensity of the flow and the thickness of the dirt took little chunks out of the skin of our legs. Many were the detours we had to make where the path had been swept into the valley below the night before and many more were the places that, sooner than later, would also crumble.

We got back to Dharan and sore eyes kept me on my back for nineteen hours. We had walked three hundred and eighty mountain miles, averaging eighteen miles a day. On our journey and at the end, as ever, I was entirely dependent on Buddhiman.

I managed to take the lead role a month or so later as our walk in the eastern hills was not the only long journey we did together that year. We went to England, he for the very first time. He very nearly failed to get a passport as none was being issued. It took him a week on top of the four-day journey to the district offices and back. The government had got tough on smugglers of contraband or undeclared goods, with strict conditions being introduced. First a police report was required to say that the applicant's character merited a passport and, without a referee, none would be given. Luckily the senior police officer was away for two days which gave Buddhiman time to walk back to the village where Singa Bahadur lived to ask him personally to go back with him as referee, otherwise no certificate would have been given. In any case, the order was that the functionary who issued the passport had to go to jail for as long as its holder if the latter were to be convicted of smuggling, with five years the minimum sentence.

Buddhiman waited four and a half days to be called in for his passport to be signed by the Chief District Officer, only to learn that that worthy individual was refusing to sanction any passport for anybody at all. Time was running out and he had to make a move back. "I said to myself that, if I can not get in front of the CDO today, there will be NO CHANCE of going to England and I was very sad," he told me. He barged into the CDO's office, in front of everybody, just before the end of the working day, stood to attention and firmly announced that he had a request to make. On grudgingly being allowed to speak, Buddhiman, having heard that the CDO was anti-British Gurkhas, told him that "an English professor" had looked after him after a life time with the military, that this professor had worked for four years in Tribhuvan university and had asked him back to his English home as part of Buddhiman's general education. "He has written a request to you," he said and gave the CDO the nicely worded, English-language request, written just for this eventuality. It worked! Buddhiman's was the only passport that particular CDO ever issued. That was not the end of the processing business but the rest was routine.

Buddhiman's visit to England (and Scotland and Wales!), to meet mother, David and the rest of his English family was a storybook in its joy. They had long heard of him but, apart from photographs, had yet to meet him in the flesh. It passed all my expectations in appreciation and love shown on all sides—in shops, in trains, on station platforms, in buses, at the dentist's, in Edinburgh castle, in Canterbury cathedral, addressing the four-year-olds at assembly at the local primary school: everywhere he went. Life was full of surprises: a hot air balloon, a nuclear power station and a dead badger on the road. He broke down in tears once at the intensity of his emotions as he remembered how far he had come since he and I met. His English improved out of all recognition. It also gave him a different, harsher and more critical view of the country of his birth and the methods it used.

Back in Pokhara Buddhiman met an elderly woman from Nalma, the village opposite his birthplace. Talking about his experiences with me, she said that, of course, he and I had been son and father in a previous incarnation, had got separated and did not find each other ever again. We had to meet up in this life and, somehow, that had been ordained.

The idea tickled me and made good sense to her. Buddhiman did not dismiss it out of hand. What was of no doubt was the way both of us "felt" for each other when we were not together. Both Buddhiman and Singa Bahadur knew, from their dreams, when my eyes were giving me trouble and Buddhiman would come back from the village to see what was wrong. Twice, when I was in England, he telephoned as he knew I had hurt myself, once when I nearly knocked myself out and once when my eyes flared up badly enough to put me on my back. He learnt how to drive a car when I was in England and, on his first long journey, yearned to tell me. He "visited" me as I was lying in bed. I was staying with an uncle and aunt and only, two days later, when back in Dorset, did I ring to find out what he wanted to say. That was it, and the time lag exactly fitted. I had to get used to the idea of incarnations and let it all "dwell a pause" at the back of my mind, surfacing from time to time when our conversation touched on it.

Back in Nepal the political situation deteriorated. Roads were blocked on orders from those unauthorized to give such an order. A grave shortage of fuel for vehicles left tourists stranded. On the pretext of no agreement on a new trade treaty being reached, India slapped on an embargo, the third since the non-party system came into force. The behavior of the Mongoloid hill students caused me to worry if there would ever be enough of the right material to get the type of soldier who had made the name Gurkha famous for so long. I remembered a worry I had had twenty-two years before when I saw Aryan Nepalis from other areas take over village schools and came across cases of old family and village traditions either not understood or merely ignored. What would be the cumulative effect of such a policy, I had wondered. Now I knew: no discipline, fewer morals and a pervasive idea of Nepalese scholastic qualifications not counting for much so let us cheat and get away with what we can. Yet, even so, this sad trait is not as virulent in Nepal as it is in the more powerful countries of the Indian subcontinent.

By now Buddhiman had a son, weighing over nine pounds at birth. I was asked to carry him from the gate to the house, which I did most gingerly. "You are so heavy you'll be a wrestler," I said, using the Nepali word, Pahalman, which is also a name. His father was delighted and that is his name, with the addition of one before that, in honour of me, Jon. We held a large party when it was time to wean him. We were hit by a severe drought and Bhim Kumari had to go and get her Proof of Citizenship papers from the district she was born in. It involved a fifty-mile walk, both ways, and when the office was reached, so hot was it that her milk for her baby dried up. Luckily Buddhiman found some glucose and that did the trick so the baby was able to be breast fed again.

We got our telephone and there was difficulty in installing it as, somehow, we were not on the list. However, Buddhiman discovered that the man in charge, a Brahman, was the first cousin to a man who had a life-time binding friendship pact between non-relatives, as a first cousin, with a first cousin of Buddhiman's first cousin and even that tenuous relationship was enough for the job to be done outside office hours for no extra charge!

Two years after I had been asked to write the history of the Royal Nepal Army I went to see the Chief Of Army Staff. I had first met him maybe thirty years previously and felt I could talk to him frankly. I told him it had been two years since he had asked me to undertake this job, but I had not started as there was no authority to have a view of any of the archives. He did not seem worried and felt I needed some payment. He arranged for 15,000 rupees [then about £230] to be paid to me, a gesture I appreciated but felt I had not deserved. However, I took it gladly as that, allegedly, was the sum one of the assessors of my work in CNAS had been paid when, after borrowing my copy of the project, he had "lifted" one section in its entirety and had it published in his name. Forty-four months after being asked to be the historian the Chief retired and I had not even started my project.

In the meantime I had written an article for a university publication, *Has Communism Failed?* Most of its references came from Soviet publications. A year later I asked if it was going to be published but that was not possible as, by then, paper was one of the commodities the embargo had affected. Instead, on 1 January 1990, I managed to arrange a seminar and half of those attending had been educated in Moscow. The other half were people who had come to know me in CNAS and came in a supportive role. I was only allowed to mention such a contentious subject at all because I had scored Brownie points when at CNAS. When Communism did fail, my stock rose accordingly. How had I known?

It was ironic that I should have ushered in the New Year with such a topic as 1990, apart from being one of the most tumultuous on the world stage in the past forty years, was to prove as significant as any in the whole of Nepal's history. The king and queen undertook an extended visit centred on Pokhara and I was invited to two functions when the queen was present. Whatever the cynical and the opportunists may aver to the contrary, I believe that the absolute aspect of the Nepalese monarchy was of paramount importance in dealing with situations that no other aspect of governance pertaining at that time could have bettered. Nevertheless, nothing that man puts his hand to has undiluted positive benefits for all time. The magic of the Nepalese monarchy does not have to be sustained by absolutism alone—nor will it be after "light has been let in on the magic."

I had tried to get an audience with the king to thank him personally for his munificence but this proved impossible. When I told a friend the reason for my request, he said that would never have been allowed and I would have to tell the authorities something else. During this period the Chief of the General Staff of the British Army and a life-long officer of Gurkhas, General Sir John Chapple (and a long-time friend of mine), had an audience with His Majesty and we had a chat afterwards. He, a historian of note, was happy that Buddhiman and I had been invited to India to take part in the celebration of the 175th anniversary of raising 1/1 Gorkha Rifles, as he was keen that links be established more firmly between Indian Gorkhas and British Gurkhas than hitherto.

Before we went down to India Buddhiman and I had to go to Kathmandu, against my gut instinct, to do some shopping. The day after we arrived coincided with yet another "shut-down-Nepal" day and everywhere was closed. That evening, as had been the case for many months, gangs of youths went around ordering people to turn off their lights for an hour or so to show how unhappy they were with conditions. Next morning, shortly before 7 o'clock, His Majesty came on the air and announced that a multi-party system would be promulgated.

I wondered if multi-party government was capable of creating in the mind of a Nepali a feeling of moral obligation to obey it. Only time would tell. Out in the streets that morning we were both forcibly struck at how everybody, whether on their own or in company, was smiling at the king's proclamation about political plurality. The mood of euphoria quickly changed. By noon Buddhiman knew what tear gas smelt like. By late afternoon many thousands of people had marched to the palace to give in a petition. This was refused and as the crowd, for the most part slowly and quietly dispersed, the army fired on them with automatic weapons, killing quite a number.

That evening a thirty-hour curfew was imposed. Next morning we were the only two people who managed to escape out of it, brazening our way through patrols until picked up by the Defence Attaché. The city looked as though it had been through a siege. Two other towns, Patan and Kirtipur, were "no-go" areas, with trenches dug around them and, for the latter, trees felled across the road to stop entry.

No kid gloves were used: two young boys who taunted a couple of policemen had their skulls cracked open with staves; a helicopter flew over Kirtipur (whose inhabitants still mistrust the Gorkha ruler from more than two centuries ago) and killed six people; a woman with four babies whose husband had left the house to get them some milk and was shot and killed to quote only three instances. Many and varied were the reports of deaths but all carried a common thread of over-reaction, under-training and heavy-handedness.

Rumors proliferated. One local newspaper later alleged that General Chapple's visit to Nepal was to arrange for ex-servicemen, both British and Gurkha, to teach urban guerilla warfare to the Nepalese army against their own people. I was quoted as having been one of the teachers; three trucks carrying stranded British tourists to the airport were alleged to be carrying dead Nepalese bodies that had been killed because of me.

Despite, on the surface, an entirely Nepalese dimension to the disturbances, sadly Nepal was not helped by influences alien to it. One morning at the gates of the Indian embassy, I overheard an Indian talking to an Australian tourist. The former said he was a journalist from Calcutta, with links to the embassy. He boasted that the Nepalis would do anything Indians told them. He further said that he had been hard at work inciting young Nepalis to demonstrate against the system, in other words, that he was responsible for "rent-a-crowd." I listened with exasperation as I heard this man joyfully boasting and saw him strike heroic postures. The Australian was embarrassed and tried to break off the conversation. This only made the Indian sing his own praises even more. The Australian moved away and the Indian disappeared, I saw not where. Even though this man may have been exaggerating and wanting to show off, I firmly believed that, at base, he was being truthful. I prayed that there would not be an unleashing of that most dangerous thing in the world: the lust for tyrannical power which grows on what it consumes, even if, in part, it can be put down to the "nation's will to live", in part it must also be seen as the "foul vent of tortured and suppressed instincts" arising because those in authority under the king had not translated his coronation oath for the nation's benefit as had been sworn during that ceremony.

This brief couplet, written on the inside of a bus, neatly summed up people's feelings:

Don't give me your tears, by weeping so much is my tiredness begotten,

Rather I ask that you teach me to laugh, as how to is what I've forgotten.

Our visit to 1/1 Gorkha Rifles was hard work. The three-day journey south to Puné, "travel" with its old meaning of "travail" both ways, was more than worthwhile. The sincerity of the Indian officers and Gorkhas of all ranks was unforgettable. I was asked to address the battalion and enjoyed reminding them of the two old soldiers I had found in Dharmsala when I joined the First Gurkhas in 1944. The elder had first enlisted in 1891, so I was a ninety-nine year link between then and 1990.

We had been invited to a missionary school on our way back, by Andrew McCabe, the delightful Scot in charge. When we eventually did get there it coincided with Muslim-Hindu controversy about the holy place of Ayodhya—1990 was quite a year. I had never lived in a missionary establishment before and found it disconcerting to be prayed over, around and with before and after every meal, as though the Lord Jesus was hiding behind the wainscot and was too embarrassed or busy to come out. On the Sunday we attended church service, conducted according to the Church of North India. One unusual feature was for members of the congregation to be called on to offer prayers. The language was Hindi. One such thanked us for attending from so far away and asked us to stand up to be recognized. It then struck me that I might be called on to utter a prayer and I composed one in Nepali as my religious Hindi was not up to scratch. In the event I was not asked. The dedication and sincerity of those in charge cannot be put in doubt. Our journey back to Nepal was fraught— hardly any trains running—and the hundred and ten miles from the border to Pokhara took over twelve hours in the bus. Since the political upheaval students stopped any bus as and how they wanted to and travelled without paying. Woe betide any bus driver who thought he knew better and had qualms about over-loading.

That year Buddhiman and I also went to visit the Seventh Gurkhas in Hong Kong, another first for him. Once again the journey was agonizingly frustrating. Having confirmed our seats with Royal Nepal Airlines one month, one week and again the day before, we were horror-struck to find, when we reported in at the desk, that they had been deleted during the night. Two hundred and fifty-two tickets had been sold for a 'plane that had only one hundred and ninety-six seats. Fifteen and a half hours and $200 later, we got away, only to have the same trouble on the return journey. However, our stay was wonderful: it is not many Hill men who get looked after as an officer in the messes of two armies in one year!

On our return I was shown yet another mention I had been given by a Nepali in a book called *Unseen Truths in Nepalese Politics*. The author, a hill man from Darjeeling, waxed strongly against British Gurkhas, saying, and I quote, "the British exploited their men, treated them like animals, showed them disrespect, hatred, treachery, tyranny and injustice and have as much regard for them when in their off time in the army as dolls bought in the bazaar and, when they end their service, they are looked down on as lower than those who are uncivilized, jungly, illiterate and foolish … " and a whole lot more. Rank and name given, I was one of the guilty men now living in Nepal. Nepalis have a touching faith in the sanctity and infallibility of the written word.

So why stay on?

The 1980 referendum for non-party or multi-party government caused much excitement. Up in Buddhiman's village, Dharmasing, the man who had told him that I would look after him, was by then a belligerent Christian and he accused Mandhoj, the seer, of being Satanic. "Let me have proof of your powers," he taunted. Dharmasing had wanted to know if "the king would win," that is to say would the non-party faction, hence the monarchy, remain, or if "the king would lose," meaning the multi-party faction would win, the reverse. Mandhoj went into a trance and said that, if the referendum were held on the originally declared date, the king would lose, otherwise the king would win. Some time later the date was indeed changed and the king "won." The monarchical system was retained in the constitution. I only learnt about this is 1992. I turned to Buddhiman and said that if Mandhoj was such a successful and accurate foreteller, could we not ask him to confirm the suggestion of the woman from Nalma that we had been father and son in a previous incarnation?

Looking back on my life with its twists and turns, high and low points, successes and disappointments, was it all for a reason? I started thinking of those turning points, significant events and coincidences that had played their part. Taking them in order: the war; the delay in going to Colchester so being sent to India as part of the first draft ever; brother Tim's death and the infusion of his spirit into me so making me a linguist; being commissioned into the Gurkhas when I had never volunteered for them; passing the Nepali obligatory examination; visiting Kathmandu and not getting back in time to be sent away to a British battalion; talking to Field Marshal Slim about the Brigade of Gurkhas' officer policy; failing the Staff College Entrance examination so not having to have "conventional" postings; the innumerable times my love life turned sour even before it had started to be sweet; sister Gillian's death; the failure of my eyesight; and the uniqueness of my status in Nepal. Was there any other coincidence? Even the throwaway remark when a child that I needed a coloured man to look after me now rang true! When I was sent to be DRO it was against the rules. As for getting approval for my unique status exactly ten months to the day, so making me a "reborn" Nepali, that could make sense if what the old lady from Nalma said was confirmed by Mandhoj, as indeed

Buddhiman's intuitively knowing when I needed help. But we did nothing about it. As for Buddhiman, he had planned to go to Assam a week before I called him over but the man who had said he would take him did not call into the camp as expected, having taken the other, bus-route, road to the border. Another coincidence!

As an example of the intuitiveness of our relationship, the following incident is indicative. Buddhiman had gone up to his hill village prior to going on to Lamjung district capital, Besi Shahar, to complete a land transaction. He was to be away for a week to ten days. A few days after he had left Pokhara, Bhimraj of Luwang came to the house to tell me that the Silver Jubilee celebrations of a school, in Kaski, I had helped were a month earlier than had been previously announced. Buddhiman had said he would give me a 'phone call from Besi Shahar and I knew I could recall him to take part in the celebrations. However, the call never came and there was nothing I could do to get my son back except to invoke whatever gods were listening. So, one morning around 10 o'clock, back from my morning walk with the dogs, I openly said, "Whatever gods are listening to me, please get my son back so that we can go to the school celebration together."

Exactly at that time, so we later discovered, Buddhiman, delayed for three days from his original plan so unable to get to the district capital, left the house he had had his morning meal in and, bidding farewell to his host, started out on the last lap of his journey—going east. After no more than a dozen paces, he turned and said to his host, "I must go back to

Pokhara. Father wants me." And he did get back just in time for us to go with me and Bhimraj to the school.

Then again: one Sunday evening in March 1992, I was told that a European woman, a complete stranger, had come to see me. She had bowled in as though it was the most natural thing in the world; she had with her a Gurkha I had enlisted. Her name, she told me, was June Andrews, "they call me Jun Kumari" [Moon Princess], she announced. She was a nurse in Aldershot ("voluntary, my dear"). She had helped in nursing Gurkhas for the past ten years and the men had always asked her if she knew a J.P. Cross. She had not, although she had been to Nepal on a number of occasions, and she was making sure about it this time. She had been told about my book, *In Gurkha Company*, and she had, after some initial hesitation in that she feared it would be "just another book written by another ignorant colonel," read it. She had started to "relate" from the very first page and it had so intrigued her that she found herself even more wanting to meet the man whose name was on the lips of all Gurkhas and who so obviously loved Gurkhas when he wrote about them. She told me it had taken her a year to get a pristine copy of the book.

By that time she was halfway through her coffee and Buddhiman had come in from outside. She further surprised us by speaking Nepali, and even more by writing her Nepali nickname in the script in the visitors' book. The most surprising part of all was when she told us that she had been a Nepali woman, a Gurung, in a previous incarnation. When in Kathmandu on her first visit some years ago, she had fallen sick and had been taken to the hospital, she knew that she had been killed in Kathmandu in her previous existence and that she would die there again if she did not get away quickly, which she did, still uncured.

On another occasion, a couple of Nepalis visited her in her hotel with a message from King Birendra asking her to stay in Nepal and be a "Mother Theresa" and write a book on Nepal. She had refused both requests, saying, for the former, that Mother Theresa was "in at the end" but that she was happier with saving younger people from dying, while for the latter, that she would be too outspoken so would not be welcome in the future. Nor had she realized that one of her visitors was intimately connected with the royal family and the other with the palace.

Of course she wanted to be introduced to the family, and, as luck would have it, Hom Bahadur and his brood were with us. She took lots of photographs and called me John without any prompting. She asked me for my autograph, to have proof that she had met me, so I wrote out a message, plus signature, that she could stick in her copy of the book. Now sixty and divorced many years ago, she asked me if I had ever been married. When I told her never, she asked me how many children would I have had since I had so many without being married? The only answer I could think of was that, had she been around, she would have known. We had never been so swamped before and, after she had gone, I asked Buddhiman if she had been our mother from before? The effect of her visit was for us to go and see Mandhoj.

As he is almost stone deaf I had written my questions out and asked Buddhiman to go and show them to him the evening before. The first question was; was Buddhiman my son during my last incarnation? The second question was: will Buddhiman be my son in my next incarnation? Thirdly I asked him who my last wife was now?

Mandhoj came at dawn, the best time of day for him to perform, carrying a bag. Inside and so out of the cold, we all sat on the floor. We were offered a drink of tea and then preparations started. A plate was produced on which rice was put and, on the rice, a small goddess (strangely a Hindu one but one of whose epithets is of the Buddha, yet Mandhoj is neither, but an animist) was placed, as was a rosary. On the left of the plate was the bag in which he had brought the goddess and rosary which now only contained some leaves, though of what plants I could not say. On the right was a receptacle on which burning embers from the fireplace were put. On this raw and precious incense, from up in the mountains, made strong and thick smoke. We three sat together, cross-legged in front; the other two with us, the man and woman of the house, sat apart.

Incantations began, using language I started to understand but which trailed off into meaningless mumbling. The spirit was being called down and Buddhiman and I were being introduced. After a short while Mandhoj, hands clasped tightly in front of him, started violently to tremble. Mostly his hands were in front of his chest but sometimes they rose to head level. Then the spirit entered him and it started to talk through him, his voice having a clearer and different timbre than when normal or when the spirit was being invoked.

Then the answers came out: Buddhiman and I had been uterine brothers, not son and father, living farther to the east, as Christians, low caste sweepers, both very good men. My mind raced; to the east lay Kathmandu and, up to 1768, six Capuchin monks had been there for over a century. We were separated and simply had to meet in this incarnation, but as son and father. If we are both pure in this life, not only will my only perceived task, writing, be successful but we will be uterine brothers once more in our next incarnation. We are probably to be born in the royal palace in Kathmandu as Christians and I, using Buddhiman's help, will become the leader of the country. If that were to happen, we will both be allowed respite from this mortal coil and can join the godhead. However, what did emerge from Mandhoj's mouth was that, at their primeval level, both Hinduism and Christianity did not contradict one another.

By the end of the second question Mandhoj was so tired and dripping with sweat that he could not sustain his trance and I felt asking the third question was unfair. Out of his trance, he talked about what had been relayed through him. Surprisingly, for a brief spell he clearly heard what we were saying before his deafness re-asserted itself.

It is quite possible that "religion" need play no part in this experience. Morphic resonance or collective thinking, as I hinted at the very beginning, could be the answer, with Mandhoj having, to a very advanced degree, the gift of linking spheres of knowledge, which is given to very few others. However, if "religion" is the medium of Mandhoj's efforts, how does it square with our own Christian teachings, how was

Mandhoj told by his non-Christian spiritual informant—through what is essentially an animist thought-pattern, and is not so far, in its basic form, from Hinduism—the part that Christianity played, does play and will play for both Buddhiman and me in three incarnations?

I find it impossible to hazard the answer: what I do know is that I now feel superbly at ease, as though I have now reached where I was heading for all the time. I am not scared of it: I don't disbelieve it, nor do I find it hard to believe. I suppose, as a baptized Christian, I should feel repugnance, if not repentance, but I don't. After all, there is so much left unexplained in Christianity that there need be no basic clash. All I do know is that those personal points I have listed, haphazard, coincidental and not understood at the time, do now seem to fall into a preordained pattern. For whatever reason, Buddhiman and I have now been initiated into the something that makes sense of this life, if not the other two.

... AND TOMORROW?

... and what of the morrow? On a number of occasions I have been asked what I think about various subjects and to give my opinion. I am always faced with a dilemma: shall I stay quiet and be thought stupid or open my mouth and be proved so? If I do venture to air what the tactful would call knowledge, I am reminded or that old saw "old men's wisdom is often arrogance aggravated by flattery." Quite so.

However, remembering the other adage of the "spectator seeing most of the game," and having an intense interest in Nepal, I venture to put my thoughts of the future on paper.

Every country, which is a convenient way of jumbling together all the many aspects and strands of society and nature, has its roots in history, which is dead politics. The chief ingredient of human wisdom is an ability to learn from experience which, by definition, can never be any time except in the past, be it the immediate past or the long-dead version. The peace of a country is preserved by a habit, nearly unconscious, of constant subordination of its people. Anyone who doubts that only has to look at other countries in southwest, south and southeast Asia to acknowledge its truth.

Politics, in this context I mean "conditions that allow people to live at as pleasant and rewarding a standard of comfort and happiness as circumstances provide," is living history, be it caused by governments, religion or the family. Implementation of required improvements is a complicated, difficult and on-going process. One of my sanest Kathmandu friends says thirty years from 1990 we will be where we should have been in 1990.

I personally believe that there are a minimum of four fundamental requirements that need to be constantly guarded and improved upon at all times if my definition is to withstand, namely a firm economic base, clean and efficient legal and administrative systems, full use of manpower resources—in particular of youth—and a positive method of education. These will not pertain, however, until another four fundamental requirements are implemented; a public conscience, accountability for responsibilities, dedicated civic duty and honesty in public life. The impression that "direct pecuniary malversation" pervades public offices must be eradicated by government transparency before a suspicious public accepts that government is "on its side" so that belief and confidence in it are widespread enough for consent of approval rather than consent by apathy. The real essence of work is concentrated energy: without that all governments are doomed to being "more of the same in the past."

Looked at another way, the primary aim of any government should be to abolish poverty, to diminish unemployment and to reduce inefficiency. Regrettably many representatives of governments, all over the world I am bold enough to suggest, are not wise enough, disinterested enough or technically competent enough for that to happen.

If developed countries with so much more going for them cannot get those points right, what chance has Nepal, certainly in the short term? I believe a good one, with a firm start embedded in the constitution of 1991.

I must, however, hark back to the three "time bombs" I postulated at the very beginning. They are intertwined and need to be defused as expeditiously and contemporaneously as possible as, by now, the fuses have burnt very near the detonator.

As object lessons I refer to Gorbachev defusing his political tensions before economic and agrarian tensions—and what happened to the Soviet Union?—as well as to China's Whoever-he-was-behind-the-scenes deciding to defuse economic and agrarian tensions before any political equivalent. That country is out of kilter and the only question is not will the elasticity of government snap but when will it? The implosion of the dead weight of inertia is all-powerful.

In Nepal ethnic tensions have been exacerbated by the introduction of democracy and the retention of Hindu values as promulgated in *Manusmrti*. The question here that Nepal must answer is can the first be resolved and are the second and third compatible or must there be an explosive polarization?

I have described some of the latent pressures and problems I personally encountered in my narrative. The modern tendency is for Mongoloid ethnic groups to discard Hinduism in favor of animism. In a democracy who can stop us? they ask. These people see democracy equaling freedom in the social equation. Within every adult Nepali is an urge for freedom of expression trying to get out and exert itself. Sadly there also seems to be an ethnic tension outside waiting to get in. I think the safest type of freedom for Nepal is that every person has freedom to do all that he wills provided that he does not infringe the equal freedom of any other person. To achieve this a system of removable inequalities is needed where, in theory, all may hope for social improvement. In all this public opinion—pressure?—is a permeating influence which exacts obedience to itself: it requires men to think other men's thoughts, to speak other men's words, to follow other men's habits. If Nepal is not far from what I have written, the democracy "time bomb" has the status of a damp squib.

The spread of ethnic minorities' animism is a recent but potentially potent phenomenon. Animism, as a religion, is too feeble to be of use to a nation. Animists live largely by what they see and hear, not much by what they feel. I cannot believe that this trend will be intrinsically fulfilling as many of its proponents believe it will. There is a very fine balance indeed between the retention of sufficient hereditary values of the ethnic variety to keep aware of them and their overindulgence leading to such stresses that the fabric of the nation is ripped apart. Wisdom, tolerance and self-discipline are needed.

Another, to me disturbing, facet of ethnic tension is the status of various languages other than Nepali in parliamentary and educational business. I know what ruling has been given about what part ethnic languages play in Nepal but there are dangers that must be made known. Let me quote only two: as French has been allowed equal status with English in Quebec province in Canada, it has "won over" culturally and there are great ideas about secession from the rest of Canada.

In South Africa the Boer language vied with English and "won over" culturally. I very much doubt if apartheid would have lasted so long and caused so much misery to so many had there been the restraining liberal voice of the English language to moderate behavior.

Language problems are endemic in India—at what expense!

An enervating and destabilizing reaction is not beyond the realms of probability in Nepal.

I next let my mind wander over the "moral philosophy" and "ethical" side of Nepalis. Some of Nepal's problems seem, to an outsider, so easy to solve but, as they have not been, they obviously are not so easy. Each person will have his own horror story. Mine, for instance, include: not keeping to office hours; not being on time for a meeting; not keeping a school free of debris and the grounds from looking like a dirty mush of self-recycling paper; not correcting examination papers properly or on time; medical malpractice, such as the clean plaster put on the broken arm of boy injured in the earthquake of 1988 without any cleaning or treatment just to impress one near The Highest In The Land, so it set badly and had to be broken again and reset; throwing hospital waste away outside the hospital compound so that the cows and the crows can pick through it, with no thought of the spread of disease; picking new stamps off unfranked envelopes; opening registered parcels instead of sending them through the mail; land-measuring *amins* with differing measurements for the same piece of land; burning forests because the "wrong" political party won a seat in that area...to name but a few. Only a few people may be involved but all get a bad name. As the Nepalis say, "one is at fault and the family suffers."

Many of these anti-social traits are not uniquely Hindu and worse could be quoted, I am sure, from elsewhere but, I ask, does the Hindu mind-set make them more difficult to rectify?

I was reminded of that old Russian story of the man who played chess against himself, would be winning, would leave the board and go to bed. In his sleep the chessboard was thrown about the place by evil spirits who were angry with the old man winning against himself. Try hard though he might, he could never catch them at this grotesque antic, nor could he escape from them, even though he always changed his rooms after each untoward occurrence. He virtually became a fugitive in his own country. He would never accept that it was not evil spirits that threw his chess board around so disturbing the pieces on it, but he himself who, sleep walking, did it. In other words, he was trying to escape from himself. How many of us are guilty of "sleep walking" to excuse habits taken for granted? Looked on thus, we can see that unconscious attitudes of mind which have only begun to stand out as strange in the eyes of the new generation might be one cause for potential instability.

And was that chess player insane? Maybe, but collective insanity is possible when conformity and stress on collective harmony help produce frustration at the unfulfilled flowering of countless individuals' potential or, for instance, the persecution of intellectuals, such as in Communist China, when there was no contact with the outside world.

Or the old fable about the dog with fleas—it went into the river and fully immersed itself less its nose. The fleas, trying to escape to the only dry place, jumped too often and were drowned. The dog was rid of his fleas. Although foxes are known to get rid of fleas this way, how few dogs can work out such a simple solution? And how does the dog's owner teach it? Mind set is all.

So, back to my moral philosophy and thought of ethics of Nepal. I presume that Nepalis accept the great natural laws governing the world which are often looked at with religious eyes; the strong instinct for preservation, natural affection, love of approbation, self-respect, sympathy with misfortune and suffering, and a sense of responsibility to the family, community and ruler.

Then there are ethics in a purely profane context, as most normal intelligent members of society see them. They seek cooperation, do deeds on trust, share confidences with associates, and get ahead by building friendships and alliances. Those who betray their employers and confederates and do not care what other people think of them are the exception, not the rule. How much moral good is "sunk without trace" by low quality "video nasties" invading the market or the insidious spread of AIDS through ignorance? Western diseases—in both senses of the word—encroach on all fronts.

Ethics often clashes with logic as does instinct with reason. A good example of this is seen with the Maoris of New Zealand. These people would never criticize one in authority at any level, be it village or state, or even mention his name. However, if a superior could not be tolerated, he was killed and eaten. This had an added advantage in that, to a degree, food stocks and population could be equated.

How many Nepalis ask themselves if there is an Ultimate Human Duty which is laid down not by men, but by some Authoritative Principle—for want of a better name—which is external to and beyond all human desires and is superior to any of them? And if their answer is affirmative, how many of them stick to it? Some would say that Nepal was, until recently, like Russia was in 1839 when all was calm on the surface yet starting to seethe underneath as the high moral ground was barren and religion had left its basic purity: Peace without tranquility, Laws without a social contract, People without a society. The king, parliament and democracy have greatly steadied what was developing into a dangerous situation. Nepal could suffer badly if ethnic tensions get out of hand. What can be said without argument is that those who really want mankind to become less wretched will do well to recognize that conflict of interests is the chief obstacle to this development.

Who and where is the leader in Nepal who has the breadth and width of knowledge, the personality, the authority, the power, the experience, the time to spare, the willingness to sacrifice much to unite the common will and translate it into a common good? What moral philosophy and ethical conduct can guide him, and the country, into this Time of Great Change and Challenge, to accept that which has to alter based on that which need not? Such a person is very rare but, without such a person when he is wanted, the situation must surely become exacerbated, as history has shown countless times in other countries.

I admit I have to be very careful when I talk about any such Principle as people see this in differing ways, if they see it at all. I personally have come to a belief that there is a Great Life Force that can be accepted by every religion as its basic premise. Force from its centre should, I also believe, come to us all undiluted, but, if it is ignored or mutated through ill use, it can only be seen as a Law of Chain Reaction, an Inverse Square Law or even a Law of Diminishing Returns. In other words, none can be permanently sustained by or joined with it then.

To explain what I mean by such descriptions: The Law of Chain Reaction is of a self-accelerating explosion, alike in the growth of the rabbit population of Australia, the spread of bracken in England, or nuclear physics. Once started it goes on and on and on, yet is in danger of mutating into something never envisaged when the original started.

Energy often diminishes; on a physical plain this can be seen in nuclear fission. An exceedingly rapid reaction occurs but not self-acceleration. As the explosive wave moves outwards from the centre, its energy is dispersed over a wider and wider radius and its intensity is correspondingly diminished. Such a process follows what is called the Inverse Square Law. There is yet another law that operates when the expansive process actually produces factors that resist its own development. In economics it is known as the Law of Diminishing Returns, or the Principle of Saturation.

These laws can be found working with the spread of ideas and of spiritual forces that reach us indiscriminately and adulterated. I firmly believe that, without pure acceptance of the Great Life Force, many of our troubles not only proliferate but are in danger of being misunderstood. This is true for all religions, all of which, as a basic tenet, embrace this concept. Many modern religious teachers and preachers, tenets and practices, seem bent on perpetuating modes that no longer reflect a universal Great Life Force. This affects both ethics and moral philosophy which, in turn, guide the conduct of a country, a society, a family, an individual.

Civilization is the adaptation to all circumstances that have already taken place. Nepal has so much already in her favor: through the Gurkhas, world renown; through the traditional ambience of the country, a haven of good will; through the majority of her population, a blessed sense of balance, self-respect and integral goodness. All those whom I have ever met who come to Nepal for the first time, especially having spent a month or two in India, always mention the politeness and pleasantness of the Nepali people. Sadly there are less of these two facets than used to be the case and I put this down to a diminution of the "Feel-Good Factor" and I detect a spreading mood of skepticism. Contentment, if not happiness, is a prerequisite for the enhancement of the lighter side of human nature. Happiness spreads down from the top. It does not move up from below. In any organization with a happy and efficient team at the top, the work force will be happy also. Nowhere is this more obvious than in the army. For civilians the task of producing and maintaining happiness is much harder but not impossible.

Let me put it this way: when I was in hospital having my eyes cut open, I was worried if I would ever be able to see again. The surgeon cheered me up immeasurably by telling me that his philosophy was to take the burden of worry off the patient's shoulders and put it on his. I had never thought of healing in that context before. Why can not that philosophy be applicable in a national, political and leadership context also?

I believe the bedrock for an enhanced future in Nepal must rest on national, material and spiritual peace of mind and that can only spring from the purity of regenerated Hinduism, which should then see no clash with other religions, and that will be the strength for a metamorphosis of that which is needed so much by this country. It is of the greatest significance that, certainly from what I have met with in the Pokhara area, more converts to Christianity come from Nepalis who once embraced communism than from those of the Congress Party. If purity of concept is not achieved, the desire to be good may operate as an actual hindrance to good activity. Moreover, if this world is seen chiefly as an area for the performance of self-sacrificing actions, one will not be very anxious to get rid of the conditions which seem to call for them.

In the past Nepalis have obeyed orders and social conventions for one or more of three reasons; *dar, kar, rahar*— fear, compulsion or desire. Is there a moral force to be found in a revised Hinduism that will supersede these three goads for a higher moral standard?

Taking my beliefs as a blue print for ethical behavior in politics, business and trade, a whole new and productive mind

457

set might well evolve, at no expense to correct and with unadulterated religious beliefs, in this case back to the pureness of original Hinduism. Mind set is all.

In other words, national revival cannot and will not emerge as all we lovers of Nepal wish it to unless and until the core concept of ethics and moral behavior is undiluted by selfishness and bolstered by trust by those in positions of authority at all levels. The high moral ground must be regained before the fullness of life can be attained. That will show itself, not so much in levels of social and political strife, educational attainment and urbanism, or even richness or poverty; rather it will be social co-operation of active citizen participation based on tolerance, trust and tact. Economic development does not explain political development but rather long established patterns of a civic community living in harmony explain a country's capacity for democratic self-government and will make Nepal happier and greater than she is now.

This is where I postulate on the second "time bomb," *Manusmrti*. The question I have to ask, without wishing to appear as one guilty of apostasy, is *Manusmrti* capable of enhancing Nepali Hindu ideas into what is known as the twenty-first century? The biggest internal danger Nepal faces is polarization on ethnic lines. There are faults on both sides of the Aryan/Mongoloid divide. I envisage one of two options to prevent this, built on the axiom that Nepal is a Hindu kingdom. It must remain so. The Hindu faith is understood, its main message easy to comprehend. The concept of a king and queen is an easy and comforting one. A strengthened pure

Hinduism could live at peace with all other major religions. The national will on such an issue can be bent to accommodate such an idea but can never be broken to accelerate it.

Were this to happen I am sure the name Nepal could become as world famous as the name Gurkha as, by liberating talents that have flowered when unsuppressed overseas, but are sadly untapped on home ground. Much of the world-famous name stems from a fusion of impeccable standards, maintenance of the old discipline, acquisition of new skills and an act of faith that Gurkhas will always prove better than even the most optimistically minded felt they were capable of performing. To allow such a blessed state to happen in Nepal such talent must be allowed to flower in the country as well as outside it. That, with an enhanced educational system that allows for more than rote and improvisation, would work wonders.

One option is to revert to basic Hinduism where all are free to pursue their gods to their own fashion untrammeled by what can be seen, basically, as social constrictions. The second option must be to look ahead and try to create political, economic, social and other relevant conditions equal to those predicted in the Age of Truth. I do not believe Nepal can possibly wait until its originally suggested arrival, 18 February 4,28,898 AD, that is probably 3 Chait 4,28,954 BS.

The better option, surely, was what King Mahendra had in mind when, in 1960, he announced that "all Nepalis are one." Other indications are that a return to pure basic Hinduism is possible. When the king of the country that glorifies bull-fighting, Spain, paid a state visit to Nepal, where such activity must be the gravest anathema, I was not aware of any murmur of dissent that such a visit was incompatible with the Hindu religion. To me this shows that the potential for a change back is buried within the psyche of the majority of Nepalis. However, many invested interests, some holy some otherwise, make this all the harder to achieve.

Eight days after I wrote those last two paragraphs in draft form I turned on the radio and found myself listening to the grandson of Mahatma Gandhi, Dr. Ram Chander Gandhi, postulating exactly the same point but in a slightly different context. I then recalled that I had met this man, in Vientiane, the capital of Laos, on 13 January 1976, and we two had talked about the same subject. We were both very worried about the moral high ground, so to speak, of the Laotian people now that the communists had taken the country over. In a Nepalese context, was that interview on the World Service of the BBC coincidence of our thoughts or catalyst for them—or both?

A start has to be made somewhere; who will the Nepali starter be? And then the thirst of expectation must be quenched slowly. For, as the last Viceroy of India but one, Field Marshal Lord Wavell mused: Speed is an expensive commodity. Alike in race horses, battleships and women, a small increase in speed may double the price of the article. He could well have added national uplift to the list...

...and can Nepal gear herself up to meet the many challenges and defuse the "time bombs" before they explode?

Not only I, but all her many myriads of friends and, I am sure, all her countrymen and women, fervently hope so.

[November 1993]

CURRICULUM VITAE

Name   John Philip Cross.

Address

PO Box 144, Pokhara, Kaski district, NEPAL or British Gurkhas Pokhara, BFPO 4, c/o GPO London NW7 1PX.

Telephone: **-977-(0)61-431139. Fax (and private room telephone): **-977-(0)61-431181. e-mail: jpx@fewamail.com.np

Occupation   Retired.

Biographical Information:

Date of birth   21 June 1925 in London, England.

Nationality: nil: originally British; not yet of Nepal.

Marital status   Single.

Education

Shrewsbury (matriculation); Member of the Chartered Institute of Linguists (Nepali) [only person so qualified in Nepali]; passed various British/Indian Army/Malayan (Malaysian) Government exams in Urdu, Chinese (Cantonese), Malay, Temiar [6th European ever to speak it and 2nd ever to pass exam], Iban (never officially tested but used it as "working language" for a year), Thai, Vietnamese, Lao (reading and writing for these last three) and French.

Career

Military (39 years 80 days of which 37 years 324 days were in Asia, mostly with the Gurkhas - Major 12+ years, Lt Col 15+

years); university researcher in Kathmandu (history - British Army Gurkhas and linguistic - comparison of Nepali of today with that of 60+ years ago, for 43 months and 5 days; only foreigner ever to be asked for by name and permission given by the King of Nepal); official historian for the Royal Nepal Army. Asked for data by Who's Who in the World, 1985; Dictionary of International Biographers, 1991; American Biographical Institute, 1990. Featured in Asia Magazine, Vol. 28, No. E-24, as *The Man For All Seasons*. Featured by Australian TV twice in 1990 by Channel 9 and 60 Minutes, and once in 1998, Foreign Affairs. On panel for a Talk Programme on *Nepalis in Foreign Uniform*, held in Kathmandu in 1990.

Hobbies

Walking, writing and Playing with Words—read a paper at annual meeting of Linguistic Society of Nepal for eight years.

Present "Appointments"

Convenor of Advisory Committee for private campus in Pokhara; member of Advisory Committee for High School in Ward 15 and the Amarsing Blind School in Pokhara; member of Advisory Committee for Lalitpur High School, Kathmandu, of one village school in the mountains, life member of the Old Peoples' Homes Association in Pokhara and of the Buddhist Crematorium, also in Pokhara, hon. life member of the Nepal chapter of the World Hindu Federation.

1943

Joined British Army as private soldier. Promoted to Lance-Corporal in the Oxfordshire and Buckinghamshire Light Infantry and chosen to go to India for officer training in India

1944

At the Indian Military Academy in Dehra Dun until December of that year when I was commissioned into the British Army, Somerset Light Infantry, but attached for service with the First Gurkha Rifles.

1945

Trained for jungle warfare in India and, six weeks before the end of the war, went to a battalion in Burma (1/1 Gurkha Rifles). Saw tail end of war in Burma before being sent to Cochin-China to disarm Japanese. In one action commanded a battalion [Yamagishi Butai] of surrendered Japanese troops against the Vietminh and the CO personally surrendered his 300-year-old sword and blade damaged in five places, to me.

1946

After handing over to the French, moved back to India by way of Singapore (where I attended and passed a board for a regular commission in the British Army). For rest of that year engaged in work in aid of the civil power in the geographical epicentre of India (Nagpur) and moved up to the North-West Frontier [now Pakistan] in the autumn.

1947

Until partition in August operated to keep hostile tribesmen off the government road and preventing them from attacking the army. After partition moved back into India and was deployed over the Jammu/ Kashmir border until December when went to Burma to join British Army Gurkhas. (Earlier in the year went to Nepal on the invitation of the Maharaja - only two Englishmen a year were allowed in.)

1948

From Burma went to Malaya where I was until 1959. During this time I was the chief instructor at the Army School of Education (Gurkhas) in Malaya from ...

1949-1951

... and discovered Communist-inspired plot to penetrate Gurkhas and disseminate anti-British propaganda from the school. I wrote *English For Gurkha Soldiers*, a "teach yourself English" type book that was later accepted as an HMSO publication for its third printing.

1951-1956

Except for one period of UK leave I was commanding a rifle company against the Communist Terrorists on operations in the jungle during this time. Recommended for at least one bravery award which was downgraded. Had many successes, personal and corporate. [Mention-in-Dispatches twice]. On language front became the first commentator to broadcast the Nepal cup (football) final in Gurkhali (Nepali), something I did on 13 occasions. [I don't think I was ever taken for a foreigner.]

1957-1959

After leave took Staff College Entrance Examination and failed (49.8% with a 50% pass mark). Next year failed again as I drank too much beer before the exam, while on the staff. Started a programme of visiting Gurkha TB and leper patients in a rehabilitation rôle. Went to Hong Kong for a 2-year tour. First time no need for loaded weapons to be carried (at one time or another during the year) since 1944.

1959

Travelled in Assam and made my first long walk in Nepal. Went round the world on leave and returned to Hong Kong in ...

1960

...where I took the lowest level army exam in oral Cantonese. I also won the Services 440 yard race (at just under 35 years of age). Never drank again. Toward the end of the year returned to Malaya and started on an unusually demanding series of military operations against the rump of the Malayan Communist Terrorists on the Malay/Thai border. Used a weapon "for real" every year up till 1976.

1961-1963

During this period I managed to nullify the effects of what the great Spencer Chapman had instituted with the Chinese communists 20 years beforehand in relation to the aboriginal population near the Malay/Thai border. With ten Gurkhas, lived on ¬ rations and carried up to 128 lbs. Managed to win over the Temiar tribe from the Chinese communist guerillas to me personally. I was given name of Tata, "Old Man," an accolade in their society. I passed the Temiar examination (Malay Govt exam, a British Army first) after my last long period in the jungle. I was sent to recuperate on leave in England. Accepted for a Malayan decoration by Malayan PM (Ali Menku Negara) but professional British Army jealousy had it stopped. I was made MBE [instead] for my work with the Temiar (later I thought it was as a result of working on short commons for such a long period that made me go blind in the early 1980s).

1964

While in England I was recalled early to be the commandant of the [Borneo] Border Scouts during the Confrontation of Malay/si/a by Indonesia. [I was on an army-wide short list of 1.] This too was a most taxing task. I was unique as I was a Lt Col in two armies (British and Malaysian) and a Superintendent of three Police Forces (Sarawak Constabulary, Sabah Police Force and the Royal Malaysian Police). Was very nearly decapitated by Iban headhunters and only narrowly escaped death on a number other of occasions. I was then earmarked to command the Gurkha Independent Parachute Company so, after another spell of leave, I became a parachutist (nearer 40 than 39 years old). From ...

1965-1968

... I commanded the Gurkha Independent Parachute Company. I operated over the border of Borneo/Indonesia during Confrontation (in what is now known as "in an SAS rôle"). Was sent on a mission to Sarawak, on the orders of the British PM, with the mother of a dead Marine who was convinced that he was alive. Secretly sent up to the area of the aborigines by the Malaysian Police who did not believe what their army told them about terrorist situation.

1968-1971

Was Chief Instructor of Jungle Warfare School for one year then Commandant for the next 2½. Ran training for 5-nation exercise that tested UK, Australia, New Zealand, Singapore and Malaysia how to react to a hostile threat from out of country. Much media coverage ensued. Was the "personality spokesman" for the Anglia feature on Jungle Warfare, called

The Jungle Fighters. Best known Lieutenant Colonel in British Army according to the Army Board in Ministry of Defence. Wrote the text of *Gurkha, The Legendary Soldier,* in English and Roman Nepali, a book of photographs by Robin Adshead.

1971

This year saw the pull out from "East of Suez." The Jungle Warfare School was to be changed into a 5-nation [Australia, New Zealand, Malaysia, Singapore and United Kingdom] Commonwealth Jungle Warfare Centre of which I was to have been the senior Briton and the Chief Instructor. It fell through. I was asked by the Thais to be a Major General in their army as the adviser on jungle warfare. The Foreign Office in London had a scheme whereby I was an adviser on jungle warfare to the Thais and the South Vietnamese for six alternating months of each year and the Singapore government put out feelers that I raise, train and command a battalion of their Commandos. In the event I was warned that I would be an attaché in an Asian country. At the end of the year I went on a 107-day walk in Nepal, more as a good-bye pilgrimage than anything else, believing I would never go there again. (I met someone I knew, or who knew me every single day.) In the February of ...

1972

... I was warned that I would be the next Defence Attaché in Laos, so I returned to England from Nepal for training, which included 160 hours of French language and 60 hours of Lao language training. At the end of the year I went to Vientiane and took up my duties, which resulted my watching the defeat of the Royalists by the Communists between ...

1972-1976

It was a period quite unlike any I had ever witnessed before, despite having been operating against the Malayan Communists (and against the Indonesians whose tactics were similarly based), and teaching about them virtually non-stop since 1948, resulting in my having spent ten years in the jungle. I was made OBE for work in Laos, a most unusual event for an attaché, made even more unusual as my assistant was also made MBE. I was suggested as attaché to Vietnam or consul in Shanghai. Neither eventuated.

1976

In February I left Laos and went to Nepal, by way of Hong Kong, on a 4-month trek, both to the east and west of Kathmandu. My task was to visit 40 Hill High Schools and assess their requirements for enhancement by Canadian welfare sources. I was due to be the next Deputy Recruiting Officer for the west of the country and the walk was useful for that as well as being therapeutic after life under the Communists. I took up my duties in November 1976. One of the people I came across was an orphan, Buddhiman Gurung, too short to be a soldier, and who had run away from home to escape the hardship of hunger. As all his friends were made into soldiers I allowed him to stay in camp, where he could survive in comfort, pending finding some sort of job.

1976-1982

During this period I was responsible for recruiting one quarter of the strength of the Brigade of Gurkhas (50% of the western content) and moving the camp from 200 yards from

469

the Nepal/India border to the epicentre of the country, Pokhara. I also walked, maybe, 5,000 hill miles.

1979

I employed Buddhiman Gurung as my servant. Instead of pay I gave him enough money for enough land so he, a future wife and two children need never know hunger again. From then we saw each other as father and son. Towards the end of that year I started to lose my sight and, for the next 30 months, I came to rely more and more on Buddhiman both in camp and walking in the mountains. As "the Colonel's son" his marriage was the social event of the year in his district in the Hills. I was unable to attend as our camp was attacked by pro-Communist Nepalese and I had to make a quick assessment of a very delicate situation for Hong Kong (the Gurkha HQ), London and Kathmandu.

1980

I should have retired on reaching 55 years of age but I was, most unusually, given a 2-year extension. I went home to England for a short break and had the eyes looked at; I also sat (and failed) the Final Diploma of the Institute of Linguists. When HRH The Prince of Wales visited us in December he asked me what I intended to do after retirement and, on my saying I had no idea, he said that he would have to find me a job. Offered CO Gurkha Contingent (Polis Republic Singapura) and Head of Intelligence, Brunei: both declined.

1981

I worked with one eye for three months and until two hours of the other not being of any use. I went to Hong Kong to be operated on. The doctor put me right but warned me that my eyesight might be permanently impaired if I hit my head. I took the one paper I had failed for the Final Diploma (with virtually no sight) and was made a Member of the (later Chartered) Institute of Linguists.

1982

After an adult lifetime in the Gurkhas I went on pension. By then I had walked a total of not less than 10,000 miles in 65 of Nepal's 75 districts. As I passed through Kathmandu on my way home I called in on the Vice-Chancellor of the Tribhuvan University and was asked if I would come and work for it. He confirmed my acceptance with the palace. I returned after six months (the longest time at home since 1935 and in England since 1943) in the December, hoping to be accepted as a Nepalese resident so that, if I went blind, my "son" could look after me. Professor Sir Ralph Turner asked me to rewrite his *Comparative and Etymological Dictionary of the Nepali Language*.

1982-1986

My first research project, *Nepal's Contribution To The British Army*, was assessed by two Nepalese of a political persuasion that disliked the idea of British Gurkhas and their verdict was that my work was "without value." This shattered any hopes of being considered a suitable subject for "academic" recognition. I was made the official adviser to the International Affairs Section of where I worked (the Research Centre for Nepal and Asian Studies) on the cold war between USSR and PRC in Asia.

1983

HE the British Ambassador mentioned my predicament to HM the King of Nepal who ordered his Principal Private Secretary to make a note of it. I petitioned HM to be a permanent resident of Nepal. No news for over a year.

1984

New 2-year linguistic project started. More eye trouble and, after an interview with HM's Principal Private Secretary, submitted another petition to HM. Wrote the text of a photographic book, *Gurkhas*, by Sandro Tucci, with a foreword by HRH The Prince Of Wales.

1985

Royal Seal affixed to a document allowing me a unique status, that of permanent residential status in Nepal, with the right to buy land and one house in my own name, without being a Nepalese citizen.

1986

Work rejected by university rewritten and published in UK by Arms & Armour as *In Gurkha Company* (print run of 5,000 copies). Started to build my own house in Pokhara. Finished linguistic project and left university. I had also written some articles for university journals. Included in article on Gurkha recruiting in *Asia Magazine*.

1987

I was to have been asked by the Chief of the Army Staff, Royal Nepal Army, to be the Director of the Military Boys Campus near Kathmandu but, in the event, he asked me to be the official historian of the Royal Nepal Army. Locally, sometimes asked to talk to schools and religious gatherings of Hindus and Buddhists. Continued to write occasional articles for University journals.

1988

Undertook 5-week walk in eastern Nepal, during monsoon, to explain to ex-servicemen need to close main camp, at Dharan, in eastern Nepal.

1989

Jungle Warfare published by Arms & Armour Press in April as Editor's Choice—Military & Aviation Book Society. 23,000+ print run. Held a seminar in University in Kathmandu on *"Has Communism Failed?"*

1990

Visited ex-Indian Army unit, 1/1 GR, for its 175 anniversary, in Poona; addressed battalion. Visited ex-British Army unit, 7 GR, in Hong Kong; addressed other ranks (476 men); asked to be the Editor-in-Chief for a new (updated Turner) Nepali-English dictionary. Included in two Australian TV programmes.

1991

Kept low profile after last year's revolution and this year's elections; addressed 398 all ranks in 7 GR, in UK.

1992

First In, Last Out, published in April, by Brassey's, (UK), Ltd. Indian edition of *Jungle Warfare* published in November.

1993

The International Biographical Centre, Cambridge, England included me as number 167 in their fully revised edition of *The First Five Hundred*, 1993. The American Biographical Institute awarded me the title *Most Admired Man of the Decade*, and International Award of Recognition, in Edition Four of 5000 *Personalities of the World* for Outstanding Linguist Achievements in Nine Asian Languages. Reviewed *Nepalko Sainik Itihas* [Nepal's Military History] for the Chief Of Army Staff, Royal Nepal Army. In Hong Kong, interviewed 59 Gurkhas soldiers enlisted when I was DRO (30 by me), to test the effects of Rote Learning, the basis of all that is taught in Nepal, on their career prospects in British Army, especially when in UK.

1994

Elected Fellow of the American Biographical Institute (FABI) and Life Fellow of the American Biographical Institute Research Association (LFABI).

1995

[Three score and ten years has seen] Biodata for obituary asked for by *The Times* newspaper and made an Honorary Life Member of the local Buddhist crematorium.

1996

The Call Of Nepal: A Personal Nepalese Odyssey In A Different Dimension, New Millennium and "A Face Like A Chicken's Backside": An Unconventional Soldier In South-East Asia, Greenhill Books, both published in April. Editor's Choice—Military & Aviation Book Society, UK and Australia.

Invited to be Visiting Professor of Central Department of Linguistics, Tribhuvan University, Kathmandu.

1997

Included in *International Biography*, 25th edition, by International Biographical Centre and 5000 Personalities of the World, by American Biographical Institute.

1998

Included in First Five Hundred, Vol 5, by International Biographical Centre. *The Call Of Nepal* published in Nepal. Subject of a New Zealand telecoms advertisement: making cuckoo noises when training jungle warfare students in Malaysia in 1970.

1999

Visited 2 RGR and Training Team, Brunei (a jungle warfare training establishment) and the Gurkha Contingent of the Singapore Police on a lecture tour.

2000

The Throne of Stone, Mandala Book Point, Kathmandu. Recommended as compulsory reading for Indian Army Gorkha unit subalterns. Japanese eager to translate it.

2001

Allotted 16 April of each year, permanently, by American Biographical Institute as *J. P. CROSS DAY*. Included in Asian/American Who's Who, Vol. 2.

2002

Gurkhas At War The Gurkha Experience 1939 to the Present, published by Greenhill Books; Whatabouts and Whereabouts in Asia published by Serendipity.

2003

"A Face Like A Chicken's Backside": An Unconventional Soldier in Malaya & Borneo, 1948-1971, published by Cultured Lotus, Singapore.

2004

Official member of advisory committee for Royal visit to Pokhara.

2005

The Restless Quest: Britain and Nepal on Collision Course and the Start of the British-Gurkha Connection, 1746-1815 Koselee Prakashan, Bag Bazar, Kathmandu, Nepal, 2005. ISBN 99946-50-09-2

2006

Fiftieth article for *The Kukri* (the Brigade of Gurkhas journal) published.

2007

Gurkhas At War: Eyewitness Accounts from World War II to Iraq, re-published by Greenhill Books, paperback, in UK, USA, Malaysia and Singapore.

2008

Jungle Warfare republished by Pen & Sword; *First In, Last Out* republished by Hailer Publishing, USA *The Crown of*

Renown, in preparation by Hallmark International Publishing, UK

Family Background

Directly descended, paternally, from Cadwalon, king of the Britons, AD 676, north Wales, through Cynvyn, Prince of Powys, through wife of Llewellyn, the last Prince of Wales who died fighting Edward 1 between 1282-84. Maternally, from one of Louis XIV's mistresses.

Father was a wartime soldier in both wars (MC, MiD) and a partner in a firm of solicitors in London. He was the private solicitor to Lord Portman and the Royal College of Surgeons. He died in 1949. Elder brother, a first-class classical scholar, was killed in the Second World War. My younger, and only, sister, was killed in a road accident in 1980. My younger brother helps his son farm organically in Dorset: mother, who was awarded the BEM for social services in 1990 at the age of 91, died in 1998, five days into her hundredth year. I have nearly been wed at least four times so still do not know the magic, mystery, misconceptions and muck of marriage.

www.ingramcontent.com/pod-product-compliance
Lightning Source LLC
Chambersburg PA
CBHW050547270326
41926CB00012B/1947